D.W. GRIFFITH'S
THE BIRTH OF A NATION:
Controversy, Suppression,
and the First Amendment
As It Applies to Filmic Expression,
1915-1973

This is a volume in the Arno Press Collection

DISSERTATIONS ON FILM 1980

Advisory Editor
Garth S. Jowett

*See last pages of this volume
for a complete list of titles*

D.W. GRIFFITH'S
THE BIRTH OF A NATION:
Controversy, Suppression, and the First Amendment As It Applies to Filmic Expression, 1915-1973

Nickieann Fleener-Marzec

ARNO PRESS
A New York Times Company
New York • 1980

Editorial Supervision: Steve Bedney

First publication in book form 1980 by Arno Press Inc.

Copyright © 1980 by Nickieann Fleener-Marzec

Reproduced by permission of Nickieann Fleeneer-Marzec

DISSERTATIONS ON FILM 1980
ISBN for complete set: 0-405-12900-9
See last pages of this volume for titles.

Manufactured in the United States of America

Library of Congress Cataloging in Publication Data

Fleener-Marzec, Nickieann.
   D. W. Griffith's The birth of a nation.

   (Dissetations on film 1980)
   Originally presented as the author's thesis,
University of Wisconsin-Madison, 1977.
   Bibliography: p.
   1. Moving-pictures--Censorship--United States.
2. Birth of a nation (Motion picture) I. Title.
II. Series.
KF4300.F54 1980   344.73'0531   79-6675
ISBN 0-405-12909-2

D. W. GRIFFITH'S THE BIRTH OF A NATION: CONTROVERSY,
SUPPRESSION, AND THE FIRST AMENDMENT AS IT
APPLIES TO FILMIC EXPRESSION, 1915-1973

BY

NICKIEANN FLEENER-MARZEC

A thesis submitted in partial fulfillment of the
requirements for the degree of

DOCTOR OF PHILOSOPHY
(Journalism and Mass Communication)

at the

UNIVERSITY OF WISCONSIN-MADISON

1977

D.W. Griffith's The Birth of a Nation: Controversy, Suppression, and
The First Amendment As It Applies to Filmic Expression, 1915-1973

Nickieann Fleener-Marzec

Under the supervision of Associate Professor
Mary Ann Yodelis Smith

This study was designed to determine whether arguments for and against legal and extra-legal restraints against The Birth of a Nation changed as the U.S. Supreme Court's interpretation of the First Amendment as it applied to filmic expression changed during the time period 1915-1973. Also, the study sought to identify the extent to which The Birth was censored and to document the extent to which different tactics were used by both sides during censorship debates. The research also sought to isolate factors influencing censor/no censor decisions resolving controversies.

To accomplish this, a search was conducted through secondary sources and major manuscript collections concerning the film. If a censorship controversy was mentioned in a primary source or in multiple secondary sources, it was coded for analysis. Information recorded for each controversy included: tactics used; rationales expressed by both sides; manner of resolution; year of resolution; ultimate censor/no censor decision; and, rationale for ultimate decision. Censorship controversies thus documented were categorized by tactic accomplishing resolution and analysed accordingly.

The study found that in general, arguments for and against censorship did not change as the U.S. Supreme Court's interpretation of film's First Amendment status changed. The study found that from 1915-1973 The Birth was involved in at least 120 censorship controversies.

The five major tactics employed during controversies were: initiating court action or criminal proceedings; petitioning officials; seeking censorship legislation; and, utilizing extra-legal means. The number of times the tactics were operationalized in the 120 controversies was 356. In terms of individual actions taken, no tactic accomplished controversy resolution with a frequency differing from chance. However, in terms of individual controversies rather than actions taken, the tactic of court action resolved controversies with a frequency greater than random. Courts resolving controversies supported no censor resolutions with a frequency differing from chance. Officials resolving controversies supported censorship with a frequency differing from chance. Regardless of tactic implemented, controversies were resolved by decisions supportive of some form of censorship (prior restraint, prior restraint partial, subsequent restraint, subsequent restraint partial) with a frequency differing from chance. Specifically, of the 94 controversies with known resolution, 59 were resolved with some form of censorship and 35 were resolved with no censor decisions. Controversy resolution was found to be independent of both controversy level (state, local, or national) and controversy year. Arguments for and against censorship centered on content, procedural, and effects issues. The rationale expressed most frequently to justify censorship was that the film engendered racial prejudice. Among other rationales justifying censorship were: after black protest; film immoral; film unpatriotic; and film detrimental to public peace. Rationales used to justify censorship appeared to be tactic dependent but not time dependent. Also, censorship action and rationale justifying that action did not function independently. Rationales justifying no censor resolutions were expressed in less than half the controversies thus resolved. The tactic of seeking censorship legislation was not found to be implemented directly toward accomplishing controversy resolution. Also, the majority of extra-legal actions were designed to influence opinion concerning the film's acceptability rather than to resolve a given controversy.

Mary Ann Yodelis Smith

TABLE OF CONTENTS

LIST OF TABLES iv

PREFACE vi

Chapter
I. CENSORSHIP OF THE BIRTH OF A NATION: AN OVERVIEW . 1

    The *Birth* in Film History
    Questions
    Procedures

II. THE CENSORSHIP ARENA 57

    Censorship Before U.S. Supreme Court Decisions
    U.S. Supreme Court: Film Censorship and
      Obscenity, 1915-1973
    The Supreme Court and the Film Color Line

III. CENSORSHIP CONTROVERSIES INVOLVING COURT ACTION . . 94

    Censorship Cases Involving Court Action: An
      Overview
    Court Decisions Upholding Censorship
    Court Decisions Which Forbade Censorship
    Racial Stereotyping Argument Rejected
    Censorship Based on Rationale That Film Would
      Engander Public Peace
    Procedural Decisions Not Allowing Censorship
    Cases Heard But Not Adjudicated
    Summary
    Conclusions

IV. CONTROVERSIES INVOLVING CRIMINAL PROCEEDINGS . . . 175

    Cases Excluding First Amendment Considerations
    Cases In Which Free Speech Was A Specific Issue
    Summary and Conclusions

V. ADMINISTRATIVE ACTIONS IN THE *BIRTH* CENSORSHIP
    CONTROVERSIES 213

    Overview
    Municipal Censorship
    Mayoral Decisions
    Police Censors

iii

        Municipal Boards
        City Councils
        Actions by Other Municipal Officials
        State Authorities
        Governors
        State Censorship Boards
        World War I Defense Councils
        Analysis

VI.   LEGISLATIVE ACTIONS AND THE BIRTH OF A NATION . . .   329

        City Councils As Lawmakers
        State Legislatures As Lawmakers
        National Authorities
        Analysis

VII. EXTRA-LEGAL TACTICS IN THE BIRTH OF A NATION
     CENSORSHIP CONTROVERSIES   351

        Overview
        Film Self-Regulation
        Film As An Extra-Legal Tactic
        Sermons
        Pamphlets
        Demonstrations
        Resolution
        Editorials and Letters to the Editor
        Other
        Spin-Off Efforts
        Summary
        Conclusions

VIII. SUMMARY AND CONCLUSIONS   483

        Resolution of Controversies In Which Censorship
          Directly Debated
        Actions Resolving and Not Resolving Controver-
          sies
        Conclusions

BIBLIOGRAPHY   542

LIST OF TABLES

1.	Types of Specific Actions Taken By Courts Resolving Controversies	144
2.	Court Decisions Resolving Controversies By Year	145
3.	Court Decisions Resolving Controversies By Level	146
4.	Rationales Justifying Court Decisions Resolving Controversies	147
5.	Initiators of Court Action and Result	148
6.	Initiators of Court Action Not Resolving Controversy and Court Action Taken	151
7.	Dispositions of Cases of Individuals Arrested in Connection With Screenings of The Birth	200
8.	Municipal Authorities and Controversy Resolution Status	279
9.	Controversies Resolved By Official and Action	291
10.	Specific Type of Restraint Exercised By Officials Resolving Controversies	291
11.	Controversy Resolution by Officials and Rationales For Censorship Actions	293
12.	Officials Resolving Controversies By Refusing to Censor and Rationale Rejected	294
13.	Local Controversies Resolved By Year and Decision	296
14.	State Controversies Resolved By Year and Decision	297
15.	Controversies Resolved By Censorship and Rationale For Action By Year	297
16.	Petitioned Officials Resolving and Not Resolving Controversies By Year	299
17.	Actions of Officials Not Resolving Controversies	300
18.	Controversies In Which Censorship Sought Through Extra-Legal Means By Year and Resolution	437
19.	Range of Extra-Legal Tactics and Position Concerning Film	440
20.	Extra-Legal Tactics By Year	441
21.	Rationales Underlying Extra-Legal Actions Designed To Sway Public Opinion Against The Film By Year	443
22.	Rationales Underlying Extra-Legal Tactics Designed To Sway Public Opinion In Favor of the Film By Year	444
23.	Extra-Legal Tactics To Influence Opinion By Year, Controversy, and Censor or No Censor Resolution	446
24.	Controversy Independent Extra-Legal Actions By Position Regarding Film	447
25.	Types of Specific Actions Resolving Controversies	485
26.	Controversy Resolution By Tactic	487
27.	Actions Resolving Controversies By Tactic	490
28.	Controversy Resolution By Level	492
29.	Specific Actions Resolving Controversies By Level	494

30.	Controversy Resolution By Year	496
31.	Tactics Resolving Controversies By Year	499
32.	Rationales Justifying Censorship By Specific Action	500
33.	Rationales For Censorship By Tactic	503
34.	Rationales Justifying Censorship By Year	504
35.	Rationales Justifying No Censorship By Tactic	505
36.	Rationales Justifying No Censorship By Year	507
37.	Success of Tactics in Achieving Controversy Resolution	509
38.	Actions Resolving and Not Resolving Controversies By Year and Tactic	513
39.	Actions Not Resolving Controversies By Tactic	515
40	Nature of Extra-Legal Actions Tied To Specific Controversies	520
41.	Extra-Legal Actions Not Controversy Specific	522

PREFACE

D.W. Griffith once explained his goal as a film maker was to make people see. Griffith strove not only to expand people's visions through the images he presented on the screen. He also wanted people to see that the motion picture medium was a legitimate member of the nation's press entitled to First Amendment rights equal to those established for the print media. In terms of his first goal, Griffith was clearly successful as he is acknowledged as one of the greatest film makers in history. In terms of his second purpose, Griffith was not as successful because film has never had a First Amendment status equivalent to print media. This study analyzes the consequences of that status for the most famous and controversial of all Griffith's films, The Birth of a Nation. No one aware of the censorship climate of today can fail to see the link between The Birth which was opposed because of the force of its racial stereotypes and current agitations for federally enforced censorship standards to eliminate all stereotypes from film and television. In addition, although much had been written about The Birth, there had been no systematic accounting of specific censorship controversies. This study provides that accounting and may serve to provide some perspective on the historical application of a censorship standard still very much alive.

The assistance of a variety of people made this study possible. First, I owe a great deal to Professor Mary Ann Yodelis Smith who not only directed this dissertation but who also guided my graduate career and my professional development. During the past five years as my adviser, she generously shared her time, her knowledge, and her enthusiasm. Her critical eye gave direction to my research and refined the manuscript as it evolved. The standard of excellence set for communication history research by Professor Harold L. Nelson challenged the effort, and his perceptive comments on my earlier research helped channel this study. I also wish to thank the other three members of my committee: Professor Charles Higbie whose gentle encouragement helped move this project along to completion; Professor Tino Balio, who provided a model of substantive film research; and Professor David Cronon who provided historical perspective for the study by adding greatly to my understanding of the early time period in which The Birth controversies took place.

I also wish to thank all my fellow graduate students for their support and encouragement. Particularly, Hazel Garcia and Gerald Baldasty offered valuable insights into the conceptual framework of this study. I am also grateful to the University of Wisconsin for the financial assistance extended in the form of a University travel grant.

The study would have been impossible without the aid of countless librarians. The staffs of the State Historical Society of Wisconsin manuscript collections and microform rooms were most helpful. The staff of Memorial Library also was helpful. I would also like to thank the staffs of the Museum of Modern Art Archives, Lincoln Center Archives, Ohio State Historical Society Archives, New York City Archives, Library of Congress Manuscript Division, Library of Congress

Microfilm Division, and Massachusetts State Legislative Library.

I would also like to thank five friends who now know more about The Birth of a Nation than they ever wanted to know, but who never complained about acquiring the knowledge: Judy Evans, Jim Payne, Kristi Petersen, Ramona Rush, and Marcia Thompson Williams. I also extend my gratitude to the two typists who worked long hours to prepare the final draft of this manuscript: Gaye Gordon and Donna Stout.

Finally, this effort would have been much more difficult without the assistance and support of my friend (and husband) Robert Marzec who never doubted that the manuscript would become a reality and who efficiently supervised the final production effort. I would also like to thank my parents and all my family for their encouragement. Because I am one of those people who do not care to find out whether she can write without a cat present, I must also thank Sassafras, Jeremiah, Daisy, and Bunter whose warm purring presences at all hours of the day and night supervised the creation of this dissertation.

CHAPTER I

CENSORSHIP OF THE BIRTH OF A NATION: AN OVERVIEW

Today the censorship of moving pictures . . . is seriously hampering the growth of the art. Had intelligent opposition to censorship been employed when it first made itself manifest it could easily have been overcome. But the pygmy child of that day has grown to be, not merely a man, but a giant, and I tell you who read this, whether you will or not, he is a giant whose forces of evil are so strong that he threatens that priceless heritage of our nation--freedom of expression.

. . . censorship . . . before publication . . . directly controverts the most valuable of all our liberties under the Constitution. **The moving picture is simply the pictorial press.** The pictorial press claims the same constitutional freedom as the printed press.

--David Wark Griffith
The Rise and Fall of Free
Speech in America

David Wark Griffith, pioneer film maker, waged direct combat with the "giant" of suppression. His fight began in 1915 when censors assaulted his first masterwork The Birth of a Nation and continued until his death in 1948. Others joined the fight, but Griffith's contention that constitutionally the motion picture should be equated with the printed press has yet to be recognized by the U. S. Supreme Court. Although the Court extended First Amendment protection to the motion picture and narrowed acceptable censorship standards,[2] prior restraint of film remains constitutional.[3] Within this context The Birth of a Nation continues to incite censorship controversies,[4] and that is the focus of this study.

Although Griffith recorded limited success in his struggle

to free film from prior restraint, his contributions to the development of the American cinema were at least as significant. By combining technical innovations with thematic significance, Griffith created motion pictures which illustrated for the first time the power of the medium as a communicative art. Griffith's genius conferred respectability upon a medium which before his guidance was tainted by "an air of disrepute."[5] In 1972, 40 years after the completion of Griffith's last picture, Robert M. Henderson, a Griffith biographer, said of the continued influence of this artistic vision:

> In every film made by anyone anywhere, there is the mark of Griffith. His films can be analyzed, deprecated, dismissed as quaint voiceless antiques, but his mind and spirit sit in every director's chair and every editing room.[6]

Of all Griffith's films, The Birth of a Nation is one of the most well known, because it awakened film makers, critics, and the public to the vast potential of the fledgling medium. With the film's first screening came both exclamations of praise over the emergence of a new art form and displays of concern at the birth of a a new propaganda vehicle. Stressing the importance of the latter influence, film historians Edward Wagenknecht and Anthony Slide have concluded that with The Birth film ". . . became a weapon in the battle for men's minds and the attacks on it made this particular specimen . . . a gambit in the struggle for freedom of thought and expression."[7]

In spite of The Birth's significance, the film's history, recorded in court proceedings, manuscript collections, newspapers, magazines and other works contains contradictory accounts of significant events. Recognizing the need for critical evaluation of the inconsistencies, film scholar Fred Silva wrote:

> D. W. Griffith's The Birth of a Nation exploded into American culture at the Liberty Theater in New York City on a bitterly cold night March 3, 1915. The critical dust has yet to settle. From the beginning so much contradictory legend, half-truth, rancor, and praise have swirled around the film that only now have film scholars and critics begun to assemble the pieces of history, sociology, aesthetic, and biography which will enable future viewers to see Griffith's masterwork not only as an outmoded, biased account of Reconstruction, filled with unquestionably racist attitudes, but as a genuine cinematic achievement.[8]

The purpose of this inquiry is to evaluate critically those contradictory pieces of The Birth of a Nation's chronicle which center on First Amendment issues in a research arena bounded by law, history, and mass communications.

To provide historical perspective, introductory sections of this chapter discuss the significance of The Birth in cinema history and outline the philosophical battlelines along which the censorship controversies were fought. A review of existing literature concerning the film follows. The final section delineates specific research questions and methods for this study which documents The Birth of a Nation's censorship history.

The Birth in Film History

Griffith said that all drama must necessarily be conflict, battle, fight. "How are we to depict the right unless we show the wrong? Unless we show the evils of a vicious past, how are we allowed to be the means of building the footsteps of the present generation?"[9] The Birth of a Nation is the cinematic embodiment of this theory.

Several film scholars have commented on the film's place in cinema history. One prominent film critic called <u>The</u> <u>Birth</u> "the most influential and controversial film in the entire history of motion pictures." In a dissertation concerning the motion picture in American society, Garth S. Jowell said of <u>The</u> <u>Birth</u> that "no single cinematic event in this early period (1884-1936) emphasized to the movie's detractors and defenders the power yielded by the medium than the furor surrounding the release of D. W. Griffith's <u>The</u> <u>Birth</u> <u>of</u> <u>a</u> <u>Nation</u> in 1915."[10] Cinema historians Edward Wagenknecht and Anthony Slide classified <u>The</u> <u>Birth</u> as ". . .an aesthetic achievement, a monument, and a cultural and sociological phenomenon."[11] One prominent film critic called the film "the most influential and controversial film in the entire history of motion pictures."[12]

Likewise, stressing the importance of <u>The</u> <u>Birth</u>, early Griffith scholar Seymour Stern said "without a full study of its history, the birth of the cinema as we know it. . .would remain a story without a beginning. . .this powerful. . .and violently controversial film. . .was. . .an event of far-reaching consequence in the political and social history of the United States."[13]

Other critics have singled out the film as a unique event in film history. <u>The</u> <u>Birth</u> has also been dubbed the first genuine feature film, the first two-dollar admission movie, the first gold-mine money-making movie, the first movie to be shown complete with ushers and theatre trappings, and the first film to generate re-

views and advertising in many non-trade papers.[14] More important
for the purposes of this research:

> . . .it was the first film to reveal the vast potentialities of
> the motion picture as a vehicle for propaganda. It was the
> first film to be taken seriously as a political statement and
> it has never failed to be regarded seriously as a 'sociological
> document.' Violent controversy, nation-wide demand for federal
> or state censorship of the motion picture, and sometimes riots
> (as in Boston) followed in its wake, so that a crude entertain-
> ment suddenly realized that they had become the century's most
> potent and provocative medium of expression. . .The Birth of a
> Nation was the film that conferred 'respectability' on the
> medium.[15]

Film historian Lewis Jacobs said of the film "The Birth of a Nation
pulsates; it is life itself."[16] Andrew Sarris, cinema professor,
characterized the film "as one of the embarrassments of film scholar-
ship. It can't be ignored. . .and yet it was regarded as outrageously racist even at a time when racism was hardly a household word."[17]
Summarizing the factors which distinguished The Birth from earlier
pictures, black film historian Donald Bogle concluded:

> In almost every way, The Birth of a Nation was a stupendous
> undertaking, unlike any film that had preceded it. Up to
> then American movies had been two-or-three-reel affairs,
> shorts running no longer than ten or fifteen minutes, crudely
> and casually filmed. But The Birth of a Nation was rehearsed
> for six weeks, filmed in nine, later edited in three months,
> and finally released as a record-breaking hundred-thousand
> dollar spectacle, twelve reels in length and over three hours
> in running time. It altered the entire course and concept of
> American movie-making, developing the close-up, cross-cutting,
> rapid-fire editing, the iris, the split-screen shot, and
> realistic and impressionistic lighting. Creating sequences
> and images yet to be surpassed, the film's magnitude and epic
> grandeur swept audiences off their feet.[18]

This film, pulsating with life and outrageously racist,
opened for a special run at the Clune Theatre in Los Angeles,
California, on February 8, 1915, bearing the title The Clansman.

When the film opened officially at New York's Liberty Theatre on March 3, 1915, the primary film title was The Birth of a Nation.[19]

The story line of The Birth is drawn basically from two of Thomas Dixon's novels, The Clansman and The Leopard's Spots.[20] The film is divided into two parts. The first act focuses on the Civil War and contains battle scenes which one reviewer termed "the greatest achievement of photo-drama."[21] Griffith recreated in this segment the assembly of two armies, the battle strategies at Atlanta and Petersburg, Sherman's march to the sea, Lee's surrender and Lincoln's assassination.[22] In the second half of the picture Griffith developed a controversial portrait of Reconstruction which presented the Ku Klux Klan as the saviours of the white South from black misrule.[23]

Critically the motion picture met with a mixture of damnation and praise. Tributes included "it is grand opera in picture form,"[24] and "the spectators actually rise from their seats and burst into cheers."[25] Critics termed the film "aggressively vicious and defamatory,"[26] "unfair to the negro race,"[27] and "a piece of Klan propaganda."[28] Lewis Jacobs concluded that the tremendous popularity of the film, coupled with the accompanying controversy stemming from the film's portrayal of blacks awakened the country to the social importance of the medium.[29]

Philosophical Battlelines

The philosophical underpinnings of both the film's advocates and the film's opponents rest in free speech arguments. The film's supporters argued from an almost absolutist position that the motion picture medium was entitled to First Amendment protection. The film's opponents argued that there should be distinctions made between acceptable speech and unacceptable speech; that what was acceptable speech in the form of a book might not be acceptable speech in the form of a motion picture; and that The Birth clearly fit into the realm of unacceptable speech.

The case for the film was clearly stated by Thomas Dixon. Dixon expressed his beliefs concerning appropriate First Amendment status for the film medium in a statement in opposition to a proposed federal censorship statute submitted to the House of Representatives, Committee on Education. In part, Dixon said:

> Censorship of motion pictures is the most dangerous attack on American liberty since the foundation of the Republic. The motion picture is a process of recording thought on yellow parchment without the use of printer's ink, and is as great an advance on printing as Gutenberg's invention was over the quill and pen. . . .A censorship of opinion is the aim of our enemies. Our fathers fled the Old World to escape this and founded the Republic to free the human mind from shackles. . . .I first preached the Clansman as a sermon. No censor dared to silence my pulpit. I turned my sermon into a lecture and delivered it from Maine to California without license. I turned the lecture into a novel and no censor has yet stopped the press of Doubleday, Page & Co. I turned the novel into a spoken play, and no censor has dared to interfere. I turned the play into a motion picture and it has cost me $75,000 in lawyers' fees to fight the local censors in the first ten months.[30]

Within Dixon's statement is a First Amendment question central to all controversies over The Birth of a Nation's right to the screen. That question is, does First Amendment protection belong to the message or does it belong to the medium. Dixon argued that First Amendment protection belonged to the message regardless of the medium. The film's opponents (and in a larger context the U. S. Supreme Court) disagreed.

The position of the film's opponents concerning the free speech status of communications like The Birth was well summarized by W. E. B. DuBois in a memo to Walter White. In part, DuBois explained:

> The fight. . .against. . .The Birth of a Nation illustrates the peculiar contradictions into which the Negro problem forces this organization. The NAACP stands for liberty: physical liberty, political liberty, and particularly liberty in artistic expression. Other things being equal we would not think of trying to suppress a book by Claude Bowers or a speech by Senator Blease: but there are situations when something has to be done.
>
> In 1914, 60 Negroes were lynched; in 1915, 99; in 1916, 65; and the number of lynchings per year kept on at the rate of at least one a week from 1915 until 1922. More Negroes were lynched in 1915 than in any other year since the beginning of the century. The chief alleged excuse for this lynching was the attacks upon white women by colored men. In 1915 Thomas Dixon's 'Clansman' was picturized (sic) by the greatest master of the new art of the cinema. . .
>
> Here then was a special case. A new art was used deliberately to slander and vilify a race. There was no chance to reply. We had neither the money nor the influence. . .What were we to do? We decided to try to make the authorities stop the picture on the ground that it was a public menace: that it was not art but vicious propaganda. If anyone came to New York today with as brutal an attack upon women or Italians we would have a right to decide that freedom of art expression was going too far. We are aware now as then that it is dangerous to limit expression, and yet, without some limitations civilization could not endure.[31]

Within this statement DuBois justified censorship of The Birth not only on the grounds of the medium in which it was presented but also on intent grounds. DuBois also indicated that although censorship in general was a dangerous beast, in certain circumstances it was a necessary evil. Thus, the philosophical battleground on which The Birth of a Nation censorship controversies was established.

Literature Review. . .The Existing Pieces

Although a number of works consider The Birth of a Nation from a variety of viewpoints, no single work authoritatively chronicles attempts to suppress the film. With minor exception, discussion of censorship is generally descriptive in nature and often written without specific source attribution. Works which discuss censorship of the film may be divided into the following categories: general histories of film; monographs and articles specifically about the film; monographs and articles about individuals involved in the censorship controversies; general histories of film censorship; and, works which consider the motion picture medium as capable of dispelling or reinforcing racial prejudice.

General Histories of Film

An example of a general film history's discussion of The Birth is Lewis Jacobs' The Rise of the American Film.[32] Jacobs asserted that The Birth "aroused a storm of protest above the Mason and Dixon line" and that "in Boston and other abolitionist cities race riots broke out."[33] As the authority for this discussion, Jacobs cited only Terry Ramsaye's anecdotal A Million And One Nights.[34] Jacobs' history terminated with 1930.

In his 1926 two-volume history of cinema, Terry Ramsaye interpreted attempts to censor the film in political terms:

> The whole negro race and its white defenders rose in a clamor for the suppression of the picture with local oppositions of serious strength developing in every community where there was a sufficient negro vote to influence the politicians and office holders. The voters were there at home, whereas the picture was merely a movie from New York.[35]

However, Ramsaye did not specify in which cities such actions were initiated. A similar generalization concerning response to the film is in Ralph Ellison's Shadow and Act. According to Ellison, The Birth's release "resulted in controversy, riots, heavy profits and the growth of the Klan."[36]

John Howard Lawson,[37] Edward Wagenknecht,[38] Richard Griffith and Arthur Mayer[39] connect 1915 protests in Boston with the film's screening. Lawson contended that "crowds demonstrated for 24 hours in front of the theatre."[40] Griffith and Mayer's account of the protests included the reproduction of two headlines from the Boston establishment press indicating the occurrence of a riot in connection with the film's screening.[41] Wagenknecht added three other specific censorship references. Without citation, Wagenknecht stated that "an injunction against The Birth of a Nation was issued in Louisville, Kentucky, two bills were introduced to prevent the screening of the film in the District of Columbia, and the film was banned from Ohio until 1917."[42]

Several film historians also have speculated about the influence of censorship upon the content of the film which has survived. For example, Edward Wagenknecht commented it would be impossible to determine specifically how The Birth of a Nation originally depicted the black man because "Griffith cut many of the scenes which gave most offense and these are not extant."[43] Parker Tyler also summarized the effect of censorship upon the surviving version of the film. Tyler said the original print "was badly cut up, so much so in some sequences as to look absurd--how can we tell, even in 'restored' versions what it was meant to be or should have been?"[44]

From these basic works, representative of general film histories, a typical pattern for discussion of The Birth can be discerned. General film histories have stressed the film's plot and production without an authoritative analysis of the film's censorship problems. Protests against The Birth are mentioned, but an exhaustive interpretive analysis of censorship actions involving the film is not presented.

Monographs and Articles Specific to The Birth of a Nation

References to censorship of The Birth are scattered throughout monographs and articles considering the film. Two of the most important documents considering the film's right to the screen are the National Association for the Advancement of Colored People (NAACP) sponsored Fighting a Vicious Film: Protest Against The Birth of a Nation[45] and D. W. Griffith's The Rise and Fall of Free Speech in America.[46] Fighting a Vicious Film, a 47-page pamphlet, was published by the Boston Branch of the NAACP as a final protest after The Birth had been approved in 1915 by the Boston censorship board under a law "plainly intended to stop the play."[47] The work contained a series of 25 short articles chronicling the branch's efforts against the film and explaining the organization's opposition to the film. The pamphlet was published "with a view to giving some idea of the scope of the agitation and spirit in which it was conducted. . .with the further purpose of aiding other communities in opposing this and all such productions."[48] Included articles justify suppression of the film on grounds ranging from group libel to historical untruth. In Griffith's answer to the NAACP and all others who sought to suppress the motion picture, the film maker contended that the medium was simply a pictorial form of the press and consequently within the protection of the First Amendment.[49]

A sample of articles which discuss freedom of expression and The Birth are included in Focus on The Birth of a Nation.[50] Edited by Fred Silva, the work reprinted a selection of reviews, commentaries, and essays about the film. Several documents concern 1915 censorship efforts in New York and Boston. Of particular relevance to this study was the inclusion of commentaries by members of the NAACP, D. W. Griffith, and Thomas Dixon, debating the film's right to the screen. The NAACP commentaries outlined: the organization's fight against the film from February 27 through May 15, 1915;[51] expressed the opinion that the film should be censored because it falsified history, glorified lynching, and falsely represented black Americans;[52] and, charged that the film was "aggressively vicious and defamatory."[53] Griffith contended that the motion picture was on a par with the spoken word and therefore should not be subjected to unique censorship standards.[54] Griffith also spoke consistently against legislation designed to censor The Birth. In particular, Griffith called the proposed Massachusetts law forbidding films judged "to excite racial or religious prejudice, or tends to a breach of the peace" unwise and designed to allow "any disgruntled or venomous adversaries" to suppress a film.[55] Dixon defended the film's historical accuracy and called the attacks on the film "slander and personal vilification,"[56] and suggested that in a free country "only a Negro or his color-blind associate could be child enough to ask such protection from historical discussion."[57]

Several authors indicate that protests against the film occurred in a variety of locations. For example, New York and Boston are identified as cities in which specific actions were taken against the film by Roy E. Aitken in The Birth of a Nation Story.[58] Unfortunately, this informal and highly anecdotal recollection of the film's early years is not footnoted. However, it does contain a reproduction of the first page of a resolution in opposition to The Birth adopted March 7, n.y., by the Dayton, Ohio, City Commissioners.[59] Aitken concluded ". . .the NAACP was never to relax its efforts to keep The Birth of a Nation off the movie screens of the U. S. They are still protesting the showing of the picture today."[60] Similarly, Milton MacKaye in a 1937 retrospective asserted that wherever the film played "there was trouble. . .In Boston. . . there were riots and there were riots and continued legal difficulties in many other cities."[61] MacKaye also noted that the film was shown under a permanent injunction in Chicago (1915) and that the threat of Negro opposition "was used by many politicians in a futile effort to 'shake down' the management."[62] The cities of Newark, Atlantic City, and St. Louis and the states of Kansas, Ohio, and West Virginia are identified by Bosley Crowther as places where the film was banned.[63] Mass demonstrations and riots in a dozen cities are attributed to the film in a program written to accompany a 1948 revival.[64] According to the program notes, "a high pitch of fury" was reached in Boston and "in Philadelphia while the film was being unreeled to enthusiastic audiences inside the Forrest Theater, 3,000 Negroes battled in the street with 500 police."[65]

A scholarly analysis of the NAACP's initial fight against the film is included in Thomas Cripps' article "The Reaction of the Negro to the Motion Picture Birth of a Nation."[66] Drawing from primary sources, Cripps traced the 1915 New York and Boston protests and outlined the National Board of Censorship's refusal to stop the film.[67] Cripps identified Chicago, Illinois; Wilmington, Delaware; Cleveland, Ohio; Baltimore, Maryland; Charleston, West Virginia; Philadelphia, Pennsylvania; and Atlantic City, New Jersey, as cities where "agitators were at work against the picture" in 1915.[68] He concluded that the NAACP-led battle to censor was unsuccessful.

In spite of speculation by several critics that the film could not be shown successfully in the South, John Hammond Moore reported the positive response of North and South Carolinas' residents to the film's initial screenings.[69] Moore concluded that

South Carolina's reaction to The Birth was "one of almost unanimous approval."[70] However, in the North, Moore contended the film caused violent controversy ". . .hundreds rioted in Boston and irate patrons in other cities 'egged' the screen, usually as Gus was chasing Flora Cameron."[71]

Although several authors have speculated that viewing the film hampered race relations at least one author has developed the theme that protests against the film also harmed race relations. Andrew Sarris concluded that early efforts against the film merely drove racism underground without successfully negating Griffith's racism. Another negative result of the controversy, he said, was the precedent set whereby "Southern theater owners exercised veto power over the slightest intimation of black-white miscegenation, and this veto power was never challenged" for decades.[72]

At least one film historian has focused attention on later censorship controversies. For example, protests in the 1920's based on the film's portrayal of the Ku Klux Klan are summarized by Maxim Simcovitch.[73] He related that "due to Klan growth and 'riots' in various cities. . .The Birth of a Nation was prohibited by the police in different areas throughout the country."[74] Simcovitch specifically identified Chicago, Detroit, Kansas and New York as scenes of such protest.[75]

Seymour Stern has written a number of monographs and articles focusing on The Birth. Most mention protests against the film. In one of his earliest articles, Stern said about the film that "aside from its single artistic merit the world-wide waves of purely external commotion which the picture stirred up form a teeming chapter in the annals of the cinema."[76] The controversy surrounding the film kept "it on exhibition for more than a decade to come."[77] In another article Stern stated "flare ups were especially bloody in Portland, Seattle, St. Louis, Louisville, and other cities."[78]

A longer analysis of the film by Stern was published in 1945 as a special supplement to Sight and Sound and it contained one section on litigation involving the film.[79] Here, Stern identified: 1915, New York, as the scene of a demonstration; 1915, Boston, as the scene of a "race riot allegedly incited" by the film; 1921, New York, as the scene of street demonstrations; and, 1924, Chicago, as the scene of violent clashes which spread into city-wide "bloody riots."[80] In addition demonstrations "shattered the peace of various other communities" and "where the Negro vote meant money and power The Birth of a Nation was banned."[81] As a result "dangerous screen censorship" and the move for national censorship legislation began.[82]

In a later monograph for Film Culture, Stern developed this theme further and said that many scenes were cut from the film during its original New York screening.[83] However, Stern asserted that attacks against the film per se did not last. Rather, three specific periods of protest existed. The first, upon the film itself, lasted only one month; the second, against Thomas Dixon, lasted another two months; and, the third, against Griffith, began after the third month of the film's initial run and continues into modern times.[84] Stern reasoned that the early NAACP campaign against Griffith and the film failed because racial prejudice was firmly established in the U. S. by 1915, and therefore, the NAACP could not prove in court that the film would automatically be responsible for black persecution.[85] Because the film itself could not be stopped, Stern concluded that blacks and white liberals turned their attack toward Dixon and then toward Griffith.[86] Thus, the "campaign against The Birth of a Nation soon became as it remained, a classic. . .application of what Charles Beard termed the devil theory of history."[87] The attacks against Griffith are of two types: the accusation that Griffith created The Birth specifically as anti-black propaganda, and the accusation that the effect of the film on race relations justifies suppression regardless of Griffith's motive.[88] Stern rejected the first accusation and concluded that although the film probably "retarded by at least half a century the progress of white negro relations"[89] the second set of objections drew attention from the "basic causes" of black oppression and helped the film at the box office.[90] In the 1930's and 1940's, the Stalinists in the U. S. became and remained the major exponent of suppression of the film.[91]

In the late 1940's, Stern engaged in a correspondence debate centering on the film in Sight and Sound. The series of four articles began with what Stern considered an attack on Griffith by Peter Noble. Noting that the film was originally banned in California and "a dozen other states" Noble contended that The Birth was a blot on Griffith's name and that "thirty years ago it constituted a direct incitement to race riot and seeing it today still tends to leave a nasty taste in the mouth."[92]

Prefaced by a short statement from Griffith, Stern replied that the film was never banned in California and that the film merely reflected existing racial attitudes rather than created them.[93] Stern concluded his criticism by stating ". . .it is all too clear to us that what really annoys his [Griffith's] critics. . .that Griffith in his films fails to reflect the Stalinist ideologies of our day which pass for liberalism."[94] As an insert with this article, Sight and Sound ran a short statement from the Museum of Modern Art outlining the decision not to include The Birth in the Museum's 1946 film retrospective because "we have. . .had sufficient and repeated evidence of the potency of the anti-Negro bias and believe that exhibiting it at this time of heightened social tensions cannot be justified."[95]

E. L. Cranstone described Stern's reply to Noble as "red baiting."[96] Cranstone asserted that proof of the film's "distorted nature" existed because of the long line of criticism against it and "that it has started riots, that its exhibition has been banned by the Museum of Modern Art, that the tests carried out in American schools confirmed that it creates racial bias."[97]

Stern's reply to Cranstone is framed within Stern's theory of a communist/Stalinist conspiracy against the film and Griffith.[98] In part Stern said "the religiously political garbage dumped on the subject by self-styled critics and historians such as Peter Noble,

Lewis Jacobs, and Mr. Cranstone more than ever convinces me that I am right. . .similarly the fact that its exhibition has been banned by the Museum of Modern Art film library proves nothing. Almost everyone today knows where the political sympathies of the film library lie. . ."[99] Stern also repudiated Cranstone's assertion that Stern admitted the film started riots:

> I wrote that riots accompanied or followed the film. I have never denied that its effect on the Negro people has been extremely damaging. But who began the riots is another question. Recently The Birth of a Nation in a cut version was revived at the Republic Theater across the street from the old Liberty where it first played in New York City. Communist partisans tried in various ways to foment a riot. No riot ensued. But suppose it had; would this then have been the fault of the film?[100]

After the conclusion of this letter, Sight and Sound printed an editorial note stating "these correspondences must cease" and thus ended the brief public interchange of ideas on the censorship controversy.[101]

Although Stern frequently mentioned censorship throughout his works concerning The Birth, he interpreted censorship efforts after the first month of the film's existence to be primarily against Griffith rather than the film. In addition, after 1930 he said these efforts became part of a Stalinist conspiracy to discredit Griffith and further the communist ideology. When Stern specifically identified censorship attempts, he usually did so without specific source attribution.

At least two Master of Arts theses have analyzed specific areas of controversy stemming from The Birth. Tom Murray White identified and evaluated five major historical assertions of the film.[102] Although censorship of the film is not one of his major themes, White briefly discussed whether the controversial race question and the possibility of race riots were used as part of promotional campaigns to increase attendance. White concluded that although there was considerable opposition to The Birth, both legal and extra-legal, no evidence existed to support the theory that publicity men working for the film's distribution company staged demonstrations to promote the film.[103] White asserted "demonstrations which did take place were apparently conducted by people who were honestly opposed to the showing of the film."[104] Concerning an alleged riot at New York's Liberty Theatre, White concluded there was "never anything approaching a riot in New York City."[105]

Rather than testing the major historical themes in The Birth, Charles Larry Hutchins strove to isolate and evaluate the controversies engendered by sociological and historical issues present in the film.[106] Hutchins did not deal specifically with censorship but, in his conclusion stated:

> As a final comment on the controversy engendered by The Birth of a Nation. . .the effects of the controversy itself have probably been as influential in publicizing the film as any organized advertising campaign could have been. The NAACP began its organized attempts to censor and stop the film only days after the New York premier. They made protests in newspapers, sent committees to various governmental officials, and even organized the mass demonstration in Boston. . .The Birth of a Nation is probably the first major example of film censorship in America. . .the attention which such censorship brought to the film has done as much to produce its mass audiences as any publicity campaign Griffith could have carried out. It is hard to imagine the people of Boston staying home from the showing of a film which was publicized on the front page of their newspapers for three days in a row.[107]

Hutchins drew from Stern's analysis of cut scenes when discussing specifically how the film was censored.[108]

An article evaluating historical inaccuracies in the film without specifically discussing censorship is "Cultural History Written With Lightning: The Significance of _The Birth of a Nation_."[109] In this article historian Everett Carter contended that the film visualized a "whole set of irrational cultural assumptions which may be termed the 'plantation illusion.'"[110] This false vision was dangerous, Carter believed, because those who saw the film "forever viewed themselves and their country's history through its colorations."[111]

Thus, although articles and monographs focusing on the film contain references to censorship of the film, these references tend to be scattered, presented without primary source attribution, and, at times, conflict with one another.

Articles and Monographs About Individuals Important in the Controversies

Articles and monographs about Griffith often discuss his reaction to censorship of _The Birth_. For example, a selection of commentaries by and about Griffith which contain references to censorship are reprinted in _Focus on D. W. Griffith_.[112] In one article Griffith termed suppression of the film "a drooling travesty of sense."[113] Griffith concluded:

> We spent over $250,000 the first six months combatting stupid persecution brought against the picture by ill-minded censors and politicians who were playing for the Negro vote. Lawyers had to be retained every place we took the picture and we paid

out enough in rents for theaters where we were not allowed to show the picture to make an average film profitable. But we finally won. Now we are showing the picture with no hindrance.[114]

Lillian Gish recalled that Griffith "reacted to the violence and censorship with astonishment, shock, and sorrow. . .then slowly his reaction turned to anger."[115] Gish also speculated that part of the immediate box office success of the film might have come from the controversy stirred by the NAACP and the Booker T. Washington clubs:

Fist fights and picket lines occurred at many premieres. . . The opening at Clune's had nearly been halted by rumors of a race riot. . .When it opened at the Tremont Theater, 5,000 Negroes marched on the state capitol building demanding that the film be banned. Outside the Forrest Theater in Philadelphia fights and rioting broke out between 500 policemen and 3,000 Negroes. War news in the papers gave way to stories of this violence. Cities all over the country clamored to see the film. . .Ugly attacks of violence flared up wherever the film was shown and have continued to this day.[116]

Robert Henderson, a Griffith biographer, agreed that "Griffith was more disturbed by the attacks on *The Birth* than he was elated by its success. . .the campaigns to censor. . .seemed to him attacks on truth."[117] Henderson identified the following footage as censored: the most inflammatory racist scenes, references to the hypocrisy of New England abolitionists, and a reference to a letter from Lincoln to Stanton stating that the black race was inferior to the white race.[118]

In his dissertation concerning Griffith, Russell Merritt, film scholar, observed that the footage showing blacks being transported back to Africa was censored and that the censorship boards of New York, Boston, Ohio, and Washington, D. C. were forced to cut the most inflammatory anti-black scenes.[119]

William Monroe Trotter's role in the 1915 Boston protest is described in a biography by Stephen R. Fox.[120] Fox concluded that Trotter's 1915 arrest outside the Tremont Theatre occurred because the ticket seller refused to sell him a ticket. Fox did not call the incident a riot, but did dub it "the most ominous racial incident in Boston in anyone's memory."[121] Although the film proved "impregnable" in 1915, Trotter and others joined in 1921 to stop the film's scheduled Boston revival.[122] As all accounts of Trotter's role in the 1915 incident, Fox's story suffered because no issues of Trotter's newspaper The Boston Guardian for that time period are extant.

A somewhat different interpretation of the Tremont Theatre incident is found in one of Raymond Cook's biographies of Thomas Dixon. Cook contended that at the Tremont "a riot occurred during which the police fought with a crowd of ten thousand people for 24 hours."[123] Cook did not mention Trotter and credited Moorfield Storey with leading the Boston protest. Cook concluded that "no theater was permanently closed" to the film and that although "the company spent thousands of dollars in legal fees it gained rewards many times greater."[124] In an earlier Dixon biography, Cook asserted that New York's Liberty Theatre was the scene of a "near riot" in 1915 when people sitting in the front row began throwing eggs at the screen.[125] Cook said that Dixon felt the protests stemmed from a "sectional conspiracy."[126]

Two letters from black author Charles Waddell Chesnutt to Ohio officials protesting a proposed Ohio revival of the film are reprinted in a Chesnutt biography.[127]

Thus, a conflicting picture of the issues involved in fighting for and against suppression of the film emerges from the works which discuss individuals directly involved in censorship controversies.

The Birth of a Nation in General Film Censorship Works

When individuals interested in the legal history of film discuss early film censorship, The Birth of a Nation is frequently mentioned. Richard Randall, for example, identified The Birth as the first film for which courts sustained the right of communities to censor films touching upon race questions.[128] As supporting evidence Randall cited Bainbridge v. Minneapolis, a case involving a mayor's ban on the film.[129]

Ira Carmen discussed two other instances of censorship of The Birth. One involved a Kansas Supreme Court decision which ordered the film returned to the Board of Review for additional consideration.[131] Carmen speculated that the decision came as the result of public pressure "against the (censor) bureau for allowing a permit to issue."[132] In an interview with a member of the Atlanta, Georgia, film censorship board, Carmen found that the film had been banned from that city in 1959 because the board considered it "a race-baiter from way back."[133] Carmen interpreted this action as "undoubtedly a violation of the Burstyn doctrine."[134]

According to Murray Schumach, the early fight against the film was led by the NAACP because the film "was a hateful thing to Negroes since it portrayed them as vicious and stupid. . ."[135] Schumach did not identify specific actions against the film.

Early censorship of The Birth in Ohio is discussed by Ivan Brychta in his analysis of the Ohio film censorship laws. Brychta summarized three court decisions involving the film during the time period 1916-1917. According to Brychta the most important decision in the series was rendered by the Cuyahoga Court of Common Pleas.[136] In this case, the court "rendered an historical decision laying down the principle that municipalities had no jurisdiction in film censorship matters after the censorship function was assumed by the state government."[137] A Youngstown, Ohio, mayoral ban on the film is related in a work on censorship during World War I by James R. Mack.[138] Mack also said that Dr. Frederick P. Keppel, the third assistant secretary of war, wrote a letter to the Committee on Public Information of the Moving Picture Industry requesting that The Birth be withdrawn from circulation during the duration of the war. In his letter, Keppel expressed the belief that because the North and the South had become united "in a common struggle for democracy. . . such a bitter film should not be allowed to keep open the wounds of the Civil War."[139] Other film censorship articles identified Boston,[140] Colorado, and New Jersey[141] as scenes of actions against the film.

Thus, although monographs and articles considering film censorship in general do contain specific references to court cases involving the film, no single work brings together and analyzes the range of restraints utilized against the film.

The Motion Picture Medium
and Racial Prejudice

Authors who consider the issue of whether the motion picture medium is a force capable of either dispelling or reinforcing racial prejudice often discuss The Birth. Noting what he considered an overall negative contribution of the film industry to race relations, writer Dalton Trumbo said that "The most gigantic milestones of our appeal to public patronage have been the anti-Negro pictures The Birth of a Nation and Gone With the Wind."[142] Further, the motion picture industry code of ethics established originally by the Hays office spoke against only one form of racial portrayal, miscegenation.[143]

Asserting the power of the media to form public opinion, critic L. D. Reddick characterized The Birth as the first motion picture to merge with "the stream of anti-Negro propaganda which pollutes the mind of people."[144] Reddick concluded that although the picture was "the most vicious anti-Negro film that has ever appeared on the American screen,"[145] initial censorship efforts were successful in less than a dozen cities and served primarily "as a great advertisement to thousands who might have never heard of it."[146] However, contemporary (1940) attempts to revive the film "have been beaten back."[147] Reddick applauded such successes and concluded that the suppression of negative black images in mass communications was the necessary forerunner of racial equality.

In contrast, historian Thomas Cripps asserted that the existence of censorship for racial portrayal "has been one of the most persistent influences on the maintenance of stereotypes."[148] Cripps interpreted the racial vision present in films from The Birth to Gone With the Wind as reflective of the attitudes of society as a whole rather than the creator of that vision. Precedents allowing censorship of films for racial presentations allowed censorship boards (primarily in the South) to suppress films which even "implied equality" between blacks and whites.[149] Further, "where there is no censorship on racial grounds producers sensitive to protest from both negroes and whites have reduced negro roles to ambivalent ciphers."[150] Cripps identified three periods of blacks in films to support his theory. The periods involve the establishment of seven black stereotypes: "up to 1954, negroes as a social problem; through the 1950's negroes as emerging characters yet bearing the vestiges of Rastus; and, finally from the varied themes of the 1960's the beginnings of the fully articulated character."[151]

Several authors have speculated about the relationship between The Birth and negative racial stereotypes in society. Seven stereotypes are identified by Sterling Brown in an analysis of black characters portrayed by white authors prior to 1933.[152] Brown characterized The Birth of a Nation as particularly harmful because it "fixed the stereotype in the mass mind."[153] Another analyst of black film stereotypes concluded that The Birth of a Nation "harmed good race relations by depicting Negroes as rapists and slaves."[154] As a foremost example of prejudicial attitudes depicted in film,

Anne K. and Hart M. Nelsen called The Birth "manifestly inflammatory freely manipulating as it does the obviously stereotyped characters to drive home its message of racial hatred."[155] Thomas Cripps[156] and Donald Bogle[157] concluded in separate articles that The Birth was influential as an expression of anti-black sentiments because it was the first technically superior film to bring together existing black stereotypes. Bogle contended that to the existing black stereotypes (the Tom, the Coon, the Tragic Mulatto, and the Mammy), Griffith added a fifth, the Brutal Black Buck.[158] These types were presented "with such force and power that his [Griffith's] film touched off a wave of controversy and was denounced as the most slanderous anti-Negro movie ever released."[159] Because of the excessive and powerful stock characterizations, Bogle concluded that blacks did not "meekly" accept the film in 1915.[160] According to Bogle, the NAACP picketed the New York premiere and later demonstrated against the picture in Chicago and Boston. Also, "riots broke out in a number of cities."[161] The banning of the film in five states and 19 cities was the tangible result of the early protest.[162] Bogle also outlined continued efforts against the film including 1921 opposition urging censorship because the film glorified the Ku Klux Klan; the Museum of Modern Art's refusal to include The Birth in its 1946 motion picture retrospective; the NAACP pickets at the 1947 New York revival; and, the "aborted" plans to show the film on television in 1959.[163]

Two general histories of blacks in film discuss briefly censorship of The Birth. James P. Murray charged "that the passions it aroused and the tensions it created were not forgotten outside the theatre, patrons overflowed the streets and race riots and mob action followed."[164] Murray identified New York, Connecticut, Illinois, Kansas, Massachusetts, Minnesota, New Jersey, Wisconsin, and Ohio as states which refused to license the film for exhibition.[165] Peter Noble is somewhat more specific in his censorship references. Noble said that the film was banned "for a time" during "the war years and into the 1920's" in New York, Connecticut, Illinois, Kansas, Massachusetts, Minnesota, New Jersey, Wisconsin, Ohio, "and many other states."[166] Specifically, Noble noted that the film was banned from Philadelphia in 1931 because the mayor declared the film "prejudicial to peace between the black and white citizens."[167] Also the film's 1942 New York revival was stopped because of "the opposition of the Negro press."[168]

Chronicles of black history often interpret The Birth's role in race relations. Black historian John Hope Franklin contended that the film bore witness to deteriorating race relations because it "proved' that he [the Negro] was unfit for citizenship to say nothing of equality."[169] The NAACP fight against the film was also based on the assumption that the picture would accelerate racial prejudice. In her history of the NAACP, Mary White Ovington recalled her initial testimony against the film in Boston, 1915:

> I had decided to speak only of that part that treated the Negro as a dangerous, half-insane brute. To me the whole picture was false. . .But the picture. . .was the South's side of the story and I was not there to ask that sectional history be censored. If I could show, however, that the method of presentation might injure the Negro in the city where it was shown, if it was so

bestial as to create antagonism, even violence then it should not be produced. I made my plea on this line, dwelling especially on the flight of the white girl whose pursuer, his great clutching hands repeatedly pictured, was enough to make a Bostonian on Beacon Hill double-lock the door at night.[170]

Ovington further reported that the beginning and end of the pursuit scene were subsequently cut, leaving the audience to wonder why the white girl was found dead.[171] Although NAACP efforts "had a considerable nuisance value," the film was more victorious in its efforts to discredit blacks.[172] In his history of the Association, Langston Hughes said that efforts against the film were significant because they were "the first campaign against the malicious misrepresentation of the Negro people in films. . ."[173] However, "the campaign had little effect on the film's distribution" other than an occasional banning or elimination of the "worst of its anti-Negro footage."[174] Another author described the Association's efforts against The Birth as a "crushing defeat."[175] Charles Flint Kellog observed that "the problem of combatting the evil effects of the picture presented the liberal leadership of the NAACP with a dilemma."[176] A few leaders opposed censorship for First Amendment reasons, defended the individual's right to judge, and advocated vigorous protest without suppression. Others urged the association to retain legal council to fight the film. Kellog credited Lillian Wald with the suggestion which formed the initial action of the national organization, a procession of 500 members to New York Mayor John Mitchell to request censorship.[177] After the New York campaign failed, the NAACP worked primarily through its branches to attain censorship at local or state levels. A tactic evolving during World War I was an appeal to all governors and state councils of national defense, asking them to "ban the picture on the grounds of its being detrimental to the war effort because it fostered race hatred and disunity in a time of crisis."[178] Kellog concluded that the West Virginia Council of Defense specifically and "several other states" banned the film on the suggested grounds.[179] In his analysis of the 1919 Chicago race riot, William M. Tuttle noted that Omaha, Nebraska's mayor, Edward P. Smith, banned the film because of "the precarious state of race relations" in his city.[130]

Representative of the Marxist attacks against the film which concerned Seymour Stern is V. J. Jerome's history The Negro in Hollywood Films.[181] Jerome identified The Birth as part of a Hollywood "tactic to counteract the new liberation movement of the Negro people as well as to hold back Negro and white unity."[132] Of The Birth Jerome said:

> The Foulness of capitalist 'culture' has never been more glaringly revealed. By viciously falsifying the Negro's role in the Reconstruction period following the Civil War, by monstrously contriving scenes like that of the Negro legislators in session. . .this picture set the style for all future slanders of the Negro people and distortions of the Reconstruction period. The film, concretely, aimed to 'justify' the denial of civil rights and equal opportunities to Negroes and to rationalize flare-ups, terror, and lynchings as both 'necessary' and 'romantic.'[183]

Jerome credited the NAACP with original opposition to the film. Then, the Communists joined the blacks and protested vigorously against the film particularly through the Communist press.[134] In the late 1940's the film's revival was met with picket lines in a variety of cities throughout the country.[185] In spite of these efforts, Jerome concluded that "this foul and vicious spectacle is again on display in various parts of the country."[186]

Attorneys Theodore Kupferman and Philip O'Brien who defended the film <u>Curley</u> against censorship in the South stemming from the film's positive portrayal of blacks criticized the U. S. Supreme Court for consistently avoiding what they considered the constitutional question of whether films can be censored for racial or ethnic portrayals.[187] According to Kupferman and O'Brien "motion picture censorship started with sex and was nurtured on scandal. . .it has expanded on racial and political grounds."[188] <u>The Birth</u> is identified as the film responsible for the first municipal ordinances forbidding the derision of minorities in films. The attorneys also tied the film to the problem of the hostile audience. This rationale argues that a film may be censored because its subject matter may incite viewers to violence because of their hostility toward the topic presented. Speaking specifically of this problem, a writer in the <u>Columbia Law Review</u> said:

> The hostile audience. . .is the extent to which the conduct of persons present at the scene of a speech may render governmental prohibition of otherwise lawful expression constitutionally permissible. . .the problem here begins where that of the typical free speech ends. . .with the finding that the combination of speaker, speech and audience creates a clear and present danger of imminent substantial harm in the form of a riot or serious breach of the peace.[189]

However, Kupferman and O'Brien did not mention specific cases in which the hostile audience censorship rationale was used against <u>The Birth</u>.

Zechariah Chafee interpreted the federal sedition law of 1919-1920 as a First Amendment violation in part because the statutes forbade publication of that which appealed to race prejudice or was intended to cause rioting. Chafee felt that such a provision would "suppress all but the most carefully guarded presentations of the wrongs of the Negro."[190] An example of the form of free press abridgement offered by Chafee is the West Virginia censorship law passed to suppress The Birth. Chafee also cites the case of Epoch v. Davis as evidence in this context.[191]

John Haynes Holmes termed the censorship of film for racial reasons "a serious situation in the field of civil liberties."[192] Holmes called The Birth the supreme example of a film attacked on racial grounds:

> Here is a screen play which must stand technically memorable in the history of the movie. Its appearance marked the opening of a new era on the screen. But, the material of the picture is vicious. It undoubtedly was a contributing factor in the revival of the KKK. What more natural than the fact that our colored friends have for years sought to suppress this picture wherever it has appeared? Its revival is now practically impossible. This is understandable enough, but what about the principle of freedom? Instead of outlawing serious literary and dramatic works in which offensive or careless material appears let the sensitively maimed rise up and protest. . .every means for the expression of free opinion is as available for good as for evil uses. It is only when such means are fanatically denied us, that we need to be afraid.[193]

In another article, James Mason Brown termed censorship for racial reasons a force which might destroy freedom of speech. Brown concluded that minority group members were wrong in believing that "safety and esteem can be guaranteed by the placing of a ban or the action of a censor."[194]

On the other hand, Dore Shary, a former production executive with Metro-Goldwyn-Mayer, likened the racial situation in the United States to a war, a war against prejudice. In this context, Shary reasoned that certain censorship measures must be taken in war time which would otherwise be inappropriate in times of peace. Shary termed The Birth "a legitimate cause for alarm to the Negro minority."[195] Shary concluded that when the battle against prejudice was won, censorship for racial reasons would no longer be necessary.

Two early empirical studies attempted to determine if viewing The Birth increased racial prejudice expressed by young people.[196] Hubert Blumer secured motion picture autobiographies from over a thousand young adults and conducted open-ended interviews with part of his sample.[197] Blumer concluded from what individuals said about The Birth that "sometimes the meaning which movie goers may get from the same picture are diametrically opposite."[198]

Ruth C. Petersen and L. L. Thurstone's experiment involved 434 Crystal Lake, Illinois, sixth to twelfth grade children. Crystal Lake, Illinois, was chosen because the school superintendent assured the researchers that very few children in the town had ever seen or known blacks. In a test given to the children prior to The Birth's screening, "most showed a pronounced liberality toward the Negro race."[199] After The Birth was shown to the children, their attitude scores bore "a definite record of a shift toward anti-Negro prejudice."[200] After five months, the children were retested and "62% of the prejudice found the day after seeing the adverse film was present in these young minds."[201] The tests were given eight

months after initial viewing and prejudice was still in evidence.
From this study the author of the Payne study summary volume concluded that:

> Prejudice against the Negro had been quite clearly increased in these children's minds by the movie The Birth of a Nation. The virgin unmarked slates had been all but indelibly written upon with a pencil of peculiar force. The motion picture which can be a tremendous power for good, can as obviously be a powerful force for evil depending upon its content and use.[202]

Some individuals who objected to The Birth suggested a film containing positive images of blacks would be a viable alternative to censorship. Thomas Cripps explained:

> To deal with the racist social propaganda of The Birth of a Nation blacks needed to choose a tactic that allowed maximum control of rhetoric, theme, imagery, much as Griffith and Thomas Dixon had controlled their movie. . . .either that or they would be forced to exhaust themselves in sterile campaigns advocating censorship.
>
> Black leaders knew early in the struggle against Birth of a Nation that blind advocacy of censorship was a dead end. No matter how many new members flocked to the NAACP; how many flagging branches blossomed or new ones sprouted; how many whites were converted or scared by the new black unity; how many producers backed off from the subject of race, in the final battle censorship was a rear guard action rather than a direct assault on racist attitudes in American life.[203]

Although the NAACP and the Booker T. Washington Tuskegee circle attempted to join forces to produce a picture to counter The Birth, its production was delayed because of financial problems. When finished in 1918, the film had little resemblance to the production originally planned.[204]

Thus, works which consider the motion picture as capable of dispelling or reinforcing racial prejudice frequently mention The

Birth. Within these discussions are references of varying specificity to attempts to ban the film on the grounds that it slandered the black race, would incite racial hatred, or would precipitate race rioting or lynching.

The Pieces Together

From this literature, it is clear that contradictory accounts of censorship controversies centering around The Birth are evident in the literature concerning the film. No single author has dealt systematically with freedom of expression issues as applied to the film throughout its history. A rigorous examination of primary sources to identify the range of restraints used against the film will yield a more complete picture of censorial actions involving The Birth of a Nation.

Questions

The basic research question guiding the study, then, is: Did arguments for and against legal and extra-legal restraints against The Birth of a Nation change from 1915-1973 as the U. S. Supreme Court's interpretation of the First Amendment applied to filmic expression changed? Evidence relating to the question has been gathered and interpreted within a framework provided by the following series of secondary questions:

1) Has there been a change in the U. S. Supreme Court's interpretation of the First Amendment as it applies to filmic expression from 1915 to 1973?

2) What kind of restraints (prior restraint, subsequent restraint, prior restraint partial, subsequent restraint

partial) have been used against *The Birth of a Nation* during the film's history, 1915 to 1973?

3) What arguments have been presented in courts at all levels for and against censorship of *The Birth of a Nation* from 1915 to 1973, and how do these follow the direction of the U. S. Supreme Court in dealing with restraints against filmic expression?

4) When administrative bodies acted in a quasi-judicial capacity concerning *The Birth of a Nation,* did they follow the direction of the U. S. Supreme Court in dealing with restraint of filmic expression?

5) Does the legislative history of specific censorship laws suggest that these laws were designed specifically to restrain *The Birth of a Nation*?

6) What interest groups advocated censorship of the film and what arguments did they offer to support restraint of the film and what interest groups supported the film and what arguments did they offer in support of the film's right to the screen?

7) What kind of extra-legal actions have been taken for and against censorship of *The Birth of a Nation* and how do these follow the direction of the U. S. Supreme Court in dealing with restraints against filmic expression?

8) Were tactics other than court action, administrative intervention, legislative action, and extra-legal means used for and against *The Birth of a Nation* during debates over the film's right to the screen, and if so, how did these tactics follow the direction of the U. S. Supreme Court in dealing with restraints against filmic expression?

These questions aided the development of a data pool from which an in-depth analysis of censorship will emerge. The first question will establish the legal parameters within which individuals interested in censorship of the film operated in various historical periods. Data relating to questions two through eight will identify the range of censorial actions and rationales for and against censorship of the film.

Procedures

Because historical evidence always is incomplete, historian Louis Gottschalk wrote:

> . . .only a part of what was observed in the past was remembered by those who observed it; only a part of what was recorded has survived; only a part of what has survived has come to the historian's attention; only a part of what has come to their attention is credible; only a part of what has been grasped can be expounded or narrated by the historian.[205]

Consequently, the goal of the historian is "verisimilitude with regard to a perished past."[206] Therefore, this study cannot identify every instance of censorship involving The Birth of a Nation. Rather there is presented as much evidence as possible to re-create a "verisimilar image" of as much of the film's censorship history as possible. To accomplish this, a literature search was conducted through secondary sources and the major manuscript collections concerning the film. If a controversy was mentioned in a primary source, it was coded for analysis. If a controversy was mentioned in a secondary source, it was noted for further verification. If the controversy was confirmed in another secondary source or in a primary source, it was coded for analysis. If the controversy could not be verified either through primary sources or through more than one secondary source, it was not included in this study for the purpose of analysis.[207] The information recorded for each controversy included the specific issue involved in the controversy, the parties involved on each side of the issue, and the tactics employed by the parties involved to accomplish controversy resolution. Also, the manner in which the controversy was resolved, the year of resolution, and the eventual censorship/no censorship decision were noted. The rationales for censorship/no censorship actions were also recorded. Censorship controversies thus identified were then categorized according to tactics utilized to accomplish controversy resolution and analyzed accordingly.

Within the context of this research the terms "censor," "censorship," "restraint," and "suppression" are used interchangeably and refer to a successful or unsuccessful attempt to "examine, review, expurgate, or change" any or all of the film.[208] A source was considered to be neutral concerning the film if it did not take a specific pro-or-anti-censorship position concerning the film.

Kinds of restraints were defined: (1) prior restraint, the alteration of the content of the film before it was shown to the general public of a given geographic area or the banning of the film in its entirety from a given geographic area before it was shown to the general public of that area; (2) subsequent restraint, the alteration of the content of the film or the banning of the film in its entirety from a given geographic area after it had been shown to the general public of that area.

Existing analyses of censored motion picture content tend to be descriptive rather than quantitative. An example of a well-known descriptive analysis is Chief Justice Earl Warren's dissent in the Times Film decision.[209] Pointing to what he considered the inadequacies of the majority decision, Warren discussed a variety of censorship cases. Although several of these examples are grouped according to kind of censorship rationale employed, the Chief

Justice, as one would expect, did not attempt a quantitative study.

One of the earliest and few quantified studies of film censorship was Morris Ernst and Pare Lorentz's Censored: The Private Life of the Movie. Ernst and Lorentz used 19 categories to examine 2,960 cuts ordered by state licensing boards in 1928.[210] Categories included: improper reference to women, reference to drinking, derogatory reference to countries, and references to suicide or cruelty.[211] Unfortunately, the authors did not explain how the data concerning the scenes cut was obtained, nor did they present operational definitions for their categories.

A more thoroughly delineated set of censorship categories was developed by Richard Randall.[212] Randall examined existing censorship ordinances and found the following standards: obscenity, indecency; immorality; scenes likely to induce unlawful behavior, incite crime, or cause disturbance of the public peace; scenes portraying crime or criminal behavior; scenes which cast reproach or derision on class, race, or religion, or which encourage racial, religious, or sectional prejudice; particularly shocking scenes; and the general standard of scenes containing anything objectionable, questionable, or harmful to the public.[213] The censorship rationale categories utilized in this study were developed from the standards found by Randall.

To view censorship of The Birth of a Nation in as many periods of the film's history as possible, the study spanned the years 1915 to 1973. The time period began with 1915, the year of both the film's first screening and the U. S. Supreme Court's first film censorship decision.[214] The study terminated with 1973 because this was judged the most recent complete year for which pertinent materials might reasonably be expected to be available and because the Supreme Court issued a series of obscenity rulings that year which bear on the history of film censorship.

The data for this analysis were drawn from censorship arguments in court opinions, legislative documents, censorship board records, newspaper articles, and manuscript collections. The findings are supplemented by descriptive information.

An overview of motion picture censorship in the United States is included as Chapter II to provide a frame of reference for evaluating censorship actions involving The Birth. Chapter III considers The Birth of a Nation censorship controversies fought in the courts. Criminal proceedings regarding the film are discussed in Chapter IV. Controversies in which officials were asked to use their administrative power of office against the film are analyzed in Chapter V. Chapter VI outlines legislative actions tied to The Birth. Extra-legal actions taken in connection with the film are documented in Chapter VII. The findings are summarized and analyzed in Chapter VIII.

NOTES TO CHAPTER I

[1] D. W. Griffith, *The Rise and Fall of Free Speech in America* (Los Angeles: D. W. Griffith, 1916). A prefatory note by Griffith stated: "This book is not copyrighted. The press is invited to freely use its contents." Part of the pamphlet is reprinted in Harry M. Geduld, ed., *Focus on D. W. Griffith* (Englewood Cliffs, N. J.: Prentice-Hall, 1971), pp. 43-45.

[2] *Joseph Burstyn, Inc. v. Wilson*, 343 U. S. 495, 96 L. Ed. 1098, 72 S. Ct. 777 (1952).

[3] *Times Film Corp. v. Chicago*, 355 U. S. 35, 35 L. Ed. 2d 403, 78 S. Ct. 115 (1961).

[4] Don Samelson, "Night Riders Strike Again," *The Badger Herald*, 24-27 October 1974, p. 4. Samelson related a protest by the Committee Against Racism (CAR) against a scheduled showing of the film sponsored by a university film society at the University of Wisconsin-Madison. CAR members blocked the entrances to the auditorium where the screening was scheduled and stopped the public showing.

[5] William Rivers, Theodore Peterson, and Jay Jensen, *The Mass Media and Modern Society*, 2nd ed. (San Francisco: Rinehart Press, 1971), p. 53.

[6] Robert M. Henderson, *D. W. Griffith: His Life and Work* (New York: Oxford University Press, 1972), p. vi.

[7] Edward Wagenknecht and Anthony Slide, *The Films of D. W. Griffith* (New York: Crown, 1975), p. 59

[8] Fred Silva, ed., *Focus on the Birth of a Nation* (Englewood Cliffs, N. J.: Prentice-Hall, 1971), p. 1.

[9] I. C. Jarvie, *Movies and Society* (New York: Basic Books, Inc., 1971), p. 164.

[10] Garth Samuel Jowett, "Media Power and Social Control: The Motion Picture in America, 1894-1936" (unpublished Ph.D. dissertation, University of Pennsylvania, 1972), p. 111.

[11] Wagenknecht and Slide, p. 58.

[12] Geduld, p. 1.

[13] Seymour Stern, "Griffith: *The Birth of a Nation*, Part I," *Film Culture*, 36 (Spring-Summer, 1965): 7.

[14] Silva, p. 3.

[15] Geduld, p. 1.

[16] Lewis Jacobs, The Rise of the American Film (New York: Harcourt Brace and Co., 1939), p. 179.

[17] Andrew Sarris, "Birth of a Nation or White Power Back When," in Andrew Sarris, The Primal Screen (New York: Simon and Schuster, 1973), p. 27. Originally published in The Village Voice, 17 July 1969, p. 45 and 24 July 1969, pp. 37 and 45; reprinted in Silva, pp. 106-110.

[18] Donald Bogle, Toms, Coons, Mulattoes, Mammies and Bucks (New York: Bantam Books, 1973), pp. 10-11.

[19] Silva, p. 4. The rationale for the shift in primary title is not precisely recorded. Terry Ramsaye suggested in his history of film, A Million and One Nights (New York: Simon & Schuster, 1926) that Dixon initiated the title change after a private screening of the film in New York on February 20, 1915. The story is repeated frequently throughout The Birth of a Nation literature. See for example, Iris Barry and Eileen Bowser, D. W. Griffith: American Film Master (New York: Museum of Modern Art, 1965), p. 47; Jacobs, pp. 147-175; and Henderson, p. 156. Roy Aitken, financial backer of the film, attributed the name change to Dixon's suggestion during the film's opening on February 8, 1915, at the Clune Theatre, Los Angeles. See Roy Aitken as told to Al Nelson, Birth of a Nation Story (Middleburg, Va.: Denlinger, 1965), p. 46. Lillian Gish recalled a different origin. In The Movies, Mr. Griffith, and Me with Ann Pinchot (New York: Avon, 1961), Gish suggested that Griffith initiated the title change after a private screening for Thomas Dixon prior to the New York opening . . . "After Mr. Griffith ran the film for Thomas Dixon, the author exclaimed 'That isn't my story, at all. It isn't The Clansman. It could be called anything else.' 'Would you mind,' Mr. Griffith asked, 'if I call it The Birth of a Nation?' 'Certainly not,' Dixon replied," See Gish, p. 154). However, both original copyright listings for the film are under the primary title The Birth of a Nation. The first copyright entry for the film lists February 8, 1915, as the date of publication for the motion picture. The entry reads "The Birth of a Nation, 1915, 12 reels. Based on the novel The Clansman by Thomas Dixon. Credits: Director, David W. Griffith, scenario, D. W. Griffith and Frank E. Woods." Epoch Producing Corp. and Thomas Dixon are listed as copyright claimant. See U. S. Library of Congress, Copyright Office, Catalog of Copyright Entries, Motion Pictures, 1912-1939 (Washington D. C.: Government Printing Office, 1951), p. 69. Griffith apparently wished to copyright the film separately because copyright records indicate that on February 13, 1915, a request was filed that "The Birth of a Nation, or The Clansman, adapted from The Clansman by Thomas Dixon," be copyrighted in the name of the D. W. Griffith Corporation. See U. S.

Library of Congress, Copyright Office, Catalog p. 69. In this entry only D. W. Griffith and Frank E. Woods are listed as authors of the film and William Bitzer is credited with photography. Also advertisements for the film's Los Angeles opening contained The Birth of a Nation as an alternate title. For example, see "Griffith's startling picture The Clansman or The Birth of a Nation," Los Angeles Times, 8 February 1915, Part III, p. 1.

[20] Thomas Dixon, The Clansman (New York: Grosset & Dunlap, 1905) and Thomas Dixon, The Leopards Spots (New York: Doubleday, 1902). Griffith used no formal shooting script. As Lillian Gish recalled rather than relying on a written scenario Griffith "carried the ideas in his head." See Richard Griffith and Arthur Mayer, The Movies, revised edition, with the assistance of Eileen Bowser (New York: Simon & Schuster, 1971), p. 31 and Gish, pp. 131-163. Eileen Bowser, curator of the Griffith collection, Museum of Modern Art (MOMA), speculated that Griffith worked from playscripts of the stage version of Dixon's The Clansman. See Barry and Bowser, p. 47. A shooting script shot by shot analysis made from a print of the film donated to MOMA by Griffith was made by Theodore Huff in 1961. See Theodore Huff, A Shot Analysis of D. W. Griffith's The Birth of a Nation (New York: The Museum of Modern Art, 1961).

[21] Carlos Hurd, "Birth of Mob is Shown in Birth of Nation Film," St. Louis Post Dispatch, 30 August 1915, p. 6.

[22] See Theodore Huff.

[23] Ibid.

[24] New York American, 7 March 1915, n.t., n.p., clipping in Griffith's Personal Scrapbook, The Birth of a Nation Openings, MOMA.

[25] Gish, p. 155.

[26] Frances Hackett, "Brotherly Love," The New Republic, 20 March 1915, p. 185.

[27] "Clansman With One Scene Removed Approved," Sacramento Bee, 28 May 1915, p. 2.

[28] "A New Era of Good Will and Racial Co-operation," Kansas City Call, 8 February 1924, p. 4.

[29] Jacobs, pp. 71-88.

[30] Hearings Before The Committee on Education, House of Representatives, 64th Congress, 1st Session, on H. R. 456, A Bill to Create a New Division of the Bureau of Education to be Known as The Federal Motion Picture Commission & Defining its Powers and Duties, 13-19

January 1916. Dixon was not totally accurate in his portrait of the freedom enjoyed by The Birth in its other forms. The play The Clansman was censored at least once (See Theatre Company v. Weaver, 18 Pennsylvania District Reports 794).

[31] W. E. B. DuBois, Memorandum to Walter White, n.d., NAACP Archives, File C301, Library of Congress Manuscript Collection, Washington, D. C. (Hereafter referred to as NAACP Archives).

[32] Jacobs, pp. 171-178. Jacobs is of particular influence because contemporary media scholars often draw from this work. For examples, see Don Pember, Mass Media in America (Chicago: Science Research Associates, 1974), pp. 234-236; and, David Clark & William Blankenburg, You and Media (San Francisco: Canfield Press, 1973), pp. 69-81. See also Peter Noble, The Negro in Film (London: Skelton-Robinson, 1948). Jacobs chapter about The Birth of a Nation is reprinted in Silva, pp. 154-170.

[33] Ibid., p. 178.

[34] Ibid.

[35] Ramsaye, p. 642.

[36] Ralph Ellison, Shadow and Act (New York: Random House, 1953), p. 275.

[37] John Howard Lawson, Film: The Creative Process, 2nd ed. (New York: Hill and Wang, 1967), p. 31.

[38] Edward Wagenknecht, The Movies in the Age of Innocence (Norman: University of Oklahoma Press, 1962), p. 100.

[39] Griffith and Mayer, pp. 36-39.

[40] Lawson, p. 31.

[41] Griffith and Mayer, pp. 36-39.

[42] Wagenknecht, p. 100.

[43] Ibid., p. 101.

[44] Parker Tyler, Sex, Psyche Et Cetera in the Film (New York: Horizon Press, 1969), p. 139.

[45] Fighting a Vicious Film: Protest Against the Birth of a Nation (Boston: Boston Branch of the National Association for the Advancement of Colored People, 1915). Selections from the pamphlet are reprinted in Geduld, pp. 94-102.

[46] Griffith, The Rise and Fall of Free Speech in America.

[47] Fighting a Vicious Film, p. 7.

[48] Ibid., p. 8.

[49] Griffith, The Rise and Fall of Free Speech in America.

[50] See Silva. A selection of these articles is also reprinted in Richard A. Maynard, ed., The Black Man on Film: Racial Stereotyping (Rochelle Park, N. J.: Hayden Book Company, Inc., 1974), pp. 25-40.

[51] "Fighting Race Calumny," The Crisis, May-June 1915, Silva, pp. 66-73.

[52] Rolfe Cobleigh, "Why I Oppose The Birth of a Nation," Fighting a Vicious Film, pp. 12-16. Also in Silva, pp. 80-83.

[53] Frances Hackett, "Analysis of the Play," in Fighting a Vicious Film, pp. 9-11. Also in Silva, pp. 84-86.

[54] D. W. Griffith, "The Motion Picture & Witch Burners," in Silva, pp. 96-99.

[55] D. W. Griffith, "Defense of The Birth of a Nation and Attack on the Sullivan Bill," in Silva, pp. 88-90.

[56] Thomas Dixon, "Fair Play for The Birth of a Nation," in Silva, p. 91.

[57] Ibid., p. 95.

[58] Aitken.

[59] City Commissioners, Dayton, Ohio, "Why We Fight The Birth of a Nation," in Aitken, p. 56.

[60] Aitken, p. 57.

[61] Milton MacKaye, "The Birth of a Nation," Scribner's Magazine, November 1937, pp. 46 & 69.

[62] Ibid., p. 69.

[63] Bosley Crowther, "The Birth of The Birth of a Nation," New York Times Magazine, 7 February 1965, Section 6, p. 84.

[64] "The Great Films Society Presents The Birth of a Nation," Beverly Vista School Auditorium, Beverly Hills, California, October 21, 1948. Three page mimeographed program in Lincoln Center Clipping

File, The Birth of a Nation.

[65] Ibid., p. 2.

[66] Thomas Cripps, "The Reaction of the Negro to the Motion Picture Birth of a Nation," The Historian, 26 (P63): 244-262. Also in Silva, pp. 111-124.

[67] Ibid.

[68] Ibid., pp. 122-123.

[69] John Hammond Moore, "South Carolina's Reaction to the Photoplay The Birth of a Nation," Proceedings South Carolina Historical Association (1963), 30-40.

[70] Ibid., p. 40.

[71] Ibid., p. 37.

[72] Sarris.

[73] Maxim Simcovitch, "The Impact of Griffith's Birth of a Nation on the Modern Ku Klux Klan," Journal Of Popular Film (Winter, 1972): 45-54.

[74] Ibid., p. 49.

[75] Ibid.

[76] Seymour Stern, "The Birth of a Nation in Retrospect," The International Photographer, (April, 1935): 4.

[77] Ibid.

[78] Seymour Stern, "Cinemages Special Issue No. 1 Published on the Screening of The Birth of a Nation, Atlanta, Georgia, Premiere," Cinemages, April 1955, p. 9.

[79] Seymour Stern, "The Birth of a Nation," Special Supplement to Sight and Sound, Index Series No. 4, July 1945.

[80] Ibid., p. 10.

[81] Ibid.

[82] Ibid., p. 11.

[83] Seymour Stern, Film Culture, p. 66. Stern stated the original release length of the film was 13,068 feet or 13 reels running

three hours. After the initial New York censorship battle the film was 12,500 feet long, or 12 1/2 reels running 2 hours and 45 minutes. Scenes identified as cut were "negroes running amuck through Piedmont . . . the opening sequences of the original prologue showing Yankee kidnappers raiding African villages and bringing the slaves to New England in chains, and then tracing the rise of the abolitionist movement to the hypocrisy of the slave-raiders' descendants who as a subtitle explained had no further use of the slaves themselves were among the first scenes to be deleted. The actual rape of Flora by Gus on the rock was also eliminated. Flashes of screaming white girls being whisked by negro rapists into doorways in back-alleys of the town were omitted after the initial showing; and the major portion of the original epilogue featuring first Lincoln's forgotten letter to Stanton wherein Lincoln affirms that he does not believe in the equality of the black race with the white; and second, fullscale images of the deportation of masses of negroes from New York harbor to the jungles of Africa as a peacable solution for America and the Negroes--all this footage was eliminated." See also, p. 1.

[84] Ibid., p. 8.

[85] Ibid., p. 10.

[86] Ibid.

[87] Ibid.

[88] Ibid.

[89] Ibid.

[90] Ibid. The Stalinist/communist plot conspiracy to destroy Griffith and suppress The Birth theme is developed by Stern in several other articles. In particular see "The Cold War Against D. W. Griffith," Films in Review, February 1956, pp. 49-59.

[91] Ibid.

[92] Peter Noble, "A Note on an Idol," Sight and Sound, Autumn 1946, p. 82. Noble also identified 1931 Philadelphia as the scene of censorship.

[93] Seymour Stern, "The Birth of a Nation: A Reply to Noble's Article in Autumn Sight and Sound," Sight and Sound, Spring 1947, p. 32.

[94] Ibid., pp. 34-35.

[95] "Without Comment," Sight and Sound, Spring 1947, p. 35.

[96] E. L. Cranstone, "The Birth of a Nation Controversy," Sight and Sound, Autumn 1947, p. 119.

[97] Ibid.

[98] Seymour Stern, "The Griffith Controversy," Sight and Sound, Spring 1948, pp. 49-50.

[99] Ibid.

[100] Ibid.

[101] "Editor note," Sight and Sound, Spring 1948, p. 50.

[102] Tom Murray White, "The Birth of a Nation: An Analysis of its Sources, Content and Assertions about Reconstruction (Unpublished AM Thesis History Department: University of Chicago, 1952), p. 4.

[103] Murray is probably basing this part of his analysis upon reports that some opposition to the film was part of a publicity stunt. See Virginia MacPherson's "Nostalgia Rampant in H'wood," New York Telegraph, 17 May 1950, n.p., clipping in Birth of a Nation File, Lincoln Center Archives, New York, New York. In this, an interview with Bill Keefe, a Los Angeles reporter, is summarized. Keefe stated that he hired 60 blacks to picket the opening of the film as "unfair propaganda against their race. We cooked up a regular riot. It got the city council so scared they ordered the movie censors . . . to stop us from premiering the picture. I rounded up the three censors, got 'em all good and drunk and they gave us no trouble at all. Thus, the council ordered the chief of police to call off the opening. He went through the motions and slapped a sign on the theatre. We fixed it up a little so it read Birth of Nation closed by chief of police--will open tonight."

[104] Ibid., p. 104.

[105] Ibid., p. 103.

[106] Charles Larry Hutchins, "A Critical Evaluation of the Controversies Engendered by D. W. Griffith's The Birth of a Nation," (unpublished Masters Thesis: University of Iowa, 1961).

[107] Ibid., pp. 109-110.

[108] Ibid., p. 11.

[109] Everett Carter, "Cultural History Written with Lightning: The Significance of The Birth of a Nation," American Quarterly, XII Fall, 1960, pp. 347-357. Also in Silva, pp. 133-143.

[110] Ibid., p. 350.

[111] Ibid., p. 348.

[112] Geduld.

[113] D. W. Griffith, "How I made The Birth of a Nation," in Ibid., pp. 39-45. Excerpted from Henry Stephen Gordon, "The Story of David Wark Griffith," Photoplay, October 1916, pp. 90-94.

[114] Ibid., p. 41.

[115] Gish, p. 161.

[116] Ibid., pp. 159-160.

[117] Henderson, p. 161.

[118] Ibid., p. 160.

[119] Russell LaMonte Merritt, "The Impact of D. W. Griffith's Motion Pictures From 1908-1914 on Contemporary American Culture," (unpublished Ph.D. Dissertation: Harvard University, 1970), p. 263. See also Russell Merritt, "Dixon, Griffith, and the Southern Legend," Cinema Journal, Fall, 1972, pp. 26-45 and Alan Casty, "The Films of D. W. Griffith: A Style for the Times," Journal of Popular Film, Spring, 1972, pp. 67-79.

[120] Stephen R. Fox, The Guardian of Boston: William Monroe Trotter (New York: Atheneum, 1970).

[121] Ibid., p. 193.

[122] Ibid., p. 196.

[123] Raymond A. Cook, Thomas Dixon (New York: Twayne Publishers, 1974), p. 116.

[124] Ibid.

[125] Raymond A. Cook, Fire from the Flint (Winston Salem, N. C.: John T. Blair, 1968), p. 175.

[126] Cook, Thomas Dixon, p. 114.

[127] Helen M. Chesnutt, Charles Waddell Chesnutt (Chapel Hill: University of North Carolina Press, 1952), pp. 271-273.

[128] Richard S. Randall, Censorship of the Movies; The Social and Political Control of a Mass Medium (Madison: The University of Wisconsin Press, 1968), p. 24.

[129] Bainbridge v. Minneapolis 181 N. W. 964 (1915).

[130] See Ira H. Carmen, *Movies, Censorship and the Law* (Ann Arbor: University of Michigan Press, 1966).

[131] Ibid., p. 179. *State ex rel. Brewster v. Crawford*, 103 Kansas 76 (1918).

[132] Ibid., p. 178.

[133] Ibid., p. 316.

[134] Ibid., p. 237.

[135] Murray Schumach, *The Face on the Cutting Room Floor* (New York: William Morrow & Company, 1964), p. 101.

[136] Ivan Brychta, "The Ohio Film Censorship Law," *Ohio State Law Journal*, Summer, 1952, p. 355. *Epoch Production Corp. v. Harry L. Davis, Mayor of Cleveland*, 19 Ohio N.P.N.S. 465 (1917).

[137] Ibid.

[138] James R. Mack, *Censorship 1917* (Princeton, N. J.: Princeton University Press, 1941), p. 182.

[139] Ibid.

[140] Sidney S. Grant and S. E. Angoff, "Massachusetts and Censorship," *Boston University Law Review*, January, 1930, p. 36.

[141] "Censorship of Motion Pictures," *Yale Law Journal*, 49, November, 1939, p. 101n88.

[142] Dalton Trumbo, quoted by John T. McManus and Louis Kronenberger in "Motion Picture, the Theatre and Race Relations," *Annals of the American Academy of Political and Social Science*, 244, March, 1946, p. 152.

[143] Ibid.

[144] L. D. Reddick, "Educational Programs for the Improvement of Race Relations: Motion Pictures, Radio, the Press, and Libraries," *Journal of Negro Education*, 13, Summer, 1944, p. 368. Reprinted in Maynard, pp. 3-17.

[145] Ibid., p. 370.

[146] Ibid., p. 371.

[147] Ibid., p. 372.

[148] Thomas Cripps, "The Death of Rastus: Negroes In American Films Since 1945," in David G. Gromley & Charles F. Longino, Jr., eds., White Racism and Black Americans (Cambridge, Mass.: Schenkman Publishing Co., Inc., 1972), p. 608. Reprinted in Maynars, pp. 18-23.

[149] Ibid.

[150] Ibid.

[151] Ibid.

[152] Sterling A. Brown, "Negro Character as Seen by White Authors," Journal of Negro Education, 2, April, 1933), p. 80.

[153] Ibid., p. 192.

[154] Leonard H. Hardwick, "Negro Stereotypes on the Screen," Hollywood Quarterly, January, 1946, p. 235.

[155] Anne K. Nelsen and Hart M. Nelsen, "The Prejudicial Film: Progress and Stalemate," Phylon, Summer, 1970, p. 143. The authors also mention the 1915 New York protest and concluded that "riots, fights to censor the film and the opposition of many progressives persisted throughout the spring from Chicago to St. Louis." See p. 142.

[156] Thomas Cripps, "The Myth of the Southern Box Office: A Factor in Racial Stereotyping in American Movies, 1920-1940," in James C. Curtis and Lewis L. Gould, eds., The Black Experience in America (Austin: University of Texas Press, 1970), p. 118.

[157] Bogle, pp. 10 and 21.

[158] Ibid., pp. 3-10.

[159] Ibid., p. 10.

[160] Ibid., p. 18.

[161] Ibid.

[162] Ibid., p. 19.

[163] Ibid.

[164] James Murray, To Find an Image (Indianapolis: Bobbs, Merrill, 1973), p. 15.

[165] Ibid. Unfortunately Murray did not state specifically when these refusals took place or whether the bannings were state-wide or specific to cities or counties.

[166] Noble, p. 33.

[167] Ibid., p. 40.

[168] Ibid., p. 43.

[169] John Hope Franklin, "The Two Worlds of Race: A Historical View," in Talcott Parsons and Kenneth B. Clark, eds., The Negro American (Boston: Beacon Press, 1960), p. 56.

[170] Mary White Ovington, The Walls Came Tumbling Down (New York: Harcourt Brace & Company, 1947), p. 128.

[171] Ibid., p. 129. Ovington also noted that the film was kept out of Ohio because of political power and out of Pennsylvania because it was considered a "gross libel on . . . Thaddeus Stevens."

[172] Ibid., p. 130.

[173] Langston Hughes, Fight for Freedom: The Story of the NAACP (New York: W. W. Norton & Co., 1962), p. 29.

[174] Ibid.

[175] Joyce Ross, J. E. Spingarn and the Rise of the NAACP, 1911-1939 (New York: Atheneum, 1972), p. 738.

[176] Charles Flint Kellog, NAACP: A History of the National Association for the Advancement of Colored People Vol. I (1909-1920) (Baltimore: John Hopkins Press, 1967), p. 143.

[177] Ibid.

[178] Ibid., p. 145.

[179] Ibid.

[180] William M. Tuttle, Race Riot (New York: Atheneum, 1970) p. 244.

[181] V. J. Jerome, The Negro in Hollywood Films (New York: Masses and Mainstream, 1950).

[182] Ibid., p. 17.

[183] Ibid., p. 19.

[184] Ibid.

[185] Ibid., p. 6.

[186] Ibid., p. 19.

[187] Theodore Kupferman and Philip O'Brien, "Motion Picture Censorship: The Memphis Blues," *Cornell Law Quarterly*, Winter, 1951.

[188] Ibid., p. 273.

[189] "Freedom of Speech and Assembly: The Problem of the Hostile Audience," *Columbia Law Review*, December, 1949, p. 1118.

[190] Zechariah Chafee, *Free Speech in the U. S.* (Cambridge: Harvard University Press, 1941), p. 174.

[191] Ibid.

[192] John Haynes Holmes, "Sensitivity as Censor," *Saturday Review of Literature*, 26 February 1949, p. 9.

[193] Ibid., pp. 9-10, 23.

[194] James Mason Brown, "Wishful Banning," *Saturday Review of Literature*, 26 February 1949, p. 9.

[195] Dore Shary, "Censorship and Stereotypes," *Saturday Review of Literature*, 30 April 1949, p. 10.

[196] Hubert Blumer, *Movies and Conduct* (New York: MacMillan, 1933) and Ruth C. Petersen and L. L. Thurston, *Motion Pictures and the Social Attitudes of Children* (New York: MacMillan, 1935). The Blumer and Petersen/Thurston studies are two of a series of twelve investigations of the influence of the motion picture upon youth. Conducted in the 1930's the studies were supported by the educational research committee of the Payne Fund at the request of the National Committee for the Study of Social Values in Motion Pictures. "The studies were designed to secure authoritative and impersonal data which would make possible a more complete evaluation of motion pictures and their social potentialities." See Blumer, Foreword and Introduction. The results of the twelve studies are summarized in Henry James Forman, *Our Movie Made Children* (New York: MacMillan, 1935).

[197] Blumer, p. xi.

[198] Ibid., p. 180.

[199] Petersen and Thurston, pp. 35-38, 60-61.

[200] Ibid.

[201] Ibid.

[202] Forman, p. 127.

[203] Thomas Cripps, "The Birth of a Race Company: An Early Stride Toward a Black Cinema," The Journal of Negro History, 59 January, 1974, p. 29. See also Sharon Cohen, "When the Hillsborough River Became the Nile," Florida Accent, December, 1974, pp. 10-11, Kellog, p. 144, and Murray.

[204] Cripps, "Brith of a Race Company," pp. 36-37.

[205] Louis Gottschalk, Understanding History: A Primer of Historical Method (New York: Alfred A. Knopf, 1964), p. 45.

[206] Ibid., p. 47.

[207] Using this standard 356 actions regarding The Birth's right to the screen were recorded occurring in 120 censorship controversies. There were an additional 12 controversies which could not be verified. Controversies which could not be verified allegedly occurred in Everett, Massachusetts; Norristown, Pennsylvania; Terre Haute, Indiana; Stockton, California; San Antonio, Texas; and Columbia, South Carolina (See Work, p. 115); Chelsea, Massachusetts, and New Haven, Connecticut (See Roy Nash Telegram to Rev. I. S. Wilson, 28 February 1916, NAACP Archives, File C301); Alaska and North Carolina (See John R. Shillady, Telegram to Fred Morton, n.d., NAACP Archives, File C301); and, South Carolina (See Typewritten Sheet, The Birth of a Nation File, Museum of Modern Art Archives, New York, New York).

[208] Webster's New Twentieth Century Dictionary of the English Language, Unabridged, 2nd Edition (Cleveland: World Publishing, 1973), p. 292.

[209] Times Film Corp. v. Chicago, 365 U. S. 50-78 (1961).

[210] Morris Ernst and Pare Lorentz, Censored: The Private Life of the Movies (New York: Jonathan Cape and Harrison Smith, 1930).

[211] Ibid., pp. 32-33.

[212] Richard Randall, "Control of Motion Pictures in the United States" (unpublished Ph.D. dissertation, University of Wisconsin, 1967).

[213] Ibid., pp. 251-258.

[214] *Mutual Film Corp. v. Industrial Commission of Ohio*, 236 U. S. 230, 35 S. Ct. 387, 59 L. Ed. 552 (1915).

CHAPTER II

THE CENSORSHIP ARENA

To provide a framework for the interpretation of censorial actions involving *The Birth of a Nation*, it is advisable to review the history of key film censorship cases in the United States. In this research the complex history of attempts to control motion picture content has been summarized and condensed in three categories: censorship before a United States Supreme Court decision; the constitutional question of film censorship and obscenity; and film censorship for racial reasons.

Censorship Before U.S. Supreme Court Decides

Barely two weeks after Thomas Edison's kinetoscope was introduced in April, 1894, a protest was lodged against a peep show parlor entertainment, *Dolorita in the Passion Dance*.[1] Three years later a New York judge closed a film pantomime of a bride's wedding night preparations because it was an "outrage upon public decency."[2] However, such early sundry efforts against films did little to alter film content, and censorship had not yet caused the constitutional question to surface. The early efforts ranged from informal protests to formal statutes.

Richard Randall noted initial formal attempts to regulate film employed local business licensing laws.[3] For example, in New York motion picture exhibitors were subject to potentially heavy license fees because their business was equated with that of "public cartmen . . . hawkers . . . ticket speculators . . . and bowling alleys."[4]

Similarly, a Minnesota court ruled that because movie houses were "among those pursuits which are liable to degenerate and menace the good order and morals of the people," a motion picture exhibitor was correctly subject to an annual $200 fee for operating a movie house in a town of 1,000.[5] However, these measures were against theater owners, not individual films, and proved to be an ineffective means of controlling film content. Consequently, communities tried to establish a more systematic form of control, censorship ordinances.

The first pre-exhibition film censorship ordinance was passed by the Chicago City Council on November 7, 1907.[7] The ordinance required that all films shown in the city be licensed by the police chief.[8] The police chief was given the power to withhold a permit if he judged a film to be "immoral" or "obscene."[9] The film representative had the right of appeal to Chicago's mayor.

The Illinois Supreme Court upheld this ordinance two years later in a case involving censorship of two westerns, The James Boys and Night Riders.[10] The court ruled that the ordinance was within legitimate police power because it was designed to help secure decency and morality.[11] The court was satisfied that the standards of "immoral" and "obscene" were adequate without statutory definition since "the average person of healthy and wholesome mind" knew what they meant.[12]

New York, Pennsylvania, Kansas, and Ohio followed Chicago's example and established state film censorship boards in 1909, 1911, 1912, and 1913, respectively.[13] Many of these laws were modeled after the Pennsylvania statute which stated that any film not meeting the board's standards of that which was "moral and proper" could be banned from the state.[14] The board vowed "to eliminate everything which shall tend to debase morals or inflame the mind to improper adventures or to establish false standards of conduct."[15]

Not all public officials favored film censorship laws. In 1912 New York's mayor vetoed a city motion picture ordinance and explained his actions to the Board of Aldermen:

> Ours is a government of free speech and free press. This is the cornerstone of free government. The phrase, 'the press,' includes all methods of expression by writing or pictures . . . If this ordinance be legal then a similar ordinance in respect of the newspapers and the theaters generally would be legal . . . Once revive censorship and there is no telling how far we may carry it.[16]

A citizen's group interested in an alternative to government censorship formed the National Board of Censorship in 1909.[17] Founded in direct response to threats by New York officials to close all movie houses in the city, the board functioned with strong support from the film industry. The board officially stood "in favor of voluntary, non-official, co-operative censorship of motion pictures in contrast to legal official, pre-publicity censorship by authorities, Federal, State and local."[18] Even though the board lacked legal authority, its voluntary agreements with theater owners assured that approximately 80 percent of the nation's theaters would not show a film rejected by the board.[19]

Thus, in the years prior to United States Supreme Court consideration of film censorship, several approaches to control of the medium's content existed. These included the application of local business licensing laws to motion picture theater owners, the passage of local and state film censorship laws, and the establishment of a film industry supported voluntary censorship organization.

U.S. Supreme Court: Film Censorship and Obscenity, 1915-1973

The constitutionality of pre-exhibition film censorship statutes was upheld by the U.S. Supreme Court in <u>Mutual Film Corporation v. Industrial Commission of Ohio</u>.[20] A Detroit based company, The Mutual Film Corporation, distributed films in Ohio and other states. Mutual contended the Ohio film censorship law 1) imposed an unlawful burden on interstate commerce; 2) was invalid on its face because it failed to prescribe precise standards by which films were to be approved or rejected; 3) violated the free speech guarantees of the Ohio Constitution; and 4) violated the First Amendment of the U.S. Constitution.[21] The Supreme Court disagreed. Speaking through Justice Joseph McKenna, a unanimous Court refused to interpret the free speech clause of the Ohio Constitution to include the motion picture:

> . . . exhibition of motion pictures is a business pure and simple, originated and conducted for profit . . . not to be regarded, nor intended to be regarded by the Ohio Constitution, we think, as part of the press of the country or as organs of public opinion. They are mere representations of events, of ideas, and sentiments published on known, vivid, useful, and entertaining, no doubt, but . . . capable of evil, having power for it, the greater because of their attractiveness and manner of exhibition.[22]

Therefore, pre-exhibition censorship was permissible because each state had the right to protect the public morals and welfare of its citizens. Thus, the motion picture medium was excluded from free press protection, a condition that remained for 37 years.[23]

In 1952, film was granted limited First Amendment protection by the Court's ruling in Burstyn v. Wilson.[24] Popularly referred to as the Miracle case, the decision marked a change in the status of the medium explicated in the Mutual case. Speaking for a unanimous Court, Justice Tom Clark said: ". . . It cannot be doubted that the motion pictures are a significant medium for the communication of ideas" and therefore included in the free press and free speech guarantees of the First and Fourteenth Amendments.[25]

The film in question in this case was an Italian import, The Miracle, shown as part of a trilogy known as the Ways of Love. The Miracle told the story of a young peasant girl seduced by a stranger she imagined to be St. Joseph. Later, the girl gave birth to a son she believed to be Jesus Christ. The film was declared sacrilegious under New York's licensing law and banned by the New York Board of Regents.[26] The New York Court of Appeals upheld the Regents action, stated that sacrilegious was an acceptable legal standard, found that the Regents were not unreasonable in calling the film sacrilegious, and ruled that films were not part of the the press entitled to free press/free speech protection.[27]

The Supreme Court considered only whether film was a medium protected by the Constitution and whether sacrilegious was an acceptable standard for prior restraint. In determining whether the medium could be subject to prior restraint, Justice Clark reasoned that although freedom of expression was the general rule, the Constitution did not provide an absolute right to show any motion picture, anywhere, at any time. However, prior restraint was only justified in "exceptional cases," and that in such cases the burden of proof would lie with the state advocating pre-exhibition censorship.[28] In this case, New York had not demonstrated that restraint was justified. Indeed, the standard of sacrilegious was "far from the kind of narrow exception to freedom of expression which a state may carve out to satisfy the adverse demands of other interests of society."[29] Clark concluded that the acceptance of a "broad and all-inclusive" standard such as sacrilegious would set the censor:

> . . . adrift upon a boundless sea amid a myriad of conflicting currents of religious views, with no charts but those provided by the most vocal and powerful orthodoxies. . . . Under such a standard the most tolerant censor would . . . be subject to an inevitable tendency to ban the expression of unpopular sentiments sacred to a religious minority.[30]

In 1957 the Court formulated a test for obscenity which influenced film censorship standards. The standard was established through two cases generally referred to as the Roth case.[31] The Roth decision was a landmark for it stated explicitly that obscenity was not protected speech and announced the following obscenity test:

> . . . whether to the average person, applying contemporary community standards, the dominant theme of the material taken as a whole appeals to prurient interest.[32]

Speaking for the majority in a 5-4 decision, Justice William Brennan also said that "all ideas having even the slightest redeeming social importance--unorthodox ideas, controversial ideas, even ideas hateful to the prevailing climate of opinion" were protected speech.[33]

Two years later the Court dealt with the question of ideological or thematic obscenity in Kingsley International Pictures Corp. v. New York Regents (1959).[34] The case was brought by Kingsley International, a motion picture distributor, after the New York Regents refused to license a Kingsley distributed version of D. H. Lawrence's Lady Chatterly's Lover. The Regents termed the film "immoral" because it presented adultery as a proper pattern of behavior. The Regents invoked a New York censorship statute which defined an "immoral" film as one which "portrays acts of sexual immorality, perversion, or lewdness, or which expressly or impliedly presents such acts as desirable, acceptable, or proper patterns of behavior."[35] The New York Court of Appeals upheld tha Regents' decision and reasoned that the statute applied to the film in question because "its subject matter is adultery presented as being right and desirable for certain people under certain circumstances."[36] The U.S. Supreme Court reversed and said that the statute violated the First Amendment guarantee to advocate ideas, even adultery, which is "hateful and immoral to some."[37]

In 1961 the Court faced squarely the question whether precensorship of motion pictures per se was constitutional in light of Burstyn. A narrowly drawn 5-4 decision ruled that prior restraint of film was constitutional and specifically upheld Chicago's film censorship ordinance.[38] Speaking for the majority in Times Film Corp. v. Chicago Justice Clark said the question is whether a film has the "complete and absolute freedom" to be exhibited "at least once," and whether this right extends to "every kind of motion picture."[39] Clark continued that the Court never held "that liberty of speech is absolute" and never "suggested that all previous restraints on speech are invalid."[40] Consequently, there is no constitutionally protected right to show every film at least once in public places.

The obscenity standard established in Roth was further explained in Jacobellis v. State of Ohio.[41] In this case the Court found the film Les Amants was not obscene and reversed the conviction of theatre manager Nico Jacobellis.[42] Further, Justice Brennan affirmed the "utterly" without socially redeeming value test:

> . . . material dealing with sex in a manner that advocates ideas, Kingsley Int'l Pictures Corp. v. Regents, or that has literary or scientific or artistic value or any other form of social importance, may not be branded as obscenity and denied the constitutional protection. Nor may the constitutional status of the material be made to turn on a 'weighing' of its social importance against its prurient appeal, for a work cannot be proscribed unless it is 'utterly' without social importance.[43]

Also, the "community" standard referred to in Roth was then "determined on the basis of a national standard," the Court said.[43]

The Supreme Court dealt with procedural standards for film censorship boards in Freedman v. Maryland.[45] Speaking for a unanimous Court, Justice Brennan said the Maryland censorship statute in question was unconstitutional because it did not "provide adequate safeguards against undue inhibition of expression."[46] Specifically, the system was deficient in three areas: it failed to provide prompt judicial review of censorship rulings; it failed to provide that censors must either license a film or take the matter into court and bear the burden of proof; and, it failed to provide prompt judicial determination on the merits of the case.[47] Finally, the Court suggested prior restraint procedures which might be acceptable.[48]

When considering obscenity cases between 1966 and 1968, the Court began focusing on the conduct of the supplier of the material rather than on the content of the material itself. In A Book Named

John Cleland's Memoirs of a Woman of Pleasure v. Massachusetts[49] the
Court reaffirmed the Roth obscenity standard reasserted in Jacobellis,
but added:

> Evidence that the book was commercially exploited for the
> sake of prurient appeal, to the exclusion of all other values,
> might justify the conclusion that the book was utterly with-
> out redeeming social importance.[50]

The implied standard in the dicta of the Memoirs opinion was directly
applied in Ginzburg v. United States.[51] Ralph Ginzburg was convicted
of using the U.S. mail to distribute obscene materials.[52] The manner
of promoting the materials (pandering), rather than content, was the
central consideration of the case. The Court upheld Ginzburg's conviction. It reasoned that even when materials are assumed to be not
obscene, when they are promoted, advertised, and exploited on the basis
of prurient appeal alone, the articles are not constitutionally protected.[53] Thus, material not necessarily obscene in the abstract
becomes unprotected speech by pandering. A third decision handed down
with Memoirs and Ginzburg, Mishkin v. New York, considered the "average
man" of the Roth test. Edward Mishkin published materials dealing
with sadism and masochism. He had been found guilty of producing and
selling obscene books. Mishkin appealed his conviction on the basis
that his books would not appeal to the prurient interest of the average
citizen of the Roth test. Rather, the average person would be dis-
gusted and sickened by the materials.[55] The Court did not agree with
Mishkin's reasoning. Justice Brennan summarized:

> Where the material is designed primarily for and primarily
> disseminated to a clearly defined deviant sexual group,
> rather than to the public at large, the prurient appeal
> requirement of the Roth test is satisfied if the dominant

theme of the material taken as a whole appeals to the prurient interest of the members of that group.[56]

Another decision which shifted the attention of the Court to the supplier of obscene material was Redrup v. New York.[57] In this decision, the Court said a conduct standard might be employed in an obscenity case when: evidence of pandering is found; a statute to protect juveniles is involved; and, the material is inflicted upon an individual and violates his privacy.[58] At least one scholar interpreted the Redrup decision as an admission by the Court of "its confusion over problems in the law of obscenity."[59]

In 1968 the Court acknowledged the concept of variable obscenity in Ginsburg v. State of New York.[60] The sale of "girlie" magazines to a 16-year-old boy was at issue. The Court ruled that the New York statute which forbade the sale of obscene material to minors was constitutional.[61] Justice Brennan explained:

> . . . material which is protected for distribution to adults is not necessarily constitutionally protected from restriction upon its dissemination to children. In other words, the concept of obscenity or of unprotected matter may vary according to the group to whom the questionable material is quarantined. Because of the State's exigent interest in preventing distribution to children of objectionable material, it can exercise its power to protect the health, safety, welfare and morals of its community by barring the distribution to children of books recognized to be suitable for adults.[62]

The Court applied the concept of variable obscenity to film in Interstate Circuit v. City of Dallas.[63]

The right of individuals to possess obscene materials in their own homes was established in Stanley v. Georgia.[64] Robert Stanley was convicted of harboring obscene materials after a Georgia state investigator and three federal agents operating under a federal warrant

entered his home and viewed three reels of 8mm film found there.[65]
Stanley's appeal was upheld by a unanimous Court which stresed two constitutional rights: the right to receive information regardless of its social worth, and a constitutional right to privacy tied to the right to receive information and ideas.[66] Justice Thurgood Marshall concluded:

> If the First Amendment means anything it means that a State has no business telling a man, sitting alone in his own house, what books he may read or what films he may watch. Our whole constitutional heritage rebels at the thought of giving government the power to control men's minds.[67]

In 1971 the Court in a series of three decisions attempted to revitalize state control of obscenity by determining when it was appropriate for a federal court to intervene in state obscenity prosecutions.[68] The Court ruled that even if state statutes were unconstitutional, the federal courts should not intervene unless one of three conditions were shown to exist: harassment by law enforcement officials, harassment by prosecuting the case when a prosecutor had no hope of winning, and extraordinary circumstances.[69] Shortly thereafter, the Court returned to the Roth standard in both the U.S. v. Thirty-Seven Photographs and U.S. v. Reidel.[70]

In June, 1973 the Court handed down a series of eight decisions which tightened federal guidelines for obscenity and empowered the states to legislate against obscenity at the local level.[71] Substantive legal issues were decided in five of the cases.[72] The remaining three cases involved procedural issues.[73] Of the eight rulings, the precedent of Miller v. California is perhaps most sweeping.

Marvin Miller was conviceted of mailing unsolicited sexually explicit material in violation of a California statute. Miller appealed on the grounds that the California statute involved violated his First and Fourteenth Amendment rights. The U.S. Supreme Court disagreed with Miller. In a 5-4 decision, the Court ruled that a work may be subject to state regulation where that work is found obscene by applying contemporary community standards. The Court set guidelines for determining obscenity:

1) whether the average person applying contemporary community standards would find that the work taken as a whole appeals to the prurient interest;

2) whether the work depicts or describes in a patently offensive way sexual conduct specifically defined by the applicable state law;

3) whether the work taken as a whole lacks serious literary, artistic, political, or scientific value.

These guidelines differ in at least two significant ways from the Roth standard. First, the Court rejected the "utterly without redeeming social value" test.[75] Second, the Court said community standards are local.[76] Speaking for the majority, Chief Justice Warren Burger emphasized that it was not the Court's function to write state statutes but suggested obscenity meant:

1) Patently offensive representation or descriptions of ultimate sexual acts, normal or perverted, actual of or simulated;

2) patently offensive representation or descriptions of masturbation, excretory functions, and lewd exhibition of the genitals.

The Court ruled that obscene films do not acquire constitutional immunity from state regulation because they are exhibited for consenting adults in Paris Adult Theatre v. Slaton.[78] Further, the

Court determined that the right of privacy established in Stanley "does not include any fundamental privacy right to watch obscene movies in places of public accommodation."[79] The Court asserted that even though there is no conclusive proof of correlation between antisocial behavior and obscene material, the state has a legitimate interest in regulating commercialized obscenity. In support, the Court cited the Hill-Link Minority Report of the Commission on Obscenity and Pornography.[80]

The Court further defined the right of privacy as it relates to obscene material in two other decisions handed down with Miller and Paris Adult Theatre. In U.S. v. 12 200 Ft. Reels of Super 8mm Film[81] the Court held that Congress has the right to proscribe importation of obscene material even though importation is for personal use and possession.[82] Further, the Court ruled that the right to possess obscene material in the privacy of one's home does not give rise to the correlative right to sell or give it to others nor does it allow transportation of obscene material in interstate commerce.[83] Likewise, in U.S. v. Orito,[84] the Court found that Congress has the right to prevent obscene material from entering the stream of commerce and that the constitutionally protected zone of privacy established in Stanley does not extend beyond the home. In addition, the Court through Chief Justice Burger stated:

> Viewing obscene films in commercial theatre open to the adult public or transporting such films in common carriers in interstate commerce has no claim to the special consideration and safeguards which the constitution extends to the privacy of the home . . . [84]

In Kaplan v. California[86] the Court determined that expression by words alone can be unprotected speech. The plain covered, unillustrated book, Suite 69, was of an explicitly sexual nature. The Court concluded that "a state could reasonably regard the hard core conduct described by Suite 69 as capable of encouraging or causing antisocial behavior, especially in its impact on young people."[87] The Court reaffirmed that the sale of sexually oriented obscene materials, even to consenting adults, is not constitutionally protected.

Procedures involving seizure of allegedly obscene films were central to Heller v. New York[88] and Roaden v. Kentucky.[89] In Heller, the Court sustained a New York action where a judge bought a regular ticket at a commercial theatre to see Blue Movie. The judge declared the film probably obscene because it contained footage of a nude couple "engaged in ultimate sexual acts" He issued a warrant for seizure of the film.[90] The exhibitor was free to show another copy of the film until the final obscenity determination was made. The Court held this method of seizure constitutional. However, in Roaden, the Court found seizure procedure illegal because there was no warrant.[91] Harry Roaden was the namager of a theatre in Pulaski County, Kentucy. The Pulaski County sheriff bought a ticket to the drive-in theatre to see Cindy and Donna, a film with a lesbian theme. The sheriff watched the film in its entirety and concluded it was obscene. Without a warrant, he seized a copy of the film as evidence and arrested Roaden. Roaden's conviction therefore was reversed. Further, in Alexander v. Virginia, the Court ruled that trial by jury was not constitutionally required in civil obscenity proceedings.[92]

Thus, it is evident the Supreme Court's attitudes toward the constitutional questions raised by film censorship and obscenity vacillated during the time period of this study. Initially, the Court refused to extend free press/free speech protection to the motion picture. When First Amendment protection was granted to film, the guarantee did not free the medium from prior restraint. Later, the Court ruled specifically that such prior restraint was constitutional. However, censorship standards may not be overly broad and must meet certain procedural requirements. Film remains a medium apart. There is no absolute right to show any film at least once anywhere in a place of public accommodation.

In outlining the concept of obscenity, the Court shifted primarily from a content standard to a conduct standard and back to a content standard. Simultaneously, there was a shift from national to local standards. Enduring parts of the obscenity definition state that an "average" person, applying contemporary community standards, judges the work as a whole to determine whether the work appeals to prurient interest or is patently offensive. Currently, the work is obscene if it lacks serious literary, artistic, political, or scientific value. The concept of variable obscenity has been applied to both print and film. Privacy includes the right to possess and view obscene materials in one's own home; however, it does not include selling, receiving or transporting obscene materials. Privacy does not extend to a place of public accommodation.

The Supreme Court and the Film Color Line

The Supreme Court has never squarely faced the question whether censorship of motion pictures for the treatment of racial themes is constitutional. However, the Court considered four cases involving films censored for positive portrayal of blacks.[93] Because the major argument used against The Birth of a Nation was that its unfavorable portrayal of blacks required censorship, the cases censored for the opposite action will lend some perspective. Although these cases never reached the racial question but were decided on broader First Amendment grounds, their origin as racial cases makes it necessary to deal with them separately.

During the mid-1940's, censors in the South apparently frequently cut film scenes featuring black actors and actresses. For example, Variety reported that "some local censors are attacking scenes indiscriminately leaving the continuity blurred and the entire film choppy and confused."[94] In particular, the Memphis Board of Censors, led by Lloyd Binford, has been characterized as considering all films which even hinted at equality between the races inimical to the public welfare, health, morals, and safety" of that city.[95] The Memphis censors banned the Jack Benny film Brewster's Millions because Rochester's antics were deemed "too familiar," eliminated Lena Horne from any movie in which she appeared because "white people don't want to see her," and rejected Lost Boundaries because it dealt "with social equality between whites and negroes in a way that we do not have in the South."[96] Newsreel sequences showing black troop actions during World War II also were cut in "several southern towns."[97] Variety summarized the situation:

> The crux of the problem is that although white southern audiences enjoy negro sequences in films for their entertainment value, they will not countenance any scenes showing the negro on a basis of social equality with the whites. Local censors will eliminate such scenes regardless of the effect on the artistic side or the continuity of the film.[98]

This situation came to the attention of Thurgood Marshall, then special counsel to the NAACP, who said racial censorship is "one of the worst evils that can be imagined" and petitioned the American Civil Liberties Union to combat it.[99] Marshall was disturbed particularly by the Memphis ban on the film Dixie. The ACLU reported that "certainly we will take up the matter of those southern censorships, although it is going to be a tough job.[100]

The ACLU pursued the matter with little immediate success. In early 1945, Memphis banned Brewster's Millions. The ACLU attempted to interest the film's distributor and/or the film's exhibitor in taking legal action. However, the exhibitor, Harry Kosner of Edward Small Productions, replied that his company would not "dare fight for fear the other southern theatres and circuits will ban the picture"[101] Likewise, the distributor, United Artists, said it "had no definite views one way or another" and would be guided by the exhibitor.[102]

Later in 1945, H. L. Mitchell, president of the Southern Tenant Farmers Union, notified the ACLU that censorship was becoming a major issue in Memphis because "Mr. Benford (sic) has banned a large number of pictures in the past few weeks and both newspapers have carried editorials denouncing the censorship."[103] The ACLU responded that it tried to bring a test case but that "local exhibitors and distributors

. . . are all so afraid of retaliatory action"[104] that none would initiate a lawsuit. Again, the ACLU turned to United Artists to bring a suit:

> As you probably know, the ACLU has been following closely the censorship activities of the Memphis Board of Censors. Earlier in the year when Lloyd T. Binford . . . made the headlines by barring Brewster's Millions we attempted to get a test case. Unfortunately . . . exhibitors are rather loath to defend themselves because of the pressure that can be brought upon them by the municipal authorities. It is therefore gratifying to us to note that United Artists is prepared to combat further censorship. May we offer you our assistance in any case that you may bring? We are prepared to help carry any suit to the United States Supreme Court if necessary.[105]

However, it was two more years before United Artists took the Memphis Board of Censors to court.

During summer, 1947, United Artists distributed a motion picture comedy, Curley, produced by Hal Roach. The film presented a variation upon the structure and theme of the "our gang" comedies for which Roach was well known.[106] The picture already had been approved in its entirety by the censorship boards of New York, Kansas, Ohio, Maryland, Pennsylvania, Virginia, Chicago, and Boston.[107] when it was submitted to the Memphis Board of Censors.[108]

Speaking for the board, Binford wrote United Artists:

> I am sorry to inform you that it is unable to approve your 'Curley' picture with the little Negroes as the south does not permit Negroes in white schools nor recognize social equality between the races even in children.[109]

United Artists (UA) interpreted this to mean the film had been banned and decided to protest. Gradwell Sears, UA president, said: "We are not going to take this lying down. I have instructed our lawyers to test the constitutionality of Binford's censorship."[110] United

Artists and Hal Roach filed a joint petition in the Circuit Court of Shelby County, Tennessee, seeking review of the censorship actions.[111] The petition alleged that the board banned the film without legal authority; that the film censorship ordinance in question was unconstitutional; that the board banned the film solely because negroes appeared in it; and that the board had acted in a "capricious and arbitrary" manner and thus violated the due process guarantees of the Tennessee and U.S. Constitutions.[112] The petition was dismissed by Circuit Court Judge Floyd Henderson, Jr.[113] United Artists and Hal Roach appealed to the Tennessee Supreme Court.[114] The Tennessee Supreme Court heard the case and affirmed Henderson's position. The Tennessee court held that "petitioners were doing business in Tennessee and having failed to comply with statutory provisions for qualification of a foreign corporation to do business in the state could not maintain in the proceeding."[115] In dicta, the court stated that motion picture censorship *might* not be based solely on race or color, but that the constitutionality of the Memphis ordinance could be contested only by someone with standing in the state.[116]

United Artists planned an appeal to the U.S. Supreme Court.[117] The Motion Picture Producers and Distributors Association (MPPDA) supported this, viewing the case an excellent opportunity to ask reversal of the *Mutual* ruling and to forbid film censorship on racial grounds. MPPDA executive Sidney Schreiber wrote to Memphis attorney Hamilton Little:

> There is no reason to assume that the motion picture should forever remain outside the full protections of the First Amendment. We expect that the Supreme Court will overrule

this anachronism when the question is re-presented to it. We expect that the case of United Artists v. Memphis will furnish the occasion for the disapproval of the principle enunciated in the Mutual Film Corp. case.[118]

Marie Wathen, Film Daily's correspondent in Memphis, wrote editor Chester Bahn that she was sure "no picture could be banned because of Negro and White children playing together--not in the U.S. Supreme Court."[119] Similarly, the Louisville Courier-Journal editorialized that the outcome of the case was "foregone" because "as long as the Constitution guarantees equality of man, it must imply the equality of the pictures of children."[120]

In October, 1949, United Artists and Hal Roach filed their petition for a writ of certiorari with the U.S. Supreme Court. The petitioners claimed "the basic issue presented is the constitutionality of previous restraint or censorship of talking motion pictures."[121] Major questions in the petition included:

1) Are state laws which provide for previous restraint or censorship of talking pictures, in derogation of the freedoms secured by the First Amendment and protected against State abridgment by the 'due process' and 'equal protection' clauses of the Fourteenth Amendment?

2) Even though previous restraint or censorship is not unconstitutional per se, may race or color, or the fact that Negro children appear along with white children in school room scenes, constitute a valid ground on which a talking motion picture may be censored and its exhibition banned?

3) Can state courts evade primary federal constitutional issues by interposing non-federal grounds of decision which, in substance and effect, deny fundamental constitutional rights?[122]

In addition, United Artists asked whether a film's producer and distributor have standing to sue.[123]

On May 8, 1950, the Court refused <u>certiorari</u> without dissent.[124] The case seems to have been dismissed because of procedural issues stressed by the Tennessee Supreme Court, rather than on constitutional grounds. United Artists and the film industry turned its attention to another film censored because of a racial theme, <u>Lost Boundaries</u>.

In early 1950 <u>Lost Boundaries</u> was submitted to Christine Smith, Atlanta, Georgia's film censor, for approval.[125] Smith ruled the film could not be shown in Atlanta because the picture would "adversely affect the peace, morals and good order of said city."[126]

RD-DR Corporation, producer, and Film Classics, distributor, sued Smith in the U.S. District Court to enjoin enforcement of Atlanta's censorship ordinance.[127] However, the three-judge federal court upheld the censor's ban and declared the ordinance constitutional.[128] Thus, unlike the Tennessee Supreme Court disposition of the <u>United Artists</u> case on procedural grounds, the Atlanta federal court directly tackled the constitutional issue.

Speaking for the federal court, Chief Justice Neil Andrews said the basic question was "whether motion pictures are entitled to the protection constitutionally accorded the press."[129] Citing the <u>Mutual</u> decision, Andrews stated that the motion picture could not be considered part of the press. In spite of Supreme Court Justice William O. Douglas's dicta in <u>U.S. v. Paramount Pictures</u>,[130] "we have no doubt that motion pictures, like newspapers and radio, are included in the press whose freedom is guaranteed by the First Amendment," Andrews said he could not "anticipate that the Court will overrule the <u>Mutual Film</u> case."[131] Expressing his personal opinion, however,

Andrews wrote that the ordinance should be interred:

> . . . in the attic which contains the ghosts of those, who arrayed in the robe of Bigotry, armed with the spear of Intolerance and mounted on the steed of Hatred have through all ages sought to patrol the highways of the mind. In essence that part of the ordinance presently under scrutiny empowers the Censor to determine what is good and what is bad for the community and that without any standard other than the Censor's personal opinion. As here applied it attempts a degree of thought control but unless motion pictures can be afforded the coverage extended the press it is clear that the police power of the State has not been exceeded.[132]

RD-DR Corporation appealed to the Fifth U.S. Circuit Court of Appeals. Not only did that court affirm, but indicated its conviction that there was no need for a review of the Mutual decision.[133]

RD-DR Corporation petitioned the U.S. Supreme Court for a writ of certiorari.[134] Though Justice Douglas stated the petition should be granted,[135] the Court refused. So when the U.S. Supreme Court was asked to face squarely the constitutional question of press freedom for motion pictures, it refused.

A few days later, the motion picture industry turned its support to another film censored for racial content, Pinky. William Gelling was convicted in the County Court of Harrison County, Texas, for exhibiting Pinky without a permit.[136] Gelling submitted the film to the Marshall, Texas, Board of Censors which denied a film permit. The board held the film "was of such character as to be prejudicial to the best interests of the people of the city."[137] Gelling exhibited the film without a permit and was arrested.[138]

Gelling appealed his conviction to the Texas Court of Criminal Appeals. He contended the ordinance under which he was arrested was invalid on its face, violating the First and Fourteenth Amendments.[139] The Appeals Court disagreed. In its opinion, the unanimous court drew heavily from Judge Hutchenson's opinion in RD-DR Corp. v. Smith.[140] In part, Judge J. Beauchamp, speaking for the court, stated:

> We cannot concede that the motion picture industry has emerged from the business of amusement and become propagators of ideas entitling it to freedom of speech. . . . The desire of a great industry to reap greater fruits from its operations should not be indulged at the expense of Christian character upon which America must rely for its future existence. Every boy and every girl reaching man or womanhood is to an extent the product of that community from which he comes. If the citizens of that community are divested of all power to surround them with wholesome entertainment and character building education then the product will go forth weak indeed.[141]

The court also said that "the name and character of the picture exhibited are immaterial."[142]

Gelling then appealed to the U.S. Supreme Court. The case was adjudicated just one week after the Court ruled in the Burstyn case. In a one sentence per curiam decision the Court reversed Gelling's conviction on the authority of Burstyn and Winters v. New York.[143]

Justices Felix Frankfurter and William Douglas filed concurring opinions. Frankfurter contended that the censorship ordinance "offends the Due Process Clause of the Fourteenth Amendment on the score of indefiniteness."[144] Douglas said the First Amendment had been violated:

> The evil of prior restraint, condemned by Near v. Minnesota in the case of newspapers and by Burstyn in the case of motion pictures is present here in flagrant form. If a board of censors can tell the American people what it is in their best interests to see or read or to hear then thought is regimented, authority substituted for liberty, and the great purpose of the First Amendment to keep uncontrolled the freedom of expression defeated.[145]

Thus, two members of the Court seemed to dispatch as unconstitutional the licensing criterion of "prejudicial to the best interests of the people" without considering the specific film involved or the fact that the film had been found potentially prejudicial because of its treatment of a racial theme.

Next, in 1954 the Ohio Supreme Court upheld the censorship of two films, M and Native Son.[146] Although three separate cases were involved, the court considered the three at once because "the same or similar questions are involved."[147] Nevertheless, the fact situations varied significantly.

The motion picture M was banned by the Ohio Department of Education "on account of being harmful."[148] The film's American producer, Superior Films, appealed the ban on the grounds that the film "artistically and dramatically" treated at least five important social problems and was not harmful.[149] Further, Superior Films claimed that the Ohio film censorship statutes violated the First and Fourteenth amendments of the Constitution and the First Article of the Ohio Constitution because of indefinite and vague censorship criteria.[150]

The two other cases involved censorship of the film Native Son.[151] One was an action in mandamus by Classic Pictures, Inc., to require the Department of Education to reexamine the film. Prior to this action, the Department of Education denied another review of the film because it was considered on three previous occasions. Despite cuts and deletions, the film was pronounced:

> . . . harmful: because--contributes to racial misunderstanding presenting situations undesireable to the mutual interests of both races; against public interest in

undermining confidence that justice can be carried out; presents racial frictions at a time when all groups should be united against everything that is subversive.[152]

The other case asked that these censorship orders be set aside and the Ohio film censorship statutes declared unconstitutional.[153]

The Ohio Supreme Court ruled the censorship of M valid and the Ohio film censorship statutes constitutional.[154] Relying upon the U.S. Supreme Court decisions in Burstyn and Gelling, the Court stated:

> From these expressions of the U.S. Supreme Court and otherwise, we conclude that, although a motion picture film may not be rejected because of 'sacrilegious' expressions or portrayals, there still remains a limited field in which decency and morals may be protected from the impact of an offending motion picture film by prior restraint under proper criteria. There can be no inherent right to publicity which tends to destroy the very social fabric of the community and consequently in such instances there is no right of free speech or free press to be infringed. As we view it, the United States Supreme Court has not ipso facto taken away all community control of moving pictures by censorship, and this court will not do so under the claim of complete unconstitutionality of censorship laws.[155]

Further, the Ohio court ordered the Department of Education to reconsider Native Son.[156]

The three cases were joined in an appeal to the U.S. Supreme Court.[157] The Court decided the cases with Commercial Pictures Corp. v. Regents of the University of the State of New York.[158] In a one sentence per curiam decision, the judgments were reversed on the authority of Burstyn.[159] Justice Douglas filed a concurring opinion, with which Justice Black agreed, expressing the broader view that the First Amendment guarantees of freedom of expression prevented a state from establishing censorship over motion pictures. In part Douglas stated "in this nation every writer, actor, or producer no matter what medium of expression he may use should be freed from the censor."[160]

Thus, the Court struck down as overbroad the standard that only films "of a moral, educational, amusing, or harmless character" under which Ohio had censored <u>M</u> and the standard "immoral or tended to corrupt morals" under which New York had censored <u>La Ronda</u>.[161] Whether the Court considered the censorship rationale utilized in the <u>Native Son</u> cases when deciding the <u>Superior Film</u> case is unclear. Although the Supreme Court has been asked four times to consider cases involving films censored because of racial themes, the Court never resolved the constitutionality of this censorhip standard.

Notes to Chapter II

[1] Richard Randall, "Control of Motion Pictures in the United States," (Ph.D. dissertation, University of Wisconsin, 1967), p. 18.

[2] People v. Doris, 14 App. Div. 117, 43 N.Y. Supp. 571 (1st Dept., 1897).

[3] Randall, p. 19.

[4] People v. Gaynor, 77 Misc. 576, 137 N.Y. Supp. 196 (Sup. Ct. N.Y. County, 1912).

[5] Higgins v. La Croix, 119 Minn. 145, 137 NW 417 (1912).

[6] Randall, p. 20.

[7] City of Chicago Charter Act 5, Cl. 45 (1907) as quoted in Block v. Chicago, 239 Ill. 251, 87 NE 1011 (1909). In 1907 there were at least 116 nickelodeon theatres in Chicago. See Randall, p. 21 and Terry Ramsaye, A Million and One Nights (New York, Simon & Schuster, 1926), p. 474.

[8] Ibid.

[9] Ibid.

[10] Block v. Chicago, 239 Ill. 251 (1909).

[11] Ibid., at 258.

[12] Ibid., at 264.

[13] Bosley Crowther, Movies and Censorship, Pamphlet No. 332, (Public Affairs Committee, Inc.: PAIS, 1962), p. 10.

[14] Pennsylvania, State Board of Censors (of Motion Pictures), Rules and Standards: Act passed May 15, 1915, P.L. 534 (Harrisburg, Pa.: Wm. Stanley Ray, 1915), p. 4.

[15] Ibid., p. 14.

[16] Mayor Gaynor as quoted by James N. Rosenberg, Censorship in the U.S.: An Address Before the Association of the Bar of the City of New York on March 15, 1928 (New York: The Court Press, n.d.), pp. 12-13.

[17] Ruth Inglis, Freedom of the Movies (Chicago: University of Chicago Press, 1947), p. 76.

[18] National Board of Censorship of Motion Pictures, *The Question of Motion Picture Censorship* (New York: National Board of Censors, 1914), pp. 4 & 12. In 1914 the board was composed of a general committee of 32 representatives from 13 New York civic agencies, an executive committee chosen from the general committee, and a censoring committee of 105 members. The censoring committee was subdivided into smaller work units.

[19] John Collier, "Censorship in Action," *Survey*, 7 August 1915, p. 23.

[20] *Mutual Film Corp. v. Industrial Commission of Ohio*, 236 U.S. 230, 355 S.Ct. 387. 59 L.Ed. 552 (1915).

[21] 103 Ohio Laws 399, Section 3 required mandatory pre-exhibition censorship without specifying who had to send the film for review or pay the inspection fee. Section 7 imposed a penalty for the exhibition of unapproved films. Because of this exhibitors "refused to rent unlicensed films for fear of prosecution. Thus, the burden of prior restraint fell upon the distributor." See Randall, p. 47. Section 11, Article 1 of the Ohio Constitution stipulated that "every citizen may freely speak, write, and publish his sentiments on all subjects being responsible for the abuse of the right; and no law shall be passed to restrain or bridge the liberty of speech or the press."

[22] 236 U.S. 230, 241. It is interesting to note that the National Board of Censors assumed a position concerning the medium similar to McKenna's. In 1914 the board stated that it recognized "that moving picture houses and the vaudeville theatres are primarily places of amusement and not of serious discussion and education." See National Board of Censorship of Motion Pictures, *The Policy and Standards of the National Board of Censorship of Motion Pictures* (New York: National Board of Censorship, 1914), p. 19.

[23] The Court did not specifically identify the "evil" states had the right to protect citizens from, but it seems likely to lay in the realm of sexual morality rather than in the area of political or social ideas. McKenna said that films can be more "insidious in corruption" because the audience is made up "not of women alone or of men alone, but together" and that the threat comes from showing "things which should not have pictorial representation in public places." See 236 U.S. 230, 242.

[24] *Joseph Burstyn, Inc. v. Wilson*, 343 U.S. 495, 96 L.Ed. 1098, 72 S.CT. 777 (1952).

[25] Ibid., at 501-502.

[26] For a more detailed account of the film's story line and early litigation see Bosley Crowther, "The Strange Case of 'The Miracle," *Atlantic*, April 1951, p. 35.

[27] Burstyn v. Wilson, 303 NY 242, 101 NE 2d 665 (1951).

[28] 343 U.S. 495, 503-504.

[29] Ibid., at 504-505.

[30] Ibid.

[31] U.S. v. Roth, 237 F2d 796 (1956); People of California v. Alberts, 138 Cal. App. 2d Supp. 999, 292 P. 2d 90, (1956).

[32] Roth v. U.S.; Alberts v. People of California, 354 U.S. 476, 487, 1 L.ed. 2d 1498, 77 S.Ct. 1304 (1952).

[33] Ibid. at 484. In a later attempt to clarify the Roth standard the Court added the element "patent offensiveness" to its definition of obscenity. See MANual Enterprises, Inc. v. Day, 370 U.S. 478, 8 L.Ed. 2d 639, 82 S.Ct. 1432 (1962).

[34] Kingsley International Pictures Corp. v. Regents, 360 U.S. 684, 3 L.Ed. 2d 1512, 79 S.Ct. 1362 (1959). Ideological or thematic obscenity refers to depictions judged obscene or immoral because they represent ideas in conflict with social norms. See Donald Gillmor and Jerome Barron, Mass Communication Law (St. Paul, Minn.: West Publishing, 1969), p. 310.

[35] N. Y. Educ. Law, s. 122-9 (1954). See Randall, p. 169.

[36] Kingsley International v. Regents, 4 N.Y. 2d 349, 351, 551 N.E. 2d 197 (1958).

[37] 360 U.S. 684, 687 (1959).

[38] Times Film Corp. v. Chicago, 355 U.S. 35, 35 L.Ed. 2d 403, 78 S.Ct. 115 (1961).

[39] Ibid., at 47

[40] Ibid.

[41] Jacobellis v. State of Ohio, 378 U.S. 184, 12 L.Ed. 2d 793, 84 S.Ct. 1676 (1964).

[42] Ibid. Jacobellis had been convicted on two counts of possessing and exhibiting an obscene film after he exhibited Les Amanto at his Cleveland Heights, Ohio, theatre.

[43] 378 U.S. 184, 191.

[44] Ibid.

[45]Freedman v. Maryland, 380 U.S. 51, 13 L.Ed. 2d 649, 85 S.Ct. 734 (1965). Several years later the Court struck down Washington's film censorship statute as overbroad because it did not provide for fair notice to theatre personnel. The case involved a drive-in theatre manager arrested for showing an allegedly obscene film after the police viewed the film on two consecutive evenings from outside the theatre. See Rabe v. State of Washington, 405 U.S. 313, 92 S.Ct. 993, 31 L. Ed. 2d 258 (1972).

[46]Ibid., at 60.

[47]Ibid., at 57-58.

[48]Ibid., at 61.

[49]A Book Named John Cleland's Memoirs of a Woman of Pleasure v. Massachusetts, 383 U.S. 413, 16 L.Ed. 2d 1, 86 S.Ct. 975 (1966). Speaking for the majority Justice Brennan insisted that the work could not be considered obscene unless it was found to be utterly without redeeming social value--even if the work were found to possess the requisite prurient appeal and to be patently offensive.

[50]Ibid., at 420.

[51]Ginzburg v. U.S., 383 U.S. 463, 16 L.Ed. 2d 31, 86 S.Ct. 942 (1966).

[52]Ibid. The publications involved were the magazine Eros; a bi-weekly paper Liason; and a book, The Housewife's Handbook on Selective Promiscuity.

[53]Ibid., at 470.

[54]Mishkin v. New York, 383 U.S. 502, 16 L.Ed. 2d 56, 86 S.Ct. 958 (1966).

[55]Ibid., at 508

[56]Ibid., at 508-509.

[57]Redrup v. New York, 386 U.S. 767, 18 L.Ed. 2d 515, 87 S.Ct. 1414 (1967).

[58]Ibid., at 769.

[59]Harold Nelson and Dwight Teter, Law of Mass Communications (Mineola, N.Y.: Foundation Press, 1973), pp. 413-414.

[60]Ginzburg v. New York, 390 U.S. 629, 20 L.Ed. 2d 195, 88 S.Ct. 1274 (1968). Under the concept of variable obscenity a distinction is drawn between obscenity standards for adults and those for juveniles.

[61]Ibid., at 632.

[62]Ibid., at 633. Brennan quoting <u>Bookcase, Inc. v. Broderick</u>, 18 N.Y. 2d 71, 75, 271 NYS 2d 947, 952, 218 N.E. 2d 668, 671.

[63]<u>Interstate Circuit v. City of Dallas</u>, 390 U.S. 676, 20 L.Ed. 2d 225, 88 S.Ct. 1298 (1968).

[64]<u>Stanley v. Georgia</u>, 394 U.S. 557, 89 S.Ct. 1243, 22 L.Ed. 2d 542 (1969).

[65]Ibid. The agents had been searching for bookmaking records and when they found none decided to view the films.

[66]Ibid., at 564-565.

[67]Ibid., at 568-569.

[68]<u>Leander H. Perez, Jr. v. August M. Ledesma, Jr.</u>, 401 U.S. 82, 91 S.Ct. 674, 27 L.Ed. 2d 701 (1971); <u>Frank Dyson v. Brent Stein</u>, 401 U.S. 200, 91 S.Ct. 769, 27 L.Ed 2d 781 (1971); <u>Garret Byrne v. Serafim Karalex</u>, 401 U.S. 216, 91 S.Ct. 777, 27 L.Ed 792 (1971).

[69]401 U.S. 82.

[70]<u>U.S. v. Thirty-Seven Photographs</u>, 402 U.S. 363, 91 S.Ct. 769, 28 L.Ed. 2d 822 (1971) and <u>U.S. v. Reidel</u>, 402 U.S. 351, 91 S.Ct. 1410, 28 L.Ed. 2d 813 (1971).

[71]<u>Marvin Miller v. California</u>, 413 U.S. 15, 37 L.Ed. 2d 419, 93 S.Ct. 2607; <u>Paris Adult Theatre I v. Slaton</u>, 413 U.S. 39, 37 L.Ed. 446, 93 S.Ct. 2628 (1973); <u>U.S. v. 12 1200 ft. Reels of Super 8mm Film</u>, 413 U.S. 123, 37 L.Ed 2d 500, 93 S.Ct. 2665 (1973); <u>U.S. v. Orito</u>, 413 U.S. 139, 37 L.Ed. 2d 513, 93 S.Ct. 2674 (1973); <u>Kaplan v. California</u>, 413 U.S. 115, 37 L.Ed. 2d 492, 93 S.Ct. 2680 (1973); <u>Heller v. New York</u>, 413 U.S. 483, 37 L.Ed. 2d 745, 93 S.Ct. 2689 (1973); <u>Roaden v. Kentucky</u>, 413 U.S. 496, 37 L.Ed. 2d 757, 93 S.Ct. 2796 (1973); <u>Alexander v. Virginia</u>, 413 U.S. 836, 37 L.Ed. 2d 993, 93 S.Ct. 2803 (1973).

[72]413 U.S. 15; 413 U.S. 39; 413 U.S. 123; 413 U.S. 139; 413 U.S. 115.

[73]413 U.S. 483; 413 U.S. 496; 413 U.S. 836.

[74]413 U.S. 15, 413 U.S. 16.

[75]Ibid., at 17.

[76]Ibid.

[77]Ibid., at 23.

[78] 413 U.S. 39.

[79] Ibid., at 49-50..

[80] Ibid., at 56.

[81] 413 U.S. 123.

[82] Ibid.

[83] Ibid.

[84] 413 U.S. 139-140.

[85] Ibid., at 144-145.

[86] 413 U.S. 115.

[87] Ibid., at 119.

[88] 413 U.S. 483.

[89] 413 U.S. 496.

[90] 413 U.S. 483.

[91] 413 U.S. 496.

[92] 413 U.S. 836.

[93] The four cases are United Artists Corp. v. Board of Censors of the City of Memphis, 339 U.S. 952, 70 S.Ct. 839, 94 L.Ed. 1365 (1950); RD-DR Corp. v. Smith, 340 U.S. 853, 71 S.Ct. 80, 95 L.Ed. 625 (1950); Gelling v. Texas, 343 U.S. 960, 72 S.Ct. 1002, 96 L.Ed. 1359 (1952); Superior Films v. Department of Education of Ohio, 346 U.S. 587, 74 S.Ct. 286, 98 L.Ed 329 (1954).

[94] "More Negro Scenes Cut Out in Dixie Set New Problem for Pix Producers," Variety, 16 July 1944, n.p., clipping in Americal Civil Liberties Union (ACLU) Archives, Vol. 2548, Wisconsin State Historical Society Microfilm Room, Madison, Wisconsin. Hereafter referred to as ACLU Archives.

[95] Ibid.

[96] See Lester Velie, "Censorship in Action," Colliers, 6 May 1950, p. 11; "Censor Board Draw Blast of Newsmen," Memphis Press Scimitar, 29 October, 1947; Theodore Kupferman and Philip O'Erien, "Motion Picture Censorship: The Memphis Blues," Cornell Law Quarterly 36 (Winter 1951): 273; and, Ira Carmen, Movies, Censorship, and the Law, (Ann Arbor, University of Michigan Press, 1966) pp. 206-210.

[97] "More Negro Scenes Cut."

[98] Ibid.

[99] Thurgood Marshall to Roger Baldwin, 19 July 1944, ACLU Archives, Vol. 2548.

[100] Roger Baldwin to Thurgood Marshall, 20 July 1944, ACLU Archives, Vol. 2548.

[101] Wolff, Greenbaum, and Ernst law firm representative, initials lbm, to Roger Baldwin, 10 April 1945, ACLU Archives, Vol. 2637.

[102] Transcript of telephone conversation between initials lbm and Harry Kosner, 10 April 1945, ACLU Archives, Vol. 2637.

[103] H. L. Mitchell to Roger Baldwin, 4 August 1945, ACLU Archives, Vol..2637.

[104] Clifford Forster to H. L. Mitchell, 7 August 1945, ACLU Archives, Vol. 2637.

[105] Clifford Forster to Gradwell Sears (vice-president in charge of distribution, United Artists) 23 August 1945, ACLU Archives, Vol. 2637.

[106] The film "relates a simple story of how a young and pretty girl is about to assume a new job as a school teacher, how the pupils expect her to be stern and are apprehensive of the new relationship, but how she generally wins the affection of the children through her athletic prowess. Among the children in the cast is a little Negro whose part in the comedy is similar to that of the little Negro "Farina" in the former Our Gang comedies . . . in short the picture is perfectly innocuous." See Petition for Writ of Certiorari to the Supreme Court of the State of Tennessee: United Artists and Hal Roach, Petitioners v. Board of Censors of the City of Memphis and the Shelby County Board of Censors, Supreme Court of the United States, October Term, 1949, No. 680, p. 3.

[107] Kupferman and O'Brien, p. 275.

[108] Memphis, Municipal Code (1925) Sections 1131 to 1139 vested the local censors with "power to censor, supervise and regulate all exhibitions, plays, motion pictures, performances, pantomimes or other presentations" and provided that the censors "have power to prohibit any exhibition which shall be of immoral, lewd, or lascivious character or which denounces, derides, or seeks to overthrow the present form of national government."

[109] United Artists v. Board of Consors of City of Memphis, 225 S.W. 24 550, 551 (1948).

[110] "Memphis Censorship Evokes Court Fight by Film Industry," Memphis Commercial Appeal, 20 September 1947, p. 1.

[111] Harry Martin, "Movie Industry Launch Suit Against Binford Censor Board: Bejach Issues Writ Calling Memphis Judges into Court," Memphis Commercial Appeal, 8 October 1947, p. 1.

[112] 225 S.W. 2d 550, 552 (1948).

[113] Ibid., at 550.

[114] Ibid.

[115] Ibid.

[116] Ibid.

[117] Sidney Schreiber to (?) Hamilton, 17 April 1948, O'Brien Legal File, Box 40, Folder 14, Manuscript Room, Wisconsin State Historical Society, Madison, Wisconsin (Hereafter referred to as the O'Brien Legal File).

[118] Ibid.

[119] Marie Walthen to Chester Bahn, 9 March 1949, O'Brien Legal File, Box 40, Folder 14.

[120] "Memphis Censorship Needs to be Checked," Louisville Courier-Journal, 25 September 1947, n.p., clipping in O'Brien Legal File, Box 40, Folder 13.

[121] Petition for Writ, p. 2.

[122] Ibid., pp. 14-15.

[123] Ibid.

[124] 339 U.S. 952.

[125] The film Lost Boundaries, based on a book by William L. White, told the story of a black doctor and his family who passed for white in a New Hampshire community. See Samuel Bloom, "A Social Psychology Study of Motion Picture Audience Behavior: A Case Study of the Negro Image in Mass Communication," (unpublished Ph.D. dissertation, University of Wisconsin, 1956), p. 14. Atlanta Ordinance Governing the Exhibition of Motion Pictures (1944), Sect. 1-12. The ordinance stated that all pictures to be exhibited in the city must first be approved by the city's duly authorized film censor.

[126] "Atlanta Ban on 'Lost Boundaries' goes before Federal Court Tomorrow," New York Times, 5 February 1950, Section II, p. 5.

[127] RD-DR Corp. v. Smith, 89 Fed. Supp. 596 (1950).

[128] Ibid.

[129] Ibid., at 597.

[130] U.S. v. Paramount Pictures, 334 U.S. 131, 68 S.Ct. 915, 92 L.Ed. 1260 (1948). This case involved anti-trust action by the govenment against Paramount and other vertically integrated motion picture companies. It forced film producers to divest themselves of motion picture exhibition theatres.

[131] 89 Fed. Supp. 596, 598 (1950).

[132] Ibid., at 598.

[133] RD-DR Corp. v. Smith, 183 F. 2d 562 (1950).

[134] 340 U.S. 853.

[135] Ibid.

[136] Gelling v. State (Texas), 156 Tex. Crim. 516, 247 S.W. 2d 95 (1952). Pinky was produced by Stanley Kramer and distributed by Twentiety Century Fox. The film told the story of a Negro woman who returned to the South after passing for white in Boston. The story line revolved around the problems the woman had adjusting to the inferior status accorded to blacks in the South. See Edward Mapp, Blacks in American Films Today and Yesterday, (Metuchen, New Jersey: Scarecrow Press, 1972), p. 38.

[137] Carmen, op. cit., p. 54.

[138] Gelling v. State, 247 S.W. 2d 95 (1950).

[139] Ibid.

[140] RD-DR Corp. v. Smith, 183 F. 2d 562 (1950)

[141] 247 S.W. 2d 95, 97 (1952)

[142] Ibid., at 95.

[143] 343 U.S. 960. In Winters v. New York, 333 U.S. 507, 68 S. Ct. 665, 92 L.Ed. 840, the Court struck down as unconstitutionally vague a New York statute prohibiting the dissemination of printed matter devoted to the publication of criminal stories or stories of deeds of bloodshed, lust or crime. In part the Court stated: "The

line between the informing and the entertaining is too elusive for the protection of that basic right. Everyone is familiar with instances of propaganda through fiction. What is one man's amusement, teaches another's doctrine." See 333 U.S. 507, 510.

[144] Ibid.

[145] Ibid.

[146] Superior Films v. Department of Education of Ohio, 159 Ohio St. 315, 112 N.E. 2d 311 (1953).

[147] Ibid. The same or similar issue referred to by the Court was the constitutionality of the Ohio film censorship statute. Ohio Code (1943), Sect. 154-47-154-471, vest in the division of film censorship the power to allow "only such films as are in the judgment and discretion of the board of censors of a moral, educational or amusing, and harmless character" to be shown in the state.

[148] Ibid., at 316. Case No. 33265. M was a German film based on a series of child murders which spread terror among the inhabitants of Dusseldorf in 1929. One reviewer termed the film "a strong cinematic work with remarkably fine acting, it is extraordinarily effective." See "The Dusseldorf Murders," New York Times Film Reviews: A One Volume Selection (New York: Quadrangle Books, 1971), p. 133.

[149] Ibid.

[150] Ibid.

[151] Ibid., at 317. Cases No. 33282 and 33283. Native Son was described to the Court by Film Classics as follows: the action of the story takes place in Chicago, and part of the picture was filmed there. The role of the central character, Bigger Thomas, an embittered young Negro is acted by Richard Wright, the author of the book. Bigger accidentally kills a white girl. After disposing of her body he attempts to extort money from her parents. After the murder is discovered, Bigger goes into hiding with his sweetheart, Bessie Mears, and immediately before his capture murders Bessie in the mistaken belief that she betrayed him.

[152] Ibid.

[153] Ibid.

[154] Ibid., at 319-335.

[155] Ibid., at 327-328.

[156] Ibid., at 335.

[157] 346 U.S. 587.

[158] *Commercial Pictures Corp. v. Regents of the University of the State of New York.* 305 N.Y. 366, 113 N.E. 2d 502 (1953).

[159] This case involved the censorship of the movie *La Ronda* by the New York film censorship bureau on the grounds that the film was "immoral" and would "tend to corrupt morals." The decision was upheld by the N.Y. Board of Regents.

[160] 346 U.S. 587.

[161] Ibid.

CHAPTER III

CENSORSHIP CONTROVERSIES INVOLVING COURT ACTION

Throughout the years of *The Birth of a Nation*'s release, a variety of tactics were employed by individuals concerned that the film had a right to be shown. These tactics included taking court action, seeking legislative remedy, requesting administrative intervention, generating counter-propaganda, launching editorial campaigns, demonstrating against the film and ignoring the film. Commenting upon the range of tactics employed by just the NAACP against the film, Mary White Ovington, NAACP Vice-President, said:

> It would be very difficult to tell you the methods employed to prevent its production in all the cities of this country where it has been booked to appear. A method successful in one place has been unsuccessful in another.[1]

Although many censorship controversies involved a blend of tactics, some basic distinctions may be drawn among those instances which were dependent upon administrative action, those instances which were ultimately decided by legislative action, and those instances which were primarily extra-legal in nature. Each of these major tactics will be considered individually. This chapter focuses on the range of tactics which involved court actions.

Censorship Cases Involving Court Action: An Overview

During the time period 1915-1973, at least 28 *The Birth of a Nation* censorship controversies included court action. Because several controversies included multiple court rulings, the number of court involvements discussed in this chapter is 39. Twenty-two controversies ultimately were resolved by court action. The remainder of the court actions did not resolve the given controversies. Court actions were initiated by both those who asserted the film's right to the screen and those who requested censorship. Decisions were rendered by a variety of courts. However, no case was appealed to the U. S. Supreme Court. The majority of court rulings were made prior to 1926. Only one case was decided after Burstyn v. Wilson,[2] the U. S. Supreme Court ruling which granted limited First Amendment protection to film.

Court Decisions Upholding Censorship

During the time period studied, six courts resolved The Birth censorship controversies by upholding either total or partial censorship. The judges decided the question asked either by ruling specifically in favor of censorship or by refusing to hear the case and thus upholding an existing censorship order. Three of the controversies involved state censorship[3] and three involved municipal censorship.[4] Two other courts upheld censorship of The Birth.[5] In each case the judge made the final court ruling, but the actions did not resolve the controversies. One such decision upheld a mayor's fight to censor the film, and the mayor resolved the controversy. In the remaining instance, a municipal court supported partial censorship, but the controversy continued and was resolved by a municipal censorship board. Because the specific issues brought before each court differed substantially, each case is discussed separately.

Court Resolved Controversies Supportive of Censorship

During the years covered by this study, six courts resolved *The Birth of a Nation* controversies by upholding censorship. Five of the decisions were based on procedural grounds. Although the judge in the remaining case was asked specifically to consider the possible negative effect of the film, the actual basis of his decision in favor of censorship was not recorded.

Procedural decisions

The first court to uphold censorship of *The Birth* for procedural reasons was the Ohio State Supreme Court. The controversy resolved by the court began when the Ohio state censorship board refused to license *The Birth*, January 6, 1916.[6] The Board's ruling indicated simply that *The Birth* was "not harmless and . . . not such a motion picture as the Board is authorized to pass and approve."[7] When asked by Epoch, the film's distributor, to explain this action and to reconsider the film, the board refused.[8] Epoch then sought from the U. S. Court of the Southern District of Ohio an order enjoining the board from interfering with *The Birth*'s production in the state.[9] However, reasoning that his court had no jurisdiction in the matter, District Court Judge John Sater refused to grant the order.[10]

Epoch next appealed to the Ohio Supreme Court asking that the board's decision be reversed.[11] In its petition, Epoch contended that The Birth was "in character and tone highly moral, educational, and instructive, as well as harmless and in no way justly engenders or tends to excite racial or religious prejudice or animosity."[12] The court dismissed the petition on the grounds that the censorship board failed to supply a complete transcript of the censorship record as required by law.[13] Epoch filed an application for a rehearing which was denied.[14]

Thus, the censor's decision was upheld and The Birth of a Nation was barred from Ohio.[15] The censors had publicly justified their actions by asserting that the film was "not harmless" without specifying what type of harm the film potentially represented. The Ohio Supreme Court refused to consider the case on procedural grounds and did not consider the film.

Nine years later the West Virginia Supreme Court refused to hear a censorship case questioning the power of a mayor to ban a film from a given community.[16] Unlike the 1916 Ohio case, Virginia Amusement Company v. W. W. Wertz[17] reached the West Virginia Supreme Court on appeal from conflicting lower court decisions. Like the Ohio case, only procedural issues and not film content were considered by the court.

The West Virginia controversy began when a committee from the Charleston Branch of the NAACP protested the planned exhibition of The Birth to Charleston's mayor, W. W. Wertz.[18] After the protest, Wertz notified the management of the Rialto Theatre that if The Birth was screened as scheduled, he would order the picture confiscated and all theatre employees arrested.[19] As authority for this threatened action, Wertz cited a 1919 state statute which made it unlawful to "advertise, exhibit, display or show" any film which engendered racial prejudice.[20] He also relied upon the police power of his administrative office.[21]

The Rialto management responded to Wertz' threat by seeking an injunction in the Kanawha County Common Pleas Court, forbidding interference with the film's production.[22] In its petition for injunction, the theatre interests contended Wertz' threat to confiscate the film and projector and to arrest all theatre employees was a potential violation of due process.[23] Wertz countered that he had lawful right to stop the film and seize it as evidence.[24]

Common Pleas Court Judge Morgan Owen heard the arguments and decided in favor of the theatre interests. Owen held that although warrants could be served and arrests made within the law, the threatened seizure of the film and projector would constitute a violation of due process.[25] Owen issued the injunction but required that the theatre post $500 bond with the court.[26] The management posted the bond and The Birth was screened twice in Charleston, April 1, 1925.[27]

The following day Wertz appealed to Circuit Court Judge Arthur Hudson. Hudson lifted the injunction issued by Owen reasoning that:

> City authorities had a right to make the arrest under proper warrants charging that a crime had been committed and to seize the film, machine, and other paraphernalia used in the reproduction of the picture as evidence of the crime.[28]

The Rialto management countered with an appeal to the West Virginia Supreme Court, requesting supersedeas (a writ having in general the effect of a command to stay, on good cause shown, some ordinary proceedings which ought otherwise to have proceeded) from Hudson's order. However, the court refused to hear the case.[29]

In this controversy, the lower courts ruled upon questions concerning a mayor's right to seize evidence in a threatened arrest situation and did not consider the constitutionality of the 1919 censorship law, the validity of the mayor's right to act as municipal censor, or any free speech questions. As in the 1916 Ohio case, the decision was based upon procedural questions. Although the courts did not specifically consider film content, the mayor stated that the film violated the 1919 statute only in the pursuit of Flora by Gus sequence.[30] Because the film was screened publicly twice during the controversy, ultimate action taken against the film was subsequent restraint.

The Birth of a Nation was banned a second time from Ohio in February 1925, when the state's censor board again refused to pass the film.[31] As in 1916, the board refused to approve The Birth "on account of being harmful."[32] Again, the censorship division did not elaborate upon the specific type of harm the film potentially represented.[33]

Epoch appealed the censor's ruling directly to the Ohio Supreme Court.[34] In addition to its petition for a hearing on behalf of the film, Epoch filed approximately ninety affidavits attesting to The Birth's quality.[35] The court apparently refused to hear the case and thus sustained the censor's decision.[36] During the duration of the controversy, the film was not screened publicly in Ohio.

The remaining procedural decision upheld variable censorship of the film. The right to designate the film for an adult-only audience was first applied to The Birth by Judge William Fenimore Cooper of the Cook County Illinois Superior Court in 1915.[37] In a decision discussed in more detail later, Cooper restrained Chicago Mayor William Thompson from interfering with the film's showing to adults bud did stipulate the theatre management could not admit anyone under 18 to the film.[38]

Children under 18 also were prohibited from seeing The Birth when the film returned to Chicago in 1917. After announcing plans to revive The Birth in Chicago, Epoch went to court to petition for mandamus to compel Chicago police superintendent Herman Schuettler to issue a general permit which would allow juveniles to attend the film.[39]

Judge Joseph B. David, Cook County Superior Court, granted the writ and Schuettler appealed to the Illinois Supreme Court.[40] The court heard the case, but decided it was without jurisdiction to resolve the issue in question because the constitutionality of the statute under which the film had been censored was not challenged.[41]

The case was transferred from the Illinois Supreme Court to

the Appellate Court of the 1st District of Illinois. In a decision which dealt solely with procedural questions, the Appellate Court reversed, reasoning that the original court had "disregarded the material issues of fact and remanded.[42] If the case was reconsidered by the lower court, the outcome is unknown."[43] Thus, because of procedural considerations, the original censorship order supporting variable viewing was apparently upheld.

Rationale Underlying Censorship Decisions Unclear

In two cases courts resolved controversies by upholding censorship, but the rationales underlying the decisions are unclear. Both decisions supported prior restraint. One case concerned censorship at the local level and other dealt with censorship at the state level.

The first case of this nature was decided by District Court Judge T. Stewart in Lincoln, Nebraska, June 1918.[44] Stewart issued an order forbidding the scheduled opening of The Birth after Lincoln Attorney Willis E. Reed charged in court that the film would generate racial prejudice and create disharmony "at a time when harmony should prevail and hence was a hindrance to the successful prosecution of the war."[45] Reed asked Stewart to consider the effect the film would have upon "the large number of colored men now serving in the army."[46] Reed also called the film a detriment to public morals. Stewart responded to Reed's request by forbidding the scheduled showing. Although Reed argued against the film on effects grounds, the actual rationale underlying Stewart's decision is not reported in the sources consulted.[47]

Because of the issues involved and timing of the other court ruling supportive of censorship with unknown rationale, the case is of particular importance within the context of this research. This case concerned censorship of The Birth ordered by the Maryland state censorship board in May 1952.[48] The board's decision was challenged in the courts by the film's distributor and the case was adjudicated after the U. S. Supreme Court ruling in Burstyn v. Wilson.[49]

The Maryland State Board of Censors banned The Birth by refusing to renew the license necessary to exhibit the film on May 23, 1952.[50] The Board acted on the authority of a state statute which gave it the authority to reject any film it considered "sacrilegious, obscene, indecent, inhuman or immoral . . . or that tends . . . to corrupt morals or incite to crime."[51] In a public statement explaining the action, censor Sydney Traub said that the board had consulted with the state police and with members of the Maryland Commission on Interracial Problems and all parties "were definitely of the opinion that the film was morally bad and crime-inciting."[52] In addition, Traub said the film was given "utmost consideration" by the board which decided that because of the nature "of many of its scenes and subtitles 'Birth of a Nation' could easily incite to riots and other crimes . . ."[53] Specifically, Traub objected to scenes depicting the post Civil War South Carolina legislative which he termed "a drunken orgy," the glorification of the Klan, and the "subtitle about crushing the white South under the black heel."[54]

Traub concluded that the film should not be shown because "times have changed and trends of thought are largely at variance with some previously held ideas."[55]

Three days following the board's decision the U. S. Supreme Court extended limited First Amendment protection to the motion picture medium in *Burstyn v. Wilson*.[56] Harry R. Shull, Maryland distributor of *The Birth* announced immediately that he would initiate legal action against the censor board.[57] Traub announced that the *Burstyn* ruling would have minimal impact on Maryland board decisions "because cases of sacrilegious movie treatment are so rare . . ."[58] The *Baltimore Sun* editorially was not as sure as Traub that the ruling would have minimal effect. The *Sun* noted that the board would no longer be able to use sacrilegious as a censorship standard and said "whether the new opinion will further restrict its (the board's) activities has not been definitely decided."[59] In this context, the *Sun* mentioned the legal proceedings involving *The Birth* as a potential text case.[60]

On June 13, 1952, attorneys Marvin Skiar and Irwin Cohen filed a suit on behalf of Harry Shull in Maryland Circuit Court alleging that the Maryland film censorship law violated the First and Fourteenth Amendments of the U. S. Constitution and Article 40 of the Declaration of Rights of the Maryland Constitution because it exercised prior restraint against what Shull contended was now protected speech.[61] Circuit Court Judge Michael J. Manley gave the board and Baltimore Police Commissioner Beverly Ober ten days to answer the charges.[62] Manley indicated that if the ban on the film was not adequately explained, it would be lifted.[63]

Seven days later Maryland Attorney General Hall Hammond filed demurrers (pleas to dismiss a suit on the grounds that even if the statements of the opposition are true, they do not sustain the claim because they are insufficient or legally defective) on behalf of the board and Ober.[64] Hall contended that Shull's suit was insufficient in law and that Shull was not entitled "to relief in the Circuit Court."[65] Hall also alleged that other legal remedies were available to Shull.[66] Judge Manley's ruling in this case was not recorded in the sources consulted.[67] However, he must have accepted Hall's argument because other sources indicate that the ban was not lifted until 1958.[68] Thus, in what was probably a procedural decision a judge upheld a state ban on the film even though the film's supporters initiated the action on First Amendment grounds.

Other Court Decisions Supportive of Censorship

During the time period studied, two courts favored censorship of The Birth, but the rulings did not resolve the censorship controversies involved. One of the decisions involved barring the film from a city. The other decision involved partial censorship of the film.

In the former case, the Minnesota Supreme Court considered only procedural questions when deciding whether Minneapolis Mayor Wallace Nye had the legal right to revoke a license issued to The Birth by the Minneapolis City Council, October, 1915.[69] This controversy began when the City Council, after lengthy debate, granted the Shubert Theatre a permit to exhibit The Birth. Black citizens who testified at the Council meeting against the film asked Mayor Nye to revoke the license.[70] In answer, Nye appointed a 50-member jury to review the film and advise him concerning its acceptability.[71] After consulting the jury, Nye announced that he would revoke the Shubert's license if The Birth were shown.

Shubert manager A. G. Bainbridge, Jr. sought an injunction in the Hennepin County District Court, restraining Nye from interfering with The Birth's production. Bainbridge also sought and received a court order permitting exhibition of the film pending the outcome of the injunction hearing.[72] Because of this order, The Birth opened at the Shubert October 31, 1915.[73]

The following day, Hennepin County District Court Judge John Steele heard arguments concerning the requested injunction. Representing Nye, City Attorney Charles Gould argued in part that the film would "endanger public morals by inciting race prejudice,"[74] and contended that the mayor had the legal right to revoke a license granted by the city council. For Bainbridge, attorney F. H. Stinchfield argued that the court had a right to overrule the mayor in this case and that they mayor had no absolute right to revoke licenses granted by the city.[75] Further, Stinchfield said that the mayor was interfering unlawfully with his client's right to do business and that Bainbridge had contracted debts in order to produce the film.[76]

After a nine-day hearing, Steele held that the power to revoke licenses was properly within the mayor's official police power.[77] Steele concluded that the "power vested in the mayor must be vested somewhere" and that unless the mayor acted in "bad faith, arbitrarily or without cause," the court could not intervene.[78] In this particular instance, Steele stated that Nye had exercised his power appropriately. Steele also said that the fact that Bainbridge had contracted debts in order to produce the film was "only one of the hazards of the business."[79] However, Steele ruled that the film could be shown for two more days while Stinchfield perfected an appeal to the state supreme court. In this decision, no attempt was made by the court to pass upon the merits of the film.

Stinchfield quickly perfected his appeal and the Minnesota Supreme Court accepted the case and gave it an almost immediate hearing. The court defined the question as "whether the court can enjoin the mayor from exercising this power which the law expressly gives him."[80] The court indicated its role in such cases was to "Inquire whether a fair legal discretion was exercised."[81] The court also indicated that the revocation of licenses per se was not subject to judicial control.

The court decided that in this case Nye had in fact "set out in an apparently honest effort to determine the fitness of this play."[82] Therefore, the mayor had acted within his power, and Steele's decision was affirmed. Although the court summarized the "objectionable portions" of the film and discussed several other censorship cases involving the film in dicta accompanying the decision, it did not specifically consider the merits of The Birth in its decision.

Because the courts had specifically upheld Nye's right to stop the film, he was free to revoke the theatre license if the film were continued. However, after the supreme court ruling, Nye requested that a second advisory committee review the film. This committee viewed The Birth and "saw no harm in the play."[83] In response to the committee's decision, Nye apparently did not revoke the Shubert's license.[84]

Thus, Bainbridge v. Minnesota reached the Minnesota Supreme Court on appeal from a district court decision and was decided upon procedural questions. In spite of the ruling which upheld the right of the mayor to stop The Birth, the mayor did not choose to exercise that right. Because the film was screened publicly during the initial trial period and because Nye did not carry out his threat against the film, efforts for restraint in this case were totally unsuccessful even though a state supreme court ruled that the film might be stopped. Therefore, the controversy was actually resolved by the mayor who refused to stop the film.

The remaining court decision which upheld partial censorship of the film but did not resolve the censorship question was handed down in Boston Municipal Court, First Session, in April, 1915.[85] This case concerned a charge brought by NAACP representatives Butler Wilson, William R. Lewis, and J. Mott Hallowell that The Birth was obscene.[86] Judge Thomas Dowd heard the case.

During the hearing, Hallowell argued that the "word immoral should be construed in its broad sense as anything hostile to the welfare of the general public or contrary to good order and public welfare."[87] After one day of testimony, Dowd advised that he would see the film before deciding the case. That evening Dowd viewed the film and when he returned to court he refused to hear further evidence. Dowd declared that on the basis of his viewing the film he considered only one scene to be objectionable and ordered that scene cut:

> I am convinced the statute covers this play. There is one scene which is offensive and immoral. This is the scene where the renegade Negro Gus pursues a child of 12, yes with an expression upon his face which leaves no doubt of his state of mind. He is plainly actuated by the lowest passions of mankind. This would be the same for a white man.
>
> This is the only scene which in my mind is covered by the statutes. . .I have no doubt that parts of it are more or less disgusting to the colored people, but there is nothing in the statutes which covers them. It is unfortunate in my opinion that our stage has descended to dealing with filth. . .
>
> This is a splendid production. . .This does not mean I condone the nauseating scene I have mentioned. But I would say that with the exception of that scene the play is within the law. It must be remembered that in reaching a decision I have not taken into account any question of color.[88]

As a result of Dowd's ruling, the pursuit of Flora by Gus sequence was modified by the theatre management. However, this action did not silence NAACP opposition to the film. The organization continued to oppose the film with a variety of tactics discussed in later chapters. This is the only case found during the time period studied in which a judge ordered a specific scene censored from the film. The scene was cut because the judge considered it to be obscene.

In summary, two courts ruled in favor of individuals requesting censorship of The Birth, but the rulings did not resolve the question of censorship. One of these decisions considered specifically the content of the film and ordered a scene cut from the film because it was considered obscene. The other decision considered only procedural issues.

Court Decisions Which Forbade Censorship

During the time period studied, sixteen courts upheld The Birth's right to the screen by either restraining local officials from interfering with the film's production or by sustaining the decisions of censorship boards which had approved the film. Although in five cases existing records did not indicate what rationale each judge used when deciding the cases, the remaining 11 cases were decided by judges who reasoned either that the film could not be censored for racial reasons; that the film could not be censored because someone felt that it threatened public peace; or, that procedural guidelines had been violated by those ordering censorship. In three cases, courts asserted the film's right to the screen, but the decisions did not actually resolve the censorship controversies.

Racial Stereotyping Argument Rejected

Four judges during the time period rejected censorship requests based upon the argument that the film would incite racial prejudice because of the uncomplimentary stereotyping of blacks.

All cases involved censorship of the film at the municipal level. Three of the cases were decided during 1915; one was decided in 1924.

The first judge to indicate that racial stereotyping was not an acceptable standard for censorship was also the first judge to hear a censorship case involving The Birth. This first challenge to The Birth's right to the screen came before the film's public premiere February 8, 1915.[89] The challenge came primarily from two organizations: The Los Angeles Brnach of the NAACP and the Los Angeles Ministers Alliance. Although neither group had seen The Birth, both groups requested that the Los Angeles film censorship board ban the film from the city.[90] The board allowed representatives from both groups to view the film and listened to the subsequent protests. However, the board approved the film.

After the board's action, the NAACP branch notified the organization's national office of the film's content and requested that the national office attempt to convince the National Censor Board to revoke its approval of the film.[91] Both groups met with Los Angeles mayor and police chief and requested that those individuals use the powers of their offices to stop the film. However, the mayor and police chief responded that the censorship board had exclusive jurisdiction in such matters and that "they were powerless."[92]

The protesters next petitioned the Los Angeles city council and requested that the council pass a resolution asking the censorship board to remove its approval of the film.[93] As is discussed in more detail in Chapter V, the NAACP opposed the film because it would stir up racial prejudice and lead to breaches of peace. They said the film "characterized the Negro as an ignorant fool, a vicious rapist, a venal and unscrupulous politician, or a faithful but doddering idiot."[94]

The NAACP filed a petition against the film with the city council. The council was receptive to the petition and issued an order instructing the police chief not to allow the film to be shown.[95] The police chief ordered The Birth's premiere 2 o'clock matinee performance cancelled at the Clune Theatre.[96] D. W. Griffith challenged this action by seeking an injunction restraining the police chief. A temporary injunction was granted to Griffith and The Birth opened at the Clune February 8, 1915, to an estimated audience of 3,000.[97]

The following day, the police chief was ordered to appear in court to show cause why the injunction should not be made permanent. At this hearing a group of black citizens testified that The Birth was inflammatory and would incite racial prejudice.[98] Nevertheless, Judge U. Jackson sustained the injunction.

In explaining his decision, Jackson said in part: "I do not approve of this play, but that does not alter my position as judge of this court."[99] Speaking particularly to those who had testified against the film, Jackson continued, "my advice to you is to wholly disregard this matter. The only harm that can come from the affair is through constant agitation of the matter. The mere reproduction of the pictures cannot change your standing in this community."[100] After Jackson's ruling, the film continued at Clune's for seven months establishing records for length of run and attendance.[101]

This is the first censorship case involving The Birth when a judge refused to accept the argument that the film should be censored because of its racist content. Prior to court intervention, one screening of the film was cancelled by police order. It is interesting to note that the judge advised those opposed to the film that the best course of action would be to ignore the film and indicated a belief that, at least in Los Angeles, the film would not affect the status of blacks.

Judge William Fennimore Cooper of the Illinois Cook County Superior Court was even more explicit in his rejection of racial stereotyping as an acceptable censorship criterion when he issued an injunction in June, 1915, restraining Chicago Mayor William Thompson and Police Chief Herman Schuettler from interfering with The Birth's showing.[102] Cooper's ruling came after Thompson refused to allow the film to be exhibited in Chicago even though his predecessor had issued a license approving the film.[103] Theatre owner Joseph J. McCarthy challenged Thompson's action in Cooper's Court and won the injunction.

During the hearing, attorneys for the city contended that the film would engender racial animosity against Chicago's black citizens.[104] Cooper refused to accept that argument and stated in his decision that films should not be censored because they presented members of one race or nationality in an unfavorable light.[105] In part Cooper stated:

> No race or nationality has greater right under the law than any other has. Any race or nationality so offended can best give the lie to the bad characters so presented by continuing to conduct themselves as law abiding citizens who do not expect greater rights from the law than it allows all other men or nationalities . . . If white men appealed to the courts to restrain production of a play because its characters portrayed thereof a dissolute white man whose acting would bring race hatred against the nation which his stage character assumed, their plea would be denied for want of law to support the same, and law should be and is the same for black and white men.[106]

During the hearing, Cooper refused to consider any pamphlets, newspaper clippings against the film which one NAACP attorney wished to submit as evidence.[107] Rather, Cooper accepted only evidence against the film from individuals who had actually seen the film. Because none of the film's opponents had seen the film, NAACP attorney C. E. Bentley described his case against the film as "weak."[108] Four individuals, including Griffith, testified for the film. Bentley described Griffith's testimony as "practically" winning the case.[109]

Although Cooper issued the injunction, he did stipulate that the management could not admit anyone under 18 to the film.[110] Thompson appealed the decision to the Appellate Court, but that court placed the case on its fall docket and effectively ended censorship efforts.[111] In this case, efforts for total prior restraint were negated by a court decision which explicitly refused to accept the argument that the film should be stopped because of its racial content.

The potential impact of The Birth's content was also the central question in a Philadelphia controversy later in 1915. The controversy began in Philadelphia after The Birth had been approved by the Pennsylvania State Board of Censors, but before the film opened in Philadelphia.[112] When an announcement was made that The Birth was scheduled for screening in the city, representatives from the city's black organizations met with city officials and asked that they stop the film.[113] After the meeting, Philadelphia's director of public safety informed the theatre which had scheduled the film that it would not be allowed.[114]

Representing the theatre, Joseph P. McCullen immediately sought and received an injunction restraining the police from interfering with The Birth's production.[115] When arguing the case, McCullen contended that the film "in no ways engenders or tends to excite racial or religious prejudice."[116] The trial judge agreed.

In his decision, Judge U. Ferguson, Court of Common Pleas, indicated that he had seen The Birth in Atlantic City and did not recall anything that could be called objectionable in it.[117] Ferguson said that he had found the film "interesting and that while some Negroes might criticize it because of their temperament, their judgment should not be the rule as many spoken plays could be criticized by other races because of reflections on race and nationality."[118] In this way, Ferguson rejected censorship for racial or ethnic reasons as an acceptable censorship standard and the film continued in Philadelphia.

U. S. Circuit Court Judge John C. Pollock also resolved a

controversy rejecting the argument that the film would engender racial strife.[119] The controversy began after C. W. Stater, Oklahoma City attorney who owned the Kansas state's rights to The Birth, announced he would submit the film to the Kansas state board of censors.[120] This announcement conjured what one newspaper termed "a wild storm" involving top state officials and a variety of interest groups.

Immediately upon learning of the planned Kansas revival of the film, the NAACP telegraphed Kansas Governor Jonathan M. Davis, requesting that Davis prevent the film from being shown. In its telegram, the NAACP charged that The Birth was a "dangerous film in its deliberate distortion of known historical facts and its glorification of the infamous Ku Klux Klan and has caused numberous racial clashes and is largely responsible for present day revival of the Klan."[121] The NAACP concluded by urging Davis to take action against the film because it spread "vicious racial prejudices."[122]

Davis responded that he did not object to The Birth and said that he would not direct a recall if the film were approved by the state censors. Davis indicated that he had seen the film and "saw nothing objectionable about the picture."[123]

Davis' position was severely criticized by a variety of individuals. For example, former Kansas Governor Henry Allen called Davis' position "sordid and inconsiderate" and indicated his belief that the film should be stopped because "it will arouse bitter racial sentiment and hatred."[124] Likewise, Charles Scott, Iowa

Daily Register editor, branded the film subtle propaganda to stir up race hatred in the state.[125] State Attorney General Charles B. Griffith said that Davis should stop the film because there was "no excuse or justification for its admission" to the state.[126] Griffith took his argument directly to the state censorship board and in testimony before the board asked that The Birth be rejected because its exhibition would endanger "the existing peace of the state by stirring up race prejudice and reopening old wounds."[127] The board assured Griffith that it would consider his appeal. However, the board approved The Birth later the same day.[128]

The board's action did not stop the protesters. For example, a group of citizens led by representatives of the Wichita Branch of the NAACP and Wichita's black newspaper the Protest filed a petition with the Wichita city commissioners requesting that The Birth be banned in their city.[129] The city commissioners responded by passing an ordinance forbidding the screening of any film which was obscene, depicted prize fighting, or tended to create sectional strife or race prejudice.[130] Stater filed a bill of complaint in the Eighth Federal District Court, Kansas City, requesting that the city commissioners be restrained from interfering with The Birth.[131] Stater's complaint alleged that the Wichita ordinance was "unconstitutional, invalid, unreasonable and void."[132]

Judge John C. Pollock heard the case. State Attorney General Griffith and R. C. Foulton, Wichita City Attorney, represented the city commissioners. Stater represented the film. Foulton and Griffith contended that the city had the power to prevent the exhibition of undesirable films and presented affidavits from city officials, ministers, and black citizens condemning the film.[133] However, Pollock granted a temporary injunction restraining the commissioners from interfering with the film and termed the Wichita ordinance "race legislation."[134] Pollock also asserted that the film had been shown in seven Kansas cities without racial difficulties and that Wichita citizens were not "likely to be misled by a motion picture."[135] However, Pollock did require Stater to post a bond of $2,500 which would be forfeited if racial trouble occurred in Wichita while the film was exhibited.[136]

After The Birth had been shown for one week with no evidence of disorder, a second hearing was held to determine if the injunction should be made permanent. After hearing arguments for both sides, Pollock continued the injunction. In this decision Pollock stressed that the events shown in the film occurred over 60 years ago when black citizens "needed the protection of all states."[137] However, Pollock continued:

> The worst thing in the world is to throw protection around people who don't need it. The colored people have so lived in Kansas that they need no more protection than whites. There are certain sections of the south perhaps where this picture could not be shown without a disturbance, but there is no better place in the U. S. where it might be shown with perfect safety than Wichita for there the people are intelligent and liberal.[138]

Pollock also indicated that the Wichita ordinance was null and void because it "impaired contracts which had been made by exhibitors and playhouse proprietors."[139]

Thus, during the time period studied, four judges rejected specifically the argument that The Birth should be censored because of its racial stereotyping. All of the controversies involved requests that the film be restrained in a given city. All cases involved decisions which restrained local officials from interfering with the film's production.

Censorship Based on Rationale that Film
Would Endanger Public Peace

During the time period studied, only one judge was found to assert the film's right to the screen by rejecting the argument that the film represented a potential threat to the public peace. This decision involved censorship of The Birth in St. Louis, Missouri, September, 1915.[140] The controversy began with the announcement three weeks prior to the film's scheduled opening, August 29, 1915.[141]

After the advertising campaign announcing the film's scheduled run, black citizens met with St. Louis Mayor Kiel and City Prosecuting Attorney Sidener and requested that the film be stopped. However, Kiel convinced the group that he was without power to act. On the other hand, Sidener promised to forbid the presentation.[142]

Responding to Sidener's promise to stop The Birth, representatives of the Olympia Theatre, where The Birth was scheduled to open, went to court and received a temporary injunction restraining both Sidener and the St. Louis police department from interfering with the film's production.[143]

A hearing to determine whether to allow demurrers filed on

behalf of both Sidener and the police was delayed twice. During the delays, the film was screened under the protection of the original injunction.

On September 10, 1915, Judge Henning of the Circuit Court overruled the demurrer filed on behalf of the police department and continued the temporary injunction restraining the police from interfering with The Birth.[144] However, Henning sustained the demurrer of Sidener and dismissed a temporary injunction restraining him from issuing warrants in the case.[145]

Five days later Henning indefinitely continued the injunction against the police department. In part Henning indicated that the best evidence to support the film's right to the screen was the fact that it had been running at the Olympia for several weeks without incident.[146] Therefore, Henning refused to accept the argument that The Birth would cause a breach of peace. In spite of the judge's earlier decision concerning his demurrer, Sidener apparently did not issue warrants in the case and the film continued at the theatre.

This is the only case found in which a judge refused to allow censorship of the film by specifically rejecting the argument that the film would lead to breach of peace. The case took several weeks to arrive at its ultimate resolution and the judge indicated that since the film had been shown without incident during the course of the hearings, it was not likely to cause violence in the future.

Procedural Decisions Not Allowing Censorship

During the years studied, six courts refused to allow censorship of The Birth for procedural reasons. The most interesting and detailed of these decisions was rendered in 1917 by Judge Foran of the Common Pleas Court of Cuyahoga County, Ohio.[147] This case questioned a mayor's right to censor a film from a given community within a state after the state board of censors had approved the film for presentation in the entire state.

The controversy began when Cleveland Mayor Harry L. Davis refused to allow The Birth to be shown in Cleveland even though the film had previously been approved by the Ohio Industrial Commission and the State Board of Censors.[148] Epoch, the film's distributor, sought an injunction in the Cuyahoga County Common Pleas Court restraining Mayor Davis, the Cleveland director of public safety, and the Cleveland chief of police from preventing the exhibition of the film. Judge Foran heard the case and ruled in favor of Epoch. In part Foran reasoned that after a film was approved by the Ohio Board of Censors, its exhibition in the state may not be questioned except "by application to that board for a review of its action, or by bringing suit in the Supreme Court to have the order amended, vacated, or set aside."[149]

Although the decision itself is rather straightforward, Foran included with his ruling 19 pages of dicta in which he explained his decision, analyzed the arguments of each side in the case, and interpreted film as a communications medium. Foran began his analysis with a description of the fact situation in the case and summarized the city's petition. According to Foran, the city cased its argument for censorship upon the position of the mayor as chief conservator of the public peace within the city. The city contended that the film "would have a tendency to create and would probably result in a serious breach of the peace."[150] The city further contended that the mayor's actions in stopping the film were justified because the film was "calculated to cast disgrace upon a large body of self-respecting and law-abiding citizens" and that certain scenes in the film depicted individuals engaged in a conspiracy against governmental authority.[151] Thus, the city argued that the mayor was within his authority when censoring this film because it represented a threat to public peace; misrepresented a large group of Cleveland's citizens; and, presented a sedicious conspiracy.

After summarizing the city petition, Foran stated that the court could only rule on the facts presented and rules of law prescribed and not on "any question of sentiment or expediency."[152] Foran said that "there may be an underlying suggestion that is political in character" which was of no concern to his court.[153] However, Foran said that this statement was not to be considered a reflection upon Davis, whose motives Foran described as "undoubtedly above suspicion."[154]

Foran then indicated that he had seen The Birth and did not like the film. Specifically, he stated: "If I had known in advance as much as I now know of the character of this exhibition, I could not have been induced by any consideration to witness it."[155] Foran explained his negative feelings concerning the film in an extended passage which contains references to Greek mythology, quotations from the Hindu religion, quotations from the *Bible*, quotations from the Declaration of Independence, and an analysis of slavery, the status of black people in the United States, the Civil War, pre-revolutionary American history, reconstruction and carpet-bagging![156] During this extended passage, Foran revealed that he was a Civil War veteran and was in essence judging the truth of *The Birth* against his personal experiences. Although he does deny the historical accuracy of certain scenes in the film,[157] Foran indicated that his actual disapproval of the film came from the fact that it brought to his memories which he described as "harsh and bitter thoughts" best left to the "abysmal past."[158]

In this passage, Foran also analyzed the status of film and concluded, much as Justice McKenna had in *Mutual Film Corp. v. Industrial Commission of Ohio*,[159] that the purpose of the film medium was to entertain, not educate, socially benefit or morally improve.[160] Expressing his dislike of the medium, Foran stated that film:

> . . . caters to the base passions and the hedonistic, and not to the classical taste of the community. Men prefer to see the foibles and idiosyncracies of their neighbors exploited rather than to see the mirror held to nature when it exposes their own sins and short-comings. Hence we have the stage Irishman, the unseemly and grotesque caricature, which, if taken seriously, frequently reflects odiously upon the racial characteristics of these people; but, these crude, clownish exhibitions appeal only to ignorant, depraved, satiated pleasure seekers. A real man is disgusted by them.[161]

In spite of Foran's conclusion that the exhibition of <u>The Birth</u> could serve "no useful purpose,"[162] Foran said that the film would not cause a breach of peace.[163] Admitting that the film would cause a breach of peace, Foran said, was admitting that black Americans were not law-abiding citizens and that admission Foran termed an "uncalled for slander upon these citizens."[164] Defining the "tendency to provoke a breach of the peace," Foran said:

> . . . something the natural effect and tendency of which would be to unconsciously and spontaneously cause men to lose control of their reason and permit passion and anger to dominate judgment. The very absurdity of the travesties presented by this play precludes such a possibility upon the part of men of reason and of common sense.[165]

Foran said that he sympathized with the individuals who opposed the film, but that the "only way to treat this so-called drama is to treat it with the silence of contempt."[166] Offering advice to those opposing the film much as Judge Jackson had done in Los Angeles two years before,[167] Foran said that wide-spread black opposition to the film had only saved the film's management "thousands upon thousands of dollars in advertising."[168] Blacks should ignore the film and allow it to be "buried in the limbo of forgotten things."[169]

In spite of Foran's detailed opposition to the film and his opinion that the film had no real artistic, historic or educational merit, Foran concluded that the case could not be decided on any of those points. Rather, his decision had to be based upon whether the mayor had acted within his rights as given him by state statute. Foran then turned to his interpretation of the Ohio film censorship statute and concluded that the statute allowed anyone dissatisfied with the censorship board's decision the right to appeal directly to the Ohio Supreme Court. These procedural alternatives were ruled sufficient protection against arbitrary or unreasonable censoring actions in <u>Mutual Film Corp. v. Industrial Commission of Ohio</u>,[170] a decision affirmed by the U. S. Supreme Court.[171] Because the mayor had not followed the appropriate procedure outlined by state statute, his actions in banning the film were judged "without authority . . . contrary to law, and therefore void."[172]

Thus, in a lengthy decision which decried the content of the film, a judge overruled a threatened censorship on procedural grounds, stating specifically as precedent <u>Mutual Film Corp. v. Industrial Commission of Ohio</u>.[173] In this case a mayor was enjoined from stopping <u>The Birth</u> because he did not follow censorship appeal guidelines outlined by state statute. The judge affirmed the sovereignty of the state in censorship cases and said that the power of home rule did not give individual communities the right to censor films with procedures that conflicted with those established by the state.

The following year, citing <u>Epoch v. Davis</u>[174] as precedent, Judge Frank W. Greger denied an NAACP petition requesting that <u>The Birth</u>'s production be prohibited in Springfield, Ohio.[175] Greger said that it was unlawful to show "any theatrical performance in Ohio on Sunday including <u>The Birth of a Nation</u>."[176] However, after a film had been passed by the state censor board, weekday performances could not be enjoined by any court other than the state supreme court. Otherwise, the board of censors "was the tribunal of last result."[177] Greger cited as authority for his decision Epoch v. Davis[178] and therefore refused to issue the injunction on procedural grounds.[179]

Another decision which refused to allow local authorities to interfere with the exhibition of The Birth after it had been passed by a state board of censors was handed down by a Common Pleas Court judge in Pittsburgh, Pennsylvania, September 1915.[180] In this instance, Pittsburgh Mayor Joseph Armstrong served notice on the management of the Nixon theatre where The Birth was scheduled to open that he would suppress the film.[181] Armstrong's action came after a delegation of more than 100 black citizens representing a variety of local organizations requested that he stop The Birth.[182]

The Nixon management requested and received a temporary injunction from Common Pleas Court of Allegeny County Judge Ambrose Reid, restraining Armstrong and all other city officials from stopping the film.[183] In its bill in equity filed with the court, the Nixon interests stated that The Birth had been approved by the state and national board of censors and contended that the film did not engender racial prejudice.[184] The city countered that the film would definitely incite race hatred and violence.[185]

Reid granted the temporary injunction, but required the Nixon to post a $500 bond for protection against what the city attorney had termed "possible violence by the display of the race-prejudice picture."[186] As a result of Reid's decision, The Birth opened at the Nixon as scheduled.

Four days later, Reid heard arguments concerning whether the injunction should be continued. In its arguments, the Nixon interests again stressed that the film had been passed by the Pennsylvania State Board of Censors which deemed the film "of a moral and proper character," had been passed by the national board of censors and had been passed by censoring agencies in "Boston, Chicago, and other cities."[187] The theatre interests also contended that the film in no way tended to "excite racial or religious prejudice or animosities, but is clean, wholesome, and elevating in tone and sentiment."[188] Finally, the Nixon attorneys stated that the theatre had always been a place of "high class amusement and entertainment and it had always been conducted in a quiet and orderly manner."[189] The theatre concluded its case by calling Armstrong's threatened action "arbitrary, without just and lawful cause," and if carried out would deprive the theatre of property without the authority of law.[190] The theatre attorneys called witnesses who testified that The Birth was "highly historical and educational" and that there should be no fear of disorder for while there were portions of the film "which the Negroes might object to. . .history is often distasteful."[191] The city countered with the argument that the film would cause racial prejudice and possibly an actual breach of peace.[192]

Reid once again ruled in favor of the theatre interests and justified his decision on procedural grounds. Reid indicated that the power to censor films had been placed by the state legislature in the hands of a state censorship board. This body was "established by law and unless it has acted fraudulently or from improper motives its decision is entitled to respect."[193] Therefore, the courts should not intervene. Reid said that the city had not tried to prove that the state board had acted improperly. Because of this, Reid concluded:

> The result is that the burden is on those who oppose it to show that it tends to cause a breach of peace. In my opinion it has not been shown that such a result is at all probable because the consensus of opinion seems to be and the face proved that it has not produced a breach of peace although exhibits have been made before more than 1,500,000 people. The picture to a great extent presents scenes that are undoubtedly historical and many of them are uplifting.[194]

In this decision, Reid indicated that if it could be proven that the film would cause an actual breach of peace, he might overrule the censorship board. However, the burden of proof in such cases was with the individuals requesting that the board's actions be overruled. Also, if the individuals requesting that the board's action be overruled could prove that the board had not done its duty by passing a given film, court intervention might be justified. Reid also specifically rejected the argument that the board's decision could be overruled by a local authority because that authority believed that a given film might cause racial prejudice. However, the circumstances were such in this case that the court would not interfere with the board's decision.

One case studied in which film censorship was enjoined on procedural grounds differed substantially from the others because the case dealt with the application of a local censorship ordinance and did not concern prior approval of the film by a state censorship board. This controversy began when Detroit Police Commissioner James Inches notified the management of the New Detroit theatre that *The Birth* would not be permitted to open as scheduled, on the order of Detroit's mayor.[195]

Acting for the film, Epoch sought and received a temporary injunction preventing interference with the scheduled opening.[196] The injunction was made permanent at a second hearing.[197]

At the second hearing, Inches justified censorship of the film on the grounds that the film's screening would "almost certainly lead to serious public disturbances."[198] However, Judge John Goff ruled that the censorship standard applied by Inches was not a legitimate one in Detroit because the local film censorship ordinance stated that films could only be censored when shown to be "immoral and indecent."[199] Since the question of whether the film was immoral or indecent was not in the original letter to the theatre management explaining the ban on the film, the question could not be addressed by the court.[200] Goff cited as authority for his decision a U. S. Supreme Court ruling which stated in part:

> ...when a party gives a reason for his conduct and decision concluding anything involved in a controversy, after litigation as begun, change his ground and put his conduct upon another and different consideration he is not thus permitted to mend his hold.[201]

Goff concluded that since the power to censor films on the belief that they might lead to breach of peace was not part of the Detroit censorship statute, the mayor and police chief had no authority to act. Thus, the injunction against Inches was made permanent upon procedural grounds. However, in spite of the decision, one source indicated that Epoch agreed voluntarily to eliminate certain scenes from the film relating to the Ku Klux Klan.[202]

In August 1915, an Oakland, California, judge ruled that local authorities did not have the power under that city's censorship ordinances to stop the film.[203] The controversy began when Oakland's mayor ordered The Birth stopped locally after a group of black citizens protested the film's screening. Acting on the mayor's direction, the Oakland police ordered the management of the MacDonough theatre to stop showing The Birth. The theatre management went to "Superior Court" and obtained an injunction restraining the Oakland authorities from interfering with the film's production.[204] Sources indicate that the injunction was issued on procedural grounds. Specifically, the judge ruled that the mayor and police had no statutory authority to stop the film.[205]

Likewise, the mayor and director of public safety of Atlantic City, New Jersey, were enjoined in 1915 from stopping The Birth.[206] In this case, the mayor instructed the director of public safety to stop the film after a group of 200 blacks indicated to the mayor that the film would engender racial prejudice.[207] After receiving notice that The Birth had to be discontinued, the management of the New Nixon theatre sought an injunction restraining city officials from interfering with the film's screening.[208] At the hearing concerning the injunction, attorneys for the film argued that The Birth was "highly moral and instructive and. . .denied that it was meant to excite race prejudice."[209] After hearing the arguments, Judge

Edwin R. Walker issued the injunction. Walker said that opposition to the film was political rather than moral and under existing statutes that was not a legitimate reason for stopping a film.[210]

In these ways six courts refused to allow censorship of The Birth for procedural reasons during the years 1915-1973. Three of the decisions refused to permit local authorities to censor the film after it had been approved by state censorship agencies. The remaining three decisions indicated that municipal authorities had no authority to act against the film under existing local ordinances. One of the decisions stated specifically as authority the Supreme Court's decision in Mutual Film Corporation v. Industrial Commission of Ohio.[211] A second decision was based upon the former and thus indirectly stated the Mutual case as authority.

Censorship Rejected But Rationale Unknown

Five courts were found to resolve censorship controversies by refusing to allow restraint of The Birth, but the details of these cases are not known.[212] The cases were adjudicated between 1915 and 1931. All decisions enjoined officials from interfering with the film's screening.

Three court rulings without written opinions were rendered during 1915. In one case city officials who censored the film on the grounds that it was immoral and would engender racial prejudice were enjoined.[213] This controversy began when a committee of black Charleston, West Virginia, businesspeople met with that city's mayor and protested the film's screening because, in their opinions, the film would "disturb the happy relations existing between the races."[214] After hearing the protests, Charleston mayor George E. Breese viewed the film and banned it.[215] The manager of the Burlew Theatre, where the film was being screened, applied to Judge Samuel D. Littlepage of the Circuit Court for an injunction restraining Breese and all other Charleston officials from stopping the film.[216] In the following debate which one newspaper termed "a forensic battle long to be remembered," attorney W. B. Byrne represented the Burlew and attorneys T. G. Nutter and George McClintic, City Solicitor, represented the city.[217] After hearing arguments from both sides, Littlepage issued the injunction.[218] Why Littlepage decided for the theatre interests is not recorded in the sources consulted, but his action effectively determined the film's right to the screen in this instance.

Under somewhat different circumstances a district court judge in Denver, Colorado, restrained city officials from interfering with the film.[219] In this case, which involved criminal proceedings as discussed in Chapter IV, a judge ruled that although the city could act against the theatre manager or the film owner, they could not act against the film itself. During the hearing to determine whether or not an injunction should be issued, the film's supporters argued that the film had been shown in many other cities for lengthy periods of time without problem.[220] The film's opponents argued that city officials had full power to stop The Birth because the film was immoral.[221] Although the judge issued the injunction prohibiting city officials from interfering with the film, he also indicated that officials could act directly against the theatre manager and required the film interests to post $2,000 bond.[222] The film's producers posted the bond and in spite of the threat of arrest, the theatre manager continued the film.[223]

In the remaining 1915 decision, the Providence, Rhode Island, police commission was enjoined from stopping <u>The Birth</u>.[224] The commission banned the film after representatives of the Providence NAACP Branch protested the exhibition (See Chapter V). The NAACP-led opposition argued that the film would engender racial prejudice, was historically inaccurate, and was a negative reflection on black patriotism.[225] The details of the hearing on injunction are unclear, but sources report that an injunction enjoining the commission's action was obtained by the film's supporters and the controversy resolved.[226]

In at least two other cases, city officials were enjoined from interfering with the film, but the details of both cases are unclear. However, in both cases, opposition to the film was led by the NAACP. One 1924 case occurred in Gary, Indiana.[227] In this instance, the NAACP reported that Gary mayor R. O. Johnson banned the film but the film's supporters secured an injunction nullifying the censorship order.[228] Likewise, the NAACP reported in 1931 that an injunction had been issued which restrained Minneapolis, Minnesota, officials from interfering with the film's production.[229]

No Censorship Decisions Which
Did Not Resolve Controversies

During the time period studied, at least an additional five

judges refused to permit censorship of The Birth, but the decisions did not resolve the controversies involved. In two cases, judges actually refused to censor the film. In the remaining three cases, judges enjoined administratively ordered censorship.

Extant facts concerning the first decision not to censor the film are somewhat contradictory. However, the case was adjudicated in San Francisco, California, shortly after The Birth's 1915 Los Angeles premier.[230] A northern California black newspaper, The Western Outlook reported that an injunction against The Birth was brought by E. J. Speede, secretary of a "non-partisan league."[231] The suit was considered "in Judge Crothers' court" but the injunction was denied.[232] On the other hand, J. B. Jefferson, a representative of the Northern California Branch of the NAACP, described the details of the incident somewhat differently in a letter to NAACP National.[233] Jefferson contended that the:

> . . .action for an injunction was brought by a colored man representing the 'Welfare League' a defunct organization of questionable repute, revived it is asserted for this occasion to bring this action in consideration of $200.00 surreptitiously advanced by the management of The Clansman. The ruse was effective. Unhealthy public interest was aroused by the press accounts of the action and crowded houses was the rule. It is needless to say that the action for the injunction being improperly drafted came to naught.[234]

In a later letter to Mary Childs Nerney, W. Butler, president of the NAACP Northern California Branch, said that "parties without the sanction or cooperation of our Branch brought an injunction against the picture, but were defeated in court."[235] Regardless of the inconsistencies in the reported details of this controversy, it seems clear that an injunction was sought against The Birth and was denied and the controversy continued. As discussed in Chapter V, the controversy was resolved when the San Francisco Municipal Censorship Board approved the film.[236]

The other case of this nature concerned the NAACP's request that Judge William McAdoo, New York Court of General Sessions, issue an injunction stopping the 1915 New York premiere of The Birth on the grounds that the film endangered public peace.[237] In this request, the NAACP reminded the court that the play, The Clansman, upon which the film was based had been banned from Philadelphia, Pennsylvania, after a racial demonstration started in the theatre during a performance.[238] McAdoo ruled that the NAACP presented insufficient evidence against the film and that unless an actual breach of peace occurred, the court was powerless to act.[239] The controversy continued and was eventually resolved by New York mayor John P. Mitchell (See Chapter V).[240]

Unlike the New York cases in which courts were asked to order censorship of The Birth, the remaining cases which did not resolve the controversies involved injunctions against municipal officials who had threatened to stop the film. Two cases were decided by Judge V. Kline and Judge George Whitcomb, respectively, in two separate actions as part of the same controversy in Topeka, Kansas.[241] The final case was decided by Judge Morgan Owen in Charleston, West Virginia.[242]

Two different courts refused to support censorship of The Birth in Topeka, Kansas, 1931, and neither resolved the censorship controversy. In this controversy, the NAACP had requested that

Topeka's mayor stop The Birth under his police power.[243] The mayor responded to the request by instructing Topeka Police Chief Perry Brush to notify the manager of the theatre scheduled to show The Birth that the film could not be shown.

Ralph Christy and R. A. Hartman, theatre operators, and Sam Silverman, distributor of The Birth in Kansas at the time, petitioned for an injunction in the District Court of Shawnee County to restrain the authorities from stopping the film.[244] In their petition for injunction, Christy, Hartman, and Silverman contended that the Topeka authorities had threatened to stop the film because they considered it "distasteful and offensive to the colored citizens of this community."[245] The petitioners said that the threatened censorship action would deprive them of property rights in violation of the Kansas Constitution and in violation of the Fourteenth Amendment of the U. S. Constitution.[246] However, Christy, Hartman, and Silverman did not discuss the content of the film and based their entire petition upon the property rights argument. Judge Kline of the District Court issued the injunction.[247]

Topeka officials countered by filing a petition for injunction against the theatre management in the Third District Court, Second Division. In its petition, the city argued that the version of The Birth scheduled for exhibition in Topeka had never been submitted to the Kansas Board of Censors as required by law.[248] Acting State Attorney General Roland Boynton based the city's argument on the grounds that the film to be shown in Topeka had a sound synchronization whereas the film previously approved by the Kansas censors was a silent film. Further, Boynton argued that the film in both versions was against public policy, immoral in nature, calculated to disturb the peace, designed to incite racial hatred, and was "treasonable in its tendency."[249] Thus, the argument against The Birth was based on both procedural and content grounds. However, Whitcomb refused to issue the injunction.[250]

In a subsequent letter to the NAACP, Whitcomb indicated that his decision was made entirely upon procedural grounds.[251] In part, Whitcomb said:

> Unfortunately for the application there is a statute in this state which commits the matter of showing of films to a board. Under several decisions of our Supreme Court, the decision of a board of this character is binding on the courts, so I was unable to give any relief. . .So far as my personal feelings are concerned. . .I am entirely in sympathy with the purpose of your organization. . .but you will understand judges of courts cannot be guided by their feelings where a question of law is involved.[252]

After Whitcomb's decision, the city appealed to another District Court, Third District, Judge Otis Hungate who was hearing the case when the Kansas State Board of Censors recalled The Birth and eventually resolved the controversy.[253]

One judge enjoined censorship of The Birth only to have his decision overruled by a higher court. This case which has already been discussed involved the 1925 West Virginia controversy.[254] In this case, Common Pleas Court Judge Morgan Owen issued an injunction on procedural grounds prohibiting Charleston, West Virginia, officials from interfering with The Birth's production.[255] However, Owen's injunction was dissolved by a subsequent ruling by Circuit Court Judge Arthur Hudson.[256] The case was resolved by the state supreme court which upheld Hudson's decision by refusing to hear the case.[257]

In these ways, five judges refused to permit censorship of The Birth of a Nation, but the rulings did not resolve the censorship controversies involved. Two cases involved refusals to issue injunctions against the film. Three cases involved the issuing of injunctions against public officials who threatened to stop the film. Three cases were ultimately resolved by censorship boards. One case was resolved by a mayor. The remaining case was ultimately resolved by a higher court.

Cases Heard But Not Adjudicated

At least three cases involving censorship of The Birth were heard by courts, but were not adjudicated. None of the cases resolved the controversies involved. The issues in each case differed substantially.

Perhaps the most bitterly fought of these cases occurred in Chicago, 1924. As discussed earlier, The Birth was originally shown in Chicago in May, 1915, under a temporary injunction restraining city officials from interfering with the film issued by Cook County Superior Court Judge William F. Cooper.[258] The injunction was made permanent in 1917.[259]

Also in 1917, Robert Jackson, Illinois state representative from Chicago's predominately black Third District, sponsored a bill in the state legislature designed to bar The Birth from Illinois.[260] Referred to as the Jackson law, the statute forbade the public exhibition of any entertainment which:

> . . .portrays depravity, criminality, unchastity, or lack of virtue, of a class of citizens, of any race, color, or religion or which exposes the citizens of any race, color, creed or religion to contempt, derision or which is productive of breach of the peace or riots.[261]

In spite of the Jackson law, United Artists in late January, 1924, announced plans to reopen The Birth at Chicago's Auditorium theatre the following February.[262] Opposition in Chicago organized immediately to force United Artists to abandon its plans. Alderpersons Louis B. Anderson and Robert Jackson, no longer a state representative, called upon Chicago Mayor William E. Dever to ascertain his stand concerning the film.[263] The Chicago Defender reported in part that Dever told Anderson and Jackson:

> Personally, I am opposed to the exhibition and you have my word for it that everything possible will be done to prevent the exhibition of The Birth of a Nation in this city even to the extent of employing the police department to stop the exhibition. I shall take the matter up with the law department.[264]

Dever then instructed Chicago Police Chief Morgan Collins to send a letter to Epoch informing them that the film would not be permitted in the city.[265] Collins indicated that this action was justified because the injunction issued in 1917 was invalidated by the Jackson law.[266]

The film interests immediately went before Judge Dennis E. Sullivan, Cook County Superior Court, on a contempt motion Saturday, February 2, 1924. Sullivan said that he would not hear the case until Collins and the city had a chance to answer and show cause why they should not be held in contempt for threatening to violate the 1917 injunction.[267] Sullivan ordered Collins to appear in court the following Monday.

February 3, 1924, The Birth opened in Chicago at the Auditorium to a capacity audience. Among those present were Chicago Police Captain Charles L. Larkin, a squad of 20 policemen, Judge John Rooney, Chicago Municipal Court, Rooney's court bailiff, and his court clerk.

During the final scenes of the film, Rooney and his court officials moved to the auditorium lobby and Rooney signed four warrants for the arrest of the projectionists Jay Webb and Nathaniel Galup.[268] The warrants were issued on the grounds that the film violated the Jackson law.[269] Larkin and his squad acted on the warrants and when the projector operators were arrested, the film was stopped. Rooney later explained his action:

> It was a great picture. I do not think it would hurt reasonable men and women to see it. It might incite others, but my own views are not important. I was acting under the law compelling me to issue a warrant under proper complaint.[270]

The Chicago Defender described the events as follows:

> The theatre was filled to its capacity Sunday evening. The large audience was pitched into a high state of excitement and feeling as it watched the various scenes depicted which tended to forment race antagonism, prejudice, and hatred. . . The audience thrilled through the enactment of scene after scene which so grossly and infamously misrepresented Negro citizens blackening their character and portraying them as depraved unchaste criminals. The audience waited for the dastardly scene to be shown where a white woman flees from a man of color. His face was pictured as flaming with passion as he pursued the woman through a forest bent on criminal attack. To escape him she flees to the edge of a high cliff and leaps to her death. At this point the police cut short the remainder of the exhibition by placing the operators of the film machines under arrest.[271]

The Chicago Tribune reported that the theatre audience first "believed that the film had broken."[272] However, when the announcement was made that the police had stopped the film, members of the audience rose and shouted among other things, "where do they get that stuff."[273] The Tribune commented that the police "made ready for a riot, but the disturbance was only vocal."[274]

The following day Sullivan announced that he could not hear the contempt suit brought by the film interests because he had discovered that when the original injunction was requested in 1915, the petitioner had obtained a change of venue stating that he could not have a fair hearing before Judge Sullivan, or Judges Foell, Goodnow, Kavanagh and McKinley.[275]

The Auditorium returned the film to the screen that night and the police again arrested the projectionists and stopped The Birth.[276] The Auditorium's management substituted another Griffith film, Way Down East, for The Birth and the theatre reopened.[277]

The next day Sullivan changed his mind and decided that he could hear the case. When attorneys for both the film and the city agreed to limit discussion to two hours, Sullivan adjourned a jury trial in his court to consider the case.[278] However, the arguments lasted two days.

A number of arguments were presented against the film. For the city, attorney Busch argued that the arrests technically violated the injunction, but it was a necessary violation to enforce the law.[279] Busch also contended that the Chicago race riot of 1919 was directly connected with the film's screening and consequently, The Birth might easily stir "the flame of a new riot."[280] Busch also said that the city's objection to the film was the "scene in which the Negro chased the white girl over the hill...also shots of the Klansmen."[281] For the film interest, attorney Charles J. Trainor disputed the charge that the film was in direct violation of the Jackson law and argued that the injunction was still valid.[282]

Sullivan stated that the burden of proof in this case lay with the city:

> Here is a valid law of the state. The Court will have to determine whether the chief of police acted within his duty or whether his action was a mere subterfuge for getting around the injunction. Certain allegations are made here that this picture is in violation of this law. This will have to be proven.[283]

While Sullivan was considering the case, Harry Aitken, representing the film, and Busch, the city, were negotiating the controversy out of court. Finally, the men reached an agreement which stipulated that The Birth could be shown without police interference until the court case was settled.[284] Aitken described the situation in a telegram to D. W. Griffith:

> Having wonderful time. Operator arrested. Sunday and Monday night shows had Chief of Police and Cop Counsel in Court yesterday and all day today for contempt. Papers carrying front page story such as quote crowd grumble as police close birth...nothing before or since like it...city hall agreed tonight no further police interference until cases to be tried in court. 4 operators arrested so far--manager, 2 operators, and I submit again to arrest...everything favorable on paper with us.[285]

After the attorneys concluded their arguments, Sullivan

adjourned the case indefinitely.[286] Apparently the city decided not to press the case[287] and the film continued at the Auditorium for a four-week run setting a box office record for that theatre.[288] The criminal actions against the theatre personnel were heard at a different time and are discussed in the following chapter.

After two District Court judges in Topeka, Kansas, upheld The Birth's right to the screen in that city as previously discussed, the Topeka officials appealed to Judge Otis Hungate, Third District Court, and requested that a restraining order be issued against the motion picture interests forbidding them to show the film.[289] However, Hungate indefinitely continued the case when Kansas Governor Harry Woodring ordered the state board of censors to recall the film. Upon reinspection of The Birth, the board voted not to approve the film and thus resolved the controversy.[290]

In a somewhat different case, the NAACP attempted to block the film in its initial New York run by swearing warrants against D. W. Griffith and Harry Aitken, charging that the film was vicious and a menace to public morals.[291] Griffith and Aitken were summoned to the Jefferson Market Police Court to answer the charges, March 12, 1915.[292] However, the case was transferred to the West Farms Police Court and continued.[293] Next, the case was transferred back to the Jefferson Market Police Court and again continued.[294] March 31, 1915, the case was postponed until April 8, 1915.[295] April 8, 1915, the case was adjourned until April 12, 1915.[296] Shortly thereafter the case was dismissed.[297] Throughout the entire proceeding, the film was screened at the Liberty theatre and this effort by the NAACP to stop the film failed.

Summary

During the time period studied, 28 controversies concerning The Birth of a Nation's right to the screen included the tactic of court action. Because several of the controversies included multiple court rulings, the actual number of documented court involvements was 39. Courts ultimately resolved 22 of the 28 controversies in which they were involved. These figures are significant (x^2 = 9.14, $<.01$). Therefore, the general tactic of court action accomplished controversy resolution with a frequency differing from chance. Of the six controversies not resolved by court involvement, five were ultimately resolved by officials and one was resolved through acquiescence. However, the 28 controversies actually included 39 petitions to court officials. Of these 39 petitions, only 22 were successful in terms of accomplishing controversy resolution. These figures are not significant (x^2 = .641, $>.02$). Therefore, in terms of individual actions other than controversies, the tactic did not accomplish controversy resolution with a frequency differing from chance. Therefore, in general if an individual had controversy resolution as a goal and was willing to implement the tactic more than once, court action could reliably be employed.

A majority of court decisions resolving controversies supported the film's right to the screen. Specifically, 16 courts resolved controversies by rejecting censorship and only six resolved controversies by supporting censorship. However, these figures are not significant ($x^2 = 4.54$, $>.02$). Thus, courts resolved controversies in favor of censorship or in favor of no censorship with a frequency that did not differ from chance. Specific actions taken by courts to resolve controversies are presented in table 1.

TABLE 1

TYPES OF SPECIFIC ACTIONS TAKEN BY COURTS RESOLVING CONTROVERSIES

Restraint	Prior Restraint Partial	Subsequent Restraint	Subsequent Restraint Partial	No Censorship
4	1	1	0	16

When the differences among the specific types of decisions made by courts resolving controversies are analyzed, the resulting figure is significant ($x^2 = 33.92$, $<.001$). Therefore, it can be concluded that courts resolved controversies with actions regarding the film as a whole with a frequency that differs from random.

To determine whether the film was screened or not screened during controversies resolved by courts with a frequency differing from chance, the categories prior restraint partial, subsequent restraint, subsequent restraint partial and no censorship were combined. The resulting figures are significant ($x^2 = 8.9$, $<.01$). Therefore, the film was more likely than not to be screened for some time or in some form during controversies resolved by court action.

Court decisions resolved controversies during the time period 1915-1952. Censorship/no censorship court decisions by year are presented in table 2.

TABLE 2

COURT DECISIONS RESOLVING CONTROVERSIES BY YEAR

Year	Censor	No Censor
1915	0	10
1916	1	0
1917	0	1
1918	2	1
1921	0	1
1924	0	2
1925	2	0
1931	0	1
1952	1	0

The number of controversies resolved during only one year, 1915, was judged sufficient for independent statistical analysis. During 1915, 10 courts supported the film and none supported censorship. These figures are significant ($x^2 = 10$, $< .001$). Therefore, if a court resolved a controversy during 1915, it ruled in favor of no censorship with a frequency differing from chance. The number of controversies resolved during each of the remaining years was not large enough for independent analysis. However, if the categories are collapsed, the resulting figures are not significant ($x^2 = 0$, $> .02$). Thus, it appears that if a court resolved a controversy after 1915, the decision supported censorship or no censorship with a frequency not differing from chance. Therefore, it can be concluded that the manner in which courts resolved controversies was time dependent during only one of the years studied.

Controversies resolved by courts occurred at the state and local levels. The majority of court resolved controversies concerned censorship of the film at the local level. Specifically, courts resolved 19 controversies concerning the film's right to the screen in a given municipality and three controversies concerning the film's right at the state level. Court decisions resolving controversies by controversy level are presented in table 3.

TABLE 3

COURT DECISIONS RESOLVING CONTROVERSIES BY LEVEL

Level	Censorship	No Censorship
Local	3	16
State	3	0

The split between censorship/no censorship decisions at the local level is significant ($x^2 = 8.89, < .01$). Therefore, if a court resolved a local controversy, the resolution would support no censorship with a frequency differing from chance. Although the number of state controversies was judged too small for statistical analysis, all state controversies were resolved with court decisions supporting censorship. Thus, overall controversies resolution and controversy level appear to be dependent. Therefore, it can be concluded that local controversies resolved by courts were more likely than not to end with no censorship decisions and state controversies would probably be resolved with decisions supportive of censorship.

Court decisions resolving controversies were based on a variety of rationales. Rationales justifying court actions resolving controversies by type of decision are presented in table 4.

TABLE 4

RATIONALES JUSTIFYING COURT DECISIONS RESOLVING CONTROVERSIES

Rationale	Censorship	No Censorship
Reject racial prejudice	0	4
Reject detrimental public peace	0	1
Procedural	5	6
Unclear	1	5

As evident in table 4, of the cases with written opinions regardless of the censorship/no censorship decision, a majority were decided on procedural rather than content grounds. In only one case was the First Amendment mentioned specifically in defense of the film and the case was apparently not decided on those grounds. In five cases, judges rejected censorship by indicating they did not think the film would have the effect feared by the film's opponent. No judge who supported censorship did so by indicating he found the film's content objectionable.

The tactic of court action was used by both the film's supporters and opponents. A majority of the court actions resolving controversies were initiated by individuals who wanted the film's right to the screen affirmed. The initiators of court actions resolving controversies and the outcome of their efforts are presented in table 5.

TABLE 5

INITIATORS OF COURT ACTION AND RESULT

Court requested to:	Censorship	Ruling Partial Censorship	No Censor
Censor film (2)	1	1	0
Overrule/enjoin censorship (20)	4	0	16

As evident in table 5, of the 22 court actions resolving controversies, 20 were begun by the film's supporters and two were initiated by the film's opponents. Of the resulting court decisions, 16 supported no censorship. All these cases were brought by the film's supporters. Six court decisions resolving controversies supported some form of censorship. Four of these cases were brought by the film's supporters and two were brought by the film's opponents. Therefore, from the standpoint of the film's supporters, initiating court action was a good tactic as courts resolving controversies ruled in their favor 16 times and against them only four times. These figures are significant (x^2 = 7.2, $<.01$). The number of court actions initiated by the film's opponents was too small to determine statistical significance.

To complete the analysis, it is necessary to also discuss court actions not resolving controversies. As mentioned previously, the tactic of court action was employed 17 times without accomplishing controversy resolution. In ten of the 17 instances, courts actually ruled concerning the film's right to the screen. Five court decisions not resolving a controversy supported some form of censorship and five supported no censorship. Thus, regardless of whether the action resolved the controversy, more courts supported the film's right to the screen (21) than supported censorship of the film (7). These figures are significant ($x^2 = 7$, $< .01$). The remaining seven appeals for court action were not adjudicated. Therefore, if a court made a specific ruling concerning the film, that ruling would support no censorship with a frequency differing from chance.

Court rulings which did not resolve controversies were based on a variety of rationales. Specifically, seven rulings were based on procedural grounds; one specifically considered the content of the film; and, the rationales underlying the remaining two actions are unclear. Thus, regardless of whether the action resolved a controversy, courts ruled concerning The Birth's right to the screen on procedural grounds. Eighteen of the 28 censorship/no censorship decisions made by courts were justified on procedural grounds. The basis for eight censorship/no censorship court decisions was unclear. Six censorship/no censorship decisions were based on the acceptance or rejection of content/effect arguments. Because the number of court actions with unknown rationale was high, statistical significance was not computed for these figures. However, 64 percent of court actions concerning *The Birth* were based on procedural grounds. Thus, it appears that if a court did act regarding the film, it usually did so on procedural rather than content/effect grounds.

Court actions which did not resolve controversies took place during the time period 1915-1931. A majority of the court actions not resolving controversies occurred in 1915. Specifically, the tactic of court action was implemented eight times that year without accomplishing controversy resolution. The tactic was employed three times without success in 1931. During both 1917 and 1925, two court actions were initiated without accomplishing controversy resolution. The tactic was implemented once in each of the following years without success: 1916 and 1924.

Thus, it can be seen that more court actions were initiated during 1915 than any other year studied. Specifically, 18 courts were asked to resolve 14 censorship controversies during 1915. Courts were successful in resolving 10 of those controversies. These figures are not significant (x^2 = 2.57, > .02). Therefore, during 1915, courts did not accomplish controversy resolution with a frequency differing from chance. The number of court actions in each of the other years was judged too small for independent statistical analysis. However, if the number of controversies resolved by court action after 1915 (12) are compared with the number of controversies not resolved by court action after 1915 (2), the resulting figures are significant ($x^2 = 7.14$, $< .01$). Therefore, after 1915, courts resolved controversies with a frequency differing from chance.

Court involvements not resolving controversies were initiated by both the film's supporters and opponents. Seven court actions which did not resolve controversies were begun by the film's supporters and ten court actions which did not resolve controversies were initiated by the film's opponents. Initiators of court actions not resolving controversies and actions taken are presented in table 6.

TABLE 6

INITIATORS OF COURT ACTION NOT RESOLVING
CONTROVERSIES AND COURT ACTION TAKEN

Court requested to:	Court Action			
	Censor	Censor Partial	No Censor	Not Adjudicated
Censor film (10)	2	1	2	5
Enjoin Censorship (7)	2	0	3	2

Thus, in general, initiating court action was a tactic used by the film's supporters 27 times and by the film's opponents 12 times. In terms of accomplishing controversy resolution, the tactic was successful for the film's supporters but not for the film's opponents. Specifically, 20 of the actions initiated by the film's supporters resolved controversies and seven did not. These figures are significant ($x^2 = 6.25$, $< .02$). Also, in terms of accomplishing the desired goal, initiating court action was a good tactic for the film's supporters because 16 courts asked to do so resolved controversies in their favor and only four courts ruled against them. As mentioned previously, these figures are significant (x^2 = 7.2, < .01). However, initiating court action was not a successful tactic from the viewpoint of the film's opponents. Only two of the court actions brought by the film's opponents resulted in controversy resolution. These figures are not significant (x^2 = 5.22, > .02). Also, although both court actions initiated by the film's opponents resulted in censorship, these numbers were judged too small to determine statistical significance.

Conclusions

Thus, it can be seen that court action as a tactic was more successfully and more frequently utilized by individuals asserting the film's right to the screen than by individuals who wanted the film suppressed. Perhaps this can in part be explained because fewer cases were initiated by individuals requesting censorship. This may in part have occurred because one major organization opposing the film, the NAACP, advised its membership in the spring of 1915 that because court cases were virtually impossible to win against the film, other tactics should be used. Specifically, the NAACP advised its membership to seek relief with city officials. Evidence would suggest that this occurred because approximately two-thirds of the questions asked the courts involved actions by local officials concerning the film. More cases were decided on procedural grounds than on content grounds. Slightly less than half of the court actions initiated actually resolved the controversy in question.

Courts apparently interpreted the 1915 *Mutual* decision which specifically exempted the motion picture medium from First Amendment protection as a procedural decision. Consequently, the majority of court actions regarding The Birth were decided on procedural grounds. Ironically, all court decisions resolving controversies during 1915 supported the film and the only court decision resolving a controversy after limited First Amendment protection was extended to the medium in 1952, supported censorship.

The First Amendment question was not specifically raised in support of the film until 1952. This case asserted the film's right to the screen as protected speech. However, the case was apparently not decided on First Amendment grounds. In no case was a First Amendment right to see the film argued. Perhaps the lack of First Amendment argumentation in favor of the film can be attributed in part to the film's supporters interpreting the *Mutual* decision as effectively closing this avenue. Perhaps the film's supporters also viewed the *Mutual* decision as a procedural one and this approach would work for them.

It is also interesting to note that for censorship purposes, courts tended to support a state standard. That is, in all conflicting decisions between state censorship agencies and local censorship agencies, courts ruled in favor of state agencies. Thus, although not stating so specifically, courts appear to have defined community censorship standards as state standards rather than national or local standards.

Courts were also asked to resolve controversies concerning the individual's right to either show the film or protest its presentation. These controversies are discussed in the next chapter.

NOTES TO CHAPTER III

[1] Mary White Ovington to George H. Woodson, 5 November 1915, National Association for the Advancement of Colored People Archives, File C301, Library of Congress Manuscript Collection, Washington, D. C. (Hereafter referred to as NAACP Archives).

[2] Joseph Burstyn Inc. v. Wilson, 343 U. S. 495, 96 L. Ed. 1098, 72 S. Ct. 777 (1952).

[3] Two controversies involved censorship in Ohio and one in Maryland. See Epoch Producing Corp. v. The Industrial Commission of Ohio, et. al., 95 Ohio 400, 117 N. E. 10 (1916); Epoch Producing Corp. v. Vernon M. Riegel, Petition No. 1930 Filed March 19, 1925 with the Supreme Court of Ohio, Document in The Birth of a Nation File, Ohio State Historical Society Archives, Columbus, Ohio (Hereafter referred to as Ohio State Historical Society Archives); and "Suit is Filed Against Film Censor Laws," Baltimore Sun, 14 June 1952, p. 26, respectively.

[4] These controversies occurred in Charleston, West Virginia; Chicago, Illinois; and Lincoln, Nebraska. See Virginia Amusement Company v. W. W. Wertz and J. W. Johnson, copy of decision in NAACP Archives, File C302; Epoch Producing Corp. v. Herman F. Schuettler, 209 Ill. App. 596 (1918); and, "Birth of Nation' May Not Appear," n.t., 26 June 1918, n.p., clipping in NAACP Archives, File C301, respectively.

[5] These controversies occurred in Minneapolis, Minnesota, and Boston, Massachusetts. See Bainbridge v. Minneapolis, 131 Minn. 195 (1915) and "Judge Refuses to Stop 'The Birth of a Nation' Film. . . One Scene Must Be Cut Out," Boston Evening Globe, 21 April 1915, p. 2., respectively.

[6] Record of the Proceedings of the Industrial Commission of Ohio, Department of Film Censorship, entry of 6 January 1916, document in The Birth of a Nation File, Ohio State Historical Society Archives. The Ohio censorship board was established by the state legislature in 1915. The law established a Board of Censors under the authority of the Industrial Commission of Ohio and gave the board the power to approve only such films as it considered to be of a "moral, educational, or amusing and harmless character." Anyone dissatisfied with the board's decision had the right to appeal directly to the Ohio Supreme Court. See 103 Ohio Laws 399 (1913). The procedures of the Ohio censorship law were upheld as constitutional by the U. S. Supreme Court in Mutual Film Corp. v. Industrial Commission of Ohio, 236 U. S. 230, 355 S. Ct. 387, 59 L. Ed. 553 (1915).

[7] Record of the Proceedings of the Industrial Commission of Ohio, Department of Film Censorship.

[8] Ibid.

[9] "In The Courts: 'Birth of a Nation Again," Press Release, n.d., NAACP Archives, File C301.

[10] Ibid.

[11] The petition is reproduced in Seba H. Miller, The Law and Practice In Error Proceedings In The Supreme Court of Ohio (Cincinnati: W. H. Anderson, 1924), pp. 341-345.

[12] Ibid., pp. 342-343. Epoch also called the board's refusal to license the film unreasonable and unlawful.

[13] Epoch Producing Corp. v. Industrial Commission of Ohio, et. al., 95 Ohio St. 400, 117 N. E. 10 (1916). At least one scholar who has analysed film censorship in Ohio has denounced the action of the supreme court in this case and called the action "a rare exception to the traditional friendly attitude of the judiciary toward private rights." See Ivan Brychta, "The Ohio Film Censorship Law," Ohio Law Journal, 13 (Spring 1952): 355.

[14] Seba Miller, p. 340.

[15] The court dismissed Epoch's petition for rehearing on 24 October 1916 (See 95 Ohio St. 400). On 1 February 1917, the board reconsidered the film and approved it. See Epoch Producing Corp. v. Harry L. Davis Mayor of the City of Cleveland, et. al., 19 Ohio NISI Pruis Reports 465 (1917).

[16] T. Gellis Nutter to J. W. Johnson, 4 April 1925, NAACP Archives, File C302.

[17] Virginia Amusement Company v. W. W. Wertz, copy of order from Judge Morgan Owen, NAACP Archives File C302; and Virginia Amusement Company v. W. W. Wertz, copy of order from Judge Arthur Hudson, NAACP Archives, File C302.

[18] T. G. Nutter to J. W. Johnson. The committee consisted of Attorney T. G. Nutter, President of the NAACP Charleston Branch; W. W. Sanders, Vice-President of the branch; and, G. E. Ferguson, former member of the branch's executive committee.

[19] Ibid.

[20] Wertz was referring to West Virginia Laws Chapter 37 (1919). The law was passed by the West Virginia legislature in January 1919. The law was based upon Senate Bill No. 176. A copy of the bill is in the NAACP Archives, File C301.

[21] Code of Ordinances of the City of Charleston, Section 596 (1924).

[22] Virginia Amusement Co. v. Wertz, Judge Morgan Owen's order.

[23] Ibid.

[24] Ibid. It is interesting to note that Wertz also told the court that the film would not be interfered with until the scene in which "a white girl is chased by Negro (sic) from a spring and she jumps from a precipice." (See T. G. Nutter to J. W. Johnson) Only at that point in Wertz' judgment did the film violate the laws.

[25] Ibid.

[26] T. G. Nutter to J. W. Johnson.

[27] Ibid.

[28] Arthur Hudson quoted in T. G. Nutter to J. W. Johnson.

[29] Ibid. See also "West Virginia Supreme Court Bars 'Birth of Nation' Film," Press Release, 10 April 1925, NAACP Archives, File C302.

[30] T. G. Nutter to J. W. Johnson.

[31] Certificate of Censorship issued by Department of Education, Division of Film Censorship, No. 128, 18 February 1925, in Birth of a Nation File, Ohio State Historical Society Archives.

[32] Ibid.

[33] Ibid.

[34] Epoch Producing Corp. v. Riegel, Petition NO. 19030.

[35] Ibid.

[36] "Ohio Bars Birth of a Nation," Press Release, 12 June 1925, NAACP ARCHIVES, File C302.

[37] Joseph M. McCarthy v. Chicago. See also "Judge Refuses to Stop 'Birth of a Nation' Film. . .One Scene Must Be Cut Out," Boston Evening Globe, 21 April 1915, p. 4.

[38] Ibid.

[39] Epoch Producing Corp. v. Schuettler, 280 Ill. 310 (1917).

[40] Ibid.

[41] *Epoch Producing Corp. v. Herman F. Schuettler*, 209 Ill. App. 596 (1918). The court indicated that a writ would be issued in cases where the petitioner presented facts to show that the film met every requisite of the censorship ordinance and to prove that the license was "arbitrarily or capriciously" refused. It is interesting to note that in another film censorship decision handed down with The Birth case, the court elaborated on what it viewed the appropriate role of the film censor. In *People of the State of Illinois, ex. rel. Walter Konzack v. Herman F. Schuettler*, 209 Ill. App. 588 (1918), the court stated that "the law does not contemplate a transfer of the censor's function to a court and jury, or that they shall sit in judgment on the exercise of his power unless it is arbitrarily or capriciously exercised. . .his duties are quasi-judicial in their nature requiring the exercise of a sound discretion which courts will not generally interfere. . ." The court further indicated that if the censor determined that different views "might reasonably be entertained" with regard to the effect of a given film within the parimeters set by law, the censor would have to exercise his discretion. In such cases the exercise of the censor's discretion was reasonable and not arbitrary or capricious. Only in cases where the content of a picture was "innocuous" could the censors actions be considered unjustified. In this particular case the court upheld Schuettler's ban on the film Margaret Sanger In Birth Control. The court considered the content of the film and concluded that "whatever views might be entertained as to its moral effect on other audiences, it requires no argument to show that its suggestions to one, including the young and unmarried might lead to immoral conditions." Consequently, the content of the film was not judged innocuous and Schuettler's action was justified.

[42] Ibid.

[43] The information was not contained in the books, newspapers, manuscripts and other materials consulted for this study listed in the bibliography.

[44] "Birth of Nation' May Not Appear."

[45] Ibid.

[46] "Would Suppress Picture," clipping in NAACP Archives, File C301, n.p., n.d. (However, the clipping is mounted on a page with the typewritten date June 26, 1918).

[47] The information was not included in the resources consulted for this study listed in the bibliography.

[48] "Birth of Nation' Banned Because of Fear of Rioting,"

Baltimore Sun, 24 May 1952, p. 9. See also "Maryland Bans 'Birth of Nation," New York Times, 24 May 1952, p. 15. The Birth was originally passed by the Maryland censors in 1917. However, the print submitted in 1952 lacked the "legally required seal" of the board and so the board reconsidered the film. The board also indicated that the film had been submitted for reconsideration in 1943 but was withdrawn when the film's distributer learned that the board would probably rule against the film. See "Birth of Nation' Banned Because of Fear of Rioting."

[49] Joseph Burstyn, Inc. v. Wilson, 343 U. W. 495, 96 L. Ed. 1098, 72 S. Ct. 777 (1952).

[50] "Birth of Nation' Banned Because of Fear of Rioting."

[51] "Suit May Test Ban of 'Birth," Baltimore Sun, 27 May 1952, p. 10.

[52] "Birth of Nation' Banned Because of Fear of Rioting."

[53] Ibid.

[54] Ibid.

[55] Ibid.

[56] "Miracle Ruling May 26, 1952," Baltimore Sun, 27 May 1952, p. 1.

[57] "Suit May Test Ban of 'Birth."

[58] "Traub Says Ruling on Movie Will Have Little Effect Here," Baltimore Sun, 28 May 1952, p. 25.

[59] "New Freedom for Movies and New Responsibilities," Baltimore Sun, 28 May 1952, p. 25.

[60] Ibid.

[61] "Suit Is Filed Against Film Censor Laws," Baltimore Sun, 14 June 1952, p. 26.

[62] "Film Ban Is Checked," New York Times, 14 June 1952, p. 8.

[63] Ibid.

[64] "Demurrers Filed To Censor Suit," Baltimore Sun, 21 June 1952, p. 7.

[65] Ibid.

[66] Ibid.

[67] The information was not included in the books, newspapers, manuscript collections and other materials consulted for this study and listed in the bibliography.

[68] "Racial Unit Aide Condemns Movie," 28 October 1958, p. 38. The Birth was licensed for exhibition after a ban "which went into effect in 1952" was lifted by the Maryland Censors in 1958. The 1958 board indicated through censor C. Morton Goldstein that the law under which it functioned had been changed in 1955 and the only censorship criteria reasons for applying censorship were obscenity, immorality, and inciting to crime. The board decided that The Birth did not violate those standards.

[69] Bainbridge v. Minneapolis, 131 Minn. 195 (1915).

[70] The Minneapolis City Charter gave the mayor the authority to revoke any license issued by the city council. See Minneapolis City Charter, Chapter 4, Subchapter 16; Special Laws 1881, Chapter 76, Subchapter 4 (1915).

[71] "Invited Censors See 'Birth of Nation," Minneapolis Tribune, 28 October 1915, p. 5. The specific make-up of the jury is never directly mentioned in any of the sources consulted. However, the Minnesota Supreme Court in dicta accompanying the Bainbridge v. Minneapolis decision was satisfied that Nye had "requested unprejudiced people of diverse callings to view the play and to give him their opinion upon it. Some of the opinions so elicited were favorable; many were not." (See Bainbridge v. Minneapolis, at 966) The jury apparently viewed the film at an invitational screening attended by around 1,000 individuals October 27th or 28th (See "1,000 Invited Censors See 'Birth of Nation," Minneapolis Tribune, 28 October 1915, p. 1) One source called the audience "representative" and stated that those invited included the mayor, the board of alderpeople, and "other city officials, including ministers, members of the drama league, of women's clubs, twenty-five of the best known of the city's Negro population, lawyers, doctors, and welfare workers." (See "The Birth of a Nation' Is Seen At Private Showing At Shubert) In a column in the Appeal a reporter indicated that he had been present at the showing and "unhesitatingly and unqualifiedly. . .failed to discover one redeeming feature in it or a plausible reason for its existence. . ." (See "The Birth of a Nation," Appeal, 28 October 1915, p. 2.)

[72] "Birth of Nation' Hearing Continued," Minneapolis Tribune, 2 November 1915, p. 7 and "Film to Show in Mill City," St. Paul Pioneer Press, 31 October 1915, p. 3.

[73] Ibid.

[74] "Birth of Nation' Decision Delayed for Several Days," Minneapolis Tribune, 3 November 1915, p. 10. However, Bainbridge later stated that the mayor refused to permit the film on the ground that it was likely to incite race riots. See "Bainbridge Tells of Strife Over 'Birth of Nation' Film," Minneapolis Tribune, 14 November 1915, p. 1.

[75] "Birth of Nation' Fate to be Determined by Court Tommorow," Minneapolis Tribune, 5 November 1915, p. 11.

[76] Ibid.

[77] "Supreme Court Last Hope of Film Show Unless Nye Relents," Minneapolis Tribune, 9 November 1915, p. 11.

[78] Ibid.

[79] Ibid.

[80] 131 Minn. 195 (1915).

[81] Ibid.

[82] Ibid.

[83] "A Means to an End," Twin City Star, 27 November 1915, p. 4. The Star severely criticized the mayor for using "his negro friends and The Birth of a Nation as a means to an end by securing a legal decision as to his power to revoke licenses and this power was an end to their appeals and protests." The Star said that Nye's actions were "political suicide" and that the mayor had "not measured up to that standard of dignity becoming a public official." See also "Minneapolis Column," Appeal, 27 November 1915, p. 4.

[84] Ibid.

[85] "Negroes Ask Warrant in Endeavor to Prevent the Photo-Play," Boston Evening Transcript, 20 April 1915, p. 2.

[86] Ibid.

[87] "Judge Refuses to Stop 'Birth of a Nation' Film. . .One Scene Must Be Cut Out," Boston Evening Globe, 21 April 1915, p. 4.

[88] Ibid. It is interesting to note that the scene which Dowd ordered cut is the same scene which Charleston, West Virginia, Mayor W. W. Wertz indicated violated the Charleston censorship statute.

[89] E. Burton Ceruti to M. Childs Nerney, 3 February 1915, NAACP Archives, File C301.

[90] Ibid.

[91] Ibid.

[92] Ibid.

[93] Ibid.

[94] "Editorial," The Crisis 10 (May 1915): 33.

[95] "The Clansman," Western Outlook, 20 February 1915, p. 2. See "L. A. Activities," New York Sun, 3 March 1915, n.p., clipping in Griffith's personal The Birth of a Nation Scrapbook, Griffith Archives. See also Henry Warnack, "Trouble Over 'The Clansman," L. A. Daily Times, 9 February 1915, p. 6.

[96] Henry Warnack, "Trouble Over 'The Clansman." Warnack attempted to attend the scheduled matinee at the theatre but reported "I couldn't see it. . ..at that hour." Warnack commented that "thousands of people" were turned away from the theatre on the order of the police chief and the city council.

[97] Ibid.

[98] Ibid.

[99] "The Clansman," Western Outlook.

[100] Ibid.

[101] Henderson, p. 156.

[102] McCarthy v. Chicago.

[103] At the time of this controversy, the power of film censorship in Chicago was vested directly within the discretion of the Second Deputy Superintendent of Police. Under this individual was a Board of Censors acting in a purely advisory capacity. The Second Deputy reported directly to the First Deputy Superintendent who reported to the Chief of Police who reported to the Mayor. Thus, the mayor had the ultimate power to grant or refuse a permit. However, apparently The Birth received its original permit in a somewhat irregular fashion. When the film was submitted for censorship in late March, 1915, it was first viewed by the wife of Chicago's mayor, Carter H. Harrison, and the mayor's secretary. A representative for the NAACP described the situation as follows: "We learn from an authentic source that the way The Birth of a Nation film permit was engineered, word came from the mayor's secretary that the room should be made ready for an inspection of this film and it was intimated that neither the Second Deputy Superintendent nor any of

the Board of Censors need be present, and we are informed that the permit under these circumstances was granted, presumably in the name of the mayor, by the mayor's secretary. We also understand from unauthentic sources that the mayor's wife, a southern woman, was present and approved the film." (See George Packard to M. Childs Nerney, 12 April 1915, NAACP Archives, File C301) However, Harrison's term expired two weeks after the permit was granted. Harrison was succeeded by William Thompson who had stated prior to his inauguration that if the film contained "anything he considered harmful to the race he would bar" it from the city (See "Mayor Thompson Bars 'Birth of Nation' From Chicago," Chicago Defender, 22 May 1915, p. 2). After he took office Thompson did refuse to issue a permit to the film. The branch was directed to protest against the film by a directive from the NAACP national office in a telegram from Mary Childs Nerney to Charles E. Bentley, 5 April 1915, NAACP Archives, File C301. In the telegram Nerney instructed Bentley to "call a meeting of executive committee of branch and protest immediately to license commissioner, police commissioner, and mayor against moving picture play on grounds that it endangers public morals and may lead to breach of peace." In response to the request the branch set up a special committee to "ascertain the facts with reference to the proposed performance of the film." (See Packard to Nerney) The National office continued to monitor the Chicago situation and on April 30, 1915, sent a letter to Charles E. Bentley encourageing the branch to "leave no stone unturned" in its fight to prevent the production of the film (See Mary Childs Nerney to Charles E. Bentley, 30 April 1915, NAACP Archives, File C301). See also McCarthy v. Chicago, "Mayor's Wife OK's 'Birth of Nation' Obnoxious Movie," Chicago Defender, 3 April 1915, p. 1, Telegram Mary Childs Nerney to C. E. Bentley, 31 March 1915, NAACP Archives, File C301, Telegram C. E. Bentley to Mary Childs Nerney, 31 March 1915, NAACP Archives, File C301, Telegram Mary Childs Nerney to J. E. Spingarn, 15 May 1915, NAACP Archives, File C301.

[104] McCarthy v. Chicago.

[105] Ibid.

[106] Ibid.

[107] C. E. Bentley to Mary Childs Nerney, 14 June 1915, in NAACP Archives, File C301.

[108] Ibid.

[109] Ibid.

[110] Epoch v. Schuettler.

[111] T. W. Allinson to Mary Childs Nerney, 19 July 1915, NAACP Archives, File C301.

[112] "New Protest Made Against 'Birth of a Nation,'" Philadelphia North American, 15 September 1915, p. 2.

[113] Ibid.

[114] "Court Lifts Ban Upon 'The Birth of a Nation," Philadelphia North American, 5 September 1915, p. 13.

[115] Ibid.

[116] Ibid.

[117] Ibid.

[118] Ibid.

[119] "Film Up to U. S.. . .Fight Over 'The Birth of a Nation' is in Federal Court," Topeka Daily State Journal, 29 December 1923, p. 1.

[120] States rights is a form of film distribution in which an individual or group purchases for a flat fee the right to distribute a film within a given geographic area. Thus, Stater more than D. W. Griffith or Epoch had a financial interest in whether or not the film was exhibited in Kansas. The Kansas State Board of Review for films was established by a 1913 statute which stated that all films intended for commercial exhibition within the state had to be licensed by the board. The three member board which was appointed by the governor could refuse any film a license if the film was found to be "cruel, obscene, indecent, or immoral" or "tended to corrupt or debase morals." The governor maintained the power to recall any film for reconsideration or to dismiss any member of the board. See General Statutes of Kansas, Chapter 294 (1913). See also Carmen, p. 176. The constitutionality of this law was upheld by the U. S. Supreme Court in Mutual Film Corp. v. Hodges, 236 U. W. 248 (1915).

[121] "Kansas Governor Asked by NAACP to Bar 'Birth of Nation' Film," Press Release, 8 June 1923, NAACP Archives, File C302.

[122] Ibid.

[123] "Won't Stop Film," Topeka Daily State Journal, 4 December 1923, p. 6.

[124] Ibid.

[125] Ibid.

[126] "A Slap at Davis: C. F. Scott Against Showing of 'The Birth of a Nation," Topeka Daily State Journal, 10 December 1923, p. 9.

[127]"Griffith Requests Rejection of 'The Birth of a Nation,'" Topeka Daily State Journal, 6 December 1923, p. 1.

[128]"Kansas Censors Pass 'Birth of Nation," Variety, 16 December 1923, p. 20.

[129]"Fight Race Film in Wichita," Topeka Daily State Journal, 26 December 1923, p. 6.

[130]"Wichita Kansas Bars 'Birth of Nation' After Protest and NAACP Action," Press Release, 8 June 1923, NAACP Archives, File C302.

[131]"Wichita Is Restrained; Ordinance Against 'The Birth of a Nation' Is Upheld," Topeka Daily State Journal, 1 January 1924, p. 1.

[132] Ibid.

[133] Ibid.

[134] Ibid.

[135]"Wichita Balked by Court in Stopping Film of the Klan," Kansas City Call, 4 January 1924, p. 1.

[136]"Birth' Under Bond," Variety, 10 January 1924, p. 20.

[137]"Birth' has Federal OK in State of Kansas," Variety, 10 January 1924, p. 19.

[138]"Klan Film given Free Rein; Ordinance of Wichita Held Null and Void," Kansas City Call, 11 January 1924, p. 1.

[139] Ibid. It is interesting to note that after Pollock's final ruling Variety concluded: "The Birth of a Nation' has caused more trouble in Kansas than any other film ever submitted for the cenosr's decision. . ." See "Nation' Arouses Politics in Kansas," Variety, 24 January 1924, p. 19.

[140]"Editorial," St. Louis Argus, 24 September 1915, p. 4.

[141]"Editorial," St. Louis Argus, 27 August 1915, p. 4.

[142]"Keep Up The Protest," St. Louis Argus, 3 September 1915, p. 4.

[143] Ibid.

[144]"Court Continues Police Injunction in Film Case," St. Louis Post Dispatch, 8 September 1915, p. 10.

[145] "Court Dissolves One Injunction in Film Case," St. Louis Argus, 10 September 1915, p. 1.

[146] "Editorial," St. Louis Argus, 24 September 1915, p. 4.

[147] Epoch Producing Corporation v. Harry L. Davis.

[148] Ibid., at 465.

[149] Ibid.

[150] Ibid., at 466.

[151] Ibid.

[152] Ibid.

[153] Ibid.

[154] Ibid.

[155] Ibid., at 466-67.

[156] Ibid., at 467-75. Specifically, Foran points to the development of the character of Flora Cameron and her choise of death rather than dishonor after being pursued by Gus. Foran said that this situation was unrealistic because it is a "well known" fact that southern men left their women in the care of "faithful slaves" and at no time during this "tragic period" was that trust "misplaced or betrayed." (See Ibid., at 474) Also Foran said that if the character Silas Lynch was intended to represent John R. Lynch of Mississippi, the characterization was "not only a caricature and a travesty, but a falsification of history." (See Ibid., at 474)

[157] Ibid.

[158] Ibid.

[159] 236 U. S. 230.

[160] Epoch v. Davis, at 467.

[161] Ibid.

[162] Ibid., at 472.

[163] Ibid.

[164] Ibid., at 471.

[165] Ibid., at 475-76.

[166] Ibid., at 476.

[167] "The Clansman," *Western Outlook*.

[168] *Epoch v. Davis*, at 476.

[169] Ibid.

[170] *Mutual Film Corp. v. Industrial Commission of Ohio*, 205 Fed. Rep. 138 (1914).

[171] 236 U. S. 230.

[172] *Epoch v. Davis*, at 483.

[173] 236 U. S. 230.

[174] *Epoch v. Davis*.

[175] Alice Gregory to James W. Johnson, 23 February 1918, NAACP Archives, File C301.

[176] Ibid.

[177] Ibid.

[178] *Epoch v. Davis*.

[179] Gregory to Johnson.

[180] "Injunction Holds in Nixon Film Case," *Pittsburgh Post*, 4 September 1915, p. 4.

[181] *Bill of Complaint filed by Nixon Theatre against Joseph Armstrong and W. N. Matthews, City of Pittsburgh in Court of Common Pleas of Allegheny County*, October Term 1915, among Griffith papers, MOMA Archives. With the Bill of Complaint, the Nixon interests filed a copy of the letter sent to them by Judge Armstrong notifying that the film would not be allowed. According to the Bill of Complaint the theatre manager Thomas Kirk received the following letter on August 25, 1915 (six days before the film's scheduled opening): "The production 'Birth of a Nation' will not be permitted to be shown in your theatre or any other place in city of Pittsburgh. Kindly make your arrangements accordingly," from Police Superintendent Matthews.

[182] S. R. Morsell to Mary Childs Nerney, Telegram, 25 August 1915, NAACP Archives File C300.

[183] "Play if Permitted to Start in Nixon," Pittsburgh Post, 31 August 1915, p. 3.

[184] Ibid.

[185] Ibid.

[186] "Scores Point on Mayor. . .Nixon Theatre May Begin 'The Birth' Film Fun," Pittsburgh Dispatch, 31 August 1915, p. 3.

[187] Bill of Complaint, Nixon v. Armstrong.

[188] Ibid.

[189] Ibid.

[190] Ibid.

[191] Ibid.

[192] Ibid.

[193] "Porter Puts Ban Upon 'Birth of Nation' Film," Philadelphia North American, 4 September 1915, p. 5.

[194] Ibid. After Reid's decision one newspaper commented that the "remarkable photo spectacle has settled down at the Nixon after all the commotion over its production to what looks like a long run." (See clipping in Griffith's personal Birth of a Nation scrapbook, No Head, Pittsburgh Gazette Times, 7 September 1915, n.p., MOMA Archives)

[195] "Ku Klux Expose Hits 'Birth of Nation' Tour," Variety, 23 September 1921, p. 45.

[196] "Michigan Judge Allows 'Nation' Injunction to Stand," Variety, 30 September 1921, p. 38.

[197] Ibid.

[198] Ibid.

[199] Ibid.

[200] Ibid.

[201] Ibid.

[202] Ibid.

[203] "Oakland Puts Ban On Birth of a Nation," Chicago Defender, 14 August 1915, p. 1.

[204] "Oakland Puts Ban On Birth of a Nation," *Chicago Defender*, 14 August 1915, p. 1.

[205] Eva B. Jones to "Mr. Randolph," 30 August 1915, NAACP Archives, File C300.

[206] "Nixon Comes Off His High Horse," *Baltimore Ledger*, 21 August 1915, p. 1.

[207] "The Birth of a Nation," *New Jersey Informer*, 21 August 1915, p. 1.

[208] "Editorial," *Philadelphia Tribune*, 4 September 1915, p. 4.

[209] "Nixon Comes Off His High Horse."

[210] Ibid.

[211] 236 U. S. 230.

[212] The information was not recorded in the books, newspapers, manuscript collections and other materials consulted for this study and listed in the bibliography.

[213] "Mayor Fights Photo-Play. . .Charleston Citizens Headed by Mayor Breese Determined To Keep Out 'Birth of a Nation," *Baltimore Ledger*, 25 December 1915, p. 1.

[214] Ibid.

[215] Ibid.

[216] Ibid.

[217] Ibid.

[218] Ibid.

[219] "A Hand At Last. . .Movie Man Refused to Cut Four Scenes As Ordered By Denver Officials and Lands in Court," *Chicago Defender*, 25 December 1915, p. 1.

[220] Ibid.

[221] Ibid. See also "Denver Suppressed Vicious Photo-Play," *New York Age*, 23 December 1915, p. 1.

[222] Ibid.

[223] Ibid.

[224] "Police Commissioner Voluntarily Refused License to Producers in Providence," Entry on Typewritten Sheet, Birth of a Nation folder, MOMA Archives.

[225] Providence Branch of the NAACP, Statement of Facts Regarding The Photo-Play 'The Birth of a Nation' by the Providence Branch of the NAACP to the Providence Board of Police Commissioners, n.d., NAACP Archives, File C302.

[226] Secretary to Mary Childs Nerney to Clifford H. Tavernier, 13 November 1915, NAACP Archives, File C301. See also Mary Childs Nerney to George W. Crawford, 13 September 1915, NAACP Archives, File C300.

[227] "Gary, Ind., NAACP Fighting to Stop 'Birth of Nation' Showing," Press Release, 12 December 1924, NAACP Archives, File C302.

[228] Ibid.

[229] "The Week's Editorial: Colored Press," Press Release, 23 January 1931, NAACP Archives, File C302.

[230] "The Clansman," Western Outlook, 13 March 1915, p. 3.

[231] Ibid.

[232] Ibid.

[233] J. B. Jefferson to Mary Childs Nerney, 6 May 1915, NAACP Archives, File C300.

[234] Ibid.

[235] W. A. Butler to Mary Childs Nerney, 19 May 1915, NAACP Archives, File C300.

[236] J. B. Jefferson to Mary Childs Nerney.

[237] "Films and Births and Censorship," The Survey, 3 April 1915, p. 4.

[238] Mary Childs Nerney to George Packard, 17 April 1915, NAACP Archives, File C300. See also Roy E. Aitken, The Birth of a Nation Story (Middleburg, Virginia: William W. Denlinger, 1965), p. 57.

[239] "Ban on Film Lifted," New York Times, 15 August 1915, Sec. II., p. 13.

[240] "A Partial Victory," New York Age, 1 April 1915, p. 4.

[241] Elisha Scott to Walter T. Andrews, 27 November 1931, NAACP Archives, File C302.

[242] *Virginia Amusement Co. v. W. W. Wertz*, copy of Judge Morgan Owen's opinion.

[243] Elisha Scott to Walter T. Andrews, 27 November 1931, NAACP Archives, File C302.

[244] *Petition for Injunction Hollywood Pictures Company and Ralph Christy v. City of Topeka, W. E. Atchison, City Attorney, Henry Dangerfield, Assistant City Attorney and Perry Brush, Chief of Police of the City of Topeka*, copy in NAACP Archives, File C302.

[245] Ibid., p. 2.

[246] Ibid.

[247] Scott to Andrews.

[248] Ibid.

[249] Ibid.

[250] George Whitcomb to Roy Wilkins, 17 October 1931, NAACP Archives, File C302.

[251] Ibid.

[252] Ibid.

[253] Scott to Andrews.

[254] *Virginia Amusement Co. v. W. W. Wertz*, copy of Judge Morgan Owen's order.

[255] Ibid.

[256] *Virginia Amusement Co. v. W. W. Wertz*, copy of Arthur Hudson's order.

[257] "West Virginia Supreme Court Bars 'Birth of Nation' Film."

[258] *McCarthy v. Chicago*.

[259] "Chicago Police Chief Faces Trial, Dollins is Summoned on Charge of Violating Injunction," *New York Times*, 3 February 1924.

[260] *Revised Statutes of Illinois*. Chapter 38, Paragraph 456 (1923). It is interesting to note that this statute is quite similar to Illinois Revised Statutes, Chapter 38, Section 404 (1949) central

to the U. S. Supreme Court's criminal libel ruling in Beauharnais v. Illinois, 343 U. S. 250, 72 S. Ct. 725, 96 L. Ed. 919 (1952). In 1924 Jackson served as a Chicago alderperson--he was no longer a state representative.

[261] Ibid.

[262] "Birth' to defy Chicago Ban," Variety, 12 January 1924, p. 22.

[263] "Chicago Chief Faces Trial," New York Times, 3 February 1924, p. 22.

[264] Mayor Dever to Put Ban on 'Birth of Nation," Chicago Defender, 2 February 1924, p. 4, Part I.

[265] "Crowd Grumbles as Police Halt 'Birth of Nation," Chicago Tribune, 4 February 1924, p. 1. Later further charges were filed against Webb and against Harry Aitken, Epoch General Manager. See "Two More Arrests Made Over 'Birth of Nation," Chicago Sunday Tribune, 10 February 1924, Part 1, p. 6, and Harry E. Aitken, Interoffice Message to D. W. Griffith, 6 February 1924, among Griffith's Papers, MOMA Archives.

[266] Ibid.

[267] Ibid.

[268] Ibid.

[269] Ibid.

[270] Ibid.

[271] "Fight 'Birth of Nation."

[272] Philip Kinsley, "Police Again Close 'Birth of Nation," Chicago Daily Tribune, 5 February 1924, p. 4.

[273] Ibid.

[274] Ibid.

[275] Ibid. Judge Cooper heard the original case and died shortly after he issued the 1917 injunction.

[276] Ibid.

[277] "Chicago Police Force 'Birth' Off Screen," Variety, 7 February 1924, p. 18.

[278] Philip Kinsley, "Birth of Nation' Shown While Lawyers Talk," *Chicago Tribune*, 6 February 1924, p. 10.

[279] "Fight 'Birth of Nation."

[280] Ibid. See also Kinsley, "Birth of Nation' Shown."

[281] Ibid.

[282] Kinsley, "Birth of Nation' Shown."

[283] Ibid.

[284] Ibid.

[285] Aitken to Griffith.

[286] "Birth's Publicity Grosses," *Variety*, 21 February 1924, p. 14.

[287] It is difficult to conlcude exactly why the city did not push for the case to be continued. The *Defender* indicated that the city gave up the fight because it feared "consequences at the hands of Judge Dennis E. Sullivan" and wanted to "avoid a heavy damage suit involving thousands of dollars at the hands of the management of the Auditorium." See "Stop Fight on Movie in City," *Chicago Defender*, 16 February 1924, p. 4.

[288] "Nation $50,000," *Variety*, 28 February 1924, p. 17. *Variety* also reported that the film during the third week of its run topped all other films in the city with a gross of over $55,000 and averaged a daily gross of $7,850. See "Nation's $55,000 Heads Chicago," *Variety*, 21 February 1924, p. 18.

[289] Scott to Andrews.

[290] "Kansas Enjoins Performance of 'Birth of Nation' Film," Press Release, 27 November 1931, NAACP Archives, File C302.

[291] "Object to Picture Play," *New York Sun*, March 12, 1915, n.p., clipping in Griffith's Personal *Birth of Nation* Scrapbook, MOMA Archives.

[292] "Court Asked to Stop Vicious Show," *New York Age*, 18 March 1915, p. 1.

[293] Ibid.

[294] Ibid.

[295] Notes on Meeting with New York Mayor, taken by Mary Childs Nerney, 31 March 1915, NAACP Archives, File C300.

[296] Mary Childs Nerney to Mrs. Whitehouse, 7 April 1915, NAACP Archives, File C300.

[297] "Editorial Graphs," *Cleveland Gazette*, 5 June 1915, p. 2.

[298] Mary Childs Nerney to Samuel R. Morsell, 26 May 1915, NAACP Archives, File C300 and also Mary Childs Nerney to Glesner Fowler, 18 May 1915, NAACP Archives, File C300.

[299] Ibid.

CHAPTER IV

CONTROVERSIES INVOLVING CRIMINAL PROCEEDINGS

The tactic of initiating criminal proceedings was found to serve two functions throughout the history of The Birth of a Nation censorship controversies. In five instances the tactic was used by the film's opponents as a tool designed to accomplish controversy resolution. In these five cases, the film's opponents initiated criminal proceedings against individuals responsible for the film's screening. Three of these criminal proceedings accomplished controversy resolution and two did not. In four cases criminal proceedings were initiated for a purpose other than controversy resolution. In these four cases individuals were arrested for participating in some form of protest action concerning The Birth. In two cases individuals arrested for their actions regarding the film argued their cases on First Amendment grounds. Because the circumstances and details of each arrest situation differ substantially, each controversy is discussed separately.

Cases Excluding First Amendment Considerations

During the time period 1915-1973, individuals were arrested during seven controversies for either showing or protesting the film. Four of these actions were intended to accomplish controversy resolution and three were not.

Actions Not Intended to Accomplish
Controversy Resolution

During three separate censorship controversies in 1915, criminal proceedings not intended to accomplish controversy resolution were initiated against individuals protesting the film's screening. In all, more than twenty people were arrested for protest activities. Many of the arrests were for actions outside the theatre where The Birth was being screened. Several of the arrests came after actions which did not seem to be planned specifically against the film, but occurred apparently because of secondary factors such as discrimination by ticket sellers.

The first incident involving the arrest of an individual for action in protest of The Birth occurred April 14, 1915, in New York's Liberty Theatre.[1] The arrest occurred during a spontaneous demonstration in the theatre which began when the pursuit-of-Flora-by-Gus sequence was screened.[2] The disturbance culminated when two eggs "splattered over the screen, blotting out portions of Flora jumping off the cliff."[3] Howard Schaeffer, described later as a white man from Maryland, was arrested for throwing the eggs after police searched him and found "a paper bag containing eggs in his overcoat pocket. . .he said he was taking the eggs home for breakfast and stopped in to see the play."[4] Schaeffer was charged with disorderly conduct.[5] Of the disturbance Schaeffer said, "It made my blood boil to see the play and I threw the eggs."[6] A second individual who protested Schaeffer's arrest and shouted "that play's a libel on a race" was escorted out of the theatre by police.[7] A third individual also was ushered out of the theatre when he began making a speech against the film.[8] He was later identified as Cleveland G. Allen, a correspondent for the *Indianapolis Freeman*. The *Freeman* reported that Allen was "hurried to the street by two officers and narrowly escaped arrest."[9]

Two weeks after the incident, Schaeffer came to trial. The case was heard before a Justice A. Duell in Jefferson Market Court.[10] Schaeffer received a suspended sentence.

Thus, in this instance although several individuals apparently were involved in a demonstration of some kind against the film, only one arrest took place. The individual arrested was charged and found guilty of disorderly conduct which took place inside the theatre. He received a suspended sentence.

During a month-long controversy over the film's right to the screen in Boston, 1915, 79 people were arrested during at least four separate incidents. This was the largest number of individuals arrested during any controversy. The first series of arrests occurred April 17, 1915, after William Monroe Trotter and a group of blacks approached the ticket window of the Tremont Theatre and were refused tickets to see *The Birth*.[11] After Trotter and his party were denied tickets ". . .the lobby was filled with a crowd of hundreds, white and colored, both pressing to reach the ticket window and angry at the refusal to sell."[12] Although existing accounts of the incident which followed vary greatly, that evening between 11 and 15 people were arrested and charged with a variety of offenses for participating in one of at least three separate incidents.[13]

The first arrests were made outside the theatre between 7:45 and 8:00 p.m. Those arrested included William Monroe Trotter and the Rev. Aaron Puller who were both charged with disturbing the peace and attempting to incite a riot.[14] Trotter also was charged with assaulting a police officer. In addition to Puller and Trotter, three others were arrested: Fred Banks was charged with public profanity; Joseph Gould, with assault and battery; and, John Hines, with sauntering and loitering.[15] All were taken to jail and freed on bond.

Later that evening, a person was arrested inside the theatre for throwing an egg at the screen. Charles Ray was taken from the theatre by plain clothes police officers after he threw the egg and was charged with malicious mischief.[16]

A disturbance of some sort occurred outside the theatre after the film screening was completed and additional arrests were made. One source described the scene:

> When the show was over scores of colored persons who had spent the evening marching back and forth in front of the theatre swarmed in front of the doors. The police ordered the crowd to fall back to enable those who had witnessed the show to leave the theatre lobbies. Men, women and children, black and white were jammed into Tremont Street between Avery and Boylston Street and retreated toward the common with the long line of reserves pressing them back.[17]

During this confusion, a black woman, Clara Foskey, was arrested for attacking a police officer with a hat pin.[18] Three individuals, Stephen Massey, James Bivens, and Lirginia Foster, were arrested for attempting to rescue Foskey from custody.[19] Foster was also charged with assaulting a man with her handbag.[20] Sometime during the evening, James L. Dunn was arrested and charged with public profanity.[21] Again, all individuals were taken to jail and released on bond.[22]

The dispositions of these arrests varied. The charges against Hines were eventually dismissed.[23] The disposition of Gould's arrest is unknown. The remaining individuals were brought to trial. Bevins was found not guilty of attempting to rescue a prisoner in police custody.[24] Foskey, Massey, Foster, and Dunn were found guilty as charged and fined $15, $5, $6, and $2, respectively.[25] Banks was found guilty of public profanity.[26] Ray pleaded guilty to malicious mischief and agreed to pay the Tremont Theatre $20 for the damages sustained when the eggs he threw hit the screen.[27] Ray was also placed on probation. Trotter and Puller were found not guilty of disorderly conduct and trying to incite a riot.[28] However, Trotter was found guilty of assaulting a police officer and fined $20.

In the decision in the Trotter and Puller cases, Judge J. Brackett of the Municipal Court said that not only was neither man guilty of disturbing the peace, but also "nothing about their conduct was riotous."[29] Brackett laid the blame for the incident with the police officer who had "punched Mr. Trotter in the jaw" and the ticket seller.[30] In part, Brackett said:

I severely criticize the ticket seller. When he testified
that he sold no more tickets after being ordered to stop I
believed him. It was the theatre's right to stop selling
tickets when it desired to. However, I find on the evidence
this agent continued to sell tickets and used unfair discrimination between white and colored people who applied for
tickets. His conduct was largely responsible for what happened.[31]

Thus, in this multi-part occurrence, at least 11 people were arrested for activities in the area of the theatre.[32] Only one action seems to have been directed at the film itself. The other incidents occurred outside the theatre and do not seem to have been planned.

Later as the controversy continued in Boston, another group of individuals was arrested outside the Tremont and charged with "sauntering, loitering, and obstructing the sidewalk."[33] Unlike the earlier incident, this march apparently was planned and included more than 100 persons marching back and forth in front of the theatre. Eight of the marchers were arrested: Eveland Washington, James Kingsley, Jacob Johnson, Augustus Granville, Carl Pinn, Raven Jones, Estelle Hill, and Jane W. Poser.[34] All were released on bond.[35] The disposition of these arrests is unknown. In this instance, individuals engaged in an organized protest against the film were arrested for loitering. Again, the incident took place outside the theatre.

A somewhat more violent demonstration against the film apparently occurred in front of Philadelphia's Forrest Theatre in September, 1915.[36] This demonstration apparently was planned to a certain extent because during the day prior to the demonstration the following announcement was circulated in predominately black sections of Philadelphia:

> RALLY--RALLY--RALLY All colored citizens and their white friends and sympathizers are earnestly urged to assemble at the Forrest Theatre Broad and Sansom Streets on Monday night at 8 o'clock to make a dignified protest against the photoplay known as The Birth of a Nation which is horrible libel on and a most aggravating insult to every Afro-American.[37]

The incident began when someone among the large group of individuals marching outside the theatre threw a brick through a theatre window.[38] The police who had been monitoring the demonstration "charged" into the crowd and a clash followed. According to several sources, the melee which followed involved 500 protesters and 100 police.[39] In spite of the numbers of people involved only four arrests were made. One individual, Arthur Linn, was charged with throwing the brick.[40] The disposition of his arrest is unknown. Three individuals, Sidney Purnell, Woodford Jackson, and Joseph Davenport, were charged with inciting to riot.[41] However, these charges were dismissed after police were unable to testify that the individuals had actually incited riot.[42]

In this instance, persons were arrested for disturbing the peace and inciting to riot. The latter charge was dropped. The disposition of the arrest of the individual charged with the former is unknown. The incident took place outside the theatre and seems to have been planned to a certain extent.

In summary, during three The Birth of a Nation censorship controversies, individuals were arrested on a variety of charges brought as a result of activities connected somehow to the film's screening. In all, more than 20 people were arrested for participation in one of six separate incidents in three different cities. The individuals arrested were charged with a variety of offenses ranging from malicious mischief to loitering to public profanity to assault and battery. None of the individuals argued in court that their arrests were invalid because of a constitutional right to free speech. Of the individuals arrested, eight were brought to trial and found guilty. Three were brought to trial and acquitted. The charges against four persons were dismissed. The disposition of ten arrests is unknown. At least two of the major demonstrations during which people were arrested apparently were planned and organized. One incident apparently was not planned and occurred after a ticket seller refused to sell tickets to blacks. Two individuals were arrested for actions performed inside the motion picture theatre against the film. The remaining persons were arrested for activities which occurred outside the theatre. In no cases were the criminal proceedings intended to accomplish controversy resolution.

Actions Intended to Accomplish Controversy Resolution

During the time period studied, at least six people were arrested for showing *The Birth of a Nation* during four controversies, and all arrests were designed to accomplish controversy resolution. In two cases people were arrested for showing the film allegedly in violation of a state statute. In one case a person was arrested for allegedly violating an administrative order directing censorship of the film. These arrests took place between the years 1915 and 1938.

Three people were charged with violating a state statute by screening the film during a 1924 Chicago, Illinois, controversy.[43] The Chicago case involved the arrests of two projectionists and a representative of the company distributing The Birth.[44]

As discussed in Chapter III, the arrests took place during a screening of the film when Judge John Rooney, Chicago Municipal Court, issued warrants in the theatre for the arrests of projectionists Jay Webb and Nathaniel Galup.[45] The warrants were issued on the grounds that the film's screening violated a state law which forbade exhibition of anything which exposed any group of citizens to "contempt, derision, or which is productive of breach of the peace or riots."[46]

The evening after the original arrests, the projectionists were arrested again for showing the film. In addition, Harry Aitken, representing the film's distributor, was arrested.[47] Although the dispositions of the Webb and Aitken arrests are not known, Galup's trial was reported in the Chicago Defender.[48]

The Defender reported that after four days of testimony and an hour's deliberation, a jury of "12 white men" found Galup not guilty of violating the Jackson law.[49] In addition to reporting the verdict, the Defender summarized the trial proceedings. According to the Defender, the case elicited "from both sides a brand of legal gymnastics seldom encountered in a courtroom where the offense charged is 'merely' a misdemeanor."[50] For the prosecution, attorney Everette Jennings called a variety of witnesses to prove that The Birth in fact violated the law in question and that a scene which specifically violated the law was on the screen at the time of Galup's arrest.[51] For the defense, attorney Charles Trainer called only two witnesses, Galup and Preston Smith, United Artists vice-president. Galup testified that he did not know whether he was operating the projector at the time the scenes allegedly in violation of the Jackson law were screened. Galup explained this by stating that "his position in the box prevented him from seeing what was on the screen."[52] During the course of the trial, the jury was shown the film.

    The Defender observed that the "most interesting part of the entire trial" came during the concluding arguments by each attorney.[53] Jennings, for the prosecution, "made an impassioned plea for America" and contended that the scenes presented in the film violated the ideals of American democracy.[54] On the other hand, the Defender interpreted Trainer's argument as "one of the most vitriolic speeches against our race that has ever been tolerated in a courtroom."[55] The Defender said that Trainer began his attack by calling Alderperson Jackson a "childish, ignorant, innocent person thriving upon the ignorance of his people."[56] The remainder of Trainer's closing statement appealed "to the racial prejudices of the jury by implying that white civilization is being threatened by the colored races."[57] Jennings countered with a final statement which "tried to remove the racial element from the case."[58] However, the Defender concluded that Jennings was unable to accomplish this after Trainer's speech and a verdict of not guilty was returned.

Thus, in this instance an individual brought to trial for allegedly violating a state law forbidding the presentation of certain kinds of information was found innocent in a jury trial. The details of the trial as reported indicate that the case was not specifically argued as a freedom of expression case. The arrests of two other individuals in connection with the same incident apparently were not reported in as much detail and the dispositions of these latter arrests are unknown. The film's opponents intended the arrests to resolve the controversy by stopping the screening. However, the arrests did not end the countroversy. As discussed in Chapter III, the controversy was resolved through acquiescence.

Adolph J. Rettig, Ormont Theatre manager, East Orange, New Jersey, was another individual arrested for allegedly violating a state statute by showing The Birth.[59] Rettig's arrest warrant was sworn out by Dr. Theodore R. Inge, president of the East Orange Branch of the NAACP. The warrant was issued under a state law which banned any film "which in any way incites, counsels, promotes, advocates or symbolizes hatred, violence or hostility against any group of persons by reasons of race, color, religion or manner of worship."[60] The statute was passed in 1935 "as a curb on Nazi activities."[61] Inge contended that the entire film tended to incite racial hatred.[62] Rettig was charged and released without bail pending a hearing.[63] However, the outcome of that hearing is unknown. Nevertheless, Rettig's arrest resolved the controversy because the film was withdrawn.

One individual was brought to trial for allegedly violating a city ordinance by showing *The Birth*. The Des Moines, Iowa, ordinance under which the theatre manager was arrested, forbade the exhibition of anything that was indecent, lewd, or immoral or that was calculated to create a feeling of prejudice, hatred or antipathy against any race of people.[64] The trial was heard by Judge J. E. Meyer, Des Moines Municipal Court, Criminal Division. The trial lasted about one week.

During the course of the trial, Meyer was asked to consider both the validity of the ordinance under which the arrest had been made and whether *The Birth* actually violated the ordinance.[65] During the trial, the defense produced a series of expert witnesses who testified that the film did not violate the ordinance. The prosecution countered by calling expert witnesses who testified that the film did violate the law.[66] After hearing all testimony, Meyer indicated that he was not satisfied that the film violated the ordinance, he found the manager of the theatre not guilty of violating the law.[67] This action resolved the controversy.

Thus, in this case a theatre manager was found not guilty of violating a city ordinance by a judge who ruled, after a trial, that although the ordinance was valid, the prosecution had not shown that the film actually violated the ordinance. The testimony in this case apparently related directly to the content of the film, but the question involved was not specifically a free speech question.

One individual was arrested for allegedly violating an administrative order to censor the film. The incident occurred in Denver, Colorado, December 1915, after the city's commissioner of safety ordered four scenes cut from the film.[68] The theatre manager, R. Mazur, refused to cut the scenes and was arrested after screening an uncensored version of the film.[69] Mazur was released on bond and the ultimate disposition of his arrest is unknown.

In spite of Mazur's arrest, the film continued at his theatre under a restraining order issued by a Judge T. Dennison of the District Court as discussed in Chapter III. Dennison's ruling is an interesting one because the judge decided that although the police could not act against the film itself, "there was nothing in the order that prevented the commissioner of safety, Mr. Nisbet, from acting directly against the manager nor the owners of the film, if the commissioner regarded the law as being violated."[70] Thus, Dennison's ruling rather than the criminal proceeding resolved the controversy.

Thus, in four controversies at least six individuals were arrested for showing the film. Individuals arrested included a representative of the film's distributor, projectionists, and theatre managers. These persons were charged with either violating a state statute, a city censorship ordinance, or a direct censorship order. Two individuals were brought to trial and found innocent. The dispositions of the remaining arrests are unknown. One individual was arrested in late 1915. One individual was brought to trial in 1916. Three individuals were arrested in connection with one 1924 controversy. One individual was arrested in 1938. In none of the cases did the defendants argue that their arrests violated their constitutional right to free speech. In two cases the criminal proceedings resolved the controversies and in two cases the controversies were resolved through other means.

    Cases In Which Free Speech Was A Specific Issue

    In two instances, individuals were brought to trial for their participation in censorship controversies and the cases were argued specifically upon freedom of expression issues. In one instance the criminal proceeding was intended to accomplish controversy resolution and in the other it was not. One case concerned the arrests of several individuals who were picketing the theatre screening The Birth and handing out circulars against the film in New York, 1921. The other controversy concerned the 1939 arrest of a Denver theatre owner for allegedly violating a city ordinance by showing The Birth. Although both cases were argued on free speech issues, only the New York case was ultimately decided on this ground.

    The New York case began when five blacks were arrested while picketing the Capitol Theatre and distributing handbills. The individuals arrested were: Helen Curtis, Laura Jean Rollock, Katherine Johnson, Edward Frazier, and Llewelyn Rollock.[71] Several of the individuals carried placards which read "We represented America in France--Why should'The Birth of a Nation' Misrepresent Us Here."[72] The two men arrested were World War I veterans. The women arrested had served during World War I as canteen workers in

France.[73] The protesters were distributing a leaflet titled "Stop the Ku Klux Klan Propaganda in New York."[74] The protesters were actually charged with distributing these leaflets allegedly in violation of a New York law which forbade the distribution of commercial or business advertising material in public places.[75]

After the individuals were arrested, the NAACP announced that it would make a test-case out of the incident and retained Aiken A. Pope and James C. Thomas to represent the defendants.[76] The case was heard by Robert E. Ten Eyck, City Magistrates Court, Seventh District Manhattan. Ten Eyck offered to dismiss the charges if the individuals involved would promise not to picket the theatre or distribute any more leaflets.[77] All defendants indicated that they would not make any such promises. Accordingly, Ten Eyck found each individual guilty of violating the ordinance, but suspended all sentences.[78]

The NAACP immediately announced plans to appeal the convictions.[79] The association's official statements on the matter both explained the nature and purpose of the protest at the theatre and indicated the central issue in the legal case as they would argue it. For the organization, Secretary James Weldon Johnson indicated that the purpose of the demonstration was "to register a peaceable protest against what is plainly propaganda for the KKK in New York City."[80] Johnson said that this form of protest was adopted only after both the film's producer and city authorities refused to stop the picture. "It was not to create violence but to protest against the end of violence which The Birth of a Nation gives rise to that the NAACP took action," Johnson explained.[81] Further, Johnson said that individuals "seemed eager" to receive the leaflets and that none were thrown on the ground.[82] Later Johnson said that "the NAACP appeal will raise the entire question as to the right of people to protest by distributing educational literature in public in New York City."[83]

The case was appealed to the New York Court of General Sessions. In the Association brief filed by attorney Pope, three specific questions were set forth for the courts consideration:

1) Whether the mere act of giving circulars to pedestrians and passersby upon the public streets of New York per se is unlawful;

2) Whether if this in fact is the case then is this a valid exercise of the charter powers conferred upon the city of New York; and

3) If passing out circulars is unlawful per se and it is properly within the charter powers of the City of New York to forbid such actions, is it constitutional within the limitations of the Constitution of the State of New York and the Constitution of the United States.[84]

Pope stressed in his statement of the face situation that there was no evidence that the defendants threw any leaflets on the streets, and there was also no charge of public disorder.[85] Further, there was no charge that the reading matter contained in the circulars was unlawful or objectionable.[86]

In its brief, the defense developed two primary points. First, Pope argued that the ordinance specifically forbade casting or throwing circulars, not the peaceful distribution of circulars

190

to individuals.[87] Pope asserted that this was the case because the ordinance under which the individuals were arrested came under the general title of street cleaning and the specific title of refuse and rubbish.[88] Thus, Pope concluded that the "intention and purpose" of the ordinance in question was to keep the "streets clean and it would seem that only when circulars are thrown or cast on the ground that their distribution may be held to be within the scope of this intent."[89] Because the defendants had not been accused of throwing or casting the leaflets generally, they could not be guilty of violating the ordinance.

Secondly, Pope argued that the statute applied only to advertising material and did not apply to "news circulars, educational leaflets, religious handbills and political pamphlets."[90] Because the NAACP-sponsored leaflet against the film and the Klan was not an advertising leaflet, it also was not covered by the statute in question. Therefore, the individuals arrested could not be guilty of violating the statute.

Judge Alfred Tally heard the case and accepted the defense's reasoning. Specifically, Tally ruled that "the defendants were well within their rights in distributing the circulars. . . ."[91] Tally indicated that the ordinance in question only applied to advertising matter and that the leaflet in question did not fall into that category. Tally indicated that to prevent the lawful distribution of any material other than advertising ". . .would be a dangerous and un-American thing."[92] The decision continued by indicating that the ordinance in question was originally intended to prevent the littering of the streets and was not invalid *per se*. Regarding the question of the right to protest the film, Tally concluded:

> The circular in question was a protest against what was believed to be a movement which encouraged discrimination against certain classes of citizens because of race, color, or religious beliefs, and whether or not there was a sound basis for that belief they were within their rights in making public their protest against such a movement and to make known their protest they used possibly the only means available by the distribution of circulars and pamphlets to the public.[93]

In this manner Tally reversed Ten Eyck's decision and dismissed the complaint against the defendants.[94]

Thus, in this case five individuals were arrested for their participation in a protest which took place outside the theatre screening *The Birth of a Nation* in 1921. The individuals arrested were charged specifically with violating a city ordinance against the distribution of advertising leaflets. The individuals were originally convicted and received suspended sentences. The convictions were reversed on appeal. The case was argued as a free speech issue with the defense claiming that the defendants were well within their constitutional rights to distribute the pamphlets in the manner in which they were distributed.

The remaining case which was argued, but not ultimately decided on free speech grounds, concerned the arrest of a Denver theatre manager who allegedly violated a city ordinance by showing the film. The case is unique among those discussed in this chapter because the American Civil Liberties Union (ACLU) intervened in this instance as a friend of the court and argued against film censorship in general.

The ACLU became involved in this controversy following a letter from a member of the Denver branch to the national office.[95] In this letter, attorney Carle Whitehead advised the national office that on the preceding evening the manager of the local theatre screening The Birth, R. E. Allan, had been arrested for violating Section 1282 of the city ordinances which forbade the exhibition of anything which was "contrary to good order and morals, and the public welfare" or which tended to stir up "or engender race prejudice" or which represented any "hanging, lynching or burning of any human being."[96] The complaint against Allan was signed by W. F. Turner, president of the NAACP's Denver chapter.[97] Whitehead asked the ACLU national office if it wanted him to appear in the case as a friend of the court to represent the viewpoint that the enforcement of "any ordinance savoring of censorship. . .is definitely unconstitutional, undemocratic, and unamerican."[98] ACLU national apparently responded affirmatively because Whitehead did appear as a friend of the court.[99]

During the trial, Allan's attorney argued that the ordinance under which Allan had been arrested was unconstitutional, vague, and tended to "give police dictatorial powers."[100] The judge, Philip Gilliam of Police Court, agreed that in some ways the ordinance was vague, but said that it was constitutional.[101] Gilliam also said that the ordinance did "everything but name this particular picture" and that The Birth was "in direct violation of the law."[102] Gilliam found Allan guilty and sentenced him to 120 days in jail and ordered him to pay a fine of $1,400.00.[103]

Allan's attorney appealed the conviction and ACLU national advised Whitehead to continue with the case.[104] The organization also explained its involvement in the case to the public through a press release. In part the organization stated:

> The ACLU offers its attorney as friend of the court, joining neither the prosecution nor the defense. It holds no brief either for or against the picture The Birth of a Nation. It holds no brief either for or against the purposes or propaganda of any group which may be sponsoring or opposing this picture. The union is concerned solely with the preservation of fundamental civil, constitutional American rights. . .in this case the rights of freedom of speech and freedom of the press--the motion picture being a means of presenting facts, opinions, ideas and points of view in common with the word of mouth and the printed word.[105]

After learning of the ACLU position in the case, the NAACP wrote the organization and requested "a statement. . .correcting the idea that you are interested in the success of The Birth of a Nation."[106] For the ACLU, Roger Baldwin responded that the organization's position was correctly stated in the press release.[107] Baldwin also restated the view that public officials should not be allowed to use their discretion in permitting or banning films.[108]

Allan's appeal was set for hearing in June, 1939, but he requested and received a continuance until September.[109] In September, a second continuance was granted until the following month.[110] Actually, the case did not come up for a hearing until February of the following year.

During the delays, the ACLU considered the strategy it would follow. Whitehead requested and received advice concerning the case from the national office.[111] Help came primarily in the form of a memorandum from communications attorney Alexander Lindey.[112] In part, Lindey advised that it would be fruitless to write a detailed argument proving that film censorship statutes had been upheld as constitutional by a variety of state and federal courts. To do this would be to belabor the obvious and not further the cause. However, Lindey said "if we were to argue solely on the basis of precedents, the law would become a static and frozen thing, and there would never be any evolutionary process. . .even fools and diehards will admit today that. . .law being an instrument of social engineering must adapt itself to the needs of the day."[113] Lindey recommended that Whitehead pursue two general lines of reasoning in his attack upon the constitutionality of motion picture censorship:

1) that such censorship was originally sustained because motion pictures in their crude and early state were analogized to circuses, prize fights and other mass exhibitions;

2) and that the character of films has undergone a vast change so that it can be reasonably argued today that movies are a medium for the dissemination of ideas akin to the press. The United States Supreme Court in 1915 could hardly have foreseen the eventual evolution of the screen as the most powerful medium (with the possible exception of the radio) for the molding of public opinion.[114]

Although Lindey concluded his memo by stating that he was "strongly persuaded" that if the proper case were presented the court would respond favorably, he did caution that he was not convinced that The Birth of a Nation was the appropriate film for the test case. In part he said:

> I need not repeat the old bromide about hard cases making bad law, but it does seem to me that in these days, when the stirring up of racial and religious hatred is giving deep concern to everybody, judges included, it is unwise to prejudice the possibility of the success of a constitutionality test-case by complicating the issue with collateral questions. It is overwhelmingly preposterous to ban a movie because it depicts (as did Giono's <u>Harvest</u>) a child born out of wedlock. It is not as absurd to suppress a film which tends to create race hatred even though the avowed purpose of motion picture censorship from the very outset was the protection of public morals. Since a constitutional attack would, on the basis of hurtful precedents, be an uphill fight anyway I'd hate to handicap myself by undertaking a case involving an unsympathetic issue.[115]

In spite of Lindey's statement of concern over the issues in the case, the ACLU continued its involvement.

Whitehead responded to Lindey's memo by stating that the case in question was not strictly a censorship case "as no board of censors" existed to judge films in advance.[116] Whitehead indicated that the strongest argument in the case was that the ordinance was "too indefinite to be enforced."[117] Also, Whitehead said that he made a distinction between films which were censored because they were immoral or indecent and films which were censored because they might engender racial prejudice. Whitehead said that the so-called immoral or indecent film was generally produced and exhibited for "the sole purpose of making money."[118] On the other hand, the "pictures which would be held to stir up race or class prejudice or hatred" contained "at least a large element of propaganda which directly involves the question of freedom of speech."[119] Whitehead concluded his response to the memo by assuring the national office that he would not base his case upon precedent or technicality, but would "properly stress the danger to liberties from the enactment and enforcement of any such legislation. . ."[120]

Whitehead argued his case before Judge C. E. Kettering and lost. Kettering ruled that the ordinance under which Allan had been arrested was valid. He refused specifically to distinguish between the censorship standards of immorality and racial prejudice. In part Kettering said:

> . . .It seems to me if a municipality. . .has the right to say in advance, and determine by a censor that one may not exhibit a lewd painting, or one may not publish a lewd or immoral book, that by the same token the municipality could say that one may not exhibit a moving picture which is contrary to good order.[121]

After Kettering's ruling, Allan's appeal was set for hearing before Judge H. Lawrence Hinkley. Shortly before this trial began, Allan's attorney withdrew from the case and Allan indicated to Whitehead that he had no funds to employ additional counsel.[122] Later, three attorneys volunteered to represent Allan.[123] When the case came to trial, the city offered to dismiss all of the charges except those stemming from the first arrest if Allan would plead guilty on that count. After conferring with his attorneys, Allan decided to accept the offer and pleaded guilty to one count of showing a motion picture which tended to incite race hatred.[124] Allan was fined $200. However, Hinkley suspended $100 of the fine and allowed Allan 60 days to pay the other $100.[125] All other charges against Allan were dismissed.[126] This action resolved the controversy.

In summary, a person was arrested for showing The Birth of a Nation in violation of a municipal ordinance which forbade the

exhibition of films which might engender racial prejudice. The
individual was brought to trial and found guilty. He appealed his
conviction, but eventually pleaded guilty to a reduced charge. The
case was argued in part on free speech grounds. In this case, the
ACLU intervened as friend of the court and argued that film censorship in general and the city ordinance in question in particular
were unconstitutional. However, at least two ACLU attorneys differed
in reasoning. One indicated that the argument should demonstrate
that the motion picture medium had evolved since the Mutual decision
and was currently clearly a medium for the dissemination of ideas.
This attorney spoke of the medium in general, but was reluctant to
base a test-case upon a film which contained racist content. On the
other hand, the other attorney involved in the case for the ACLU
indicated that he felt that censorship for racial reasons was clearly
unconstitutional. However, he did not seem convinced that film censorship per se was unconstitutional. Rather, he seemed to go back
to the Mutual decision and accept the idea that if films were purely
for commercial ends, then they were not truly vehicles of speech
entitled to First Amendment protection.

Summary and Conclusions

During the years of this study, at least 36 individuals were
arrested during nine controversies on a variety of charges related
to their activities undertaken in or around a theatre where The
Birth of a Nation was being screened. Seven individuals were arrested
for asserting the film's right to the screen by showing it. Twenty-

nine persons were arrested for their participation in protests related to the film's screening. Three of these people were charged with more than one offense. The arrests were made during nine separate censorship controversies. In five instances criminal proceedings were intended to accomplish controversy resolution. In four instances criminal proceedings were not intended to accomplish controversy resolution. In no controversy were individuals from both sides arrested.

In one controversy, individuals were arrested in connection with four different incidents. A majority of those arrested for protesting (24 persons) were arrested during 1915. The remaining five protesters were arrested together in 1921. Individuals were arrested for showing the film over a more extended time span. Individuals were arrested for showing the film in the following years: 1915; 1916; 1924; 1937, 1939. Although the disposition of 14 arrests is unknown, ten individuals were acquitted of all charges brought against them; seven individuals were found guilty of all charges brought against them; one individual was found innocent on two counts and guilty on one; and, the charges against four individuals were dropped. For a breakdown of the charges brought and the disposition of arrests, see table 7.

TABLE 7

DISPOSITIONS OF CASES OF INDIVIDUALS ARRESTED
IN CONNECTION WITH SCREENINGS OF THE BIRTH

Charge	Acquitted	Convicted	Dismissed	Unknown
Disorderly Conduct	2	1	0	1
Assault and Battery	0	3	0	1
Public Profanity	0	2	0	0
Loitering	0	0	1	8
Malicious Mischief	0	1	0	0
Attempt to Rescue Prisoner	1	2	0	0
Trying to Incite Riot	2	0	3	0
Illegally Distributing Leaflets	5	0	0	0
Showing film which might engender racial prejudice	2	12	0	3
Violating censorship order	0	0	0	1

Only two of the cases found were argued specifically on First Amendment grounds and only one of these cases was ultimately decided on these grounds.

Although the tactic was not implemented enough times to determine its statistical significance in terms of accomplishing controversy resolution, it does not appear to have been particularly successful in this regard. Specifically, in three cases criminal proceedings intended to accomplish controversy resolution did so and in two cases controversy resolution was not accomplished by the tactic. Two controversies resolved by criminal proceedings resulted in censorship of the film and one controversy resolved by criminal proceedings resulted in no censorship. Since criminal proceedings as a tactic to accomplish controversy resolution was used only by the film's opponents, the tactic also does not appear to have been particularly successful in accomplishing the purpose of which it was instituted. Both controversies not resolved by criminal proceedings were resolved through acquiescence.

NOTES TO CHAPTER IV

[1]"Egg Negro Scenes In Liberty Film Play . . . Police Quell Disturbers at 'Birth of a Nation' and Arrest Indignant Southerner," New York Times, 15 April 1915, p. 1.

[2]Ibid. The NAACP reported that the organization had nothing to do with the demonstration. See M. Childs Nerney to George Packard, 17 April 1915, NAACP Archives File C300, Library of Congress Manuscript Collection, Washington, D. C. (Hereafter referred to as NAACP Archives).

[3]Ibid.

[4]Ibid.

[5]Ibid.

[6]Ibid.

[7]Ibid.

[8]Ibid. In part it was reported that Allen said "On the Anniversary of Abe Lincoln's assassination it is inappropriate to present a play which libels 10,000,000 loyal American Negroes. I think President Lincoln wouldn't like this play."

[9]"News of the Nation's Metropolis," Indianapolis Freeman, 24 April 1915, p. 1.

[10]"Sentence Suspended in Clansman," New York Age, 29 April 1915, p. 1. See also, "Threw Eggs at Picture Film," Baltimore Ledger, 1 May 1915, p. 1.

[11]"Birth of Nation' Causes Near-Riot . . . Alleged Plot to Destroy Film Results in Wild Scenes and 11 Arrests . . . Clash Comes When Ticket Sale Ends," Boston Sunday Globe, 18 April 1915, p. 1.

[12]Ibid.

[13]Most accounts of the incident describe it as a race riot in connection with the film. For example, Lewis Jacobs in his classic film history The Rise of the American Film (New York: Harcourt Brace and Co., 1939), indicated that "in Boston and other abolitionist cities race riots broke out." (See p. 178) Jacobs' interpretation of The Birth's history is often cited by contemporary media scholars. See for example, Don Pember's Mass Media in America (Chicago: Science Research Associates, 1974), pp. 234-236 and David Clark and William Blankenburg, You and Media (San Francisco: Canfield Press, 1973), pp. 69-81. Ralph Ellison in Shadow and Act said

that the film's screening "resulted in controversy, riots . . ."
(New York: Random House, 1953), p. 275. John Howard Lawson in Film:
The Creative Process, 2nd Ed., (New York: Will and Wang, 1967) said
of the incident that "crowds demonstrated for 24 hours in front of
the theatre." (See p. 31) Richard Griffith and Arthur Mayer reproduced two headlines from the Boston Press indicating that the incident was a riot in their The Movies, Rev. Ed., (New York: Simon
and Schuster, 1970), pp. 38-39. Milton Mackaye also termed the incident a riot in a 1937 retrospective article concerning the film.
See Mackaye, "The Birth of a Nation," Scribner's Magazine, November
1937, pp. 46 & 49. Griffith scholar Seymour Stern also identified
Boston as the scene of a "race riot allegedly incited" by the film.
See Seymour Stern, "The Birth of a Nation," Special Supplement to
Sight and Sound Index Series No. 4, July 1945, p. 10. In perhaps
one of the most dramatic interpretations of the event Raymond Cook
wrote in a biography of Thomas Dixon that a "riot occurred during
which the police fought with a crowd of ten thousand people for 24
hours," See Cook, Thomas Dixon (New York: Twayne Publishers, 1974),
p. 116. On the other hand, Stephen Fox in a biography of William
Monroe Trotter called the happening "the most ominous racial incident in Boston in anyone's memory" but did not dub the occurrence
an actual riot. See Fox, The Guardian of Boston: William Monroe
Trotter (New York: Atheneum, 1970), p. 193. Newspaper accounts of
the incident also differ in their descriptions. The Boston Sunday
Globe said that "Birth of Nation' Causes Near Riot . . . Alleged Plot
To Destroy Film Resulted in Wild Scenes and 11 Arrests," 18 April
1915, p. 1. The Boston Herald reported "150 Patrolmen Guard 'Birth
of Nation' . . . Editor Trotter and Pastor Puller of Calvary Baptist
Church Among Those Arrested While Seeking Admission to Tremont
Theatre . . . Reserves In Force Forbid Big Disturbance," 18 April
1915, p. 1. The New York Times said "Negroes Mob Photo Play," 18
April 1915, p. 1. The Indianapolis Freeman reported "Editor of the
'Boston Guardian' Stormed Tremont Theatre Last Saturday Evening to
Stop Vicious Play from Running in that City," 24 April 1915, p. 1.
The Cleveland Gazette said "What Caused the Riot," 1 May 1915, p. 2.
The Chicago Defender said "Boston Race Leaders Fight 'Birth of a
Nation' . . . Editor William Monroe Trotter and Rev. Puller are arrested When They Seek Admission to Tremont Theatre," 24 April 1915,
p. 4. The Boston Morning Journal reported, "Negro Rioters Fined
and Put on Probation," 29 April 1915, p. 14. And, later the New
York Telegraph concluded "Boston Won't Ban 'Birth of Nation' . . .
Despite Race Riots, Mass Meetings, and Protests Film Censors Decide
for film," 3 June 1915, p. 1. Thus, it can be seen that many existing interpretations of the incident indicate that it was a race riot
and that there was some reasonably direct link between the film and
the riot. However, the evidence does not adequately support the
race riot interpretation. Also, the link between the film itself
and the events which occurred the evening of 17 April 1915, in Boston,
is not as direct as many of these sources would seem to indicate.
For example, although at least eleven individuals were arrested,

they were not all arrested at the same time nor were they charged with exactly the same kind of offenses. Five were arrested outside the theatre prior to the screening. (See "Birth of Nation Causes Near Riot") One individual was arrested in the theatre during the screening and the remaining individuals were arrested outside the theatre after the screening. (See "150 Patrolmen Guard Birth of Nation") Only two individuals were charged with disorderly conduct and trying to incite a riot. Both individuals were found innocent of these charges. In fact, the trial judge indicated that there was nothing riotous about the conduct of these individuals during the incident. (See "Trotter Fined for Assault Upon Officer," Boston Morning Journal, 4 May 1915, p. 4) In addition the judge in this particular case indicated that the incident was probably triggered by the actions of a ticket seller and a police officer rather than the film itself. Only one arrest came as the result of an aggressive action against the film itself (See "150 Patrolmen Guard 'Birth of Nation"). The remaining arrests occurred after the film had been shown and took place outside the theatre. These arrests were tied primarily to the arrest of one woman who apparently stabbed a police officer with a hat pin (See "Negro Rioters Fined and Put On Probation"). The link between this action (if any) and the film itself is somewhat difficult to pinpoint.

[14] Again, the statements of individuals involved in the incident differ substantially in their accounts of what happened. For example, Trotter indicated that he had gone to the Tremont to see whether or not the film's "objectionable features" had been removed. Trotter said that when he requested a ticket, the seller told him that there were none available. However, Trotter noticed that while white people were allowed to buy tickets, black people were not. Trotter challenged the ticket seller on this point and was arrested. Trotter said that after he was arrested a plain clothes police officer struck him on the jaw. (Trotter's arrest did seem somewhat violent. One reporter on hand wrote "The police had difficulty in getting Mr. Trotter and considerable rough handling was in evidence. When he finally was dragged out from behind the rail he was seized by a sergeant and another officer with one guardian holding each wrist was marched down Tremont street . . . Mr. Trotter's legs not being so long as those of his captors he apparently had difficulty in keeping up with them. He had the appearance of being partly pushed and partly dragged along and was overheard to say 'If you'll let go of my wrists, I'll go along." See "150 Patrolmen Guard 'Birth of Nation.") Also, the judge who later tried Trotter criticized the police officer who apparently hit Trotter. (See "Monroe Trotter and Dr. Puller Are Acquitted," Chicago Defender, 8 May 1915, p. 1) Puller also indicated that he had received rough handling during the incident. Puller recalled that as he spoke to a police officer outside the Tremont someone hit him over the head, knocking him to the ground. Puller said, "Policemen helped me to my feet. One had me by the back of the collar, two had their hands

on my shoulders, and still two more had me by the arms. They rushed me along the street using such force that I was almost choked. The crowd jeered and somebody yelled, 'Kill the black -- --." Puller continued that he told the police that he was a minister and that "I was only for peace, that I wanted no violence." In spite of this Puller was taken to the station house and booked. Police Superintendent Michael H. Crowley said that the police "were anxious to have no roughness of any kind and regret that anything of the kind occurred." Crowley also indicated that he did not believe that the disturbance had been planned beforehand. However, Tremont manager John Schoeffel said that he had been informed prior to the disturbance that a plot existed among blacks to raid the theatre and destroy the film. Schoeffel said that after a large number of blacks arrived at the theatre the box office was closed and no tickets were sold to blacks or whites. Schoeffel said that after the blacks were informed that no more tickets would be sold they became boisterous. The police intervened and no serious property damage or human injury occurred. Schoeffel concluded his statement by stating "the management regrets that this incident has occurred, but feels that the men and women engaged in this attempt to destroy property and disturb the performance are not representative of the colored race of Boston." For a more detailed account of the statements issued by each of these individuals see "150 Patrolmen Guard 'Birth of Nation."

[15] "150 Patrolmen Guard 'Birth of Nation."

[16] Ibid. See also, "Birth of Nation' Came Near Causing a Riot in a Boston Play House," Philadelphia Tribune, 24 April 1915, p. 1.

[17] Ibid.

[18] Ibid.

[19] Ibid.

[20] Ibid.

[21] Ibid.

[22] Ibid.

[23] "Still Fighting Obnoxious Movies," Baltimore Ledger, 1 May 1915, p. 1.

[24] "Negro Woman Fined for Rioting At The Tremont," Boston Morning Journal, 30 April 1915, p. 14. See also, "Negro Rioters Fined and Put On Probation."

[25] Ibid.

[26] Ibid.

[27] Ibid.

[28] "Trotter Fined For Assault Upon Officer . . ."

[29] Ibid.

[30] Ibid.

[31] Ibid.

[32] Two other sources indicate that more than the eleven persons named by the other sources were arrested. One source indicated that in addition to the eleven individuals previously mentioned, four others were arrested in the vicinity of the Tremont. These individuals were A. H. Benjamin, Michael Jordan, Charles F. Sullivan, and Harrison McDonald. The source does not indicate the deposition of the Benjamin and Jordan arrests nor does it indicate what the two were charged with. However, the source indicates that Sullivan and McDonald were charged with assault and battery by "patrolman Newell of the La Grange Street station." Both of these individuals were tried and found not guilty. See "Court To Rule Today on 'Birth of Nation," Boston Morning Journal, 21 April 1915, p. 12. In addition the Boston Globe reported that three black men going home after the disturbance met a group of white men in "front of 167 Shawmut Avenue" and knived four white men. See "Negroes and Whites Clash," Boston Globe, 18 April 1915, p. 1. The deposition of these arrests is unknown. In each of these instances the source mentioned is the only one which indicated that these arrests were made. The eleven arrests previously discussed were mentioned in more than one source.

[33] "Percy Hammond Denounces 'Birth of a Nation," Chicago Defender, 19 June 1915, p. 1.

[34] Ibid.

[35] Ibid.

[36] The unusual thing about the Philadelphia incident is that it was covered unevenly by the press. For example, the Philadelphia Inquirer did not cover the incident. The Philadelphia Tribune gave brief mention to the occurrence. The Philadelphia North American gave the incident extensive front page coverage. Black papers outside of Philadelphia such as the Chicago Defender and the Baltimore Afro-American Ledger also covered the incident. However, major white papers such as the New York Times did not mention the incident.

[37] "100 Cops Fight Negro Mobs in Broad Street Riot," Philadelphia North American, 21 September 1915, p. 1

[38] Ibid. See also, "Colored Women Run 'Birth of Nation' Out of Philadelphia," Chicago Defender, 25 September 1915, p. 1., and "Birth of Nation' Causes a Riot in Philadelphia," St. Louis Argus, 1 October 1915, p. 1.

[39] Ibid. See also, "Citizens Clash with Policemen," Baltimore Afro-American Ledger, 25 September 1915, p. 1.

[40] Ibid. See also, "Film Play Cause Hurt," New York Age, 23 September 1915, p. 1.

[41] Ibid.

[42] Ibid.

[43] Philip Kinsley, "Police Again Close 'Birth of Nation . . .," Chicago Tribune, 5 February 1924, p. 4.

[44] Ibid.

[45] "Crowd Grumbles As Police Halt 'Birth of Nation," Chicago Tribune, 4 February 1924, p. 1.

[46] Revised Statutes of Illinois. Chapter 38, Paragraph 456 (1923).

[47] "Two More Arrests Made over 'Birth of Nation," Chicago Tribune, 10 February 1924, Part 1, p. 6. See also, Harry E. Aitken to D. W. Griffith, Interoffice Message dated 6 February 1924, among D. W. Griffith's Personal Papers, Museum of Modern Art (MOMA) Archives, New York, New York (Hereafter referred to as MOMA Archives).

[48] "White Jury in Judge Fitch's Court Out One Hour in Film Trial," Chicago Defender, 22 March 1924, clipping in NAACP Archives, File C302.

[49] Ibid.

[50] Ibid.

[51] Ibid. Specifically, Jennings contended that The Birth violated the law because it portrayed a lynching.

[52] Ibid.

[53] Ibid.

[54] Ibid.

[55] Ibid.

[56] Ibid.

[57] Ibid.

[58] Ibid.

[59] "Cinema," Time, 30 May 1938, p. 49.

[60] "Theatre Man Arrested for Showing 'Birth of Nation,'" press release in NAACP Archives, File C302. See also, "Protest," Time, 30 May 1938, p. 49.

[61] Ibid. See also, V. F. Calverton, "Cultural Barometer," Current History, September 1938, p. 45. If convicted Rettig faced the possibility of three years in jail and a $5,000 fine. One source indicated that this was the first time the law had been invoked.

[62] "Seized on Charge 'Birth of Nation' Incites Hatred," New York World Telegram, 18 May 1937, n.p. clipping in Griffith's Personal Birth of a Nation Scrapbook, MOMA Archives.

[63] Ibid.

[64] "The Birth of a Nation' Case," Bystander, 5 May 1916, n.p., clipping in NAACP Archives, File C301.

[65] Ibid.

[66] Ibid.

[67] Ibid.

[68] "A Hand At Last . . . Movie Man Refused to Cut four Scenes As Ordered by Denver Officials and Lands In Court . . .," Chicago Defender, 25 December 1915, p. 1.

[69] Ibid.

[70] Ibid.

[71] "Negroes Oppose Film . . . Ex-Service Men Say 'Birth of Nation' Misrepresents Them," New York Times, 7 May 1921, p. 8.

[72] "War Workers Oppose 'Birth of Nation," St. Louis Argus, 20 May 1921, n.p., clipping in NAACP Archives, File C301.

[73] "Negro Pickets Found Guilty by City Court," *New York Call*, 13 May 1921, n.p., clipping in NAACP Archives File C301.

[74] "Stop the KKK Propaganda in New York," Leaflet in NAACP Archives File C301. The leaflet began with the following statement: "The Birth of a Nation exalts the infamous KKK which has been publically accused of voting to blow up or burn Negro School houses in 1921. The film distorts and falsifies history." Then the leaflet reproduced statements from four governors (Georgia, Florida, North Carolina, and South Carolina) who spoke strongly against the Klan. Then, the leaflet concluded with the following: "The best white newspapers of the South are openly opposing the revived KKK. Do you know that the KKK is not only anti-Negro but anti-Jewish and anti-Catholic. Are you going to allow KKK propaganda to be displayed in the movies in New York City?" The leaflet was one page long and was signed by the NAACP. Thus, the pamphlet dealt more with arguments against the Klan than with arguments against the film *per se*.

[75] Section 15, Article 2, Chapter 22 of the Code of Ordinances of The City of New York read: "No person shall throw, cast or distribute or cause to be thrown, cast or distributed, any handbill circular, card or other advertising matter whatsoever, in or upon any street or public place, or in a front yard or court yard or on any stoop, or in the vestibule or any hall or any building, or in a letterbox therein; provided that nothing herein contained shall be deemed to prohibit or otherwise regulate the delivery of any such matter by the postal service.

[76] "NAACP Makes Test Case of Protest Against 'Birth of Nation," *Michigan State News*, 19 May 1921, n.p., clipping in NAACP Archives, File C301.

[77] "Negro Pickets Found Guilty by City Court." See also, "Birth of Nation Pickets Freed by Higher Court."

[78] James W. Johnson to Lester A. Walton, 20 May 1921, NAACP Archives, File C301.

[79] "NAACP Makes Test Case of Protest Against 'Birth of Nation." Not all individuals interested in the protest agreed that the NAACP Tactic was correct. Lester A. Walton, a columnist for the *New York Age* indicated his disapproval of the strategy to James W. Johnson in a letter dated 25 May 1921. In part Walton stated "Personally, I do not see what good was accomplished by the demonstration you staged before the Capitol Theatre. You were playing into the hands of the enemy by giving them valuable advertising. Certainly you did not bring about the desired results: Have the picture taken off." See NAACP Archives, File C301.

[80] James W. Johnson, Statement in the form of Press Release, 7 May 1921, in NAACP Archives, File C301.

[81] Ibid.

[82] Ibid.

[83] "NAACP Makes Test Case."

[84] People of the State of New York v. Kathryn Johnson, Helen Curtis, Laura Rollock, Edward Frasier, and Llewellyn Rollock. Brief for Defendants-Appellants filed in Court of General Sessions of the Peace In and for the County of New York, p. 5, NAACP Archives, File C301.

[85] Ibid., p. 2.

[86] Ibid.

[87] Ibid., p. 6.

[88] Ibid.

[89] Ibid.

[90] Ibid., p. 21.

[91] People of the State of New York v. Kathryn Johnson, Helen Curtis, Laura Rollock, Edward Frasier and Llewellyn Rollock, Court of General Sessions of the Peace In and for the County of New York. Copy of the opinion rendered by Judge Alfred Tally, 31 November 1921, p. 2, NAACP Archives, File C301.

[92] Ibid.

[93] Ibid.

[94] Ibid., p. 3.

[95] Carle Whitehead to American Civil Liberties Union, 10 April 1939, Microform Collection, University of Wisconsin Historical Society, Madison, Wisconsin, American Civil Liberties Archives, Volume 2157 (Hereafter referred to as ACLU Archives).

[96] Ibid.

[97] "Riotous Film Costs Exhibitor $1,400 Fine," 20 May 1939, n.t., n.p., clipping in ACLU Archives, Vol. 2157.

[98] Carle Whitehead to American Civil Liberties Union.

[99] Jerome M. Britchey to Carle Whitehead, 25 April 1939, ACLU Archives, Vol. 2157.

[100] "Riotous Film Costs Exhibitor $1,400."

[101] Ibid.

[102] Ibid.

[103] "Birth of a Nation," *New York Times*, 20 April 1939, p. 1. See also, "Jail for Film Showing," *Variety*, 30 April 1939, n.p., clipping in Lincoln Center Archives, New York, New York, *Birth of a Nation* File, and "Birth of Nation' Banned in Denver," *New York Herald*, 20 April 1939, n.p., clipping in Griffith's *Birth of a Nation* Scrapbook, MOMA Archives. Allan was fined in total $1,400—$200 for the first screening of the film and $1,200 for four additional showings of the film. He was sentenced to 120 days in jail—30 days for the first offense and 90 days for the subsequent offenses.

[104] Carle Whitehead to Jerome Britchey, 28 April 1939, ACLU Archives, Vol. 2157. See also, "Birth of Nation' Ban in Denver Appealed," Press release, n.d., in ACLU Archives, Vol. 2157.

[105] Untitled Press Release, n.d., ACLU Archives, Vol. 2157.

[106] William Pickens to Roger Baldwin, 4 May 1939, ACLU Archives, Vol. 2157.

[107] Roger Baldwin to William Pickens, 5 May 1939, ACLU Archives, Vol. 2157.

[108] Ibid.

[109] W. F. Turner to Thurgood Marshall, 4 October 1939, NAACP Archives, File C302.

[110] Ibid.

[111] Jerome Britchey to Carle Whitehead, 1 November 1939, ACLU Archives, Vol. 2157.

[112] Alexander Lindey to Jerome Britchey, 30 October 1939, ACLU Archives, Vol. 2157.

[113] Ibid.

[114] Ibid.

[115] Ibid.

[116] Carle Whitehead to Jerome Britchey, 6 November 1939, ACLU Archives, Vol. 2157.

[117] Ibid.

[118] Ibid.

[119] Ibid.

[120] Ibid.

[121] *Denver v. Robert Allan*, copy of opinion by C. E. Kettering, 1 February 1940, ACLU Archives, Vol. 2157.

[122] Carle Whitehead to Jerome Britchey, 17 February 1940, ACLU Archives, Vol. 2157.

[123] Carle Whitehead to Jerome Britchey, 27 February 1940, ACLU Archives, Vol. 2157.

[124] Ibid.

[125] "$200 Fine for 'Birth,'" *Variety*, 6 March 1940, p. 4. See also, "Denverite Is Fined $200 For Showing 'Birth of A Nation," *Denver Post*, 28 February 1940, clipping, NAACP Archives, File C302.

[126] Ibid.

CHAPTER V

ADMINISTRATIVE ACTIONS IN THE BIRTH
CENSORSHIP CONTROVERSIES

The court room was not the only arena in which The Birth of a Nation censorship controversies were fought. Throughout the years of this study, the offices and meeting places of state, local and national officials were more prominent than court rooms as the scenes of debates between the film's supporters and opponents. The actual involvement of elected or appointed authorities in The Birth censorship controversies took one of two major forms: administrative power to affirm or deny the film's right to the screen or legislative authority to establish censorship laws against which the film could be judged. This chapter examines the implementation of administrative power in The Birth censorship controversies during the time period 1915-1973. Legislative actions are discussed in Chapter VI. After a discussion of the tactic in general, the involvement of authorities at the municipal level is presented. Actions of state officials regarding the film follow.

Overview

Requesting that local, state, or national authorities use the power of their offices to resolve The Birth of a Nation censorship controversies was a tactic employed primarily by individuals who opposed the film. For example, as early as April 1915, NAACP's national office advocated appeals to local, state, and national officials as a primary tactic against the film. In a memorandum to all its branches and local chapters urging a campaign against The Birth, NAACP national advised:

> The play can probably only be stopped by executive order of the Mayor whom you may be able to interest by united appeals from colored and white civic and welfare organizations, secret societies, women's clubs, etc. We urge you to be watchful and to leave no stone unturned in an effort to suppress this picture.

NAACP national also outlined the implementation of this tactic. First, the film's opponents were "to have an able lawyer, preferably a white man upon whom you can depend absolutely" examine existing local ordinances to determine if one could be applied against the film.[2] If an ordinance existed, the next step was to urge local organizations, black and white, to protest against the film to local authorities like censorship boards, police commissioners, and mayors.[3] If no ordinance existed, the film's opponents were told to seek such legislation.[4] If these alternatives failed, individuals opposing The Birth were advised "to try to have the worst scenes eliminated . . . ."[5] According to NAACP national, the "most objectionable scenes" were those depicting Gus' pursuit of Flora and those "showing the Negro politician trying to force marriage on the daughter of his white benefactor."[6]

Through summer 1915, NAACP national continued to suggest this course of action would be the most efficient. However, by September 1915, the organization's attitude toward stopping the film by

any tactic grew pessimistic. Concerning its earlier policy that
the best remedy was to secure a local executive order banning the
film, NAACP national noted:

> It will do no good to have the Mayor forbid the production because Griffith will do exactly what he had done elsewhere, that is secure an injunction against the mayor and exhibit his picture. He has done this in several cities.[7]

Nevertheless, administrative action remained popular with the
film's opponents and they continued to petition authorities for
relief from what they perceived the film's evils. The administrative involvement of municipal authorities in censorship are
discussed first.

Municipal Censorship

During the time period studied, 84 municipal authorities
were asked to censor The Birth. Forty-one of these requests resulted in the resolution of the controversy by the municipal official
petitioned.[8] More than any other category of municipal official,
mayors were asked to censor the film. The actions of 21 mayors resolved the controversies. Twenty-nine mayors were involved in censorship controversies, but the controversies were resolved by other
means. In two cases, mayors acted with other city officials to determine the film's right to the screen locally. Municipal film censorship boards resolved the debates in at least nine cases. One
other municipal film censorship board was involved in a controversy,
but did not resolve it. Of the twelve city councils involved in

censorship controversies, four made the ultimate decision concerning whether the film was screened in their cities. The remaining eight city councils asked to order censorship of The Birth did not resolve the controversies. Three boards of police commissioners acting as municipal censors resolved censorship controversies. One board of police commissioners, acting as municipal censor, could not resolve the controversy in its city. Of the remaining six municipal controversies, three were resolved by other municipal officials and three were not resolved by the petitioned officials. The actions of each category of municipal official are discusses separately.

Mayoral Decisions

In 21 censorship controversies between 1915 and 1973, the ultimate decision of the film's right to the screen was made by a mayor exercising the executive power of his office. In 13 of these instances, mayors exercised prior restraint against the film; in three instances mayors ordered total subsequent restraint of the film; in one instance a mayor ordered partial subsequent restraint of the film. Four mayors resolved censorship controversies in favor of the film.

Mayoral decisions for censorship

Seventeen mayors resolved The Birth censorship controversies by supporting either total or partial suppression of the film. The mayors employed a variety of arguments to justify their actions against the film.

During the time period studied, 12 mayors ordered the film censored arguing that the film would incite racial prejudice. Mayor R. Roth of Cedar Rapids, Iowa, apparently was the first mayor to justify censorship of *The Birth* on these grounds.[9] Roth's order banning the film came May 21, 1915, in response to a protest by a delegation of five blacks led by Mrs. Fred H. Gresham.[10] Roth said: "There shall be no picture shown in this city as long as I am mayor that will in any way cause race prejudice or bad feeling between the races."[11] A similar rationale for censorship was expressed by Minneapolis Mayor George Leach when he banned *The Birth* from that city in August 1921.[12] Leach refused to allow the film and said he was "opposed to any exhibition which has a tendency to incite race prejudice."[13] Likewise, Mayor O. Stacy of Springfield, Massachusetts, announced in June 1915, that "The Birth of a Nation and similar plays designed to forment prejudice against the negro will not be allowed to be shown."[14] Thus, three mayors banned *The Birth* from their respective communities before the film opened locally because they felt the film could engender racial prejudice.

Although they did not order the film suppressed, three other mayors resolved censorship controversies by requesting that the film not be shown in their communities because they feared the film would engender racial prejudice. For example, Mayor R. Spellacy of Hartford, Connecticut, requested the State Theatre cancel the film because in his opinion the film presented blacks in an unfavorable light particularly in "that one scene shows a Negro chasing a white woman causing her to leap from the side of a cliff."[15] Sources indicated that this was the first time any film had not been shown in Hartford for any reason other than obscenity.[16] Spellacy's position was criticized by several Hartford alderpeople and the American Civil Liberties Union (ACLU). The ACLU telegraphed Spellacy to state that Spellacy's request exceeded his legal authority and set a dangerous censorship precedent.[17] Spellacy apparently did not respond to the ACLU protest, and the theatre cancelled its scheduled run of The Birth because "it did not wish to court trouble."[18]

The Alhambra Theatre in Richmond, Virginia, also cancelled a scheduled 1918 revival of The Birth after Richmond Mayor M. Evans requested the film not be shown.[19] Evans asked the theatre not to show the film after a number of "Richmond's prominent citizens" expressed opposition to the film.[20] The protesters requested that The Birth be banned because it would stir up race feeling and "was otherwise objectionable being a reproduction of the Ku Klux days following the Civil War and in which the intermarriage between negro and white is portrayed."[21] Anna Belle Ward, Alhambra manager, responded that because "it is the policy of the management. . .not to oppose public opinion in the matter of pictures presented," the film had been cancelled.[22]

Mayor Edwin O. Childs, Newton, Massachusetts, also asked the local theatre which had scheduled The Birth in 1924 to cancel the film because of a "unanimous" protest from Newton's black community.[23] In a letter to the theatre management Childs stated:

> As long as our colored citizens feel as they do, it seems to me most unwise to stir up ill feeling at this time. . .There are forces at work in this country and in this city trying to emphasise (sic) racial and sectarian differences and separate bretheren who ought to dwell together in unity. I, therefore, request that the feelings of our colored citizens who are good citizens and who are striving for the best interests of our city and for the colored race be respected, and that The Birth of a Nation be not exhibited.[24]

Thus, reasoning *The Birth of a Nation* would engender racial prejudice in their communities, six mayors exercised prior restraint against the film.

Two mayors resolved *The Birth* controversies by ordering the film withdrawn because of its portrayal of blacks. For example, the film was withdrawn from a Detroit, Michigan, theatre after a two-day run in 1931 when Detroit Mayor Frank Murphy threatened to revoke the theatre's license if it continued the film.[25] In this instance, Murphy indicated the film should be stopped because "of its unfair presentation of the Negro and its tendency to arouse race hatred."[26] Likewise, Mayor Harry A. Mackey, Philadelphia, Pennsylvania, ordered *The Birth* discontinued in 1931 because the film was "prejudicial to the peace between the races."[27]

The specific reasoning underlying the decisions of seven mayors who exercised total prior restraint against the film are not recorded in the sources consulted.[28] However, because these mayors prohibited the film after protests from local black organizations, it appears likely that the decisions were based, at least in part, upon the idea that the film engendered racial prejudice.

For example, the mayor of Hartford, Connecticut, in 1925 ordered two theatres which had booked *The Birth* to show other films because The Birth could "not be permitted in the city."[29] The NAACP reported that the mayor's action came after he heard "the united protest" of the city's black population.[30] Likewise, Cleveland, Ohio, Mayor Harry L. Davis ordered a print of The Birth seized after the film was denied certification by the state's division of film censorship and the Ohio Supreme Court refused the film distributor a hearing on behalf of the film.[31] Although Davis' rationale for ordering the film seized is not recorded, this was the second time he banned the film. Davis first prohibited the film in April 1917, but that ban was overruled by the Cuyahoga County Common Pleas Court (See Chapter III).[32] Davis' original action against the film was based upon the argument that the film might create a breach of peace and that the film unfairly represented blacks.[33] However, whether this was also the rationale underlying Davis' 1925 ban is unknown.

Charles G. Phillips and Richard L. Metcalfe, mayors of Montclair, New Jersey, and Omaha, Nebraska, respectively, prohibited exhibitions of The Birth in separate decisions in 1931.[34] Metcalfe banned the film in March 1931 "upon the request of the Omaha branch of the NAACP."[35] Phillips ordered the Bellevue Theatre to cancel the scheduled screening of the film after a delegation of that city's blacks presented him a written protest, charging the film fostered racial prejudice.[36]

In a similar move, Mayor James Burns, Glen Cove, New York, requested that the manager of the theatre scheduled to show the film in his city cancel the film in 1931.[37] Burns issued his request after several black citizens representing the NAACP expressed their belief that The Birth should be prohibited because of "the race hatred and prejudice which the film aroused."[38] Burns responded that if the theatre would not voluntarily withdraw the film, he would "compel its withdrawal."[39] After a conference with the mayor, the theatre management agreed to withdraw the film.[40]

In another instance of a mayor supportive of total suppression of the film, Louisville, Kentucky, Mayor George W. Smith stopped a 1918 production of The Birth in his city.[41] Smith's action against the film came after a committee representing the NAACP argued that the film was a "prejudice breeder" and that it was an "insult" to Louisville's black citizens at a time when "the Race had done its share in war work and in fighting."[42] Smith assured the protesters that he would "do the wisest thing" and banned the film.[43] Likewise, the mayor of Gary, Indiana, in July 1915, banned the film after meeting with an NAACP delegation led by Judge William Dunn.[44]

One mayor banned The Birth on the grounds that "it is not fit for a decent people to look at."[45] Whether this Newark, New Jersey, mayor in 1915, believed the film was indecent because of its unfavorable portraits of blacks or for some other reason is unclear.

In one censorship controversy, a mayor ordered several scenes cut from the film and so eventually resolved the controversy. This subsequent partial restraint occurred after the NAACP petitioned New York Mayor John Mitchell to cancel the film's original New York engagement in March 1915.[46] In a letter to Mitchell, the NAACP requested that he use the power of his office to suppress the film because it represented "an offense against public decency" and endangered public morals.[47]

> We object to the film as an undisguised and unjust appeal to race prejudice and as an attempt to arouse the feeling of sectionalism and the war spirit. From a historical point of view it does not tell the whole truth and sometimes misrepresents what it tells.[48]

Immediately, Mitchell received letters from individuals supporting the NAACP's position.[49] Typical of these letters is one from Mrs. N. J. Floyd dated March 29, 1915.[50] In her letter, Floyd asked Mitchell to "use your influence" to stop the film because it was "misleading to the public to a great extent, in that it lowers the moral standard of the colored people, falsely portrays them, and also increases the deep prejudice toward them which now exists."[51]

After receiving a number of such protests, Mitchell agreed to hold a public hearing concerning the film. The hearing took place April 1, 1915. D. W. Griffith and Thomas Dixon testified in support of the film.[52] Dr. Frederick Howe, chairperson National Board of Censorship, Dr. William Brooks, pastor St. Marks ME Church, Lillian D. Wald, head of the Henry Street Settlement, Dr. W.E.B. DuBoise, editor *The Crisis*, Dr. Stephen S. Wise, rabbi of the Free Synagogue, Fred Moore, editor *New York Age*, and George Wibeoan, president Brooklyn Citizen's Club, testified against the film.[53]

During the hearing, Mitchell requested the modification of two scenes in the film:

> My personal feeling is that those scenes should be modified. Whatever your personal views on the larger questions may be, Negro citizens of this city have certain rights which ought to be observed whatever your view or mine might be on these questions and it does seem to me that the production of

parts of the play infringe on what I might call their moral
rights if not their legal rights.[54]

According to Mitchell, the "parts of the play" he objected to included a scene in which "a motherly elderly woman (white) repulses a Negro child" and parts of the Gus pursuit of Flora sequence.[55] Griffith agreed to modify the scenes and the film's run at the Liberty Theatre continued.[56]

NAACP representatives viewed the revised film and found that all the scenes they originally objected to were still in the film. The NAACP wrote Mitchell:

> . . .the two objectionable scenes in the second part have not been cut. . .certain slight changes have been made but the scene showing the colored man, Gus, pursuing the white girl and the scene showing the mulatto politician's attempting to marry the white girl. . .still form the motif of the second part.
>
> These are the scenes you promised the delegation to which you granted a hearing on Tuesday should be eliminated. . . They are the ones which are a libel on the Negro and which would likely lead to a breach of the peace. Should the film be shown in the South it would undoubtedly cause race riots . . . .Its fate in New York will determine the form in which it is to be produced all over the United States and the matter is entirely in your hands. We urge you to use your authority to compel the owner and producer Aitken and Griffith to eliminate these objectionable scenes.[57]

Mitchell assured the NAACP the scenes would be cut.[58]

The NAACP continued to monitor the film[59] and express displeasure with Mitchell's position and the edited version.[60] Mary Childs Nerney, NAACP national secretary, explained the situation to George Packard, Chicago opponent of The Birth:

> I am utterly disgusted with the situation in regard to The Birth of a Nation. . .In spite of the promise of the Mayor to cut out the two objectionable scenes in the second part, which show a white girl committing suicide to escape from

a Negro pursuer, and a mulatto politician trying to force
marriage upon the daughter of his white benefactor, these
two scenes still form the motif of the second part. All
the cut outs that have been made are vulgar but really un-
important incidents. . .I have seen the thing four times
and am positive that nothing more will be done about it.[61]

Nerney's prediction that "nothing more will be done about it" proved correct. Mitchell did not alter his position and the edited film continued at the theatre breaking all New York attendance and length-of-run records.[62] The NAACP acquiesced to Mitchell's position and directed its protests against the film elsewhere.

Thus, during the time period studied, 17 mayors resolved The Birth of a Nation censorship controversies by supporting total or partial censorship of the film. Half of the mayors censored the film specifically because they said it would engender racial prejudice in their communities. Seven other mayors censored the film after receiving protests from black organizations locally. One mayor banned the film because it was "unfit for decent people." One mayor ordered subsequent partial restraint of scenes he said violated the moral rights of blacks.

Mayoral decisions rejecting censorship

During the time period studied, at least four mayors refused to censor the film. Three of these decisions were made in 1915. The other mayoral decision rejecting censorship was in 1924.

The first mayor who refused to stop the film was Oakland, California, Mayor Frank K. Mott in May 1915.[63] In a letter to the NAACP's Northern California Branch which asked Mott to ban the film, Mott replied that he attended a San Francisco screening of the picture and concluded:

> I gave my best thought to its effect, not only upon myself, but upon the large audience present, and I must say to you that there was not the slightest indication of race hatred or mob violence, or anything likely to lead to such results manifested by the audience. The applause was mainly directed to pictures of the signing of the emancipation proclamation, the surrender of General Lee, and the allegorical picture of universal peace at the close.
>
> In my judgment, there would be much more notoriety given the play were I to suppress it, for the managers would then return it to San Francisco and advertise it to the limit on this side of the bay as the picture that had been suppressed here. It would therefore get a thousand times more publicity than if permitted to run its course.
>
> My judgment is that the play should not be withdrawn for the principal reasons here set forth.

Mott rejected the argument that the film might engender race hatred or mob violence. Mott like Judge U. Jackson who enjoined Los Angeles officials from stopping the film earlier in 1915 (See Chapter III) indicated he believed those opposed to the film should ignore it and let the film run its natural course.[65] Mott said constant agitation would only bring more attention to the film, arouse people's interest and defeat the purpose the NAACP wished to achieve.[66]

The reasons the other three mayors refused to censor the film are unclear. For example, Louisville, Kentucky, Major T. Buschmeyer refused to stop The Birth in 1915. According to the NAACP, Buschmeyer refused to stop the film "despite strong protest from local colored and white citizens and strong pressure from the NAACP officials such as Hon. Morefield Storey, Dr. Joel Spingard and others."[67] However, exactly why Buschmeyer refused to move against the film is not recorded in the sources consulted.[68]

Likewise, the NAACP reported that Baxter Springs, Kansas, Mayor L. S. Brewster refused to stop the film when it came to his city in October 1924, for a two-day run.[69] The NAACP stated in a news release Brewster promised the organization he would prohibit the film, but "despite the Mayor's assurance to the contrary" The Birth was screened.[70] The NAACP speculated that Brewster's reversal came because he was "intimidated by the Klan."[71] Whether this was the case is not verified in the sources consulted.[72]

Another mayor who apparently reversed his position concerning censorship of The Birth was Minneapolis, Minnesota, Mayor Wallace G. Nye in 1915.[73] Nye originally notified Shubert Theatre management he would revoke the theatre's license if the film were shown.[74] According to Shubert manager, A. G. Bainbridge, Nye refused to permit The Birth "upon the ground it was likely to incite race riots."[75] Bainbridge received a court order permitting the exhibition of the film (See Chapter III).[76] On appeal, the right of the mayor to censor the film was upheld of Hennepin County District Court Judge John Steele.[77] Steele's decision was affirmed by the Minnesota Supreme Court.[78] Thus, Nye's right to stop The Birth if he desired, was established. However, after the Supreme Court ruling, Nye reversed himself and allowed the film to be screened.[79] Exactly why is unclear. One source indicated after Nye's right to stop the film was affirmed, he left the actual decision concerning censorship to his advisory committee "who saw no harm in the play."[80] However, the exact character of this committee is not described. One source accused Nye of using "his Negro FRIENDS and 'The Birth of a Nation' as a means to an end by securing a legal decision as to his power to revoke licenses" and implied Nye used the controversy only to establish officially his right to censor.[81] Although the reasoning underlying Nye's decision is not specifically recorded by the sources consulted, his decision ultimately resolved this controversy.

In these differing ways, four mayors resolved *The Birth of a Nation* censorship controversies by refusing to stop the film. Only one of the four appears to have gone on public record explaining the rationale for his actions. In that instance, the mayor specifically rejected the argument that the film would engender race hatred.

Mayoral decisions with others

During the time period studied, at least two controversies were resolved by decisions made by mayors acting with at least one other public official.[82] In both cases the film was banned after the officials heard protests from representatives of black civic groups.

The Birth was banned from Lynn, Massachusetts, in April 1918, when the city's mayor and Board of Common Council revoked the license needed for the film's screening.[83] The mayor and council acted after a protest organized by the local Equal Rights League. The decision exercised prior restraint against the film.

Likewise, the permit needed to exhibit *The Birth* in New Britain, Connecticut, was cancelled in August 1924, by that city's Mayor A. M. Paonesa and its Chief of Police William Hart.[84] Paonesa conferred with Hart, and after Hart investigated, ordered the film withdrawn. The NAACP praised the action in a letter to Hart:

> If only other public officials were as prompt as you and the Mayor of New Britain in stopping such demonstrations, it is undoubtedly true that the Klan would not have been able to have capitalized as it has the most vicious racial and religious prejudices of America.[86]

Mayoral involvements resolved by other means

At least 29 additional mayors were asked to resolve The Birth censorship controversies during the time period 1915-1973, but these mayors did not do so. For example, ten of these controversies were resolved by court action. One was resolved by a state censorship board. In one case the film's opponents acquiesced after a drawn out battle. One mayor supported partial censorship of the film, but the individuals opposing the film continued to press for total suppression. Four mayors did not actually resolve the controversies, but facilitated resolution. Although apparently powerless to act against the film themselves, three mayors joined protesters by going on public record against the film. The roles played by the remaining five mayors are unclear. Because each of these controversies is discussed in more detail in other parts of the research, each is dealt with only briefly here.

Courts overruling or upholding mayoral decisions

As discussed in detail in Chapter III, nine courts resolved The Birth controversies by enjoining mayors from interfering with the film's screening. One court resolved a censorship controversy by upholding the right of the mayor to stop the film. Two courts negated mayoral ordered censorship, but the rulings did not resolve the controversies.

In four cases courts resolved controversies in which mayors ordered the film censored by either upholding or overruling the mayors' actions on procedural grounds. In two of these instances courts ruled that after a film had been approved by a state consorship board, local authorities could not interfere. The first opinion of this nature was rendered in Pittsburgh, Pennsylvania, in August, 1915, by Judge Ambrose Reid, Court of Common Pleas of Allegheny County. In his opinion, Reid said the legislature vested the power of film censorship in a state board of censors and that unless it could be shown that this board had not done its duty, "it would not be prudent for a court to interfere."[88] Reid's decision negated censorship of The Birth ordered by Pittsburgh Mayor Joseph G. Armstrong. Armstrong notified the Nixon Theatre which has scheduled The Birth that he would not allow that theatre or "any other in the city of Pittsburgh" to show the film.[89] Armstrong's action came after he heard a number of protests from Pittsburgh's black citizens who "had complained that the play tended to incite race hatred."[90]

The Common Pleas Court of Cuyahoga County Ohio was the second court to rule that after a film was approved by a state board of censorship that local authorities could not stop it.[91] In this instance, Cleveland Mayor Harry L. Davis wrote the theatre manager in 1917 that the film could not be shown.[92] In the letter, Davis indicated he was acting as chief conservator of the peace within the city and was prohibiting the film because he believed it would probably result in a serious breach of peace.[93] Epoch, the film's distributor, wanted Davis enjoined from interfering with the film's showing in Cleveland.[94] Expressing reasoning similar to the 1915 Pennsylvania opinion, the court ruled that local authorities could not stop the local performance of a moving picture "except by application to that board for a review of its action, or by bringing suit in the Supreme Court to have the order amended, vacated or set aside."[95]

The remaining judge to enjoin a mayor from interfering with the film's showing on procedural grounds was Detroit Judge John Goff in 1921.[96] In this case, Detroit's mayor instructed the city's police commissioner to notify the theatre management that The Birth would not be permitted because it would "almost certainly lead to serious public disturbances."[97] In his decision, Goff ruled that because the Detroit censorship statute stated films could only be censored when shown to be "immoral and indecent," the mayor acted beyond his authority.[98]

One court upheld the right of a mayor to censor The Birth under a state statute which forbade the presentation of any film likely to incite racial prejudice.[99] In this instance Charleston, West Virginia, Mayor W. W. Wertz banned the film in 1925 under a 1919 statute making it unlawful to "advertise, exhibit, display, or show" any film which engendered racial prejudice.[100] However, as discussed in Chapter III, the theatre scheduled to show the film sought and received an injunction against Wertz' interference and began showing the film.[101] The controversy was resolved when Wertz' power to censor was upheld on appeal and the film was withdrawn after it had been screened twice.[102] After Wertz won the court battle, the NAACP reported he rushed "to the manager of the Rialto" theatre and said of The Birth "it is the worst thing I ever saw and I cannot understand why any law-abiding citizen should bring such a picture to Charleston. . .It will not be shown so long as I am mayor. . ."[103]

One mayor was enjoined from restraining The Birth because a judge refused to accept his argument that the film might engender racial animosity against blacks.[104] As discussed in Chapter III, Judge William Fennimore Cooper, Illinois Cook County Superior Court, issued an injunction in June 1915, restraining Chicago Mayor William Thompson and other city officials from interfering with The Birth's showing by ruling that films could not be censored because they presented members of one race or nationality in an unfavorable light.[105] However, Thompson did stipulate that the theatre could not admit anyone under 18 to the film.[106]

In five cases, judges enjoined mayors from interfering with The Birth's showing but the judges' rationales for action are unclear. Mayors were enjoined from stopping the film in Oakland, California,[107] Charleston, West Virginia,[108] Atlantic City, New Jersey,[109] Gary, Indiana,[110] and Minneapolis, Minnesota.[111]

The censorship orders of two other mayors were negated by court rulings. However, the controversies in each case were not resolved by the court decisions.

In one of these instances, Chicago Mayor William E. Dever instructed Police Chief Morgan Collins to inform Epoch, the film's distributor, the film would not be allowed in 1924.[112] Dever's censorship order came after he met with individuals opposing the film because of its racial portrayal. Dever indicated he had the authority to stop the film under the Jackson law which banned from Illinois any film which either degraded any class of citizens or race or which might lead to a breach of peace or riots.[113] However, Epoch secured an injunction against Dever's interference.[114] After a rather complicated hearing the case was adjourned indefinitely. The film continued at the theatre and the film's opponents apparently did not press the issue. (See Chapter III.)

Similarly, the mayor of Topeka, Kansas, in 1931 instructed the city's police chief to notify the management of the theatre which scheduled the film that it could not be shown.[115] The theatre managers sought and received an injunction restraining Topeka authorities from interfering with the film. Topeka officials countered by filing a petition for injunction against the theatre management.[116] In this instance the judge ruled in favor of the theatre management on procedural grounds.[117] The city appealed to a different court and before the case was adjudicated, the Kansas state board of censorship recalled The Birth and resolved the controversy.

Mayoral support of partial censorship but controversy otherwise resolved

During the time period studied, one mayor recommended that several scenes be cut from The Birth, but this decision did not resolve the controversy because the film's opponents continued to press for total suppression. Boston Mayor James M. Curley in April, 1915, made the decision.[118] Curley's decision was the first in a rather complex 1915 controversy ultimately resolved by a local censorship board created by the state legislature specifically for that purpose. This facet of the controversy is discussed in more detail later.

When The Birth was announced for a 1915 Boston run, Curley did not object.[119] However, the film's opponents asked Curley to hold a public hearing.[120] Several hundred people attended. One participant wrote:

> While the Mayor was ready to hear all we had to say against the film he seemed prejudiced against us from the start. I tried to bring out the effect produced upon the audience by seeing the Negro always with a sensuous look upon his face, but the Mayor seemed quite sure that there was not harm in suggestion as long as the girl kept her shoes on and the Mulatto did nothing desperate, it was only my imagination that made the thing bad.[121]

Another source indicated those leading the protest "pleaded with the mayor insisting that he order the play stopped on the grounds that it was an unjust slur on the colored race. . .they pleaded in vain."[122] Curley concluded the hearing by saying he would have his censors view the film before deciding.[123] After the hearing, Curley commented:

> I do not want to make political (sic) out of it (the film), and I do not want to hurt a legitimate firm doing business. You people seem to want everything pertaining to the Negro cut out of this picture. Are there not good Negroes and bad? Are there not bad whites as well as good?. . .You must remember that history cannot be denied. The Photo-play will be produced. I will have the official censor of the municipality there and I will notify the police commissioner of the city of Boston to have his censor present. If this film violates

233

the law it will be stopped. I shall not take any hand in the matter. You have introduced no evidence that I could use in stopping at least one performance.[124]

After the censors viewed the film, Curley recommended one title from the first reel, scenes of the South Carolina legislature, the entire pursuit of Flora by Gus, and several shots of leering blacks be modified.[125] Apparently, Griffith agreed to the cuts and the film opened to a sold-out house.

Several days later, 25 blacks, including Boston Gazette editor William Monroe Trotter, met with Curley and requested that the film be stopped because the modifications had not been made.[126] Curley said he would "see that the eliminations he had ordered were made" but he could not stop the film under the existing statute.[127] Curley later notified Trotter that ". . .the eliminations originally requested by me have been attended to" and that there was "no way legally" he could do anything more against the film.[128] Because the Boston censorship statute empowered the mayor to stop only those sequences he and the police commissioner considered "obscene or immoral or tended to injure the morals of the community" and because Curley insisted that he had done all he legally could against the film, it appears that Curley ordered the cuts because he considered those sections of the film immoral or obscene.[129] Curley's actions did not silence protesters who continued their fight to stop the film by petitioning Massachusetts Governor David Walsh.[130] Walsh's response is discussed later.

Mayors without censorship authority

Four mayors indicated that they had no authority to stop The Birth. In each instance, the individuals opposing the film carried out their protests further.

The first mayor to indicate he had no authority to move against The Birth was a Los Angeles mayor in February 1915.[131] In response to a protest from the local NAACP the mayor said he was "without authority" to stop the film because the local film censorship board "had exclusive jurisdiction" in the matter.[132] The individuals opposing the film then filed their protests with the Los Angeles city council. This action is discussed later.

Likewise, Mayor George A. Badings, Milwaukee, Wisconsin, indicated in 1915 that he could not interfere with the film's production. Bading's comment responded to a protest against the film organized by a NAACP branch.[133] Bading said the power of film censorship had been vested solely in the local board of censors and he had no authority to intervene. The protesters then took their objections to the censorship board and its response is discussed later.[134]

Two other mayors indicated they had no authority to censor the film. One was St. Louis, Missouri, Mayor Keil who heard a protest against the film in 1915 from representatives of various local black organizations.[135] This controversy was eventually decided in the courts. (See Chapter III.) The other mayor who indicated he had no authority to censor The Birth was New York Mayor Haley in

May 1921.[136] In that case the film was screened despite the protests.[137]

Mayors facilitating resolution

Although four mayors did not specifically resolve the controversies in which they were involved, they facilitated ultimate resolution by exercising the power of their offices. For example, the film was barred by the Lynn, Massachusetts, Municipal Censorship Committee in 1922 after Lynn's mayor notified the Committee that he had received a protest from the local "colored clergymen."[138] Similarly, Philadelphia Director of Public Safety, George D. Porter, banned The Birth from that city in September 1915 after a public hearing concerning the film called by Philadelphia's mayor and held in his office.[139] However, as discussed in Chapter III, Porter was enjoined from interfering with the film's screening.[140]

The Birth was withdrawn from Los Angeles in June 1921. Although conflicting accounts of the controversy's resolution exist in the sources consulted, the city's mayor apparently facilitated resolution of this controversy. One source indicated the film's distributor voluntarily withdrew The Birth after hearing arguments against the film at a meeting called by the mayor.[141] Another source indicated the film was banned after the mayor consulted with the city prosecutor and the prosecutor ordered the police chief to stop the film.[142] In any case, the film was removed after a two week run and the mayor was somehow involved in controversy resolution.

In the final case of this nature, a mayor facilitated partial censorship of the film. In this instance the NAACP reported that Roselle, New Jersey, city officials ordered "race prejudice inciting parts" of the film deleted in November 1931.[143] A report to the NAACP stated "the mayor was terribly upset and sorry about the showing of the picture and did all he could to stop it."[144]

Mayors who joined protests

Although apparently powerless to act against the film, at least three mayors voiced their displeasure with its screening by notifying the appropriate censorship agencies that they disapproved of the film. For example, Syracuse, New York, Mayor John H. Walrath indicated his concern about The Birth's 1923 revival in a letter to the New York Motion Picture Commission.[145] The Commission responded to Walrath's letter by indicating it had approved the film with certain eliminations and could see "no legal objection to the film's being shown" in Walrath's city.[146] The Commission added it had been advised the film "never has incited riots."[147]

Lincoln, Nebraska, Mayor J. E. Miller said he opposed the film in an affidavit against The Birth in 1918.[148] The affidavit was filed with Lincoln's Attorney General, Willis Reed, who submitted it to a local court to support his petition requesting a restraining order against the film. In the affidavit Miller said the "highest class colored people" in the city had protested The Birth's screening to him and in his opinion the film "had a tendency to cause friction and stirred up criticism against Negroes."[149] Miller also said he was convinced the film should not be shown in Lincoln because it would be an insult to the black service men fighting in World War I.[150] As discussed in Chapter III, the controversy was resolved by a court.

Likewise, Columbus, Ohio, Mayor George J. Karb signed a petition protesting the film's exhibition in 1915.[151] The petition was filed with the Ohio State Censorship Board which later refused to approve the film. As discussed in Chapter III, Epoch challenged the agency's ruling to the Ohio Supreme Court. The court resolved the controversy by refusing to hear the case and upheld the censorship decision.

Mayors with undefined roles

During the time period studied at least five additional mayors were asked to resolve The Birth of a Nation censorship controversies, but the actual role in controversy resolution played by each mayor is unclear. In three of these cases mayors said they would view the film and censor it if they found objectionable content. However, whether the mayors actually viewed the film with an eye toward censorship is unclear.

Mayor U. Clarence of Hetrick, New Jersey, was the first mayor so involved. Hetrick issued the Savoy Theatre a permit to show the film in 1915, but promised those individuals opposed to the film that he would view it before it was screened to the public.[152] Clarence told the delegation protesting the film that "if he finds things as represented, he will stop further production of the film here."[153] However, whether Clarence stopped the film is not recorded in the sources consulted.

Later in 1915, Mayor A. Smith, Sioux City, Iowa, told a delegation protesting the film that he favored elimination of certain sequences.[154] However, whether Smith ordered scenes cut and if so, which scenes, is not indicated in the sources.

About one month after Smith said he favored partial censorship, Duluth, Minnesota, Mayor U. Prince received a protest from a local black citizen's committee concerning the film's scheduled showing.[155] The mayor, along with city commissioner Silberstein, met the protesters. After the meeting Silberstein assured the film's opponents that the manager of the theatre would be "glad to eliminate" the features of The Birth they opposed.[156] Whether the manager was as glad to make the cuts as Silberstein anticipated is not recorded. Also, the mayor's position on censorship is unclear.

The two other mayors whose roles in controversy resolution remain unclear did receive protests concerning the film, but the sources consulted did not indicate the mayors' responses. For example, San Francisco, California, Mayor James Rolph received a protest from a group of that city's black citizens.[157] Rolph's response is unclear, but the controversy was eventually resolved by the city's censorship board as discussed later. Also, New York Mayor O'Deyer was asked to ban The Birth in 1950 by the NAACP.[158] In a telegram to O'Deyer the NAACP called the film "totally out of step with world-wide opinion of 1950" and reminded O'Deyer that the film had previously been banned "throughout the United States" as an open incitement to violence.[159] O'Deyer's response to the telegram is not known, but the film continued at the theatre.[160]

Police Censors

Rather than designating the mayor as official local censor, several cities during the time period studied vested the power of municipal censorship in a police commission or board. At least three such boards handled complaints concerning The Birth between the years 1915-1973.

In August 1915, the Baltimore, Maryland, police board apparently became the first such censorship agency to take such action by refusing to stop The Birth.[161] The refusal came after a complaint against the film was lodged by a delegation led by Julius C. Johnson, president of the Baltimore NAACP branch.[162] Johnson said the film was likely to cause racial friction and should be censored because it was unfair to blacks and historically inaccurate.[163] Police Board president Daniel C. Ammidon said that the police board had the right to exclude films it considered vulgar or indecent.[164] Ammidon also "asserted that the protests of colored people would give the play unnecessary advertisement" and advised the delegation to abandon its protest.[165] The police board took the protest under advisement, but did not move against the film.

The attitude of the Detroit, Michigan, police censors was more sympathetic to the film's opponents and that board banned The Birth from Detroit in 1939.[166] The censors banned the film after a special screening attended by the censors and representatives of Detroit's major black organizations.[167] After the screening, censor Nate Goldstick said the film violated the local film censorship statute which forbade obscene or indecent movies.[168] When a Detroit member of the American Civil Liberties Union learned of this, he notified the ACLU national office and argued that censorship would set a dangerous precedent.[169] ACLU member W. G. Bergman said: "I see great danger in a precedent that would allow the obscenity and indecency of 'The Birth of a Nation' to be used as the cloak under which its showing is denied when the real reason is its incitement to race hatred."[170] ACLU national contacted Goldstick directly and in part said:

> . . .We disire (sic) to take issue with any such interpretation and to see that any exhibitor who is prevented from showing the film on that ground will have our support in a contest in the courts. While we hold no grief for the kind of intolerance represented by this particular film, it is obvious that power of police officials to bar films on any such grounds opens the door wide to a general exercise of prejudice or response to any sort of pressure that may be brought.[171]

ACLU national also wrote Bergman, thanked him for his attention, and said:

> . . .No official action should be taken against the showing of such a picture. Those opposed to it have the right to picket, distribute leaflets against it or to boycott it. We could not object to such private action, indeed, we would aid it if necessary. But we do object to any control or censorship by public officials. I think that the Civil Rights Federation ought to take a stand against censorship by police department for the reason you give, namely, that it lays down another precedent to include under obscenity and indecency, a theme which had nothing to do with that classification.[172]

In spite of the ACLU's position, the individuals applying for a permit to show The Birth did not press the issue and the film was not shown.[173]

The Providence, Rhode Island, police commission barred The Birth from that city in 1915.[174] The commission acted after the Providence NAACP Branch protested the film.[175] The NAACP told the commission that the "avowed intentions" of the author of the book upon which the film was based were "to create a condition in the North that will strain the friendly relations of the colored and white races."[176] Further, the branch said blacks opposed the film because:

> It is historically false, is a reflection on Negro morals, honesty and loyalty, an insult to Negro womanhood, a reflection on Negro patriotism, an insult to the white man of the north who stood loyally by the Negro in both anti-slavery days and during the reconstruction period, one more industrial advancement and a menace to peaceful race relations.[177]

The commission banned the film, but Griffith secured an injunction, enjoining the commission's interference with the film (See Chapter III).[178]

Municipal Boards

Rather than assigning censorship duties to a mayor or a police board several cities placed the power of municipal censorship in a specific board. During the time period 1915-1973, at least 10 such boards were asked to resolve The Birth of a Nation censorship controversies. Nine of these boards resolved the controversies and one did not.

Municipal boards supporting censorship

Six municipal censorship boards resolved The Birth controversies by supporting suppression of the film. Two boards resolved censorship controversies by ordering cuts in the film.

The municipal board found to be the first which suppressed The Birth was the Memphis, Tennessee, board in November 1915.[179] When announcing the censors' decision, board member John M. Dean said:

> 'The Birth of a Nation' is based on those prejudices we have tried to bury. It gets its theme from the unholy influences at work immediately after the Civil War. Wherever it has been shown, some ill effect has been noted. In Memphis we have for the most part a law-abiding set of Negroes. The whites are living at peace with them. I see no reason why the two elements should be stirred up. The play is a great moneymaker. That's all that can be said in its favor.[180]

The Board also indicated the film would have a bad moral effect on the community.[181]

The Birth was barred from Boston, Massachusetts, by a decision of that city's censorship board in May 1921.[182] The board acted after a public hearing where the film's supporters and opponents debated. The film's opponents were led by William Monroe Trotter, Boston Guardian editor, and Butler R. Wilson, secretary of the NAACP Boston Branch.[183] The film's supporters were represented by attorney David Stoneman and Judge J. Albert Brackett.[184] Stoneman and Brackett argued the film's opponents were "supersensitive," and stressed the film had shown for long periods in both New York and Boston in 1915 "without creating serious disorder."[185] On the other side, Trotter attacked former Boston Mayor James Curley for allowing the film in

1915 and cautioned the board not to "force us to the wall" by allowing the film.[186] Wilson petitioned the board to oppose the film:

> Because it is a malicious misrepresentation of the colored people, depicting them as moral perverts. . .
>
> Because it glorified the most abominable crime of the lynching of men, women and children by irresponsible mobs. . .
>
> Because it arouses sharp race antagonisms that embitter citizens against each other. . .
>
> Because it tends to a breach of the public peace.[187]

Wilson gave the board a Knights of Columbus petition protesting the film.[188] One individual asserted the film was "part of a Southern Campaign of propaganda of nationwide scope designed to stimulate the popularity of the Ku Klux Klan idea and to establish branches of gang-assassins throughout the country."[189] Several black clergymen and attorneys testified that The Birth libeled their race, exposed them to ridicule and contempt, distorted history, glorified lynching, and was immoral and obscene in certain sequences.[190]

After the hearing, the board viewed the film at a private screening and rejected it.[191] Asked specifically why the board had acted in this manner, Boston mayor and board member Andrew Peters, indicated there were several reasons, but "as they were not required by law to give reasons and as the matter may go to court he did not care to name them."[192] Peters also refused to disclose whether the vote was unanimous.[193] Apparently, the matter was not taken to court and the action of the board ended the controversy.

The next municipal censorship board to bar The Birth was Lynn, Massachusetts, in 1922.[194] The Lynn Municipal Censorship Committee banned the film on the mayor's advice. He forwarded the protests of local blacks.[195] Sources indicate that although local blacks had tried to stop the film before, The Birth had been exhibited in Lynn theatres on two previous occasions.[196]

The Birth was stopped in Milwaukee, Wisconsin, by that city's board of censors in 1939.[197] The film was being screened there when the board met and banned the film.[198] The order followed a public hearing where local blacks, represented primarily by attorney James W. Dorsey, vice-president of Milwaukee's NAACP branch, said the film contained "many scenes which were prejudicial to their race."[199] Still, the specific basis upon which the board acted is unclear.

The Atlanta, Georgia, board of censors apparently banned The Birth in 1959 and in 1961.[200] Christine Gilliam, Atlanta censorship board member recalled that The Birth was banned in 1959 because it was considered "a race baiter from way back."[201] Two years later Variety reported that Atlantans were driving to nearby Roswell, Georgia, to see The Birth because the film had been "ruled against by city Motion Picture Censor Mrs. Christine Smith Gilliam."[202] In these two instances, the film was banned from the same southern city apparently because the film might engender racial prejudice.[203]

The first municipal censorship board found to order cuts in the film was the San Francisco Moving Picture Censor Board on March 2, 1915.[204] The board viewed The Birth at the Alcazar Theatre March 1, 1915, and the next day notified the theatre that certain changes had to be made in the film. In part, the board told theatre management:

In general, whereas we recognize that a picture of this nature must necessarily be offensive in many ways to the colored people, and whereas we might question the good taste in exhibiting such a picture in a mixed community, still under the ordinance under which this board operates we cannot modify nor prohibit these objectionable features beyond the following suggestions, alterations and eliminations which we strongly urge should be made:

1. When the old white woman in the Abolitionist meeting sniffs the little colored boy and shows plainly that his odor disgusts her. This is in very bad taste and is generally unclean and offensive.

2. The scene between the mulatto housekeeper and Stoneman, where he finds her after she has torn her clothing is offensive through too much lustful detail. That part of the scene where he strokes her naked shoulder and his feelings are shown to be aroused whereby must be eliminated.

3. The brutality of the Guerillas in the Cameron house in the scene in which the women take refuge in the cellar is too long drawn out and overdone. A portion of this scene of wanton violence should be cut out.

4. The scene in the legislature showing buffoonery of negroes taking off shoes, etc., is overdone and overplayed and is therefore essentially offensive to colored people.

5. Gus chase of the girl is far too long drawn out and that part where he overtakes her on the cliff and slavers at the mouth like an animal must be eliminated. This is absolutely offensive to the moral sense.

6. In the mob scene towards the end just before the K.K.K.'s arrive, negroes are shown grabbing up white women fondling and kissing them. This part must be cut out.

7. The struggle scenes between Lynch and Miss Stoneman are too frequently flashed and in too much detail. They should be pruned and shortened.

Please be advised that we are suggesting changes No. 1, 3, 4, 7. . .but that changes 2, 5, and 6 are mandatory. . .[205]

According to Walter A. Butler, president of the NAACP's Northern California branch, the theatre made the mandatory changes, but no "attention was paid to the suggested changes."[206] Nevertheless, the film continued.

Later in 1915, the Milwaukee, Wisconsin, board of censors ordered two scenes cut from The Birth.[207] The board ordered the scenes cut because the scenes "might arouse the race passion or excite a riot."[208] However, exactly which two scenes were cut is unclear. The film continued in modified form.

Municipal boards rejecting censorship

During the time period studied at least two municipal film censorship boards refused to censor The Birth. One of these boards made the ultimate decision concerning the film's right to the screen in the controversy; the other did not.

A Boston censorship board refused to censor The Birth in 1915. As discussed later, the board was established by the Massachusetts legislature in 1915 specifically to censor the film.[209] Boston Mayor James Curley, Boston Police Chief Fred O'Meara, and Judge Warren Bolster were the 1915 board.[210] The Birth was the first film considered by the board. In a closed door, four-hour hearing the board permitted the film, but gave no explanation. Speaking for the board, Mayor Curley stated:

> Having witnessed the performance, heard counsel representing the protesters and the licensee and having given full consideration to the entire subject the Board has decided that the license of the theatre should not be revoked or suspended.[211]

Although the NAACP and other organizations complained, the film continued and established length of run, number of consecutive performances, and attendance records.[212]

The remaining municipal censorship board which refused to censor the film did not resolve the controversy. This was the Los Angeles board of censors which early in 1915 approved The Birth as submitted. The individuals protesting the film turned their efforts elsewhere. As discussed in Chapter III, the controversy was ultimately resolved by a court ruling.

City Councils

In some municipalities the city council functioned as local censor. During the time period studied, at least 12 city councils were asked to censor The Birth. Half ordered total or partial suppression of the film.

Council ordered censorship

Six city councils asked to resolve The Birth controversies ordered total or partial censorship. In four instances the council ordered censorship resolved the controversy. In the other two instances the council decisions were not the ultimate ones in the controversies.

The St. Paul, Minnesota, city council was the first to resolve a The Birth of a Nation censorship controversy.[213] Throughout this controversy which raged during October and November 1915, the council took three separate actions regarding the film. First, in spite of NAACP-led opposition, the council approved the film without a public hearing.[214] Then, the NAACP reported the council "left the city to attend a convention."[215] This upset the St. Paul NAACP branch and it continued to agitate to ban the film. When the council returned, it scheduled a public hearing and ordered the theatre management showing The Birth to attend and show cause why the film should not be stopped.[216] In an editorial, the St. Paul Pioneer Press stated the:

> ...city council finds itself in a dilemma from which it may encounter difficulty in extricating itself. If it revokes the license issued for the production of 'The Birth of a Nation' it will be called upon to explain why...the license was issued in the first place...if the production should not be exhibited, then it should have been prohibited from the outset...the councilman's life is not a happy one.[217]

The council compromised. It ordered the theatre management to eliminate certain parts of the film or face possible theatre license revocation.[218] Theatre manager H. Sherman objected, but finally agreed to two cuts "all of the Gus scene from the time the Cameron girl leaves the house for the spring, until her brother finds her at the foot of the cliff; all of the Lynch-Elsie Stoneman scene from the time Lynch proposes marriage to the return of Stoneman."[219] The film's opponents monitored the film and reported several days later that the cuts had not been made. The council revoked the theatre's license and thus effectively removed the film from the screen.[220] Thus, in three separate rulings concerning The Birth, the council ultimately suppressed the film.

The Birth was barred a second time from St. Paul by that city's council in December 1930.[221] In response to an NAACP-led protest against the film, the city council ordered St. Paul chief of police Thomas A. Brown to tell the theatre showing The Birth to stop.[222] The council unanimously banned the film under an ordinance passed during the 1915 controversy discussed previously. The passage of the ordinance is discussed later.

Using a somewhat different rationale to justify suppression, the Montclair, New Jersey, city commissioners banned The Birth in August 1924.[223] After receiving a petition signed by 550 of Montclair's blacks and hearing testimony from others, the commissioners resolved, in part:

> . . .that in the opinion of the Commission the proposed showing of the picture known as 'The Birth of a Nation' is detrimental to public peace, therefore Commissioner Robinson, director of public safety, is instructed to notify the management of the Clairidge Theatre that the picture must not be shown and to take such steps as may be necessary to carry out this order.[224]

The remaining city council to resolve a The Birth of a Nation censorship controversy was the Portland, Oregon, city council in March 1925.[225] The council unanimously voted to ban the film after opposition voiced by the Portland NAACP branch.[226] However, the sources do not indicate the ground on which the film was banned.

The city councils of Denver, Colorado, and Los Angeles, California, both ordered censorship of The Birth in 1915, but neither order resolved the controversy in question. In both cases the controversies were resolved by court rulings.

The first city council to act against The Birth was the Los Angeles city council before the film's premiere in February 1915.[227] As mentioned earlier, the film was approved by the Los Angeles censorship board before the council banned it. The council prohibited the film after an NAACP petition. The NAACP gave five reasons the film should be suppressed:

First: It serves to revive the difference and the causes of differences between the North and the South which led to Civil War. It opens afresh the wounds long healed by time. . .The Sacred cause of Liberty is caricatured, made ridiculous and repulsive by the scenes contained in the introduction. . .

Second: The Negro is made to look hideous and is invested with most repulsive habits and depraved passions. The Negro, Lynch, who, perhaps, figures as the villian in this production, is an unwarrantable, unjust and unprovoked attack upon one of the best and most honored members of our race. . .Major John R. Lynch. . .

Third: The questionable scene suggesting illicit relations between the senile Stoneham (sic) and the mulatto servant is a reflection upon the mind which inspired it and is unfit for a public performance.

Fourth: The conflict between young Cameron, "The Little Colonel," and the Negro soldiery is calculated to inspire bitterness and to suggest the solution of violence for the petty differences which might arise between members of opposite races. Without determining the equities of the situation there displayed, it would seem to be unwise to accentuate those differences, revive their memories and rekindle the flame of bitterness they engendered.

Fifth: The meeting between "The Little Colonel" a southern aristocrat, and Lynch, the villian, a mulatto politician, is a diabolical piece of art never surpassed. The flames of Hell seemed to leap from the eyes of each in expression of their intense hatred. Indeed, it seems that all the evil passions of man are focussed (sic) in the fiery, yet sullen, glare of each. We respectfully submit that this scene is injurious to the public mind and calculated to excite feelings of animosity between the races.[228]

In addition, the petition called the film "untimely, unfortunate and unwise, calculated to develop into positive dislike, distrust, and hatred, the casual antipathy of two opposite races. . .historically, inaccurate and with subtle genius designed to palliate and excuse the lynchings and other deeds of violence committed against the Negro."[239] The petition concluded that the film was an appeal to violence and "an attempt to commercialize the evil passions of man."[230]

The council responded by instructing the Los Angeles police chief to stop the film. The police chief was enjoined from interfering with the film by a court order (See Chapter III).

Likewise, the Denver, Colorado, city council ordered The Birth stopped, but its action was enjoined by a court.[231] In a 3-2 decision, the Denver council ordered the film stopped under the local ordinance "which prevents the presentation of pictures which would stir up race hatred" and under the "full power" of the council to "suppress immoral plays."[232] Individuals dissatisfied with this action protested to the council as a whole, and a majority of the council voted to suppress the film. The council said that even with the ordered omissions, the film was "objectionable and tended to create a racial feeling."[234] The court, however, prohibited the officials from interfering with the film's showing (See Chapter III).

Other city council participation

The other six city councils asked to censor The Birth apparently did not do so. However, one of these six did express sympathy with the film's opponents without resolving the controversy. The actions of the remaining five city councils regarding the film are unclear.

The council expressing agreement with the film's opponents was the Cleveland, Ohio council in 1917.[235] This group passed a resolution against the public exhibition of the film and forwarded it to Cleveland Mayor Harry L. Davis. Davis banned the film.[236] However, Epoch, the film's distributor, sought and received an injunction prohibiting interference with the film's production as discussed in

Chapter III.

In the remaining five instances, individuals who opposed the film petitioned city councils to censor the film, but the councils apparently did not do so. For example, the San Francisco board of supervisors received a protest against the film's screening in February 1915.[237] Although the supervisors' response is unclear, this controversy was resolved by the city's board of censorship which ordered several scenes cut as discussed earlier.[238] The East Orange, New Jersey, city council received a petition signed by more than 600 citizens, asking that The Birth be prohibited after the film was announced for screening there in May 1938.[239] However, as discussed in Chapter IV, the controversy was resolved when one of the film's opponents obtained a warrant against the manager of the theatre showing The Birth under a 1935 law designed originally to curb Nazi propaganda.[240]

The remaining three city councils which heard protests concerning the film apparently took the protests under advisement and did not move to block the film. The eventual resolution of each of these controversies is unclear. For example, Eugene W. Scott, Janesville, Wisconsin, resident, wrote the Chicago Defender in October 1915, indicating that he had spoken against the film before the Janesville city council.[241] Scott said that he had "put up a fight" against The Birth, but whether that fight was successful from Scott's point of view is unclear.[242]

Likewise, the Montgomery, Alabama, city commission heard protests against The Birth during a regular meeting early in 1916.[243]

However, the commission's response is unclear.[244]

The response of the Kansas City, Kansas, commissioners to a protest against The Birth's screening is also unclear.[245] Black organizations of that city protested the film's showing in December 1923.[246] The commissioners heard the protest and agreed to view the film before granting a permit. Whether the commission actually moved against the film is unclear.[247]

Actions By Other Municipal Officials

During the time period studied, a variety of other municipal officials were asked to censor The Birth. These officials responded by either ordering suppression or indicating they had no authority to act.

In two instances, other municipal officials resolved The Birth censorship controversies by ordering cuts in the film. For example, Sacramento, California, city commissioner U. Carrahar negotiated a compromise in May 1915.[248] As a result the Gus chasing Flora sequence was eliminated.[249] The Birth opened in this modified form.[250] Likewise, unspecified Roselle, New Jersey, officials deleted "race prejudice inciting parts" of the film according to the NAACP in November 1931.[251] However, exactly which scenes were deleted is unclear.

In one case, a deputy director of public safety forbade a theatre to continue screening The Birth.[252] In this way, the film was banned from Jersey City, New Jersey, in September 1931.[253] The action followed a protest from the Jersey City Branch of the NAACP to Thomas Wolfe, then Deputy Director of Public Safety.[254]

In one instance, a city commissioner assured individuals protesting the film's screening that certain cuts would be made.[255] In this case Duluth, Minnesota, city commissioner U. Silverstein said:

> . . .from what I can learn, the production has three or four scenes to which the colored people object. I am sure Manager Morriessey will be glad to eliminate these features before showing the picture. . .[256]

However, whether the Lyceum theatre manager was willing to cut the film is not recorded.

In at least two The Birth of a Nation controversies in New York, New York, individuals protesting the film requested the city commissioner of licenses to stop the film. George Bell was apparently the first New York Commissioner of Licenses to be petitioned for relief by those who objected to the film. In a letter to Bell, the NAACP in March 1915, "respectfully" requested Bell to use his power of office to stop the film.[257] The NAACP said it opposed The Birth because the film was "an undisguised appeal to race prejudice" and said its particular opposition was to the Gus pursuit of Flora sequence and the Lynch proposal to Elsie Stoneman sequence.[258] New York Mayor John Mitchell also forwarded several letters protesting the film to Bell's office.[259] However, as discussed earlier, Mitchell resolved this controversy by ordering several cuts.

During a 1921 New York controversy, several city officials indicated to NAACP-led protesters that the city was powerless to act against the film. The protesters led by James W. Johnson, NAACP New York branch representative, met with New York Commissioner of Licenses, John Gilchrist, and Commissioner of Police, Richard E.

Enright, and requested they stop the film.[260] Each indicated lack of authority to act.[261] The NAACP continued its protest through extra-legal means.

State Authorities

During the time period 1915-1973, a variety of state officials were asked to censor The Birth of a Nation. Although it is evident from the sources consulted (discussed in more detail later) that a number of governors were asked to ban The Birth, only 13 governors responded to censorship requests. Also, although many state censorship boards probably were asked to rule on The Birth during the years of this study, 12 were involved directly in censorship controversies. All State Councils of Defense in World War I were asked to stop the film. However, sources indicate that only three councils responded. Therefore, 28 state involvements in The Birth of a Nation censorship controversies are discussed.

Governors

Throughout the time period studied, many governors were asked to censor The Birth. However, apparently not all governors responded to censorship requests. For example, during World War I, the NAACP wrote to each governor, asking that the film be stopped for patriotic reasons.[262] However, the responses of only three governors are recorded. In addition, nine other governors were involved in a variety of censorship controversies during the time period 1915-1973.

Governors Resolving Controversies

Only three governors were found to resolve The Birth censorship controversies. Of the three governors who resolved controversies one suppressed The Birth and two indicated they had not authority to act against the film. The governors taking the latter position resolved the question of whether the film could be barred from the state entirely. In each instance the film's opponents shifted their focus and attempted to have the film banned from individual communities within the state.

Ohio governor James Cox was the only governor found to resolve a censorship controversy by banning the film. Cox requested in 1918 that the film be withdrawn from his state for the duration of World War I.[263] The film's distributor agreed. The NAACP called Cox' action "wise and patriotic" and thanked Cox:

> In peace and in war every effort should be made to allay lingering race antagonisms. But war conditions impose upon all good citizens a more than usual responsibility to do whatever they can to bring about that feeling of national unity which in increasing degree is the ideal of every American. In succeeding as you have in preventing the spread of race feeling by means of the appeal which this film makes to baser passions despite some of its excellencies you have earned the gratitude not of Negroes but of all Americans.[264]

This is the only instance in which a censorship controversy was actually resolved by a governor's banning the film.

Both governors who resolved controversies by indicating they had no authority to act against the film at the state level did so in 1915. The governor who explained his position in this manner more thoroughly was Michigan governor Woodbridge Ferris. In October 1915, Ferris notified the NAACP that he "would do everything" in his power to stop The Birth.[265] However, Ferris added "I doubt if the laws of Michigan will permit me to render very much assistance."[266] Ferris' statements were in response to a telegram from the NAACP asking him to prohibit the film in Michigan.[267] Ferris apparently could do nothing against the film as he had predicted and the battlegrounds over the film's rights to the screen became individual Michigan communities.[268]

The other individual who expressed sympathy with the film's opponents but who resolved a state controversy with his inability to act against the film at the state level was the governor of Minnesota in 1915.[269] Specifically, the NAACP said that the governor "threatened action" if the picture were "advertised for exhibition in Minnesota."[270] However, the governor did not have the power to operationalize his threat against the film and again the individual communities within the state became the scenes of censorship debates.

Governors Facilitating Resolution

In four instances, governors facilitated controversy resolution by either making their opposition clearly known to the state board of censorship or by advising film opponents of appropriate protest channels. For example, the latter form of aid was given The Birth's opponents by the first governor involved in a censorship controversy, Massachusetts governor David Walsh.[271] On April 19, 1915, more than one thousand blacks gathered at the Massachusetts State House and protested the screening of the film in Boston to Walsh.[272] The protesters had already asked Boston's mayor James Curley to stop the film, but as discussed earlier, Curley's actions did not appease the protesters.[273] While Walsh met in the State House with a delegation of film opponents, the remaining protesters awaited the outcome on the building's steps and alternately listened to speeches denouncing the film and "hanged Thomas Dixon, D. W. Griffith or Jeff Davis to a sour apple tree to the tune of John Brown's Body."[274] Walsh announced he was in "complete sympathy with the contention that the pictures tend to incite race prejudice and bigotry."[275] However, Walsh stated: "I doubt whether I have the authority to close the theater . . . . Of course, if the situation should become so bad as to cause race rioting, I could exercise my authority as commander-in-chief."[276] Walsh assured the delegation he would do everything in his power to stop the film, including a special law prohibiting the film if necessary.[277] Walsh advised the delegation to begin a court case immediately, charging that the film violated Chapter 367 of the Massachusetts Acts of 1910 prohibiting performance of an obscene or immoral work.[278] The delegation appeared before Judge T. Dowd, First Session of the Boston Municipal Court, and charged The Birth was obscene. Dowd ordered one scene cut from the film (See Chapter III).[279]

Disappointed with the trial outcome, the delegation returned to Walsh and asked him to send a special message to the state legislature, urging a law designed to prohibit The Birth.[280] As a result, at least five motion picture censorship bills were introduced in the state legislature.[281] These bills are discussed later. One of the bills passed and was signed into law by Walsh.[282] It established a new Boston film censorship board appointed by the Massachusetts governor.[283] Walsh named Boston mayor James Curley, Boston police chief Fred O'Meara, and Judge Warren Bolster, Chief Justice Boston Municipal Court, to the board.[284] The board refused to stop the film as discussed earlier.

Shortly after the 1915 Boston controversy subsided, The Birth was announced for showing in Ohio. Immediately, individuals protested the film's scheduled screening to Ohio governor Frank B. Willis.[285] For example, one Akron, Ohio, resident, Hazel Hall, wrote Willis and asked him to stop the film because its screening would engender racial prejudice.[286] Cleveland Gazette editor Harry C. Smith also sent Willis a letter and newspaper clippings outlining The Birth's objectionable features.[287] Willis responded he would place all protests concerning the film before the Ohio Censorship Board. Willis also said "so far as I have power to prevent it no films which reflect upon any class of our citizens will be exhibited in this state."[288] Willis then forwarded the protests to the censorship board. Board chairperson Charles G. Williams told Willis the Board had "received very many protests against" The Birth, but because the film had not been submitted to the Board he could say nothing about its "merits or demerits other than because of the protests against it, it should be carefully considered."[289] Nevertheless, Willis continued to forward protest letters to the Board and also spoke against the film. For

For example, Willis told a Knights of Pythias meeting in August 1915:

> . . . so long as I have any influence with this administration there will not be produced in the state of Ohio any photoplays that are calculated to reflect upon any class of our citizens . . . . It is entirely possible for the races to live together in peace and harmony, but it is not possible if we allow the production upon the state of picture plays that are calculated to disturb and insult any class of our citizens and I do not propose to stand for it.[290]

In late September 1915, The Birth was submitted to the Ohio censors.[291] The Board screened the film and on September 28, 1915, rejected it.[292] In a public statement explaining the decision, Williams said that Willis:

> . . . had repeatedly called the attention of the board to the fact that many protests against the film have been entered in his department . . . he had repeatedly also requested that this board give said film very careful attention and if it should be found to reflect upon the colored race and tend to arouse racial hatred and prejudice as claimed, he has urgently recommended that we reject same . . . . [293]

Willis called the decision "welcome news."[294] He also continued to publicly oppose the film.[295]

In January 1916, The Birth was resubmitted to the Ohio censors and rejected by a 2-1 vote.[296] Once again Willis praised the censors and restated his belief that any film which reflected negatively on "any portion" of Ohio's citizenship should not be shown in the state.[297] In this instance, the film's promoters sought relief in the Ohio courts (See Chapter III).

Also, in 1915, Kansas governor Arthur Capper notified The Birth's distributor he did not want the film shown in Kansas.[298]

Nevertheless, the film was submitted to the Kansas Board of Censors. The board, of which Capper was a member, considered the film and rejected it.[299] Thus, in this case a governor actively expressed his opposition to the film and in his role as board member voted to ban the film.

Harry Woodring, Kansas governor in 1931, also opposed The Birth and voiced his disapproval to the Kansas Board of Censors.[300] The governor asked the censors to recall the film after it had been approved and reconsider its acceptability. The board did recall the film and banned it.[301] Then, Woodring wrote the NAACP indicating the board's action met with his approval.[302]

Governor refusing censorship

During the time period studied, at least one governor answered individuals requesting censorship of The Birth by indicating he did not oppose the film and would not object if the state censorship board approved it. The governor was Jonathan M. Davis, Kansas 1923.[303]

Davis began receiving protests from the film's opposition shortly after the announcement was made that the film would be submitted to the Kansas Board of Censors. For example, the NAACP telegraphed Davis and requested that he "continue the splendid example of former governors of Kansas in forbidding exhibition of this film capitalizing and spreading as it does vicious racial prejudices . . ."[304] The Wichita Ministerial Association passed a resolution protesting the film's exhibition and sent it to Davis.[305] The Women's Christian Temperance Union in Kansas also publicly announced its opposition to

The Birth.[306] Davis also received a petition signed by more than 8,000 Kansans asking that he exercise "a wise discretion with the power vested in your great office prevent the showing within the state of Kansas of the iniquitous film known as 'Birth of a Nation.'"[307] The Topeka Daily Capital editorially endorsed the protest and urged Davis to ban the film.[308] However, Davis told the protesters that he viewed the film and saw "nothing objectionable" about it.[309]

Davis also said he would place the decision concerning the film's acceptability squarely in the hands of the Kansas Board of Censorship.[310] Davis said he had instructed the board to use its judgment. If the board approved the film, he would not order a recall because "I have been unable to see anything wrong with it myself . . . ."[311] The Kansas censors viewed the film and approved it. This action resolved the controversy at the state level as discussed later.[312] However, as discussed in Chapter III, the Wichita city commission passed an ordinance banning the film and that controversy was resolved in the courts.

Governors sympathetic to censorship

During the time period studied, at least two other governors indicated that they disapproved of The Birth, but the actual role each governor may have played in resolving the censorship controversy in his state is unclear. For example, Henry Allen became governor of Kansas after Arthur Capper and continued Capper's opposition to The Birth.[313] After Allen left office, he commented that during his administration "every influence from that of the practical politician to the use of money was brought to bear in an effort to induce me to permit" The Birth to be shown in Kansas.[314] Allen continued that he had seen the film in Los Angeles when it was first released and believed that its screening "would arouse bitter racial sentiment and hatred."[315] For this reason Allen said he banned the film in Kansas during his administration. Apparently, the film was not shown in Kansas during Allen's term, but whether this was specifically because of Allen's opposition to the film is unclear.[316]

Likewise, the governor of North Dakota indicated in a letter to the D. W. Griffith Corporation that he did not want The Birth shown in his state during World War I.[317] In part, the governor said "In view of the fact that the colored people of this state have evidenced the greatest loyalty to our country in the national crisis," he would recommend that the film not be shown in North Dakota.[318] Further, the governor indicated that banning the film would become a gesture so that "our colored citizens may know we appreciate the sacrifices they are making in behalf of a worldwide Democracy."[319] However, the sources do not indicate whether the film was actually banned from the state during World War I.[320]

Indecisive governors

During the time period studied, other governors were asked to censor The Birth, but the responses of these governors are unclear. For example, in 1918, the NAACP wrote the governor of each state, asking that the film be banned during World War I.[321] The NAACP said the film tended to "accentuate and engender race prejudice and race hatred" at a time when blacks were "performing their full share of patriotic service both in the fighting forces of the nation on the battlefronts of Europe and at home . . . ."[322] The NAACP said that in the interest of national morale "all divisive influences" should be "subordinated to the common good" and therefore the film should be banned.[323]

However, the actual responses of only three governors to this letter are clear. As mentioned, the governor of North Dakota wrote the D. W. Griffith Corporation indicating he did not want the film shown in his state during World War I.[324] As also discussed earlier, Ohio governor James Cox requested that the film not be shown in his state during the war.[325] The governor of Connecticut apparently forwarded his letter to the Connecticut State Council of Defense.[326] The responses, if any, of the other governors to the letters are not recorded in the sources consulted.[327]

At least one other governor received a censorship request in 1918 in addition to the NAACP plea. In November 1918, Kentucky Governor A. O. Stanley received a letter from Kentucky NAACP members Dr. A. C. McIntyre, William Warley, and Wilson Lovett.[328] However, Stanley's response to the letter is unclear.[329]

State Censorship Boards

During the time period 1915-1973, at lease 12 state censorship boards were directly involved in The Birth of a Nation censorship controversies. Nine decisions by state boards resolved 10 controversies. The rights of the remaining three boards to censor The Birth were challenged in the courts. In each case a court resolved the controversy by affirming the boards' rights to determine the film's acceptability. The boards functioned in only five different states.

The Kansas state censors banned The Birth from that state three times and approved the film once between the years 1915-1931. Through these actions the board resolved four state and one local controversy. In each instance, the board made the ultimate decision concerning the film's right to the screen in the controversy.

The Birth was first submitted to the Kansas censors in 1915.[330] The censors considered the film and banned it from the state.[331]

The Birth was resubmitted to the Kansas censors in 1917.[332] The board met and announced that if certain eliminations were made, it would approve the film.[333] The film's distributor agreed and the board issued a certificate of approval, May 7, 1917.[334] However, two days later, the board ordered:

> The Board of Review of Motion Pictures of Kansas hereby orders the recall of the film 'The Birth of a Nation' for reexamination and we are giving you the official 30 days notice. In the meantime, of course, there must be no exhibition of the picture in the state.[335]

The film was not returned to the censors and Kansas state Attorney General S. M. Brewster filed suit in the Kansas Supreme Court, requesting it to compel the film producer to resubmit the film.[336] Brewster also requested that the certificate of approval be "delivered up" to the board.[337] In a 5-2 decision, the Kansas Supreme Court accepted Brewster's argument and ordered the film returned to the censors.[338] The film was resubmitted to the censors and they withdrew the certificate of approval.[339]

The film was again submitted to the Kansas censors in 1923.[340] As previously discussed, the opposition asked Kansas Governor Jonathan Davis to tell the censors he disapproved of the film.[341] However, Davis told them that he saw nothing objectionable in the film and would leave the decision of acceptability to the state censors.[342] The film's opponents found an ally in Kansas state Attorney General Charles B. Griffith who pleaded the case directly to the state censors.[343] Griffith said:

> In the absence of any fraudulent act either specific or claimed, I have no official authority to ask this but I make the appeal as a citizen, as a father, and as the chief law enforcer of the state. The showing of the film, in my opinion endangers the existing peace of the state by stirring up race prejudice and reopening old wounds.[344]

The board assured Griffith it would consider his appeal. Nevertheless, later the same day, the board approved the film.[345] This action resolved the controversy at the state level.

Eight years later, The Birth's distributors announced the film with sound synchronization would be revived in Kansas, beginning October 10, 1931.[346] Kansas Governor Harry Woodring disapproved and asked the Kansas censorship board to consider the film.[347] The censors did and after inspecting the film, banned it.[348] As was discussed earlier in this chapter, this ruling also resolved a municipal controversy which had been occurring simultaneously in Topeka, Kansas.

The Topeka controversy was being adjudicated at the time of the censor board decision but by barring the film from the state the censors also barred the film from Topeka.[349] This is the only instance found in which any type of official directly resolved two controversies through one action.

One state censorship board resolved a 1922 controversy by ordering cuts in the film. This board was the New York State Motion Picture Commission and it acted after the NAACP filed a complaint against the film. The complaint charged the film should be banned from New York because it promoted racial prejudice and provoked civil disorder.[350] The NAACP was joined by Henry Shields, state senator elect, and George W. Harris, New York City alderperson. Specifically, the efforts were timed to stop the film's scheduled December 1922 revival at New York's Selwyn Theatre.

The New York State Motion Picture Commission agreed to hear the complaint and conducted a two-day hearing. However, before the hearing, Joseph Levenson, commission member, stressed to the complainants that The Birth had been screened in New York before and therefore was a "picture exhibited prior to the formation of the commission which received permits without the usual screening of a new picture."[351] Because of this status, the film could only have its permit revoked if the complainants could prove the film was "of an immoral nature or would tend to incite crime." [352]

Walter White, NAACP assistant executive secretary, objected to the film:

> We demand the revocation of the permit on two grounds. First, that it is a glorification of the KKK coming at a time when the Rev. Haywood has announced a drive is on for increased membership in the Klan and we believe that it has been brought here for this purpose. In the second place, it is the revival of race prejudice sentiment which has followed the picture wherever shown and has caused riots in many instances.[353]

D. W. Griffith and Thomas Dixon defended the film.[354] Griffith denied a Klan connection and insisted the film revival was justified as a work of art and as an historic document. The time of the revival was "purely for commercial reasons" according to Griffith, "and the fact that it came at the time of the proposed drive by Dr. Haywood was simply a coincidence."[355] Griffith and Dixon both stressed that the film had been shown previously in New York without incident. Griffith's attorney, Frank J. Loughlin, also denied connection between the film and the modern Klan. Loughlin attributed the opposition "to the supersensitiveness of certain members of the Negro race and not the race as a whole."[356] Alderperson Harris countered that sentiment against the film was prevalent among the majority of blacks and that lynching in the South had increased every year since The Birth was first shown.[357]

On December 8, 1922, the commission voted 2-1 to disregard the complaint filed by the NAACP against The Birth.[358] Commissioners George H. Cobb and Mrs. Eli T. Hosmer voted in favor of the picture and Commissioner Joseph Levenson recommended the revocation of the permit.[359] Levenson said he voted against the film because it tended to stir up racial prejudice.[360]

Dissatisfied with the board's action, the NAACP again asked for suppression or at least partial censorship.[361] For the NAACP, Walter White said:

> We note that in the consideration of our complaint no official action was taken upon the elimination of scenes but solely on the revocation of the license. We are herewith requesting that exactly the same procedure be gone through with in the case of this picture as in all other complaints filed with the Motion Picture Commission.[362]

The commission reconsidered and ordered several scenes modified. The commission asked for the following deletions because the sequences were "indecent, immoral, and would tend to incite crime, and some of them are inhuman:"[363]

Act 1: Shorten view of mulatto woman on floor, tearing dress waist and with dress off shoulder.

If in the picture, eliminate scene of Stoneman kissing and embracing mulatto.

Act 2: Suggest that authority be given for quotation: 'To put the white south under the heel of the black south.'

Eliminate actual scene of whipping negro.

Eliminate scene of negro removing shoes and sitting at table in Senate in bare feet.

Alter subtitle: 'We will crush the white south under the heel of the black south.'

Eliminate closeup of negro's face.

Eliminate scene where negro Gus lays his hand on girl.

Eliminate all closeups of negro Gus chasing the girl.

Eliminate view of dead girl in bier.

Change subtitle: 'This flag bears the red stain of the blood of a <u>Southern</u> woman.'

Eliminate all but one scene of the master in chains.

Shorten scene between Lynch and Elsie. Show but one view of Lynch embracing Elsie.

Eliminate all views of Elsie actually gagged.[364]

The commission also recommended a title disavowing connection between the modern Klan and the picture.[365] The commission was notified that the cuts had been made, and the edited film was screened throughout the state.[366]

Three state censorship boards resolved controversies by routinely approving the film for viewing in their states. The first board to resolve a state controversy in this manner was the Pennsylvania censorship board in 1915.[367] The Pennsylvania board approved The Birth for screening in that state, but the board's right to determine what was appropriate for all communities within the state was challenged by Pittsburgh authorities.[368] As discussed in Chapter III, Pittsburgh authorities banned The Birth after the state censorship board approved the film. The film's supporters challenged this banning in the courts and Judge Ambrose Reid, Allegeny County Common Pleas Court, ruled that because the state law vested the power of censorship in a state board, its decisions could not be overruled by a lesser authority unless it was shown that the state board acted improperly by approving the film.[369] In this case, Reid said the Pittsburgh authorities had not proven the board's action was improper; thus, the board's right to determine a film's acceptability for all communities within the state was affirmed and The Birth's right to be screened throughout Pennsylvania established.

As was also discussed in Chapter III, the right of the Ohio state censor board to determine the acceptability of films for screening throughout the state was affirmed in a court decision involving The Birth. In this instance, the Ohio censors approved The Birth in February 1917 and by this action resolved the controversy at the state level.[370] Cleveland, Ohio, mayor Harry L. Davis disagreed with this decision and banned The Birth locally. Epoch challenged Davis' action in the courts and won when the judge ruled as Reid had that once a film was approved by the state censors it could not be stopped by a lesser authority.[371]

The remaining censorship board to resolve a state controversy by approving The Birth was the Maryland Board of Censors in 1958.[372] In this instance the state censors passed the film in October 1958. This action negated censorship ordered by the same board in 1952.[373] The board's approval of the film apparently was not challenged and the film's right to be shown in the state established.

In three cases state censorship rulings concerning The Birth were challenged through court action. In each case the court petitioned resolved the controversy by affirming the right of the censor board to act regarding the film. Because all three of these controversies are discussed in more detail in Chapter III, they are only summarized here. Two of the controversies involved decisions made by the Ohio board of censors. The Ohio censors rejected The Birth as inappropriate for screening in that state in 1915, but reconsidered the film in 1916. On January 6, 1916, the board again rejected the film.[374] Epoch, the film's distributor, asked the board to reconsider; the board refused.[375] Epoch appealed to the Ohio Supreme Court. The court dismissed Epoch's petition on the grounds that the censorship agency failed to supply a satisfactory record of its administrative procedures as required by law.[376] Because the court refused to consider Epoch's petition, it effectively upheld the censorship agency's ban of the film on procedural grounds. The Ohio Supreme Court also supported the right of the Ohio censors to rule concerning the film in 1925. The controversy began when the Ohio censors rejected The Birth "on account of being harmful" in February 1925.[377] Epoch challenged the board's action to the Ohio Supreme Court which refused to hear the case and thus upheld the board's action.[378]

The remaining state board to ban the film but have its ruling directly challenged in the courts was the Maryland board of censors in 1952. In this case the Maryland censors refused to approve The Birth because it considered the film "inflammatory" and said the film's screening "could easily incite to riot and disorder."[379] Amplifying the board decision, censor Sydney Traub said many scenes in the film were "grossly exaggerated and accompanied by objectionable dialogue which might stir up some members of both the white and Negro races."[380] Specifically, Traub said he objected to scenes of blacks in the South Carolina legislature after the Civil War, scenes of the Ku Klux Klan, and the subtitle which included the phrase "crushing the white south under the black heel."[381]

Harry R. Shull, the film's distributor, challenged the board's decision in court. Judge Michael J. Manley, Maryland Circuit Court, heard the case. Shull's attorneys, Marvin P. Skiar and Irwin Cohen, argued that the board's censorship action violated the First and Fourteenth Amendments of the U. S. Constitution and Article 40 of the Declaration of Rights of the Maryland Constitution.[382] Manley gave the censorship board 10 days to explain why it should not be enjoined from interfering with the film's screening.[383] However, exactly what happened next is unclear. Nevertheless, it appears that the ban was upheld.[384] For example, the Baltimore Sun reported in October 1958, that The Birth had recently been approved by the Maryland censors and this action "lifted" a ban on the film which "went into effect in 1952."[385] Likewise, Variety reported that the 1958 action "rescinded" an earlier ban on the film.[386] Thus, in this case it appears that a ban issued by a state board of censors was challenged in the courts and upheld. As a result, The Birth was kept from that particular state for at least six years.

World War I Defense Councils

One other type of state authority was asked to censor the film in specialized circumstances, the state defense councils in World War I. In October 1918, NAACP national mounted a special campaign to censor The Birth in every state for the duration of World War I. In a letter to every state defense council, the NAACP asked that the film be banned as a "patriotic service" both at home and in Europe.[387] The organization explained that the film insulted the nation's blacks who were helping fight the war by "patriotic service."[388] Also, the film tended to create race prejudice and race hatred at a time when the country needed unity in the war effort.[389] NAACP national also asked each branch to write its state council, requesting censorship and to "secure local publicity."[390]

Records indicate that only three councils responded. One council banned the film; one indicated general support; one said it lacked authority to act.

The West Virginia State Council of Defense banned <u>The Birth</u> for World War I. The Council's action came after the McDowell County (West Virginia) Auxiliary Council of Defense passed a resolution against the film.[391] In condemning the film, the McDowell County Auxiliary said the film aroused racial hatred which would "likely retard and hinder the proper cooperation between the races in promoting the greatest efficiency in war work of all kinds."[392] The auxiliary also requested the state council to adopt a similar measure.

The state council agreed and banned the film because the film would:

> . . . Cause and produce a bad feeling between the Negro race and the white race in this State which would result in materially preventing the two races from working together in peace and harmony in inaugurating and producing the best reults (<u>sic</u>) in our national defense.[393]

The council said its ban was effective "during the war with Germany"[394] NAACP national wrote the council to express its appreciation for the ban.[395]

After being contacted by NAACP national, the Utah State Council of Defense wrote the NAACP it was: "in full sympathy" with the NAACP position on the film.[396] The council said it would "use whatever influence we have to eliminate motion pictures such as you mention."[397] In this way, the council went on record opposing the film without explicitly banning it like the West Virginia Council.

The last council answering the NAACP request was the Connecticut Council of Defense. This council told the NAACP it discussed the film and after "adequate consideration" found that the "subject in hand" was not "one which was distinctively of war character."[398] Therefore, the council said it did not have jurisdiction to act. The council also told the NAACP that The Birth was shown in the state before the war, but not during the war to that time and it knew of "no proposal for its exhibit within this state at the present time."[399]

Analysis

During the time period 1915-1973, 91 controversies over The Birth of a Nation's right to the screen included the tactic of requesting local or state officials to use administrative power to affirm or deny the film's right to the screen. Because several controversies included appeals to multiple officials, the actual number of official involvements discussed in this chapter is 113. Thus, an average 1.24 officials were involved in each controversy regardless of level (state or local). Among those asked to take administrative action were: mayors, governors, city councils, local censorship boards, state censorship boards, police censorship boards, and World War I state councils of defense. No national officials were asked to exercise administrative power concerning the film. Fifty-six of the 91 controversies were actually resolved by administrative action.

These figures are not significant ($x^2 = 4.84$, $>.02$). Because one state censorship board resolved two controversies with one action, the number of officials actually resolving controversies was 55. In terms of petitioned officials rather than controversies, 55 of the 113 officials asked to resolve censorship controversies did so by exercising administrative power. These figures are not significant ($x^2 = .078$, $>.02$). Therefore, in terms of individuals petitioned, it can be seen that petitioned individuals resolved controversies with a frequency that does not differ from random. Likewise, in terms of controversies rather than number of petitioned individuals, administrative intervention was successful in achieving resolution with a frequency that does not differ from chance. Thus, if an individual had controversy resolution as a goal over the years of this study, seeking administrative intervention was not a tactic one could reliably employ.

Overall, 43 controversies were resolved by total or partial censorship of the film and 13 controversies were resolved by decisions affirming the film's right to the screen. These figures are significant ($x^2 = 16.06$, $<.001$). Thus, it can be seen that if administrative action resolved a censorship controversy, it did so in favor of censorship with a frequency that deviates from chance. In order to determine whether the deviations from chance discussed thus far hold for all categories of officials, it is necessary to analyze administrative actions by level (state or local) and by type of official petitioned.

Administrative action was sought more at the local level than at the state level. Eighty-five municipal authorities were asked to resolve 70 censorship controversies. Thus, in each controversy an average 1.21 officials were petitioned. Forty-one of the controversies were resolved by the official petitioned. This figure is not significant (x^2 = .11, >.02). Therefore, in terms of individuals petitioned and in terms of controversy resolution status, individual municipal officials resolved controversies in a pattern that does not differ from chance. These findings are consistent with those regarding administrative intervention regardless of level. A summary of the number of municipal officials by type and controversy resolution status is presented in table 8. Of the municipal officials who resolved a controversy, 35 supported total or partial censorship and six supported the film's right to the screen. These figures are significant (x^2 = 20.5, <.001). Therefore, if an individual wished to suppress The Birth and was willing to chance that the petitioned official would resolve the controversy, the municipal official would support censorship in a pattern that deviates from random. Again, this finding is consistent with that found to be true for the manner in which controversies were resolved by officials regardless of level. To determine whether these findings hold for all categories of officials, it is necessary to look at actions taken by each category of municipal authority.

TABLE 8

MUNICIPAL AUTHORITIES AND CONTROVERSY
RESOLUTION STATUS

Type of Authority	Resolve	Not Resolve	Total
Mayor	21	29	50
Mayor plus other authority	2	0	2
Police censors	2	1	3
Municipal censor boards	9	1	10
City Council	4	8	12
Other	3	5	8
Totals	41	44	85

As shown in table 8, mayors more than any other type of municipal official were asked to resolve The Birth censorship controversies. Specifically, 21 of the 50 mayors petitioned individually acted to resolve the controversy in question. These figures are not significant (x^2 = .64, >.02). However, of the 21 mayors resolving a controversy, 17 ordered total or partial suppression of the film and 4 refused to censor The Birth. These figures are significant (x^2 = 8.04, >.01). Therefore, mayors as a class of municipal official did not resolve controversies with a frequency greater than chance. However, if a mayor did resolve a controversy, he was more likely than not to resolve that controversy in favor of censorship. Eight mayors who resolved controversies by ordering censorship of the film did so on the grounds that the film would incite racial prejudice. Seven other mayors censored the film after receiving protests from local black organizations, but the specific rationales underlying the bans are unclear. One mayor ordered two scenes cut from the film because he thought the scenes violated the "moral" rights of his city's black citizens. One mayor forbade the film by ruling it "unfit for decent people." One mayor ruled in favor of The Birth by specifically rejecting the argument that the film would incite race hatred. The rationales underlying the decisions of the remaining three mayors who refused to censor the film are unclear. All of the mayoral decisions were rendered between 1915-1938. Slightly more than half of the decisions were made between 1915-1921. The remaining decisions were rendered between 1924-1938. More censorship controversies were resolved by mayors in 1915 (eight) than any other single year. In 1915, 5 mayors decided in favor of censorship and 3 mayors decided in favor of the film. The only other mayor to decide in favor of the film did so in 1924. Thus, all mayors who decided The Birth's right to the screen after 1924 favored censorship. More of the latter type of decision were made in 1931 (five) than any other single year.

The roles played by the remaining 29 mayors involved in censorship controversies, but not resolving those controversies, varied. For example, 12 of these mayors ordered total or partial censorship of the film. But, in 10 instances the mayor's actions were challenged in the courts and the controversies resolved there. In one of these instances the controversy was resolved by a state censorship board. In the remaining instance, the film's right to the screen was determined by a municipal censorship board. Four mayors indicated they had no authority to act regarding the film. In four cases, mayors facilitated controversy resolution. In three additional cases, mayors went on public record against the film. In one instance the film's opponents continued to protest after a mayor's decision in favor of the film, but eventually acquiesced. The roles played by the remaining five mayors involved in controversies are unclear. These 29 involvements occurred between 1915-1950. Slightly over half of them occurred in 1951. Only one mayor was asked to censor The Birth without resolving the controversy after 1931.

Two mayors acted in joint power with other municipal officials to resolve the controversies in which they were involved. In both instances, the film was banned after the officials heard protests from representatives of local black groups. One of the controversies was resolved in 1918; the other in 1924. In the former instance, the mayor acted with his city's board of common council. In the latter, the mayor acted with a police chief. Because so few officials occurred in this category, its statistical significance was not measured independently.

Three police censor boards were asked to resolve The Birth controversies. Two boards did so and one did not. Of the police censor boards which resolved a controversy, one censored the film and one did not. The censorship order was issued on the rationale that the film was immoral and/or obscene. On the other hand, the board which refused to censor the film specifically rejected that same rationale. In this instance, the board told the film's opponents that unless a film was indecent or obscene, it could not censor the film. Since in its opinion, The Birth did not violate these standards, the board would not move against the film. Informally, this board also advised the protesters to abandon their efforts because it thought the agitation would only bring more attention to the film. The board which ordered the film stopped did so in 1939. The board which refused to censor the film did so in 1915. The board which ruled on the film but did not resolve the controversy ordered the film stopped in 1915. This action was based upon the rationale that the film was unfair to blacks. However, the board's decision was overruled by a court which enjoined the censorship. Because of the limited number of police boards located which dealt with The Birth a test for statistical significance was not performed on the data. However, from the board's actions which were studied it can be seen that boards resolved two-thirds of the controversies in which they were involved. Half of the boards which resolved a controversy supported censorship and half supported the film.

Of the ten municipal censorship boards asked to resolve The Birth censorship controversies, nine did so and one did not. Of the nine boards which resolved controversies, eight supported censorship and one supported the film. Thus, in 88 percent of the cases resolved by municipal censorship boards, the boards supported censor-

ship. These boards resolved controversies between 1915-1961.
Four boards supported censorship action because they judged the film
would engender racial prejudice. One board censored the film because
it considered the film indecent and/or obscene. Other board rationales are unclear. The board which did not resolve a controversy refused to censor The Birth in 1915. The film's opponents carried
their protests elsewhere and the controversy was eventually resolved
by a court injunction against city council ordered censorship. Again,
the number of instances of municipal censorship board involvement in
The Birth controversies was judged too small to compute statistical
significance. However, in the instances found, municipal censorship
boards resolved 90 percent of the controversies in which they were involved. Of the nine boards which resolved controversies, 88 percent
supported censorship.

Twelve city councils were asked to take action concerning the
film. Four resolved the controversies in which they were involved and
eight did not. This figure is not significant ($x^2 = .75$, $>.02$).
Therefore, city councils did not resolve The Birth controversies with
a frequency that differs from random. The four city councils which
resolved controversies did so by forbidding the film. These rulings
were made between 1915-1930. Once the film was banned under an ordinance which prohibited the exhibition of anything which might engender racial prejudice. One city council prohibited the film because it threatened public peace. One council prohibited the film
after promised cuts were not made. The reason underlying the other

council action resolving a controversy is unclear.

Eight other city councils involved in The Birth controversies did not resolve a controversy. Of these eight councils, two ordered the film suppressed but were enjoined from interfering with the film. One council passed a resolution against the film, but that controversy was resolved by court action. The actions of the remaining five councils regarding the film are unclear. City council involvements occurred between 1915-1923.

A variety of other municipal officials were asked to resolve eight The Birth controversies. Three of these controversies were resolved by the petitioned officials who in each case ordered total or partial suppression of the film. One official ordered the film censored, but was enjoined by court action from interfering with the film. Four petitioned officials indicated they were without authority to act regarding the film and the controversies were resolved by other means. In one instance the controversy was resolved by a mayor. In two instances the controversies were resolved by a state censorship board. The ultimate resolution of the remaining controversy is unclear. All controversies which enlisted the aid of miscellaneous city officials took place between 1915-1931. Because the number of miscellaneous city officials involved is small and because the officials petitioned varied from controversy to controversy, the figures were not tested for statistical significance. However, it can be seen that about 38 percent of petitioned miscellaneous officials resolved the controversies in which they were involved. All miscellaneous officials who resolved controversies supported censorship of the film.

Administrative action against The Birth also was sought at the state level. Specifically, governors, state censorship boards, and World War I state councils of defense were asked to censor The Birth. During the time period studied, 28 state authorities were involved in 23 controversies. Twenty-one of these controversies debated state censorship and two dealt with municipal censorship. Thus, an average 1.22 officials were involved in each controversy. Fifteen of the 23 controversies were resolved by the petitioned state authority. This figure is not significant (x^2 = 1.08, $>.02$). Therefore, it can be seen that in terms of individuals petitioned and individual controversies, state officials did not resolve controversies with a frequency that differs from random. These findings are consistent with those found for administrative intervention regardless of level.

Of the 15 controversies resolved by state authorities, eight ended with total or partial censorship and seven ended with no censorship. This figure is not significant (x^2 = .06, $>.02$). Thus, state officials who resolved controversies rejected or supported censorship with a frequency that does not differ from chance. This finding is not consistent with that determined for officials resolving controversies regardless of level. To determine whether all types of state authorities resolved controversies in a pattern that does not differ from chance it is necessary to analyze each category of state official petitioned.

Slightly more governors than any other type state official were asked to censor The Birth. Of the 13 petitioned governors only

3 actually resolved a censorship controversy. This figure is not significant (x^2 = 3.76, $>$.02). Thus, it can be seen that governors did not act regarding The Birth in a pattern that differs from chance. All governors except one were asked to resolve state controversies. One governor was asked to resolve a municipal controversy but did not do so. One governor who did resolve a state controversy forbade the film because he considered the film unfair to blacks serving in World War I. Two governors resolved state controversies by indicating they had no authority to act against the film at that level and the film's opponents shifted their attention to municipal controversies within the states. The roles played by the remaining governors who did not resolve controversies varied. For example, six governors facilitated controversy resolution. Five of these governors supported censorship and one supported the film. Four of these controversies were resolved by state censorship boards, one was resolved through court action, and one was resolved by a municipal censorship board. In all cases but one, if a censorship board resolved the controversy, it supported the governors' positions on the film. Two governors expressed sympathy with the film's opponents but apparently did not actually act regarding the film. In one instance the film was not shown during the governor's term, but the manner in which this censorship occurred is unclear. The resolution of the other controversy is unclear. One governor indicated he had no authority to act regarding the film. That controversy was resolved by a state council of defense. Both the role played by the governor and the resolution of the remaining controversy

are unclear. Gubernatorial involvements with The Birth occurred between 1915-1931.

Twelve state censorship boards were involved in thirteen The Birth controversies between 1915-1958. Twelve of the controversies were at the state level and one was at the municipal level. Ten controversies were state censorship board resolved and three were not. This figure is not significant ($x^2 = 3.76$, $> .02$). Therefore, state censorship boards resolved controversies with a frequency that did not differ from random. Six of the state board resolved controversies ended with total or partial censorship of the film. Four boards refused to censor the film. Although the number of state censor boards was not high enough to determine independent statistical significance, it can be seen that the studied boards supported censorship 60 percent of the time. Of the boards which resolved controversies by supporting censorship, one justified censorship because the film was "not harmless," one justified partial censorship because parts of the film were indecent and/or immoral, and the rationales underlying the other censorship decisions are unclear. The rationales underlying the four state board decisions in favor of the film are all unclear. The three controversies taken to state boards but not resolved there were resolved by courts which in each case supported the board's right to censor the film.

Of the three state councils of defense which responded to the NAACP's request for suppression of the film during World War I, two resolved the controversies and one did not. One of the boards which resolved a controversy supported censorship; the other supported the film. The council which supported censorship based its action on the rationale that the film would engender racial prejudice during the war. The other council specifically rejected the argument that it could censor the film as a threat to the war effort. The council which apparently did not resolve the controversy said it was in sympathy with the film's opponents, but did not specifically ban the film. All state defense council involvements were in 1918 and all judgments were for the duration of World War I. The number of defense council involvements was judged too small to compute independent statistical significance. However, since all state councils apparently were petitioned and the responses of only three are recorded, the tactic was apparently not successful from the NAACP's point of view.

Thus, it can be seen that the three overall findings concerning administrative involvements in censorship controversies do not hold for all levels of officials or types of officials petitioned. The overall findings concerning the likelihood of controversy resolution in relation to number of individuals petitioned and number of controversies held regardless of controversy level. Therefore, both state and local officials resolved controversies with a frequency that did not differ from random. However, the overall finding regarding the manner in which officials who resolved controversies determined the film's right to the screen varied with controversy level. Local authorities who resolved controversies supported censorship with a frequency that differs from random like the overall pattern of administrative resolution. However, state authorities resolved controversies in favor of the film or in favor of censorship with a frequency that does not differ from chance. This differs from the overall pattern of administrative resolution.

Also, the overall findings regarding the frequency of success of administrative intervention in terms of individuals petitioned and individual controversy resolution, held for certain categories of officials and could not be determined independently for others. Mayors, city councils, governors, and state censorship boards resolved controversies with a frequency that did not differ from chance. Thus, these four categories of officials were consistent with the overall finding. However, five categories of officials contained too few examples to be analyzed independently for statistical significance. Therefore, whether the overall findings hold for the categories of police censor boards, municipal censor boards, state councils of defense, mayors plus other official, and miscellaneous city officials is uncertain. However, if the categories are combined, the resulting figures are not significant ($x^2 = 4.8$, $>.02$). Thus, across these categories, the overall findings hold.

The general finding regarding the manner in which officials who resolved controversies determined the film's right to the screen was also analyzed by category of official. Mayors resolving controversies did so in favor of censorship with a frequency differing from random. However, the number of officials resolving controversies in each of the following categories was too small to determine independent statistical significance: governor, state censorship board, state council of defense, mayor plus other official, municipal censorship boards, police censorship boards, city councils, and miscellaneous city officials. However, if these categories are collapsed and considered for statistical significance, the findings are significant ($x^2 = 8.24$, $<.01$). Thus, when considered together these categories of officials resolved censorship controversies in a manner supportive of censorship which differs from chance. Therefore, no category of official varied from the pattern found for controversy resolution regardless of official category.

An overview of specific actions taken by each category of official resolving controversies is presented in table 9. As discussed previously and as evident in table 9, more officials regardless of category resolved controversies in favor of censorship than in favor of the film. Also, if an official supported censorship of the film, he/she supported total suppression of the film over six times more frequently than he/she supported partial censorship. This finding is also reflected in table 10 which presents a summary of the specific kind of censorship/no censorship action taken: prior restraint, prior restraint partial, subsequent restraint, subsequent restraint partial, no censorship.

Officials resolving controversies based their actions on a variety of rationales. Thirteen officials who banned the film totally did so on the rationale that the film engendered racial

TABLE 9

CONTROVERSIES RESOLVED BY OFFICIAL AND ACTION

Official	Censor Total	Censor Partial	No Censor	Total
Mayor	16	1	4	21
Mayor plus other	2	0	0	2
Police Board	1	0	1	2
Municipal Board	6	2	1	9
Miscellaneous city officials	1	2	0	3
City Council	4	0	0	4
Governor	1	0	2	3
State censor board	5	1	4	10
State defense council	1	0	1	2
Total	37	6	13	56

TABLE 10

SPECIFIC TYPE OF RESTRAINT EXERCISED BY OFFICIALS RESOLVING CONTROVERSIES

Prior Restraint	Prior Restraint Partial	Subsequent Restraint	Subsequent Restraint Partial	No Censor
27	3	10	3	13

prejudice. Eleven officials banned the film after receiving protests from black community leaders, but the officials did not state specifically why they stopped the film. One censor board suppressed the film because it was "not harmless." Two censorship decisions were justified by the censors' argument that the film violated the patriotic rights of blacks during World War I. A different official banned the film once for each of the following reasons: film "unfit for decent people;" film obscene/indecent; film threatened public peace; and, promised cuts not made in film. The reasons underlying the remaining six decisions to censor the film are unclear. Two individuals who resolved controversies by ordering cuts in the film based their decisions on the reasoning that the scenes engendered racial prejudice. In one case scenes considered immoral/obscene were ordered cut. In a similar decision, one controversy was resolved when an individual ordered scenes cut because the scenes were judged to be in violation of the moral rights of blacks. One controversy was ended when all scenes considered "indecent, inhuman," or crime inciting were ordered cut. The rationale underlying the remaining controversy resolved by partial censorship is unclear. Of the 13 decisions in favor of the film, one was based specifically on the rejection of the argument that the film would engender racial prejudice; one rejected the argument that the film was obscene; and, one rejected the argument that the film violated the patriotic rights of blacks during World War I. Two state controversies ended when the petitioned officials indicated they had no authority to act against the film. The rationales used by the remaining officials who refused to censor the film are unclear. Censorship rationales utilized by each category of official are presented in tables 11 and 12. From the tables it can be seen that 82 percent of mayors ordering censorship based the order on either the rationale that the film would engender racial prejudice or on a rationale that is unclear with censorship coming after the mayor heard protests from black organizations.

TABLE 11

CONTROVERSY RESOLUTION BY OFFICIALS AND RATIONALES FOR CENSORSHIP ACTIONS

Official	Race Prejudice	Immoral	After Black Protest	Not Harmless	Patriotism	Unclear	Other
Mayor	8	0	6	0	0	1	2
Mayor + official	0	0	2	0	0	0	0
Municipal Board	5	1	1	0	0	1	0
Police Board	0	1	0	0	0	0	0
City Council	1	0	1	0	0	0	2
Other Municipal	1	0	1	0	0	1	0
State Board	0	1	0	1	0	4	0
Governor	0	0	0	0	1	0	0
State Defense Council	0	0	0	0	1	0	0

TABLE 12

OFFICIALS RESOLVING CONTROVERSIES BY REFUSING TO CENSOR
AND RATIONALE REJECTED

Official	Race Prejudice	Immoral	Patriotism	No Authority to Act	Unclear
Mayor	1	0	0	0	3
Municipal Board	0	0	0	0	1
Police Board	0	1	0	0	0
State Board	0	0	0	0	4
State Defense Council	0	0	1	0	0
Governor	0	0	0	2	0

Municipal censor boards, city councils, mayors plus other city officials, and other municipal authorities also based the majority of their decisions against the film on this rationale. On the other hand, no state official was found to justify censorship of The Birth on either the grounds that it would engender racial prejudice or on grounds which are unclear but censorship coming after black protest. Individuals who refused to censor the film were more likely than not to refuse to make public the reasons underlying their actions.

Administrative decisions resolved The Birth of a Nation censorship controversies from 1915 to 1961. To determine whether officials resolved controversies for or against censorship consistently throughout the years of the study, it is necessary to analyze the controversies by the years in which they occurred. Because the frequency with which officials resolved controversies in favor of censorship differed from chance with local officials but not with state officials, the data have been split for this analysis. Local officials and controversies resolved by year are presented in table 13. State officials and controversies resolved by year are shown in table 14. As shown in table 13, more controversies were resolved by local officials in 1915 than in any other year. In 1915 local officials resolved 15 controversies, 10 in favor of censorship and five in favor of the film. These figures are not significant ($x^2 = 1.66$, $>.02$). Therefore, local officials in 1915 did not resolve controversies for or against censorship with a frequency that differs from chance. However, after 1915 the number of controversies resolved by total or partial suppression outnumbered controversies resolved in favor of the film 26 to 1. These figures are significant ($x^2 = 23$, $<.001$). Therefore, if a municipal official resolved a controversy after 1915, he/she resolved that controversy in favor of censorship with a frequency that deviates from chance. Thus, the overall finding of the study concerning municipal officials who resolved controversies in regards of censorship/no censorship holds for all official decisions after 1915. However, the finding does not hold for municipal decisions during 1915. However, if one analyzes the manner in which state officials resolved controversies across time, one finds that the overall finding regarding the manner in which this level of official resolved controversies in relation to censor/no censor holds. That is, state officials resolved controversies in favor of censorship or in favor of the film with a frequency that did not differ from chance. The largest number of controversies in any year resolved by state officials was five in 1915. That year officials resolved two controversies with censorship orders and three controversies by allowing the film at the state level.

Rationales expressed by individuals resolving controversies with one exception did not concentrate in any given year. For example, as shown in table 15, censors justified actions against the film on the rationale that it would engender racial prejudice from 1915-1961. The rationale which is an exception to this finding was patriotism. All decisions justifying censorship on this rationale were made in 1918. However, since this rationale was only used during World War I, this is not a surprising finding.

TABLE 13

LOCAL CONTROVERSIES RESOLVED BY YEAR AND DECISION

Year	Prior Restraint	Prior Restraint Partial	Subsequent Restraint	Subsequent Restraint Partial	No Censorship
1915	5	1	1	3	5
1918	3	0	0	0	0
1921	2	0	0	0	0
1922	1	0	0	0	0
1924	2	0	1	0	1
1925	3	0	0	0	0
1930	0	0	1	0	0
1931	3	1	4	0	0
1938	1	0	0	0	0

1939	1	0	1	0	0
1959	1	0	0	0	0
1961	1	0	0	0	0

TABLE 14

STATE CONTROVERSIES RESOLVED BY YEAR AND DECISION

Year	Prior Restraint	Prior Restraint Partial	Subsequent Restraint	Subsequent Restraint Partial	No Censorship
1915	2	0	0	0	3
1917	0	0	0	0	1
1918	2	0	1	0	1
1922	0	1	0	0	0
1923	0	0	0	0	1
1931	0	0	1	0	0
1958	0	0	0	0	1

TABLE 15

CONTROVERSIES RESOLVED BY CENSORSHIP AND
RATIONALE FOR ACTION BY YEAR

Year	Race Prejudice	Immoral	After Black Protest	Not Harmless	Patriotism	Unclear	Other
1915	4	1	0	1	0	3	3
1918	1	0	2	0	2	1	0
1921	1	0	0	0	0	1	0
1922	0	1	1	0	0	0	0
1924	1	0	1	0	0	0	1
1930	1	0	0	0	0	0	0
1931	3	0	4	0	0	2	0
1938	1	0	0	0	0	0	0
1939	1	1	0	0	0	0	0
1959	1	0	0	0	0	0	0
1961	1	0	0	0	0	0	0

To extend the data analysis it is possible to compare those administrative involvements already discussed which resolved controversies with administrative actions not resolving controversies. As evident in table 16, the split by year between the number of petitioned officials who resolved a controversy and the number of petitioned officials who did not resolve a controversy was reasonably equal with two exceptions. One exception to the reasonably equal distribution occurred in 1915. In 1915 20 of 47 petitioned officials resolved a controversy. However, these figures are not significant ($x^2 = 1.04$, $>.02$). The other exception was 1931. In 1931, eight of 12 petitioned officials resolved a controversy. These figures also are not significant ($x^2 = 1.33$, $>.02$). Therefore, at least in the extreme cases, the relationship between individuals petitioned and controversy resolution by year supports the overall finding that petitioned individuals resolved controversies with a frequency that did not differ from random. The only other year which witnessed enough petitioned officials for independent statistical analysis supports this general finding. In 1918, seven officials resolved controversies and five did not. These figures are not significant ($x^2 = .332$ $>.02$).

As shown in table 17, 21 of the 58 officials involved in but not resolving a controversy made a specific censorship decision concerning the film. Nineteen of the 21 supported total or partial suppression of the film and two supported the film. While not taking direct action concerning the film, an additional 17 officials either facilitated controversy resolution or indicated they were in sympathy with the film's opponents. In these 17 instances, only one official supported the film. Eight other officials said they had no authority to act regarding the film. The roles played by the remaining 12 officials in relation to controversy resolution are unclear.

Of the 35 controversies not resolved by administrative involvement, 19 were resolved by court action, three were resolved when either the film's opponents acquiesced or voluntary censorship occurred, one municipal decision regarding the film was overruled by a decision at the state level and one controversy was resolved through criminal proceedings. The actual resolutions of the remaining 11 con-

TABLE 16

PETITIONED OFFICIALS RESOLVING AND NOT RESOLVING CONTROVERSIES BY YEAR

Year	Resolve	Not Resolve
1915	20	27
1916	0	3
1917	1	2
1918	7	5
1920	0	1
1921	2	5
1922	2	1
1923	1	3
1924	4	2
1925	3	2
1930	1	0
1931	8	4
1938	1	1
1939	2	0
1950	0	1
1952	0	1
1958	1	0
1959	1	0
1961	1	0

troversies are unclear. Of the 19 court rulings, 14 enjoined administratively ordered censorship and five supported censorship. These figures are not significant ($x^2 = 4.26$, $>.02$). Therefore, over the time period studied, courts overruled administrative censorship with a frequency that did not differ from chance. A majority of these court decisions were made during the first year of the film's release. Specifically, during 1915, 10 courts were asked to enjoin administratively ordered censorship and all 10 did so. After 1915, court decisions of this nature were fairly evenly divided between those supporting censorship and those supporting the film. The last such decision was made in 1952 by a court which apparently affirmed the right of a state board to censor the film. Thus, after 1915 courts were almost as likely to affirm the film's right as they were to deny it.

TABLE 17

ACTIONS OF OFFICIALS NOT RESOLVING CONTROVERSIES

Official	Censor total	Censor partial	No Censor	No Authority	Facilitated	Sympathetic	Unclear
Mayor	11	1	1	4	4	3	5
Police Censors	1	0	0	0	0	0	0
Municipal Censors	0	0	1	0	0	0	0
City Council	2	0	0	0	0	1	5
Misc. city official	1	0	0	4	0	0	0

Governor	0	0	0	0	6	2	2
State Censor	3	0	0	0	0	0	0
State defense council	0	0	0	0	0	1	0
Totals	18	1	2	8	10	7	12

Thus, during the time period studied, seeking administrative relief was not a tactic which reliably resolved censorship controversies. All categories and levels of officials petitioned within the time frame did not resolve controversies with a frequency that differs from chance. However, overall if an official resolved a controversy, that official supported censorship of the film with a frequency which differs from chance. However, this generalization holds only for municipal officials. State officials resolving controversies supported censorship of the film with a frequency not differing from random. Several sources speculated that officials ruled against the film consistently to woo black voters. Because not all officials who censored the film were elected, because the generalization held for local but not for state officials, and because overall officials did not resolve controversies with a frequency that differs from random, this explanation probably does not adequately explain why officials who resolved controversies did so significantly in favor of censorship. Therefore, if the film's opponents were willing to chance that a municipal official would resolve a controversy, the tactic could be considered successful against the film.

Notes to Chapter V

[1] NAACP National, Memorandum "to our Branches and Locals" on The Birth of a Nation, 15 June 1915, NAACP Archives, File C300, Library of Congress Manuscript Collection, Washington, D. C. (Hereafter referred to as NAACP Archives).

[2] NAACP National, Memorandum "to our Branches and Locals" on The Birth of a Nation, 7 April 1915, NAACP Archives, File C300.

[3] Mary Childs Nerney to Mrs. S. B. Henderson, 24 May 1915, NAACP Archives, File C300. It is interesting to note that Nerney described this tactic as "practical but hard work."

[4] Mary White Ovington to George H. Woodson, 5 November 1915, NAACP Archives, File C301. Ovington described this tactic as "very difficult" to implement.

[5] Secretary to Miss M. C. Nerney to Clifford H. Tavernier, 13 November 1915, NAACP Archives, File C301.

[6] Ibid.

[7] Mary Childs Nerney to Dr. Stephen Lewis, 12 September 1915, NAACP Archives, File C300.

[8] Within the context of this research the phrases "resolve a controversy" or "controversy resolution" refer to the ultimate decision made or the outcome of a given controversy.

[9] "Birth of Nation' Barred by Mayor in Cedar Rapids," Chicago Defender, 5 June 1915, p. 1.

[10] Ibid.

[11] Ibid.

[12] George Leach to James W. Johnson, 15 August 1921, NAACP Archives, File C301.

[13] George Leach as quoted in Entry on Typewritten Sheet, Birth of a Nation folder, Museum of Modern Art Archives, New York, New York (Hereafter referred to as MOMA Archives).

[14] "Birth of Nation' Barred," Baltimore Ledger, 12 June 1915, p. 6.

[15] "Birth of Nation' Nix Sets Precedent by Hartford Police," Variety, 1 June 1938, n.p., clipping in D. W. Griffith's personal

Birth of a Nation scrapbook, D. W. Griffith Personal Papers, MOMA Archives, New York, New York (Hereafter referred to as Lincoln Center Archives).

[16] Ibid.

[17] Hazel L. Rice to William McKinley, 3 June 1938, ACLU Archives, Vol, 1076, Wisconsin State Historical Society, Madison, Wisconsin (Hereafter referred to as ACLU Archives).

[18] "Birth of Nation' Nix Sets Precedent. . .," Variety.

[19] "Great Picture Won't Be Shown," Daily Register, November 1918, n.p. clipping in NAACP Archives, File C301.

[20] Ibid.

[21] Ibid.

[22] Ibid. In addition Ward said "The cancellation of this picture means a loss of $225 in actual cash as the picture which costs $150 had already been paid for and $75 worth of advertising has been done on billboards and newspapers. This naturally works a hardship on us coming at this time when we have just lost over $1,500 by having to close for the past six weeks on account of the influenza epidemic. It has always been our policy to give the Richmond people all the best pictures money can buy, and for this reason we made the engagement for 'The Birth of a Nation.' However, we do not at any time want to show any picture that will be offensive to the public. . .While we are satisfied the 'Birth of a Nation' is not offensive, and would not have booked it if we thought so, we concluded not to show the wonderful production and comply with the Mayor's request. Those wishing to see the picture can do so at a later date as it will be shown in Lexington at the Ben Ali Theatre for a two day's run as soon as the flu ban is lifted."

[23] "Birth of Nation' Film Barred in Newton, Massachusetts," Press Release, 18 July 1924, NAACP Archives, File C301.

[24] Ibid.

[25] "Detroit," Variety, 19 February 1931, n.p., clipping in D. W. Griffith's personal Birth of a Nation scrapbook, D. W. Griffith Personal Papers, MOMA Archives.

[26] "NAACP Wins Barring of 'Birth of Nation' in Detroit," Press Release, 20 February 1931, NAACP Archives, File C302.

[27] "Birth of Nation' Film Barred by Philadelphia Mayor," Press Release, 4 September 1931, NAACP Archives, File C302.

[28] The information was not available in the newspapers, archive collections, and other resources consulted for this study, listed in the bibliography.

[29] "NAACP Helps Stop 'Birth of Nation' Film," Press Release, 13 February 1925, NAACP Archives, File C302.

[30] Ibid.

[31] "Ohio Bars 'Birth of Nation," Press Release, 12 June 1925, NAACP Archives, File C302. See also, *Epoch Producing Corporation v. Vernon M. Riegel*, Petition No. 1903, Filed 19 March 1925, with the Supreme Court of Ohio, Document in *Birth of a Nation* File, Ohio State Historical Society Archives, Columbus, Ohio (Hereafter referred to as Ohio State Historical Society Archives).

[32] *Epoch Producing Corporation v. Harry L. Davis Mayor of the City of Cleveland, et. al.*, 19 Ohio NISI Pruis Reports 465 (1917).

[33] Ibid., at 466.

[34] "Montclair, N. J. Bars 'Birth of a Nation," Press Release, 21 August 1931, NAACP Archives, File C302, and "Nebraska: March 30, 1931. . .,"Entry on Typewritten Sheet, *Birth of a Nation* folder, MOMA Archives.

[35] "Nebraska: March 30, 1931. . .," Entry on Typewritten Sheet.

[36] "Montclair, N. J. Bars 'Birth of a Nation," Press Release.

[37] "Glen Cove Mayor Stops Film Showing of 'Birth of a Nation," Press Release, 16 October 1931, NAACP Archives, File C302.

[38] Ibid.

[39] Ibid.

[40] Ibid.

[41] George W. Smith to John Shillady, 11 November 1918, NAACP Archives, File C302.

[42] "Infamous Picture Forbidden," n.t., n.d., n.p., clipping in NAACP Archives, File C301.

[43] Ibid.

[44] William M. Dunn, Telegram to NAACP, 21 July 1915, NAACP Archives, File C300. See also, Mary Childs Nerney to R. L. Brokenburr, 29 July 1915, NAACP Archives, File C300.

[45] P. W. Stewart to Mary Childs Nerney, 24 April 1915, NAACP Archives, File C300.

[46] NAACP to His Honor John Purroy Mitchell, 19 March 1915, NAACP Archives, File C299.

[47] Ibid.

[48] Ibid.

[49] At least seven such letters may be found among John P. Mitchell's Mayoral Papers in the New York City Archives, New York, New York (Hereafter referred to as New York City Archives).

[50] Mrs. N. J. Floyd to John P. Mitchell, letter has no date but is stamped "received March 29, 1915," John P. Mitchell Mayoral Papers, Correspondence File B, New York City Archives.

[51] Ibid.

[52] "Proceeding meeting held 4/1/15 before the Mayor at City Hall Thursday Morning, April 1, 1915," Transcript among D. W. Griffith Personal Papers, MOMA Archives.

[53] Secretary NAACP to John P. Mitchell, 30 March 1915, NAACP Archives, File C300.

[54] "Proceeding meeting held 4/1/15 before the Mayor at City Hall. . ."D. W. Griffith Papers.

[55] Ibid. Another perspective on Mitchell's attitude concerning the film was presented in the testimony of D. W. Griffith's attorney Martin W. Littleton before a U. S. House committee concerning a bill on establishing a federal censorship board. Martin represented Griffith at the April 1, 1915, hearing in Mitchell's office and recalled Mitchell said "I went to see the picture myself. I cannot see why people should complain about it; but, nevertheless, as the representative of the people of this city between whom there seems to be a line of cleavage in opinion, I very much wish to do the thing which will satisfy and placate." Littleton said that the mayor suggested certain cuts in the film as long as "those excisions do not emasculate the integrity and character of the picture and the intention and purpose of the men who made it." Although in his testimony Littleton did not indicate which specific scenes were

eliminated, he did say that in response to the mayor's suggestion certain cuts were made in the film. Littleton also stressed that they were not ordered to cut the film because the mayor's request was "only a suggestion." See Statement of the Honorable Martin W. Littleton, New York, Hearing Before the Committee on Education: House of Representatives, 64th Congress, 1st Session, on House Resolution 456--a Bill to Create a New Division of the Bureau of Education to be Known as the Federal Motion Picture Commission and Defining Its Powers and Duties, January 13-19, 1916 (Washington, D. C. Government Printing Office, 1916), pp. 252-255.

[56] Statement of Honorable Martin W. Littleton.

[57] Chairman NAACP Board of Directors to John P. Mitchell, 1 April 1915, NAACP Archives, File C300.

[58] "Fighting Race Calumny," The Crisis 10 (May 1915), p. 40.

[59] Apparently the NAACP regularly sent people to view the film. For example, Mary Childs Nerney asked Mrs. Norman Whitehouse to report on the film April 7, 1915. See Mary Childs Nerney to Mrs. Norman Whitehouse, 7 April 1915, NAACP Archives, File C300.

[60] When the film opened in New York it contained 1,544 individual shots. After cuts, the total was reduced to 1,375. There seems to be no complete record of the scenes which were actually cut. However, it is presumed that the most heavily racist shots such as those of blacks "attacking" white girls on the Piedmont streets and the original epilogue including Lincoln's letter to Stanton affirming that he did not believe in racial equality and the departation of blacks to Africa as the solution to America's racial problems were cut out. See Fred Silva, Focus on Birth of a Nation (Englewood Cliffs, N. J.: Prentice-Hall, Inc., 1971), p. 4. Mary Childs Nerney also sent a summary of scenes which had been cut from the film to Gilbert Lamb in response to Lamb's request for a record of the changes which had been made in the film. Nerney indicated that "the beating of a little white child in the presence of her mother by an old colored man who meets them on the street and who is annoyed because the child accidentally gets in his path; the showing of the dead body of the Negro 'Gus' after his murder by the Ku Klux Klan; a saloon brawl showing the most degraded types of Negroes in a drunken fight; the incident in the South Carolina legislature where a colored member takes off his shoes" had been cut. In addition to the eliminations, Nerney indicated that several modifications had been made in the following sequences: "the incident of the Southern Colonel's refusal to shake hands with the mulatto politician in the North which is cut short; when 'Gus' approaches the white girl whom he afterwards pursues he originally said, 'Missy, I'm a captain now.' This had

been changed to 'Missy, I'm a captain now and will marry.' At the beginning of the second part a new legend has been introduced reading 'This is an historical presentation of Reconstruction and is not meant to reflect upon any race of people of today.' An expansion of this sentiment is also introduced in a long legend which is run at the beginning of the performance inviting censorship: the two rape scenes have not been omitted though the first one has been shortened." (Here, Nerney is probably referring to the pursuit of Flora by Gus sequence and the attempt of Lynch to force Lucy Cameron to marry him when she refers to the two rape scenes). See Mary Childs Nerney to Gilbert D. Lamb, 13 April 1915, NAACP Archives, File C299.

[61] Mary Childs Nerney to George Packard, 17 April 1915, NAACP Archives, File C299.

[62] Seymour Stern, "The Birth of a Nation," Sight and Sound Index Series No. 4 (July 1945), p. 12.

[63] Frank K. Mott to W. A. Butler, 10 May 1915, NAACP Archives, File C300.

[64] Ibid.

[65] Ibid.

[66] Ibid. See also Harry Warnack, "Trouble Over The Clansman," Los Angeles Times, 9 February 1915, p. 6.

[67] "Infamous Picture Forbidden," Clipping in NAACP Archives.

[68] The information was not available in the newspapers, archive collections, and other resources consulted during the course of this research, listed in the bibliography.

[69] "Kansas Mayor Gets Cold Feet After Barring 'Birth of Nation' Film," Press Release, n.d., NAACP Archives, File C302.

[70] Ibid.

[71] Ibid.

[72] The information was not available in the newspapers, archive collections, and other resources consulted for this study, listed in the bibliography.

[73] "A Means to an End," Twin City Star, 27 November 1915, p. 4.

[74] Bainbridge v. Minneapolis, 131 Minn. 195 (1915).

[75] "Bainbridge Tells of Strife Over 'Birth of Nation' Film," Minneapolis Tribune, 14 November 1915, p. 1.

[76] "Film To Show in Mill City," St. Paul Pioneer Press, 31 October 1915, p. 3.

[77] "Supreme Court Last Hope of Film Show Unless Nye Relents," Minneapolis Tribune, 9 November 1915, p. 11.

[78] Bainbridge v. Minneapolis, at 196.

[79] "A Means to an End," Twin City Star.

[80] Ibid.

[81] Ibid. The Twin City Star called Nye's actions "political suicide" and said that it would have been "far better" had Nye "permitted the show without the advertising." Another area black paper The Appeal severly criticized Nye's actions also. See "Minneapolis Column," Appeal, 27 November 1915, p. 4.

[82] The controversies occurred in Lynn, Massachusetts, and New Britain, Connecticut. See "Birth of Nation Is Barred," Supreme Circle News, 18 May 1918, n.p. clipping in NAACP Archives, File C301, and "Mayor and Police Chief Stop 'Birth of Nation' in New Britain," Press Release, 29 August 1924, NAACP Archives, File C302, respectively.

[83] "Birth of Nation' Is Barred," Supreme Circle News.

[84] "Mayor and Police Chief Stop 'Birth of Nation' in New Britain," Press Release.

[85] Ibid.

[86] Unsigned but initialed WFW, Assistant Secretary NAACP, to Honorable William Hart, 27 August 1924, NAACP Archives, File C302.

[87] "Injunction Holds in Nixon Film Case. . .Court Rules Censor's Approval on 'The Birth of a Nation' is Sufficient," Pittsburgh Post, 4 September 1915, p. 4.

[88] Ibid.

[89] Nixon Theatre Company v. Joseph Armstrong and W. N. Matthews, Bill of Complaint, Filed by Reed, Smith, Shaw and Beal for the Plaintiff, document among D. W. Griffith's Personal Papers, MOMA Archives.

[90]"Play is Permitted to Start in Nixon," *Pittsburgh Post*, 31 August 1915, p. 3.

[91]*Epoch v. Davis*.

[92]Ibid., at 466.

[93]Ibid.

[94]Ibid.

[95]Ibid., at 465.

[96]"Michigan Judge Allows 'Nation' Injunction to Stand," *Variety*, 30 September 1921, p. 38.

[97]Ibid.

[98]Ibid.

[99]*Virginia Amusement Company v. W. W. Wertz and John Britton*, copy of order from Judge Morgan Owen, NAACP Archives, File C302 and *Virginia Amusement Company v. W. W. Wertz and John Britton*, copy of order from Judge Arthur Hudson, NAACP Archives, File C302.

[100]Ibid.

[101]Ibid.

[102]"West Virginia Supreme Court Bars 'Birth of Nation' Film," Press Release, 10 April 1925, NAACP Archives, File C302.

[103]Ibid.

[104]*Joseph M. McCarthy v. City of Chicago*, General No. 316145, copy of Ruling of William F. Cooper rendered 5 June 1915, State of Illinois County of Cook in the Superior Court of Cook County, document among D. W. Griffith's Personal Papers, MOMA Archives.

[105]Ibid.

[106]Ibid.

[107]"Oakland Allows 'The Clansman' To Reopen," 10 August 1915, n.p., clipping in NAACP Archives, File C300. As is discussed in Chapter III, in this case the mayor ordered the film stopped after receiving protests from individuals who contended the film was unfair to blacks and would incite racial prejudice. The court decision was apparently a procedural one.

[108]"Mayor Fights Photoplay," *Baltimore Ledger*, 25 December 1915, p. 1. In this case the mayor forbade the film because he considered it immoral, obscene, and unfair to blacks. The rationale of the judge in this case is unclear.

[109]"Ban on Film Lifted," *New York Times*, 15 August 1915, Section II, p. 13. In this case the mayor ordered the film stopped because he considered it unfair to blacks and likely to incite racial prejudice. The judge in this instance indicated he believed the decision had been made for political reasons and issued an injunction.

[110]"Gary, Indiana, NAACP Fighting to Stop 'Birth of Nation,'" Press Release, 12 December 1924, in NAACP Archives, File C302.

[111]"A Good Fight Against a Bad Thing," *Twin City Herald*, 10 January 1931, n.p., clipping in NAACP Archives, File C302.

[112]"Mayor Dever to Put Ban on 'Birth of Nation," *Chicago Defender*, 2 February 1924, Part1, p. 7.

[113]Ibid.

[114]Philip Kinsley, "Birth of Nation' Shown While Lawyers Talk," *Chicago Daily Tribune*, 6 February 1924, p. 10.

[115]*Hollywood Pictures Company and Ralph Christy V. City of Topeka, W. E. Atchison, City Attorney, Henry Dangerfield, Assistant City Attorney, and Perry Bruch, Chief of Police of the City of Topeka*, Petition for Injunction, copy in NAACP Archives, File C302.

[116]Ibid.

[117]Elisha Scott to Walter T. Andrews, 27 November 1931, NAACP Archives, File C302.

[118]"Disputed Film Play Seen at the Tremont. . .'Birth of Nation' Shown to Invited Audience," *Boston Morning Journal*, 9 April 1915, p. 4.

[119]"Theatre Notes," *Christian Science Monitor*, 3 April 1915, p. 4. It is interesting to note that although Curley said he did not object to The Birth, he did object to a film then showing in Boston called The Hypocrites. Curley said that he opposed that film because of the nudity of the woodland nymphs in it and that the film would be stopped unless the numphs were clothed with "garments of paint." Curley also said that he would not allow films of the Willard-Johnson fight to be shown in Boston on the

grounds that the films would "degrade public decency." See also "Theatre Notes," Christian Science Monitor, 6 April 1915, p. 5.

[120] Ibid.

[121] Mary Childs Nerney to Joel E. Spingarn, 9 April 1915, NAACP Archives, File C300.

[122] "The Birth of a Nation," Indianapolis Freeman, 1 May 1915, p. 4.

[123] "Censors To Decide After Viewing Protested Film," Christian Science Monitor, 8 April 1915, p. 4.

[124] "Disputed Film Play Seen at the Tremont. . .," Boston Morning Journal.

[125] Ibid.

[126] "Film Again Protested," Christian Science Monitor, 12 April 1915, p. 5.

[127] Ibid.

[128] "Birth of Nation' Causes Near-Riot," Boston Sunday Globe, 18 April 1915, p. 3.

[129] Laws and Resolves of Massachusetts, Acts 1908--Chapter 494. The statute gave the mayor the power to suspend the license of a place of public amusement which did not eliminate any scenes he and the police commissioner had requested cut because they considered them to be obscene or immoral or tended to injure the morals of the community. The Boston Guardian supported this view of the mayor's reasons for acting in a 17 April 1915 story when it stated ". . .Mayor Curley of Boston cannot stop the presentation of the film because it does not transgress the rules regarding obscenity. . ." See Boston Guardian, 17 April 1915, p. 1. Also the Cleveland Gazette reported "Mayor Curley decided that he could not stop the infamous production inasmuch as it was not established that the pictures were obscene even though indecent and mob-inciting." See "What Caused the Riot. . .," Cleveland Gazette, 1 May 1915, p. 2.

[130] "Big Negro Mass Meeting Denounces Photo-Play. . .The Film Vilifies Colored Race Says Delegate to Call on Governor Walsh," Boston Morning Journal, 19 April 1915, p. 1.

[131] E. Burton Ceruti to Mary Childs Nerney, 3 February 1915, NAACP Archives, File C301.

[132] Ibid.

[133] Genevieve Reusen, "Citizens Fight 'Birth of Nation,'" Chicago Defender, 31 July 1915, p. 4.

[134] Ibid.

[135] "Keep Up The Protest," St. Louis Argus, 3 September 1915, p. 4.

[136] James W. Johnson to Lester A. Walton, 20 May 1921, NAACP Archives, File C301.

[137] Ibid.

[138] "Film Barred at Lynn," Variety, 19 May 1922, p. 34.

[139] "Mayor Will Hear Negroes on 'Birth of Nation' Protest," Philadelphia North American, 22 September 1915, p. 6.

[140] "Court Lifts Ban Upon 'Birth of a Nation," Philadelphia North American, 5 September 1915, p. 13.

[141] "Birth of Nation' Film Barred in California," Press Release, 8 July 1921, NAACP Archives, File C301. See also Charles Alexander to James W. Johnson, 26 June 1921, NAACP Archives, File C301.

[142] "Los Angeles Bars 'Birth of Nation," Variety, 1 July 1921, p. 25.

[143] "Roselle, N. J. Deletes Parts of 'Birth of Nation' Film," Press Release, 30 November 1931, NAACP Archives, File C302.

[144] Ibid.

[145] George Cobb to John Walrath, 5 January 1923, NAACP Archives, File C302.

[146] Ibid.

[147] Ibid.

[148] "Birth of Nation' May Not Appear," n. t., 26 June 1918, n. p., clipping in NAACP Archives, File C301.

[149] Ibid.

[150] Ibid.

[151] "Birth of Nation' Kicked Out of Ohio," Chicago Defender, 2 October 1915, p. 1.

[152] "Birth of Nation' Is Coming Here Monday Aug. 23rd, What Are You Going To Do About It?" *Philadelphia Tribune*, 21 August 1915, p. 1.

[153] Ibid.

[154] "Birth of Nation' Barred Out West By J. W. Harris," *Chicago Defender*, 11 September 1915, p. 1.

[155] "Birth of a Nation' To Be Shown in Modified Form by Mayor's Order," *Chicago Defender*, 30 October 1915, p. 3.

[156] Ibid.

[157] "San Francisco Protests Against 'Clansman," *Chicago Defender*, 13 March 1915, p. 4.

[158] "Ban Film Says NAACP," *Daily Compass*, 14 May 1950, p. 5.

[159] Ibid.

[160] Clipping with no head, *New York Times*, 19 May 1950, n.p., *Birth of Nation* file, Lincoln Center Archives.

[161] "Protest Against 'Birth of Nation," *Baltimore Ledger*, 7 August 1915, p. 1.

[162] Ibid.

[163] Ibid.

[164] Ibid.

[165] Ibid.

[166] "Cargo' and 'Primrose' Censorial Jams a Bit of a Trade Shock," *Variety*, 3 April 1940, p. 7.

[167] W. G. Bergman to Roger Baldwin, 27 April 1939, ACLU Archives, Vol. 2157.

[168] Ibid.

[169] Ibid.

[170] Ibid.

[171] Arthur Garfield Hays to Nate Goldstick, 1 May 1939, ACLU Archives, Vol, 2157 (A copy of the letter is also in NAACP Archives, File C302).

[172] Roger Baldwin to W. G. Bergman, 1 May 1939, ACLU Archives, Vol. 2157.

[173] Nathanial H. Goldstick to Arthur Garfield Hays, 22 May 1939, ACLU Archives, Vol. 2157.

[174] "Police Commissioner Voluntarily Refused License to Producers in Providence," Entry on Typewritten Sheet, <u>Birth of a Nation</u> folder, MOMA Archives.

[175] Mary Childs Nerney to George W. Crawford, 13 September 1915, NAACP Archives, File C300.

[176] Providence Branch of the NAACP, <u>Statement of Facts Regarding the Photo-Play 'The Birth of a Nation' By The Providence Branch of the NAACP To The Providence Board of Police Commissioners</u>, n.d., NAACP Archives, File C302.

[177] Ibid.

[178] Ibid.

[179] "Barred from Memphis," <u>New York Age</u>, 11 November 1915, p. 1.

[180] "Memphis Acts," <u>New York Age</u>, 11 November 1915, p. 4.

[181] "Memphis Bars 'Birth of Nation," <u>Philadelphia Tribune</u>, 20 November 1915, p. 5.

[182] "Censors Bar 'The Birth of a Nation," <u>Boston Globe</u>, 17 May 1921, p. 1. The Board was composed of Boston Mayor Andrew Peters, Boston Police Commissioner Edwin Curtis, and Wilfred Bolster, Chief Justice of the Boston Municipal Court. It is interesting to note that this Board was the one established by the authority of a 1915 statute passed by the Massachusetts legislature to stop <u>The Birth</u>. But, as also discussed in this chapter the original board did not stop the film.

[183] Ibid. See also, Stephen Fox, <u>Guardian of Boston: William Monroe Trotter</u> (New York: Atheneum, 1970), pp. 191-193.

[184] Ibid.

[185] Ibid.

[186] Albert C. Wolff, "Battling for Equal Rights," <u>Boston Guardian</u>, 22 February 1947, p. 4.

[187] "NAACP v. 'The Birth of a Nation," *Crisis* (February 1965), n.p., clipping in NAACP Archives, File C302.

[188] "Censors Bar 'The Birth of a Nation," *Boston Globe*.

[189] "Despite 16 Weeks Played Once, 'Birth' Barred in Riot Charge," *Variety*, 20 May 1921, p. 47.

[190] Ibid.

[191] "Censors Bar 'The Birth of a Nation," *Boston Globe*.

[192] "Close Theatre to Stop 'Birth of Nation' Film" *Boston Herald*, 17 May 1921, p. 1.

[193] Ibid.

[194] "'Birth' Barred at Lynn," *Variety*.

[195] Ibid.

[196] Ibid.

[197] "Milwaukee Negro Protest Bans 'Birth of Nation," *Variety*, 19 April 1939, n.p., clipping in *Birth of Nation* folder, Lincoln Center Archives.

[198] Ibid.

[199] Ibid. See also, James W. Dorsey to NAACP, 30 April 1939, NAACP Archives, File C302.

[200] Statement of Christine Gilliam to Ira Carmen, in Ira Carmen, *Movies, Censorship and the Law* (Ann Arbor: University of Michigan Press, 1966), p. 316.

[201] Ibid.

[202] "'Birth of Nation' Plays Outside Atlanta," *Variety*, 5 April 1961, n.p., clipping in *Birth of Nation* folder, Lincoln Center Archives.

[203] It is interesting to note that film scholar Ira Carmen called this suppression of *The Birth* "As to protect the good order of the city" undoubtedly a violation of the *Burstyn* doctrine. See Carmen, *Movies, Censorship and the Law*, p. 237-422.

[204] Mary Ashe Miller to Gentlemen, 2 March 1915, NAACP Archives, File C300.

[205] Ibid.

[206] Walter Butler to Mary Childs Nerney, 19 May 1915, NAACP Archives, File C300. See also J. B. Jefferson to Mary Childs Nerney, 6 May 1915, NAACP Archives, File C300.

[207] Genevieve Reusen, "Citizens Fight 'Birth of Nation."

[208] Ibid.

[209] "Birth' Protest Bill Passed By Senate," *Boston Morning Journal*, 21 May 1915, p. 5.

[210] "Nation' Film Is Now Up To Censor Board. . .Governor Signs Bill," *Boston Morning Journal*, 22 May 1915, p. 2.

[211] "Board of Censors Refuses to Stop Photoplay at Tremont But Refuses to Give Reasons," *Boston Evening Transcript*, 3 June 1915, p. 14.

[212] "Birth of Nation," *Boston Morning Journal*, 23 October 1915, p. 4.

[213] "Birth of Nation' Ends Career Here Tonight," *Minneapolis Tribune*, 10 November 1915, p. 2.

[214] Jose Sherwood to Mary Childs Nerney, 31 October 1915, NAACP Archives, File C301.

[215] Ibid.

[216] Dr. V. D. Turner to W. E. B. DuBois, 25 October 1915, NAACP Archives, File C300.

[217] "Will Be Damned Either Way," *St. Paul Pioneer Press*, 27 October 1915, p. 8.

[218] Jose Sherwood to Mary Childs Nerney.

[219] Ibid.

[220] "Birth of Nation' Ends Career Here Tonight," *Minneapolis Tribune*.

[221] "St. Paul NAACP Procures Ban on Showing of 'Birth of Nation," Press Release, 2 January 1931, NAACP Archives, File C302.

[222] Ibid.

[223] "NAACP Stops 'Birth of Nation' in Montclair, New Jersey," Press Release, 8 August 1924, NAACP Archives, File C302.

[224] Ibid.

[225] "Portland, Ore. NAACP Succeeds in Barring 'Birth of Nation' Film," Press Release, 20 March 1915, NAACP Archives, File C302.

[226] Ibid.

[227] Petition Filed by Dr. Charles E. Locke and E. Burton Ceruti for the Los Angeles Branch of the NAACP with the City Council of the City of Los Angeles, State of California, 2 February 1915, NAACP Archives, File C301.

[228] Ibid.

[229] Ibid.

[230] "The Clansman," Western Outlook, 20 February 1915, p. 2.

[231] "Denver Suppressed Vicious Photo-Play," New York Age, 23 December 1915, p. 1.

[232] "A Hand At Last," Chicago Defender, 25 December 1915, p. 1.

[233] Ibid.

[234] Ibid.

[235] Epoch v. Davis at 465.

[236] Ibid.

[237] "San Francisco Protests Against 'Clansman," Chicago Defender, 13 March 1915, p. 4.

[238] Mary Asche Miller to Gentlemen.

[239] "Theatre Man Arrested for Showing 'Birth of Nation," Press Release, 20 May 1938, NAACP Archives, File C302.

[240] Ibid.

[241] Eugene Scott to Chicago Defender, Chicago Defender, 13 October 1915, p. 9. (Reprinted in Chicago Defender, 23 Obtober 1915, p. 9.)

[242] Ibid.

[243] "Montgomery Citizens Protest Vicious Film," New York Age, 24 February 1916, p. 1.

[244] Ibid.

[245] "Negro Societies Protest," Variety, 27 December 1923, p. 20.

[246] Ibid.

[247] Ibid. However, it seems likely that the Kansas City, Kansas, commission opted not to move against the film. The controversy had already been fought at the state level and lost by the film's opponents when the state censor board passed the film and the governor refused to direct a recall. (See "Won't Stop Film," Topeka Daily State Journal, 4 December 1923, p. 6.) Also, the outcome of the Wichita controversy was being decided at that time and as was discussed the city in that case was enjoined from interfering with The Birth's production and the ordinance it had passed to ban the film was declared null and void by the court. (See "Birth' has Federal O.K. In State of Kansas," Variety, 10 January 1924, p. 19).

[248] "Clansman With One Scene Removed Approved," Sacramento Bee, 28 May 1915, p. 2.

[249] Ibid.

[250] Ibid.

[251] "Roselle, New Jersey Deletes Parts of 'Birth of Nation' Film," Press Release, 20 November 1931, NAACP Archives, File C302.

[252] "Jersey City, New Jersey," Entry on Typewritten Sheet, Birth of a Nation Folder, MOMA Archives.

[253] Ibid.

[254] Ibid.

[255] "Birth of a Nation' To Be Shown in Modified Form By Mayor's Orders," Chicago Defender, 30 November 1915, p. 3.

[256] Ibid.

[257] NAACP to Commissioner of Licenses George Bell, 16 March 1915, NAACP Archives, File C300.

[258] Ibid.

[259] John Mitchell to Mary White Ovington, 1 April 1915, John P. Mitchell Mayoral Papers, Correspondence File B, New York City Archives.

[260] James W. Johnson to Lester A. Walton, 20 May 1921, NAACP Archives, File C301.

[261] Ibid.

[262] John R. Shillady to Dear Sir, 10 October 1918, copy of letter sent to each governor by NAACP National office, NAACP Archives, File C301.

[263] "Birth of Nation' Kicked Out of Ohio," Chicago Defender, 2 October 1915, p. 1.

[264] John Shillady to James M. Cox, 9 October 1918, NAACP Archives, File C301.

[265] Woodbridge N. Ferris to Mary Childs Nerney, 12 October 1915, NAACP Archives, File C300.

[266] Ibid.

[267] Mary Childs Nerney to Woodbridge N. Ferris, 9 October 1915, NAACP Archives, File C300.

[268] For example, see Roy Nash, Telegram to Rev. I. S. Wilson, 28 February 1916, NAACP Archives, File C302; James Weldon Johnson, Telegram to R. E. Wilson, 21 March 1924, NAACP Archives, File C302; and Monroe N. Work Negro Yearbook 1916-1917 (Tuskegee Institute, Alabama: The Negro Yearbook Publishing Company), 1916, pp. 48-49.

[269] John Shillady, Telegram to Fred Morton, n.d., NAACP Archives, File C301.

[270] Ibid.

[271] "Walsh Will Help Negroes," Boston Evening Transcript, 19 April 1915, p. 1.

[272] "Big Negro Mass Meeting Denounces Photo-Play," Boston Morning Journal, 19 April 1915, p. 1.

[273] "Crowd Stands for Hours," Boston Evening Transcript, 19 April 1915, p. 1.

[274] "Citizens Plead at State House for Film Ban," Christian Science Monitor, 19 April 1915, p. 4.

[275] "Walsh Promises Aid to Stop Photo-Play," Boston Morning Journal, 20 April 1915, p. 1.

[276] "Walsh Will Help Negroes," Boston Evening Transcript.

[277] Ibid.

[278] "Judge Refuses to Stop 'Birth of a Nation' Film," Boston Evening Globe, 21 April 1915, p. 4.

[279] Ibid.

[280] "Colored People Ask Governor Walsh to Urge Legislation," Boston Evening Globe, 21 April 1915, p. 2.

[281] These bills are discussed in more detail in Chapter VI. However, it seems that Walsh probably did encourage their introductions. At least those individuals who opposed the legislation were quick to lay the blame for the legislation at Walsh's door. For example, one of the attorneys who represented Griffith, John F. Cusick, indicated at a hearing concerning one of the bills that Walsh "caused a whole lot of this agitation and is much to blame for such a short-sighted policy" because Walsh had promised to have a new law passed if none existed under which the film could be stopped. See "Blames Governor for Photo-Play Agitation," Boston Morning Journal, 28 April 1915, p. 4, and "Cusick Blames Governor," Boston Evening Transcript, 27 April 1915, p. 2.

[282] "Nation' Film is Now Up to Censor Board . . . Governor Signs Bill," Boston Morning Journal, 22 May 1915, p. 2. See also, "Board of Censors Refuses to Stop Photoplay at Tremont But Refuses to Give Reasons," Boston Evening Transcript, 3 June 1915, p. 14.

[283] Ibid.

[284] Ibid.

[285] On July 3, 1915, the Cleveland Gazette ran a story urging Ohio residents to "be on the lookout" for the film and to notify immediately the governor and/or the state board of censors of their opposition to the film should it be announced for showing in their communities. See "Be on the Lookout!;" Cleveland Gazette, 3 July 1915, p. 2.

[286] Hazel Hall to Frank B. Willis, 7 July 1915, Cleveland Gazette, 17 July 1915, p. 2. Reprinted in Cleveland Gazette, 24 July 1915, p. 2.

[287] Frank B. Willis to Harry Smith, 31 August 1915, reprinted in Cleveland Gazette, 4 September 1915, p. 2. It should be noted that Willis had previously spoken against the film The Nigger and after his comments the film's permit was revoked. See "Governor of Ohio Protects Black Citizens," Chicago Defender, 17 April 1915, p. 1.

[288] Ibid.

[289] Charles G. Williams to Frank B. Willis, 7 July 1915, reprinted in Cleveland Gazette, 17 July 1915, p. 2. Reprinted in Cleveland Gazette, 24 July 1915, p. 2.

[290] "Birth of Nation," Cleveland Gazette, 28 August 1915, p. 2. Reprinted in Cleveland Gazette, 4 September 1915, p. 2.

[291] "Ohioans Protest Vicious Photoplay," New York Age, 30 September 1915, p. 1. See also "Birth of a Nation' Kicked Out of Ohio," Chicago Defender.

[292] Robert Barcus to Editor of The Crisis, The Crisis, 28 September 1915, NAACP Archives, File C300. See also, "Birth of Nation' Barred From Ohio," New York Age, 30 September 1915, p. 1., and "Leading Points in Film Play Decision . . . Board of Censors Acts in Defense of All the People," Oakland Sunshine, 16 October 1915, p. 2.

[293] "Sample of the Type of Men the State of Ohio Produces," Philadelphia Tribune, 9 October 1915, p. 1. See also "Birth of Nation' Barred From Ohio," New York Age and "Leading Points in Film Play Decision . . ." Oakland Sunshine, and reprinted in Twin City Star, 27 November 1915, p. 3.

[294] Frank B. Willis to Harry C. Smith, 31 August 1915, reprinted in Western Outlook, 16 October 1915, p. 2.

[295] For example, Mary Childs Nerney indicated that the governor promised her the film would not be shown in Ohio "while he is governor" when she visited Cleveland in November 1915. See typewritten statement headed "Rec'd November 1, 1915," NAACP Archives, File C301.

[296] Resolution in Record of Proceedings of the Industrial Commission of Ohio, 6 January 1916, p. 19, Birth of a Nation file, Ohio State Historical Society Archives.

[297] "Loving Cup for Governor Willis," Cleveland Gazette, 22 January 1916, p. 1.

[298] Arthur Capper to Mary Childs Nerney, 12 October 1915, NAACP Archives, File C300.

[299] Ibid.

[300] "Kansas Enjoins Performance of 'Birth of Nation' Film," Press Release, 27 November 1931, NAACP Archives, File C302.

[301] Ibid.

[302] "The Birth of a Nation," *Cleveland Gazette*, 12 October 1918, n.p., clipping in NAACP Archives, File C301.

[303] "Kansas Governor Asked by NAACP to Bar 'Birth of Nation' Film," Press Release, 8 June 1923, NAACP Archives, File C302.

[304] "Protest to Governor Davis," *Topeka Daily State Journal*, 4 December 1923, p. 6.

[305] Ibid.

[306] Ibid.

[307] Petition to Jonathon M. Davis, Governor Kansas, copy of petition in NAACP Archives, File C302.

[308] "An Encourager of Race Hatred," *Topeka Daily Capital*, 19 June 1923, n.p., clipping in NAACP Archives, File C302.

[309] "Won't Stop Film," *Topeka Daily State Journal*, 4 December 1923, p. 6.

[310] Ibid.

[311] Ibid.

[312] "Kansas Censors Pass 'Birth of Nation," *Variety*, 16 December 1923, p. 20.

[313] "Ex-Governor Henry J. Allen Denounces Kansas Release of 'Birth of Nation," Press Release, 14 December 1923, NAACP Archives, File C302.

[314] Ibid.

[315] Ibid.

[316] Ibid.

[317] Governor North Dakota to D. W. Griffith Corporation, 15 October 1918, NAACP Archives, File C301.

[318] Ibid.

[319] Ibid.

[320] Ibid.

[321] John R. Shillady to Dear Sir, 10 October 1918.

[322] Ibid.

[323] Ibid.

[324] Governor North Dakota to D. W. Griffith Corporation.

[325] John Shillady to James M. Cox, 9 October 1918, NAACP Archives, File C301.

[326] Henry M. Wriston to John Shillady, 5 October 1918, NAACP Archives, File C301.

[327] The information was not found in the manuscript collections, newspapers, and other sources consulted for this study, listed in the bibliography.

[328] Dr. A. C. McIntyre, William Warley, and Wilson Lovett to Governor A. O. Stanle, 19 November 1918, reprinted in "Infamous Picture Forbidden," n.t., n.p., clipping in NAACP Archives, File C301.

[329] The information was not found in the manuscript collections, newspapers, and other sources consulted for this study, listed in the bibliography.

[330] According to a 1913 statute all films intended for commercial exhibition within Kansas had to be licensed by the State Board of Review. The three member board could refuse any film a license if the film was found to be "cruel, obscene, indecent, or immoral" to "tended to corrupt or debase morals." The Governor appointed the board and maintained the power to dismiss any member or to recall any film for reconsideration. See General Statutes of Kansas, Chapter 294 (1913). See also Ira Carmen, Movies, Censorship, and the Law, p. 176. The constitutionality of the Kansas statute was upheld by the U. S. Supreme Court in Mutual Film Corporation v. Hodges, 236 U. S. 248 (1915).

[331] Arthur Capper to Mary Childs Nerney. It is interesting to note that Kansas Attorney General S. M. Brewster issued a statement justifying censorship of The Birth under the state statute by describing the film as "immoral." In part Brewster said: "Said photo-play is immoral in that it purports to represent historical facts; it is on the whole false and untrue. The senators and other officials and representatives of the federal government in the North are shown to be influenced by the basest motives. That almost without exception the northern soldiers are depicted as 'scalawags' or brutes while the Southern soldiers are depicted as the flower of chivalry." See Monroe Work, Negro Year Book, 1916-1917, p. 49.

[332] Arthur Capper to Mary Childs Nerney.

[333] S. M. Brewster v. L. M. Crawford, et. al., 103 Kansas 76 (1918).

[334] Ibid.

[335] Ibid.

[336] Ibid.

[337] Ibid.

[338] Ibid.

[339] Ibid. The permit was withdrawn after the Kansas Supreme Court ruled that the film must be sent back to the board for further inspection.

[340] "Won't Stop Film," Topeka Daily State Journal.

[341] "Kansas Governor Asked by NAACP to Bar 'Birth of Nation' Film," Press Release.

[342] "Protest to Governor Davis," Topeka Daily State Journal.

[343] "Action Is Up To Davis," Topeka Daily State Journal, 5 December 1923, p. 1.

[344] "Griffith Requests Rejection of 'The Birth of a Nation," Topeka Daily State Journal, 6 December 1923, p. 1.

[345] "Kansas Censors Pass 'Birth of Nation," Variety.

[346] "Birth' has Federal O.K. in State of Kansas," Variety.

[347] Kansas v. Sam Silverman, Petition filed in the District Court of Shawnee County Kansas by Roland Boynton, Attorney General, copy in NAACP Archives, File C302.

[348] Elisha Scott to Walter T. Andrews.

[349] Ibid.

[350] "Foes of Klan Fight 'Birth of Nation," New York Times, 3 December 1922, Section I, p. 8.

[351] Ibid. The New York State Motion Picture Commission was created in 1921 to pre-screen all new films prior to their public exhibition. The three member board was appointed by the governor. See Ira Carmen, Movies, Censorship and the Law, pp. 141-142.

[352] Ibid.

[353] Ibid. The hearing was conducted Saturday, 2 December 1922, and continued 4 December 1922. Representing the NAACP at the hearing were Walter White, Herbert Seligman, A. B. Spingarn, Henry Shields, George W. Harris, Dr. Louis Wright. Representing Epoch were Frank C. Laughlin, D. W. Griffith, Rev. Thomas Dixon, Albert Banzhaf, J. J. McCarthy, and H. W. Pierson. See copy of Opinion of Joseph Levenson on Protest filed by NAACP, New York Motion Picture Commission, 8 December 1922, NAACP Archives, File C301.

[354] Ibid.

[355] Ibid.

[356] Ibid.

[357] Ibid.

[358] Copy of Opinion of Joseph Levenson on Protest Filed by NAACP.

[359] "Ku Klux Lecturer Under Fire Three Hours," New York Times, 9 December 1922, pp. 1 & 4.

[360] Ibid.

[361] Walter White to New York State Motion Picture Commission, 15 December 1922, NAACP Archives, File C301.

[362] Ibid.

[363] George H. Cobb to Walter White, Enclosure, 18 January 1923, NAACP Archives, File C302.

[364] Ibid.

[365] The title added to the film stated that after the reconstruction of the South following the Civil War the originators of the Klan put away their uniforms and disbanded the original Klan forever. See "Griffith's 'Birth of Nation' Remains The Daddy of 'Em All," Variety, 8 December 1922, p. 33 and "Compromise on 'Birth' and Company Clucks Film Permitted on Agreement to Repudiate Secret Empire," Variety, 8 December 1922, p. 37.

[366] George H. Cobb to Walter White, 3 January 1923, NAACP Archives, File C302.

[367] State of Pennsylvania, County of Allegheny in the Court of Common Pleas of Allegheny County in Pittsburgh, Bill of Complaint of the Nixon Theatre Co. v. Joseph Armstrong and W. M. Matthews, among D. W. Griffith's Personal Papers, MOMA Archives.

[368] Ibid.

[369] Ibid.

[370] Ivan Brychta, "The Ohio Film Censorship Law," Ohio Law Journal, 13 (Spring 1952), p. 355.

[371] Epoch Production Corporation v. Harry L. Davis.

[372] "Racial Unit Aide Condemns Move," Baltimore Morning Sun, 28 October 1958, p. 38.

[373] "Baltimore Rescinds Earlier Ban," Variety, 5 November 1958, n.p., clipping in The Birth of a Nation file, Lincoln Center Archives.

[374] See Record of Proceedings of the Industrial Commission of Ohio, Department of Film Censorship, August 1914-1921, Entry of 6 January 1916, Ohio State Historical Society Archives. It is interesting to note that prior to the Board's decision concerning the film, the NAACP had sent at least one national representative, Mary Childs Nerney, to the state to assess the situation. Nerney reported back to the association in confidence that the "Board of Censors has three members - the Chairman is all right, the other man wobbly and the lady "a Southern woman,' the worst Bourbon I ever met. She went out and slammed the door, she got so mad at me. Among other things she predicted I would plunge this country in race riots, that 'The Birth of a Nation' was a great education to the North and must be shown in Ohio and that Wilbur King agreed with her. She said among other things that if it was not for us Northerners she would still be living on her plantation like a lady instead of working for a living. The Chairman of the Board said I had made her put herself on record because she had before evaded all attempts to enlighten them as to where she was on the race question." See typewritten Sheet, no name but probably from Mary Childs Nerney, recorded 1 November 1915, NAACP Archives, File C301. As Nerney anticipated the vote on The Birth was split with the woman she referred to voting in favor of the film and the two men mentioned voting against the film. See Record of Proceedings of the Industrial Commission of Ohio, Department of Film Censorship. The Ohio Board of Censors was established under a 1913 law which indicated that "only such films as are in the judgment and discretion of the board of censors of a moral, educational, or amusing and harmless character shall be passed and approved . . ." The constitutionality of this statute was upheld by the U. S. Supreme Court in Mutual Film Corporation v. Industrial Commission of Ohio, 236 U. S. 230 (1915).

327

[375] Brychta, "The Ohio Film Censorship Law." In the official ruling on the film the board indicated it rejected the film because "in the judgment and discretion of this board, is not harmless and is not such a motion picture as the Board is authorized to pass and approve under Section 871-49 of the General Code of Ohio." When Epoch attorney Sagmeister asked the board for a more detailed explanation of the ruling, the board restated its belief that the film was "Not harmless." Sagmeister "Further respectfully requested" the board to state what it took into consideration in arriving at the conclusions that it did and that the same "be spread upon the record of the Board . . Whereupon the Board denied said application for a specific statement of its conclusions other than the grounds stated upon the record . . To which counsel for applicant objected." In spite of Sagmeister's continued objections, the board refused to explain its position further. See Record of Proceedings of the Industrial Commission of Ohio, Department of Film Censorship.

[376] Brychta, "The Ohio Film Censorship Law." Brychta denounced the action of the Ohio Supreme Court in this case and called it "A rare exception to the traditional friendly attitude of the judiciary toward private rights." See p. 355.

[377] "Certificate of Censorship," Department of Education, Division of Film Censorship, State of Ohio, No. 128, 18 February 1925, Document in Birth of a Nation file, Ohio State Historical Society, Columbus, Ohio.

[378] Epoch Producing Corporation v. Vernon M. Riegel, No. 19030, Filed 9 March 1925, in the Supreme Court of Ohio, document in Birth of a Nation file, Ohio State Historical Society, Columbus, Ohio. See also "Ohio Bars 'Birth of a Nation,'" Press Release, 12 June 1925, NAACP Archives, File C302.

[379] "Birth of Nation' Banned Because of Fear of Rioting," Baltimore Morning Sun, 24 May 1952, p. 9. The Birth was originally licensed for screening in Maryland in 1917. In 1943, the film was submitted to the board for relicensing. However, when the board indicated it might reject the film, the movie was withdrawn.

[380] Ibid.

[381] Ibid.

[382] "Suit Is Filed Against Film Censor Law," Baltimore Morning Sun, 14 June 1952, p. 26. It is interesting to note that this suit was filed shortly after the U. S. Supreme Court ruled in Burstyn v. Wilson that film was entitled to limited First Amendment protection and that sacrilegious was not an acceptable criterion for censorship.

[383] "Film Ban is Checked, Maryland Judge Asks Censors to Explain 'Birth of Nation' Move," New York Times, 14 June 1952, n.p., clipping in Lincoln Center Birth of a Nation file.

[384] See "Racial Unit Aide Condemns Move," Baltimore Morning Sun, 28 October 1958, p. 38, and "Baltimore Rescinds Earlier Ban," Variety, 5 November 1958, n.p., Birth of a Nation file, Lincoln Center Archives.

[385] "Racial Unit Aide Condemns Move," Baltimore Morning Sun.

[386] "Baltimore Rescinds Earlier Ban," Variety.

[387] John R. Shillady to State Council of Defense, 10 October 1918, NAACP Archives, File C302. See also John R. Shillady to Isobel Field, 17 October 1918, NAACP Archives, File C301.

[388] John R. Shillady, NAACP Secretary to State Governors, 10 October 1918, NAACP Archives, File C301.

[389] Ibid.

[390] John R. Shillady to All Branches, 10 October 1918, NAACP Archives, File C301.

[391] Copy "Resolution" signed by Houston G. Young, West Virginia Secretary of State and Secretary of the Executive State Council of Defense, 18 June 1918, NAACP Archives, File C301.

[392] Ibid.

[393] Ibid.

[394] Ibid.

[395] John R. Shillady to West Virginia State Council of Defense, 9 October 1918, NAACP Archives, File C301.

[396] Arch. M. Thurman, Utah State Council of Defense to John Shillady, 24 October 1918, NAACP Archives, File C301.

[397] Ibid.

[398] Henry M. Wriston, Assistant Manager Connecticut Council of Defense, 15 October 1918, NAACP Archives, File C301.

[399] Ibid.

CHAPTER VI

LEGISLATIVE ACTIONS AND THE BIRTH OF A NATION

During the time period 1915-1973, elected officials were also asked to use their legislative authority regarding The Birth. Legislative actions considered regarding the film took one of three major forms: legislatively establishing censorship laws against which the film could be judged; legislatively denunciating the film; and legislatively banning the film. This chapter examines the responses of officials to requests for legislative action concerning the film. The involvement of officials at the municipal level is discussed first. Actions of state legislative bodies concerning the film are presented next. Finally, the controversy at the national level is outlined.

City Councils as Lawmakers

During the time period studied, at least five city councils passed censorship ordinances designed specifically to censor The Birth of a Nation.[1] The ordinances were passed between 1915 and 1923.

The Wilmington, Delaware, city council apparently was the first to pass an ordinance to stop The Birth. The ordinance was introduced by the only black council member, Dr. John Hopkins in June 1915.[2] The ordinance stated specifically that:

> . . . no person, firm or corporation shall exhibit within
> the limits of the City of Wilmington, any moving picture
> that is likely to provoke ill-feeling between the white
> and black races.[3]

The ordinance gave censorship power to the police department. The penalty was a fine "for each and every offense not exceeding the sum of Fifty Dollars."[4] Thus, the ordinance was highly specific, allowing censorship of films deemed by police likely to provoke ill feelings between blacks and whites.

The Tacoma, Washington, film censorship ordinance was amended to cover films "such as 'The Birth of a Nation,'" in August 1915.[5] Prior to amendment the statute covered only obscene or immoral performance.[6] After amended, the statute read:

> It shall be unlawful for any person, firm, or corporation to
> publicly show or exhibit in any place in the City of Tacoma
> any picture or series of pictures by any device known as a
> mutescope, kinetoscope, cinematograph, kinemacolor, penny
> arcade, a moving picture, or any vaudeville act, drama, play,
> theatrical song or stage or platform performance or any ad-
> vertisement or bill board display which is or tends to be
> immoral, obscene, lewd, lascivious or of any indecent char-
> acter or which portrays brutality or which tends to incite
> race riot or race hatred, or that shall represent or purport
> to represent any hanging, lynching, burning or placing in a
> position of ignominy, of any human being, the same being in-
> cited by race hatred.[7]

Even though the ordinance was amended to allow film censorship because of racial portrayal, the ordinance was not used to exclude The Birth, shown in Tacoma later in 1915.[8]

In December 1915, the Denver, Colorado, city council made it a misdemeanor to:

> . . . advertise, publish, produce, exhibit . . . at any time
> or place in the city and county of Denver any theatrical play,
> act, picture, picture show, lithograph, drama, photodrama,

drawing, sketch, or historical production which is contrary to good order and the public welfare and which tends to reflect reproach upon any race, or which incites race hatred, race riot, and which stirs up race prejudice and tends to represent any hanging, lynching, or burning of any human being incited by race hatred.[9]

The city council voted to censor The Birth under the ordinance, but as discussed earlier in Chapter III and Chapter V, the council was enjoined from doing this.

The St. Paul, Minnesota, city council also passed a film censorship ordinance designed to stop The Birth in 1915. Before passage, film censorship in St. Paul was left to the police who "maintained a sort of supervision."[10] The ordinance was prepared by St. Paul attorney W. T. Frances and vested the power of censorship with the commissioner of public safety.[11] In part, the ordinance forbade the exhibition of any film tending "to . . . incite riot or create race or religious prejudice, or purports to represent any hanging, lynching, burning or placing in a position of ignominy any human being, the same being incited by or inducive to race or religious hatred . . ."[12] The council also voted to stop The Birth, but as discussed earlier, the council did not apply the ordinance.[13] However, 15 years later, a St. Paul city council used the ordinance to ban The Birth, as discussed earlier.[14]

The Wichita city commission passed an ordinance in 1923 to ban films which "would tend to create racial strife."[15] The commission responded to persons who opposed The Birth. As discussed in Chapter III, C. W. Stater, distributing The Birth in Kansas, sought and received an injunction stopping Wichita officials from interfering with the film.[16] Stater called the Wichita ordinance "unconstitutional, invalid, unreasonable, and void."[17] Apparently Judge John C. Pollock agreed and issued the injunction. He said the Wichita ordinance was null and void.

Thus, in five instances, city councils passed ordinances specifically designed to censor The Birth of a Nation. In two cases the ordinances were passed during censorship controversies. However, in at least one of these cases the ordinance was not actually used against The Birth to resolve the controversy. In one case, a court enjoined the city council from enforcing the ordinance it had passed to stop The Birth. In one case the film was screened in spite of the fact that an ordinance to prevent its screening had been passed.

Actions by other city officials

During the time period studied, a variety of other city officials were asked to resolve The Birth of a Nation censorship controversies. These officials responded by ordering total or partial suppression of the film.

State Legislatures as Lawmakers

During the time period 1915-1973 at least five state legislatures considered bills to allow censorship of The Birth. Three of the legislatures eventually passed legislation. The bills were considered between the years 1915 and 1919.

The Massachusetts state legislature was the first to consider censorship legislation specifically designed to ban The Birth.

Introducing bills extending film censorship to anti-racial presentations was one tactic used against The Birth by the NAACP during the film's original Boston screening in 1915. Several of these tactics have been discussed in previous chapters. As discussed earlier Massachusetts governor David Walsh suggested to individuals protesting the film that if all else failed, they should attempt to have a new censorship law passed by the state legislature to stop the film. After other efforts to stop the film failed, the protesters turned to the legislature, in session in Boston. On April 22, 1915, the legislature's joint committee on rules recommended to the Massachusetts House of Representatives that its rules be suspended to allow the introduction of a motion picture censorship bill authored by Senator Lewis R. Sullivan.[18] The rules were suspended and the bill, House No. 2077, was referred to the legislature's joint Committee on the Judiciary.[19] Known as the Sullivan Bill, it amended an earlier censorship law, extending it to "any show or entertainment which tends to excite racial or religious prejudice, or tends to a breach of the public peace."[20]

Hearings on the bill began immediately. Lt. Governor Grafton Cushing favored the bill, saying: "I have not been to see the play because my curiosity does not run along that line, but I am certainly opposed to the production of anything that tends to stir up race prejudice."[21] U. S. Representative from Boston Samuel McCall wrote the Judiciary Committee to support the measure and to oppose The Birth of a Nation because it presented an historically inaccurate portrait of Thaddeus Stevens.[22] Charles W. Eliot, Harvard University President, also spoke against The Birth and in favor of censorship at a protest meeting in Cambridge's First Parish Church. Eliot said:

> I have not seen the photo-play, but from what I have heard of it, I object first to its expression of a grave historical error. This nation was not born in the Reconstruction period. It was born when the Constitution of the U. S. was accepted by the thirteen colonies.
>
> This film, or play, should not be allowed to accomplish what is probably its purpose--to inspire the white people of the North with a different feeling toward the colored people than we held at the close of the Civil War.[23]

Opposition to the bill was vocal. Rabbi Charles Fleisher and attorney John F. Cusick both charged that Walsh, Cushing, McCall and Sullivan opposed the film for political expediency rather than principle. Fleisher told the committee considering the measure that "a few excitable men" had fanned the fires of protest to win the black vote.[24] Cusick contended that Walsh damned the play without seeing it and promised a censorship law. Cusick said, "Therefore, Governor Walsh, you have caused a whole lot of this agitation and are much to blame for such a short-sighted policy."[25]

The Boston Morning Journal, the Boston Evening Transcript, and the Boston Herald took editorial stands against the Sullivan Bill. The Transcript termed the measure "the curse of a nation" and concluded "any sort of censorship is irritating to the spirit of our people and only that regulation which is in the essential interest of public decency and public morals should be tolerated."[26] The Herald called the bill "hysterical legislation, designed to limit an individual's freedom of speech.[27] The Journal favored the film and termed it "inspiring from the standpoint of broad and true Americanism."[28]

In opposition to the film, the Journal said:

> Unfortunately, a serious diversion caused by the opposition of colored leaders in this city to certain phases of Birth of a Nation has obscured temporarily--except for those who have witnessed the production with open minds and responsive hearts--the strength, beauty, and inspiration of the whole.[29]

The Journal also published letters from D. W. Griffith and Thomas Dixon for the film and against the censorship bill.[30]

Shortly after the Sullivan Bill was introduced into the legislature, individual legislators began offering alternative censorship bills. Representative Butler Wilson submitted a measure which, in addition to the provisions of the Sullivan Bill, abolished the joint censoring body in Boston and established either the mayor or the chief of police as the official censor.[31] J. Mott Hallowell drafted a measure to establish the Massachusetts district police as offical film censors. Hallowell's bill did not amend the existing obscenity statute to include race or religion and stated that a film should be judged on whether it was "sexually or otherwise immoral" or tended "to encourage, incite, or cause lawlessness or breach of peace."[32]

Two other legislators submitted censorship bills. Senator James A. Lowell also submitted a proposal establishing the district police chiefs and their aids as a state board of film censorship.[33] Senator W. Bates also proposed a state film censorship board within the State Board of Labor and Industries.[34] Bates said that the trouble over The Birth in Boston showed the defects in the existing system (which gave the mayor the power to censor obscene material) and also said "he did not think police should have power to fix the moral standards of motion pictures."[35]

All of the censorship bills were assigned to committees. However, the Sullivan Bill was the only measure reported back to the legislature and it was reported back in drastically altered form. After three days of hearings on the Sullivan Bill, the Judiciary Committee decided to draft its own bill. The Committee framed a bill which established a censoring triumverate: the mayor of Boston, the chief of Boston's police, and the Chief Justice of Boston's Municipal Court.[36] The bill gave them power to censor whatever their "common sense decides violates the canons of public decency."[37] The bill, House No. 2127, amended a different section of the Massachusetts law than the Sullivan Bill and did not specify censorship for racial portrayal as a criterion.[38] The bill as reported back to the House of Representatives stated that it would take a unanimous vote to revoke or suspend theatre licenses.[39] Four members of the joint Judiciary Committee dissented from the majority report.[40] Four days after the bill was reported back to the House floor, a representative presented "a petition of Joseph Lee and 4,534 others" supporting legislation to forbid "public entertainments" which tended "to excite racial or religious prejudice."[41] The following day another petition was read on the floor of the House and filed.[42] House Bill No. 2127 was read a second time on the House floor May 6, 1915. After debate, the bill was ordered to a third reading by a vote of 94-41.[43]

May 10, 1915, the bill was again debated. During this discussion, several questions were considered. Rowley of Brookline moved that the bill be amended so that a majority vote of the censorship board permitted censorship, opposed to the unanimous vote called for in the legislation drafted by the Judiciary Committee. Allison Catheron moved that the bill be amended to establish Boston's mayor as the sole censor.[45] Representative Fred Cross of Royalston "raised the point that the bill was improperly before the House" because that legislation applied only to the city of Boston and the original bill asked for general censorship power. The Speaker of the House replied that since the bill had advanced to third reading, it was too late to raise that point of order.[46] The Rowley and Catheron amendments were considered and defeated.[47] The following day, the House passed the bill 175-43 and was sent to the Senate.[48] On May 15, 1915, Senators proposed the amendment that the censor board be ruled by majority, instead of unanimous consent.[49] However, the amendment was defeated and the bill was advanced to third reading. In spite of this, amendment supporters pressed their case and on May 18, 1915, the Senate again considered the amendment and passed it on a roll call vote, 20-18.[50] Senators opposing the amendment then campaigned to defeat the entire bill. The next day the Senate voted to reconsider engrossment of the measure. However, the motion for reconsideration of engrossment was defeated when the president of the Senate voted against the motion and created a tie.[51] This effectively defeated the motion for reconsideration, and the Senate approved the bill in its amended form. May 18, 1915, the Senate sent the bill to the House to determine whether the lower body would consur on the amended legislation.[52] The next day, the House reconsidered the bill and after debate concurred in the Senate amendment 136-71 and sent the bill to Walsh for signature.[53] Walsh signed the bill and in accordance with the provisions of the legislation named Boston's Mayor James Curley, Boston's police Chief Fred O'Meara, and Boston Municipal Court Judge Warren Bolster to the board.[54]

However, as discussed, this board considered <u>The Birth</u> immediately and approved the film. Also, a later Boston censorship board acting under this same legislation considered <u>The Birth</u> and censored it.[55]

Later in 1915, Illinois state representative Robert Jackson introduced a film censorship bill into the Illinois house. The bill prohibited the exhibition of any film in the state that depicted "lynching or unlawful hanging" or which tended toward race hatred and rioting.[56] After debate, the House approved the bill 111-2. However, the bill failed by one vote to pass the state Senate.[57]

In 1917, Robert Jackson returned to the House, representing Chicago's predominantly black Third District, and again sponsored a bill to ban <u>The Birth of a Nation</u> from Illinois.[58] This time the bill passed and was signed into law. Referred to as the Jackson law, the statute forbade the public exhibition of anything which:

> portrays depravity, criminality, unchastity, or lack of virtue of a class of citizens, or any race, color, or religion or which exposes the citizens of any race, color, creed, or religion to contempt, derision or which is productive of breach of the peace or riots.[59]

As discussed, the law was not specifically used regarding The Birth until 1924.[60] At that time, Epoch announced that it would revive the film in Chicago under the injunction forbidding local officials from interfering with The Birth's screening which had been issued by Judge William F. Cooper in 1915. The film opened February 3, 1924, to a capacity audience. Among those present were representatives of the Chicago police force, a judge, his bailiff, and his court clerk.[61] During the performance, the judge opened court in the lobby of the theatre and issued warrants for the arrests of the theatre management after he determined that the film violated the Jackson law.[62] The theatre management countered in court that the arrests violated the injunction and were therefore illegal.[63] The film's opponents countered that the Jackson law invalidated the injunction.[64] While the case was being considered, the Chicago Tribune editorially supported the right of The Birth to the screen and editorially opposed the Jackson law by saying:

> Such a law could interfere with the artistic and intellectual freedom of the people. It might permit prejudices to be converted into dictates. In this present case we are well aware of the dangers of provocation. No intelligent person likes to see the principles of free speech within the bounds of public decency restricted for adults and if we were all sensible adults it would not need be. Sensible adults do not need censors. They exercise censorship without statutes. They withhold their patronage from what offends them. We are opposed in principle to the stopping of The Birth of a Nation.[65]

However, as discussed in Chapter Three, the court adjourned the case indefinitely and the film continued in revival for a four-week run and set a box office attendance record for the theatre screening the film.[66] Also, as discussed in Chapter Four, Nathaniel Galup, projectionist, charged with violating the Jackson law by operating the projector, was found innocent after a jury trial.[67]

In January 1919, a bill designed to censor The Birth was introduced into the West Virginia Senate. The bill made it unlawful to show any film in the state:

> which . . . in any manner injuriously reflect upon the proper and rightful progress, status, attainment or endeavor of any race or class of citizens calculated to result in arousing the prejudice, ire or feelings of one race or class of citizens against any other race or class of citizens.[68]

The legislation also provided that anyone violating the law "shall be fined not less than one hundred nor more than one thousand dollars and may, at the discretion of the court, be confined in jail not more than thirty days."[69] The measure passed the Senate with "absolutely no opposition," and was sent to the House.[70] The House concurred with the Senate and the bill was signed into law.[71]

At least two other states considered legislation designed to censor The Birth, but apparently the legislation failed. For example, Percy Carter, secretary of the Riverside, California, Branch of the NAACP, notified NAACP national that the California legislature was considering a bill "relating to shows such as the Clansman which causes bad feelings between the two races."[72] However, sources do not indicate that the legislation passed.[73]

According to Illinois representative Robert Jackson, a bill identical to the one he introduced into the Illinois House in 1915 was introduced into the Ohio Senate also in 1915.[74] However, sources indicate that this bill did not become law.[75]

In these ways five state legislatures considered legislation designed to allow for censorship of The Birth of a Nation. In three instances the censorship legislation was passed and signed into law. In one case the censorship law applied only to a given city. The effectiveness of the legislation as a tool against the film was mixed.

National Authorities

During the time period studied, at least two resolutions against The Birth of a Nation were introduced into the U. S. Congress. In addition, a bill to prohibit the exhibition of any film which reflected on any race or nationality also was introduced. However, none of the measures passed.

The bill prohibiting films reflecting on race or nationality was introduced into the U. S. House of Representatives, April 15, 1916.[76] Although the legislation did not specifically mention The Birth, the wording indicates that the bill's sponsor may have had that film in mind when framing the legislation. The bill made it unlawful for anyone to mail, send, or carry into the U. S. or across state lines:

> any film or other pictorial representation based or founded on any adaptation of any book, play, or publication under whatever name, which is designed to be used or may be used for purposes of public exhibition and which would reflect or tend to reflect on any race or nationality and subject it to unjust and unwarranted criticism or which may disturb the peaceful relations existing in a community.[77]

The bill was assigned to the Committee on Interstate and Foreign Commerce and apparently died there.

The two resolutions against the film opposed it for similar reasons. The initial resolution was introduced into the House, May 9, 1916.[78] It instructed the Commissioners of the District of Columbia to forbid the exhibition of The Birth in the District.[79] The resolution stated:

> Whereas the picture known and styled The Birth of a Nation has a tendency to, and does engender prejudice against colored people; and
>
> Whereas it is best that prejudices between the colored and white races should be eliminated as far as possible: Therefore be it
>
> Resolved by the Senate and House of Representatives . . . that the Commissioners of the District of Columbia be instructed to issue orders forbidding the display in any show house . . . of . . . The Birth of a Nation.[80]

The resolution was referred to the Committee on the District of Columbia and apparently died there.

May 10, 1916, a second resolution against The Birth was introduced into the House. This resolution both asked the Commissioners of the District to suppress the film and expressed the more general opposition of Congress to the film.[81] In part, the resolution said:

> . . . it is the sense of the Congress of the United States that the picture exhibition entitled The Birth of a Nation now being presented in Washington, is largely immoral and untrue to history, and maligns and monstrously libels and traduces the memory of one of the Nation's greatest statesmen and patriots, former Congressman Thaddeus Stevens of Pennsylvania. In response to a common demand the Commissioners of the District of Columbia are therefore called upon to suppress the invidious portrayal in which the immortal Lincoln and Grant are introduced as a mask and paliation of the evident real purpose of the picture, believing that a further exhibition can only tend to arouse and perpetuate that sectional hatred so unhappily born of civil strife . . . We . . . further voice the sentiments contained in an editorial written by Howard E. Butz . . .

Huntingdon (Pennsylvania) Globe of May fourth, nineteen hundred and sixteen, which reads as follows:

'We witnessed the production of. . .The Birth of a Nation. It is a stupendous production, one of the biggest things ever put on the American stage, but the blight it puts upon the life of Thaddeus Stevens is rank, outrageous, and black as hell. We do not wonder that the people of Lancaster, headed by Congressman Griest, prevented the production of the play in that city, where the great commoner and the founder of the public school system of Pennsylvania spent so many years of his great and useful life.[82]

This resolution also was referred to the Committee on the District of Columbia where it apparently died.

Analysis

Of the 14 legislative actions taken regarding The Birth, 12 were designed to establish censorship standards which could later be used against the film; one was designed as a renunciation of the film; and one was intended to ban the film. Five of the attempts to establish censorship laws were at the local level and six were at the state level. The remaining attempt to pass a censorship statute which would be used against The Birth was in the U. S. Congress. Congress also considered the other two pieces of legislation designed to ban or renounce the film. All five actions at the local level resulted in the passage of the proposed legislation. Four such ordinances were passed in 1915 and one was passed in 1923. Two of the state actions intended to establish state censorship laws did so and three failed. These laws were passed in 1917 and 1919. In one 1915 case a state legislature passed a bill which established a new censorship agency for a city within the state. All pieces of legislation introduced into the U. S. Congress failed.

The eight laws passed to allow for censorship of The Birth were used inconsistently against the film. For example, in at least four instances the film was screened in spite of legislation passed specifically to stop it. In one of these cases, the law involved was declared null and void by a court. In other cases, the authorities enforcing the laws apparently decided that The Birth did not violate the statutes.

Also, the statues were not used evenly against the film throughout its history. For example, in at least one instance a censorship board refused to censor the film even though it was established to do so. Several years later a censorship board functioning under the same law banned the film. Thus, in general legislative action even as a secondary tactic was not particularly effective from the standpoint of the film's opponents.

NOTES TO CHAPTER VI

[1] These were Wichita, Kansas; St. Paul, Minnesota; Denver, Colorado; Wilmington, Delaware; and Tacoma, Washington. See "Wichita Bars Birth of Nation," *Topeka Daily State Journal*, 27 December 1923, p. 3; Mrs. George M. Kenyon to *Twin City Star*, *Twin City Star*, 27 November 1915, p. 4; "Denver's City Council Prohibits Prejudice Breeding Pictures," *Chicago Defender*, November 23, 1915, p. 1; "Wilmington Bars Photoplay," *Baltimore Ledger*, 5 June 1915, p. 1; Henrietta Sadler to Mary Childs Nerney, 11 August 1915, NAACP Archives, File C300, respectively.

[2] "An Ordinance to Prohibit the Exhibition of any Moving Picture likely to Cause ill-feeling between the White and Black Races," Copy of Ordinance passed by the Wilmington, Delaware, City Council, 8 June 1915, NAACP Archives, File C300.

[3] Ibid.

[4] Ibid.

[5] Sadler to Nerney.

[6] Tacoma City Ordinance No. 5864, Section 1, passed 12 August 1914.

[7] Tacoma City Ordinance No. 6179, "An ordinance to amend Section 1, No. 5864 passed August 12, 1914," Copy of ordinance, NAACP Archives, File C300.

[8] Secretary of Mary Childs Nerney to D. H. Parker, 3 November 1915, NAACP Archives, File C300.

[9] "Denver's City Council Prohibits Prejudice Breeding Pictures," *Chicago Defender*.

[10] Kenyon to *Twin City Star*.

[11] Jose Sherwood to Mary Childs Nerney, 31 August 1915, NAACP Archives, File C301.

[12] "St. Paul," *Appeal*, 6 November 1915, p. 4.

[13] Kenyon to *Twin City Star*.

[14] "St. Paul NAACP Procures Ban on Showing of 'Birth of Nation,'" Press Release.

[15] "Wichita Bars 'Birth of Nation," *Topeka Daily State Journal*.

[16] "Wichita Is Restrained; Ordinance Against 'The Birth of a Nation' is Upheld," Topeka Daily State Journal, 1 January 1924, p. 1.

[17] "Birth' has Federal O. K. In State of Kansas," Variety, 10 January 1924, p. 19. See also, "Wichita Bars 'Birth of Nation,'" Topeka Daily State Journal, and "Klan Film Given Free Rein; Ordinance of Wichita Held Null and Void," Kansas City Call, 11 January 1924, p. 1.

[18] Journal of the Massachusetts House, 22 April 1915, p. 1030.

[19] Ibid.

[20] An Act, House No. 2077, Bill accompanying petition of Lewis R. Sullivan relative to public entertainments that are immoral or indecent or that tend to excite racial or religious prejudice, Documents Printed by the Order of the House of Representatives of the Commonwealth of Massachusetts During the General Court of 1915 (Boston: Wright & Potter Printing Co., 1915), Section 1, Lines 16-18.

[21] "Hearing Friday on Film Censor Amendment . . . Under Suspension of Rules Sullivan Bill Extending Law to Cover Anti-Race Plays Admitted by Legislature," Christian Science Monitor, 22 April 1915, p. 1.

[22] "McCall Scores Portrayal of KKK . . . Letter of Protest Against 'Birth of Nation Read at Hearing," Boston Morning Journal, 24 April 1915, p. 3.

[23] "Eliot Protests 'Birth of Nation' . . . Resents Alleged Attempt to Inspire Feeling Against Negroes," Boston Morning Journal, 26 April 1915, p. 4.

[24] "Blames Governor for Photo-Play Agitation," Boston Morning Journal, 28 April 1915, p. 4.

[25] "Says Politics Features Fight to Stop Play . . . Rabbi Criticizes Cushing, Walsh, McCall, and Speaker Cox," Boston Morning Journal," 27 April 1915, p. 4.

[26] "The Curse of a Nation," Boston Evening Transcript, 23 April 1915, p. 12.

[27] "Kill the Sullivan Bill," advertisement, Boston Evening Transcript, 26 April 1915, p. 17.

[28] "The 'Birth of a Nation," Boston Morning Journal, 23 April 1915, p. 8.

[29] Ibid.

[30] See Griffith's "Defense of 'The Birth of a Nation' and Attack on the Sullivan Bill," and Dixon's "Fair Play for 'The Birth of a Nation," Boston Morning Journal, 26 April 1915, p. 8.

[31] "Bill Extending Film Censorship Powers Urged," Christian Science Monitor, 23 April 1915, p. 1.

[32] "Another Movie Bill," Boston Evening Transcript, 29 April 1915, p. 2.

[33] "Provides State Board for Movies . . . Lowell Bill Gives Power to District Police Chief and Aids," Boston Morning Journal, 6 May 1915, p. 4.

[34] "Another 'Movie' Hearing," Boston Evening Transcript, 22 April 1915, p. 2.

[35] "Hearing on Bill to Transfer Censorship," Boston Evening Globe, 22 April 1915, p. 4.

[36] An Act, House No. 2127, Commonwealth of Massachusetts 1915, Documents Printed by Order of the House of Representatives of the Commonwealth of Massachusetts During the General Court of 1915, (Boston: Wright & Potter Printing Co., 1915).

[37] Ibid.

[38] Ibid.

[39] Ibid.

[40] Journal of the Massachusetts House 1915, (Boston: Wright & Potter Printing Co., 1915), 30 April 1915, p. 1088. It is interesting to note that three days after the bill was reported back to the House floor the legislators attended a special showing of The Birth at the Tremont. The legislators were first shown the film as it was originally seen in Boston and were then shown the scenes which had been cut. According to a report in the Boston Evening Transcript the "legislators applauded KKK rushing to rescue Elsie," See "Legislators Attend Play," Boston Evening Transcript, 3 May 1915, p. 2.

[41] Journal of the Massachusetts House, 3 May 1915, p. 1101.

[42] Journal of the Massachusetts House, 4 May 1915, p. 1112.

[43] Journal of the Massachusetts House, 6 May 1915, p. 1146.

[44] Journal of the Massachusetts House, 10 May 1915, p. 1158.

[45] Ibid.

[46] Ibid.

[47] Ibid.

[48] "Theatre Censor Bill Passed By House," *Boston Morning Journal*, 11 May 1915, p. 7.

[49] "Senate Advances Bill for 3 'Movie' Censors," *Boston Morning Journal*, 15 May 1915, p. 16.

[50] "Birth of Nation' Opponents Win Senate Fight," *Boston Morning Journal*, 18 May 1915, p. 4.

[51] "Coolidge Saves Bill Aimed at Photoplay," *Boston Morning Journal*, 19 May 1915, p. 12.

[52] *Journal of the Massachusetts House*, 18 May 1915, p. 1218

[53] *Journal of the Massachusetts House*, 19 May 1915, p. 1238.

[54] "'Nation' Film is Now Up To Censor Board," *Boston Morning Journal*, 22 May 1915, p. 2.

[55] "Censors Bar 'The Birth of a Nation," *Boston Globe*, 17 May 1921, p. 1.

[56] "Jackson Bill Bars Films From Illinois," *New York Age*, 27 May 1915, p. 1. It is interesting to note that NAACP national was originally concerned that the bill was sponsored by the film's supporters instead of its opponents. Specifically, Mary Childs Nerney said in a letter to Charles Bentley, "We are much concerned about the newspaper reports that there is a movement on foot to have state censorship in Illinois. From what I know of Griffith who produced the photoplay 'The Birth of a Nation' I think he may be back of this. Of course, moving picture men say they do not believe in censorship but if he thought a state censorship which he might be able to bribe would enable him to put on this photoplay, I am sure he would work for one." See Mary Childs Nerney to Charles E. Bentley, 21 May 1915, NAACP Archives, File C300.

[57] "Major Jackson Arouses Legislators By His Masterful Address," *Chicago Defender*, 29 May 1915, p. 1. See also "Jackson Bill Passes House By Vote of 111 to 2," *Baltimore Ledger*, 29 May 1915, p. 1.

[58] "Jackson's Moving Picture Bill Is Lost By One Vote," *Chicago Defender*, 26 June 1915, p. 1.

[59] Philip Kinsley, "Police Again Close 'Birth of Nation," *Chicago Daily Tribune*, 5 February 1924.

[60] *Revised Statutes of Illinois*, Chapter 38, Paragraph 456 (1923). It is interesting to note that this statute is quite similar to *Illinois Revised Statutes*, 1949, Chapter 38, Section 404, central to the U. S. Supreme Court's criminal libel ruling in *Beauharnais v. Illinois*, 343 U. S. 250, 72 S. Ct. 725, 96 L. Ed. 919 (1952). In 1924 Jackson served as a Chicago Alderperson, he was no longer a state representative.

[61] "Birth' to Defy Chicago Ban," *Variety*, 12 January 1924, p. 22.

[62] "Crowd Grumbles As Police Halt 'Birth of Nation," *Chicago Daily Tribune*, 4 February 1924, p. 1.

[63] Philip Kinsley, "Police Again Close 'Birth of Nation."

[64] "Fight 'Birth of Nation' Robert Abbott Heads Attack To Halt Showing of Picture," *Chicago Defender*, 9 February 1924, pp. 1 and 5.

[65] "The Birth of a Nation," *Chicago Daily Tribune*, 6 February 1924, p. 8.

[66] "Nation' $50,000," *Variety*, 21 February 1924, p. 18.

[67] "White Jury in Judge Fitch's Court Out One Hour In Film Trial," *Chicago Defender*, 22 March 1924, n.p., clipping in NAACP Archives, File C302.

[68] Copy of West Virginia Senate Bill No. 176, 1919 in NAACP Archives, File C301.

[69] Ibid.

[70] J. C. Gilmer to R. G. Randolph, 9 February 1919, NAACP Archives, File C301.

[71] J. C. Gilmer, Press Release, 24 February 1919, NAACP Archives, File C301.

[72] Percy Carter to NAACP national, 25 February 1919, NAACP Archives, File C301. Carter indicated the bill number was 179 and that he had contacted "Senator S. C. Evans and Assemblyman Chester B. Cline" to secure their support for the legislation.

[73] The information was not included in the manuscript collections, newspapers, and other sources consulted for this study.

[74] "Major Jackson Arouses Legislators By His Masterly Address," *Chicago Defender*.

[75] Ivan Brychta, "The Ohio Film Censorship Law," Ohio State Law Journal, 13 (Summer, 1952): 355.

[76] House Resolution 14668, 64th Congress, 1st Session, 15 April 1916.

[77] Ibid. It is interesting to note The Birth was based on both a book and a play.

[78] House Joint Resolution 221, 64th Congress, 1st Session, 9 May 1916.

[79] Ibid.

[80] Ibid.

[81] House Joint Resolution 222, 64th Congress, 1st Session, 10 May 1916.

[82] Ibid.

CHAPTER VII

EXTRA-LEGAL TACTICS IN <u>THE BIRTH OF A NATION</u>
CENSORSHIP CONTROVERSIES

Extra-legal tactics also were used in the battles over <u>The Birth of a Nation</u>'s right to the screen. The press, the pulpit, the picket line, and the pamphlet are examples of vehicles used to carry the messages of those attacking or supporting the film. Although it is difficult to gauge the effectiveness of extra-legal tactics in controversy resolution, no discussion of the range of tactics used for and against <u>The Birth</u> would be complete without this inclusion. This chapter summarizes categories of extra-legal efforts and analyzes the variety of extra-legal expression in each category. After an overview of the tactic, the chapter discusses the involvement of motion picture industry self-regulation mechanisms in <u>The Birth</u> censorship controversies.

Several extra-legal tactics involved in controversies over <u>The Birth</u>'s right to the screen were not directly efforts to censor the film itself. Rather, several extra-legal tactics utilized were geared to alter individual opinions concerning the film, to present alternative communications to counter the film, or to make the film itself more acceptable. The communication forms through which these approaches were operationalized ranged from films to sermons to pamphlets to newspapers to picket lines to parades. Because of the wide variety of communications involved in <u>The Birth</u> controversies, each form of expression is discussed separately. The use of film to counter the negative images of blacks in The Birth is outlined. Sermons and pamphlets concerning the acceptability of the film are presented next. Demonstrations in the form of picketing and parades are discussed in the following section. A discussion of resolutions concerning the film's right to the screen follows. Next, editorial campaigns and letters to the editor are detailed. Miscellaneous additional extra-legal tactics are described in the last section.

Overview

Although extra-legal means were used by both The Birth's opponents and supporters, the philosophical base of the tactic was embraced more heartily by the American Civil Liberties Union (ACLU). From at least 1939 on, the ACLU actively indicated its opposition to formalized, official censorship of The Birth.[1] This position was articulated by Roger Baldwin, ACLU spokesperson, in a letter to the NAACP's Walter White in April, 1939. Baldwin said in part:

> An old difficulty seems to have cropped up again with the attempts on the part of your locals to ban the film The Birth of a Nation. We can, of course, understand why Negroes generally bitterly oppose such a film. But, efforts to ban it are inevitably a boomerang. The precedent established will work against films favorable to Negroes, opposed by the other side.
>
> . . . Of course, there can be no objection to protests to motion picture distributors nor to picketing. But when appeal is made to public authorities to take action, it crosses the line of legitimate pressure, and invades the field of censorship. . .[2]

White notified Baldwin his comments would be given the NAACP Board of Directors for consideration.[3]

The Board considered the matter and passed a resolution authorizing the organization's national office to write Will Hays, president of the Motion Picture Producers and Distributors Association (MPPDA), requesting his office stop The Birth and indicating the Association's plan to "use every other means in its power to prevent the showing of the film."[4] Baldwin responded that the ACLU had "no complaint about the use of pressure on private agencies such as the Will Hays organization" but did object to the use of police power to stop the film.[5]

The ACLU reiterated its position concerning formalized censorship during the course of the 1939 Denver, Colorado, controversy (see Chapter V). Again, the ACLU stated: ". . . No official action should be taken against the showing of such a picture. Those opposed to it have the right to picket, distribute leaflets against it or to boycott it."[6]

Throughout the Denver controversy, the ACLU continued its effort to get the NAACP to alter its approach to protests concerning The Birth. For example, Baldwin called Thurgood Marshall, NAACP attorney, and requested a clarification of the NAACP's position on the film.[7] In his request, Baldwin once again stated that "picketing, protests, boycotting are justifiable means of fighting a vicious picture such as 'Birth of a Nation', but that the involving of censorship by municipal authorities through penal ordinances is a violation of the right of freedom of speech."[8] Marshall asked NAACP national to make "its position clear concerning this one item."[9]

Baldwin also wrote a letter to the NAACP publication the Crisis "for the purpose of calling the issue to the attention of your branches and your readers."[10] In the letter, Baldwin explained the ACLU's position:

> The ACLU and the NAACP have worked in harmony for so many years that it may seem ungracious to call attention to an issue on which we differ. I do so in the belief that sober second thoughts will indicate the wisdom of the position we take, and the danger of the position that has been taken by some of the branches of the NAACP.
>
> I refer to the attempts made to suppress the showing of the film The Birth of a Nation. I presume that every member of the ACLU is just as much opposed to the intolerance and brutality which that film represents as are the members of the NAACP. But the Civil Liberties Union is equally opposed to invoking the law to suppress the showing of any film on the ground of intolerance. For if an anti-Negro film can be so suppressed, a pro-Negro film (if one can conceive of such a production) can also be suppressed. Every precedent of suppression makes it that much easier to suppress something else. It is impossible to draw successful distinctions as to what should be suppressed and what should not, save where the criminal law against obscenity is plainly violated. Even those cases are difficult. We have always argued with our Jewish friends against attempts to protect them by law against anti-semitic propaganda. We know from experience that laws against attacks on a race are used in ways never intended. . . It is on this ground that we have always opposed invoking the law against showing of The Birth of a Nation. We have even defended its showing against persecution. We say to our colored friends who oppose the picture that they have in their hands the means of boycott, picketing, demonstration, letters of protest to motion picture proprietors--and they are quite a different matter. . . . We earnestly urge our Negro friends to confine themselves to those measures of protest and boycott which are the inherent right of all of us, and not to help build up a machinery of public suppression of anything.[11]

This letter was followed in the Crisis by a note from the magazine's editor, Roy Wilkins, outlining the NAACP position:

> This difference of opinion between the ACLU and the NAACP over The Birth of a Nation goes back many years because the ACLU believes some forms of an (sic) Negro propaganda had to be attacked even though it meant censorship. Into this category fell The Birth of a Nation because the NAACP felt and still

feels that in view of the Negroes struggle against a hostile public opinion we could not permit so universal a medium as the moving picture to spread race hatred without protest; the association always has opposed The Birth of a Nation.[12]

The ACLU also expressed its opposition to censorship of the film specifically in First Amendment terms. In a press release explaining its involvement in the Denver controversy, the ACLU said:

> The union is concerned solely with the preservation of fundamental civil, constitutional, American rights . . . in this case the rights of freedom of speech and freedom of the press--the motion picture being a means of presenting facts, opinions, ideas and points of view in common with the word of mouth and the printed word.[13]

An NAACP representative responded to the ACLU's statement by asserting censorship of The Birth was not a violation of free speech because the film was not "a legitimate theatrical performance of an honest endeavor in art."[14] Specifically, the NAACP regarded:

> . . . this performance as an attack on a helpless and handicapped minority, an attack masquerading under the guise of a show. We have so regarded it for 15 years or more and see no reason to change our minds. We believe in the freedom of the stage and screen, but we do not believe in mob-incitement and dangerous race-hate taking advantage of the theatre in order to claim immunity. Just as we also believe in free speech but would call the police if a free-speaker took the stump and began to yell, 'Lynch him! Lynch him!' While we believe in liberty of the press we would do our best to haul into court any editor who wrote an editorial calling upon the mob to attack us, for that is not legitimate editorial privilege, that would be a plain crime, taking advantage of editorial power.[15]

Thus, the battle lines were drawn. The range of formalized, legal tactics used for and against censorship of the film are discussed in Chapters III, IV, V, and VI. Extra-legal tactics are examined in this chapter.

Film Self-Regulation

Throughout its history, the motion picture industry devised various self-regulatory mechanisms. These mechanisms are by definition extra-legal in nature and censorship decisions rendered by these bodies have been enforced by custom and voluntary agreement rather than by law. One of the film industry's first attempts at self-regulation was through the National Board of Film Censorship. The Hays Commission was the other motion picture self-regulatory agency involved with The Birth.

National Board of Censorship

The National Board of Censorship's involvement with The Birth began when the film was submitted to the board January 12, 1915.[17] Because of the length and "difficulties of presenting" The Birth, a special meeting was called to review it.[18] About twenty members of the Censoring Committee were invited. Ten members actually saw the film and after discussion voted unanimously to pass the picture without change.[19] The film was returned to California for its Los Angeles Premiere.

The NAACP's Los Angeles branch lodged a protest against The Birth with the Los Angeles censors prior to the film's public opening (see Chapters III, V, VI). The branch was allowed to preview the film at a special showing January 29, 1915.[20] The branch then filed formal protests against the film and notified the organization's national office of the film's objectionable content.[21] In part, the Los Angeles Branch advised the national office to protest the film's production to the National Censorship Board. The branch secretary wrote:

> I have learned that the National Censor Board has also passed the picture and as this is a larger question and concerns the whole country we would urge that you take such steps as will be available and most effective to recall the approval of the National Censor Board. This method would seem to have great advantage over the waging of local fights wherever the Clansman is introduced.[22]

Next, NAACP national sent representatives to the National Censorship Board and requested the names of the individuals who approved The Birth, the names and addresses of all board members, a list of cities where the film had been released, and a list of cities where film censorship ordinances were pending. NAACP national also investigated the possibility of arranging a special showing of The Birth before the entire board and a NAACP committee.[23] The board apparently did not give the NAACP the information it requested.[24]

The NAACP then carried its protest to the National Censorship Board's chairperson, Frederic C. Howe. After hearing the NAACP protest, Howe ordered the board's General Committee to review the film.[25] The NAACP was notified and was promised 12 tickets.[26] Later the NAACP was notified it would receive only two tickets and was told that "no colored people would be admitted."[27] The two tickets were mailed to Dr. J. E. Spingarn, NAACP Board of Directors chairperson, and Mary C. Nerney, NAACP national secretary. W. D. McGuire, National Censorship Board executive secretary, explained the decreased ticket allocation to Nerney:

> I regret very much that I was disappointed in the other tickets. You will appreciate that this is due to the fact that the exhibition is a strictly private review given by Messrs. Aitken

and Griffith to some of their friends. The picture was reviewed by the National Board some time ago and had we known at this time that you were interested we would have been glad to have as many of your Board of Directors as would have cared to meet with us. As this review is Mr. Aitken's personal affair it was only out of courtesy to Dr. Howe and the Board that he was willing to provide us with a few cards of admission, and I was fortunate enough in prevailing upon him to furnish me with two extra ones.[29]

The screening was held March 1, 1915. After the performance, Spingarn briefly spoke against the film. The Board then met and decided to request several modifications in the second half of the film.[30] Although the exact cuts requested are not reported, the board later indicated the only standard it used was "whether or not the picture is objectionable from the standpoint of public morals."[31] The board indicated it would be "absurd" to judge the film by any other standard and advised "the courts are open for anyone who contends that the Board's standard was not fair."[32] The board also explained the criteria it did not use:

> Whether a picture-play is historically accurate or not does not concern the Board. It is specifically stated in the Board's printed standards that 'The National Board does not regard itself as a censor of accuracy unless the inaccuracy in question is of a kind that will result in some concrete disaster to the person whom the inaccuracy misleads.' Any historical inaccuracy in 'The Birth of a Nation' can hardly result in leading any individual into any concrete disaster. That the picture places its dramatic emphasis in such a way that sympathies are aroused for one set of characters and against another is outside the Board's province of control. If the picture tends to aggravate serious social questions and should therefore be wholly forbidden, that is a matter for the action of those who act on similar tendencies when they are expressed in books, newspapers, or on the stage. On what basis of reasoning should a film be suppressed whose subject matter has already been allowed the freest circulation in a novel and in a play?[33]

Although the NAACP did not receive official notification of the board's March 1 action regarding The Birth, unofficial word reached the

NAACP that the board had voted to disapprove the film entirely. Thinking its cause won, the NAACP noted that although the board had "no power to stop" the film, its perceived disapproval would pave the way for censorship.[35] On the basis of what proved to be misinformation, the NAACP began claiming a significant victory concerning the film. For example, Nerney telegrammed E. Burton Ceruti, Los Angeles branch secretary and said:

> Association has scored great triumph in New York. National Board of Censorship after advance performance of 'Birth of Nation' unanimously voted last evening to disapprove entire second part of film and to cut out all objectionable race allusions including that to little child in first part. Police commissioner has promised to stop production in New York. Action of Board of Censorship ought to make it possible for L.A. Branch to stop production in California.[36]

The NAACP press release concerning the triumph appeared in a variety of black newspapers throughout the country.[37] The release began "The NAACP has scored a real triumph in New York in succeeding in getting the National Board of Censorship to reverse its approval of the moving picture film called 'The Birth of a Nation' ... ."[38]

The board reviewed the modified version of The Birth on March 12, 1915, and voted to pass the film "with request that two additional changes be made."[39] Although official notification of this action did not reach the NAACP until March 15, 1915,[40] the organization was immediately aware of it and began notifying its membership. For example, in a letter to Jane Addams, Nerney said:

> You will be interested to know that despite the protest of Mr. Howe, Chairman of the National Board of Censorship and Dr. Werbasse, one of the more important members of its executive committee, after a performance yesterday the Board passed the film in toto even cheering the producer. So much for the kind of censorship we have.[41]

Although the board refused to make public either the vote or the names of the individuals actually voting on the film,[42] several newspapers reported the board was split concerning the film and that Howe was strongly opposed to the film's screening.[43] Several sources indicated Howe refused to allow his name to be used on the official statement of board approval attached to the film.[44] Howe said his opposition to the film was:

> . . .personal. It was because the story is bound to arouse race hatred which I think unjustified and have a very bad effect. It is likely to lead to race troubles. If the picture goes into the South I should think it would bring about race riots. Men might be killed as a result of it. . . I don't exactly approve of censorship in a strict sense of the word. My theory of the Board is an organization to fight where necessary to uphold public opinion.[45]

After the NAACP received notice of the board's approval, it indicated its dissatisfaction with the board in a letter attacking not only the action of the board, but the manner in which the board acted:

> Our Board feels that they have not been treated with consideration of frankness by the National Board of Censorship. Incredible as it is that a National Board supposed to represent all elements in our population should unqualifiedly approve such a pernicious and dangerous film as 'The Birth of a Nation,' still more incredible is the action of your Board in approving this film after they had once disapproved it and in doing this after two weeks deliberation during which time they did not give our Association an opportunity to make a protest or to be heard in any way; nor did they make any attempt to confer with us. . .
>
> . . .Our Board feels very strongly that our ten million colored fellow citizens. . .should be represented on the Board of Censorship. To have moving pictures which are universally acknowledged as one of the greatest educational forces of the country used to outrageously misrepresent and caricature them with the approval of the Board of Censorship indicates that colored membership is needed on the Board. . .[46]

The NAACP also outlined its version of the controversy and requested that more cuts be made in the film.

The National Board of Censorship established a special committee to investigate the matter and then responded in a letter to the NAACP:

> From a careful investigation of the facts, we do not find that the first statement made in regard to the treatment of your Association appears justified. May it not be the result of an apparent reluctance to accept the statements as made by the office of the National Board as facts, and the acceptance of unofficial reports as the Board's decisions?[47]

The board also outlined its version of the controversy and indicated it followed the "regular procedure of the office" regarding Nerney's requests for the names of the committee members voting on The Birth.[48] Nerney's request for a list of cities and states where bills for public censorship were pending was referred to the board's Executive Committee. The committee refused to supply Nerney with this information because:

> It was understood that Miss Nerney had stated that your organization intended to work in favor of legalized censorship. The Executive Committee felt morally bound not to assist in your endeavor. The Board could hardly take action assisting you in a measure by which would be annulled the non-legal, pre-publicity censorship for which it stands.[49]

The board said it believed the NAACP was well represented on the board. The board also indicated "there is a wide difference of opinion among good people" concerning The Birth and reaffirmed its position concerning legal censorship, stating:

> The approval of the courts upon technical interpretations is what the National Board wishes to avoid. Such precedents are exactly what the producers of objectionable films desire.

Therefore, the only method that will eventually prohibit the production of objectionable films is in the nature of constructive suggestion looking toward the elevation of the standard of production.[50]

By the time this letter of explanation reached NAACP national, the organization turned its energies against the film in other directions. In this instance, a self-regulatory agency of the film industry approved The Birth after modification and was vocal in its belief that extra-legal restraints were the only ones appropriate.

MPPDA

Later the NAACP protested The Birth's screening to the next major motion picture self-regulatory body, the Motion Picture Producers and Distributors Association (MPPDA), headed then by Will Hays.[51] The NAACP first protested The Birth to the Hays office in 1930. At that time the NAACP presented Hays with a formal protest against a proposed re-release of the film with an added sound track,[52] Christian Century reported the protest was based on the rationale that the film contained scenes which incited "to race hatred, to crime, and which inculcate contempt for the people of the colored race."[53] Hays apparently refused to move against the film.[54]

The NAACP next petitioned the Hays office concerning The Birth in 1939. In this instance, the NAACP's Board of Directors voted to "write to Mr. Will Hays. . .protesting against the showing of 'Birth of a Nation.'"[55] However, Hays' response to the NAACP is unclear.

In March 1940, the NAACP renewed its protest against The Birth to the Hays office. This time the NAACP was protesting a proposed remake of the film by Epoch.[56] In a letter to Hays, Walter White, NAACP national secretary, said:

> We vigorously urge that you use the full power of your office as President of the Motion Picture Producer-Distributors of America to prevent the remaking of this film.
>
> As you, of course, know, the production of 'The Birth of a Nation' in 1915 was one of the chief factors in the recrudesence of the Ku Klux Klan whose depredations during the '20s constituted one of the gravest threats to orderly and democratic government in America during recent years. It spread bitterness against and hatred of religious and racial minorities, and particularly against the Negro, with its falsification of history of the Reconstruction Period.
>
> At a time like this when forces of bigotry and racial prejudice threaten the security of the world and even of our own country, it is our contention that the distribution showing 'The Birth of a Nation' in any form would be disastrous.[57]

In addition to its own protest, the NAACP urged other organizations to write to the Hays office.[58] According to the NAACP, a number of organizations including the Commission on Interracial Cooperation, the American Jewish Congress, Harlem's Negro Labor Committee, and the Negro Work Department of the YMCA's National Council responded to the appeal and sent "vigorous" protests against the film to the Hays office.[59]

The sources consulted indicated that the Hays office answered the protests in varying ways. For example, Carl E. Milliken, MPPDA secretary, responded to White's original protest letter:

> . . .the general opinion in the motion picture industry is that this picture has been more or less constantly showing in various parts of the world ever since its first release 25 years ago. We understand that a sound version of the film was produced 8 or 9 years ago. Naturally, the circulation of the film has not been great, and we have had practically no comment from the public.[60]

White answered Milliken by commenting that the lack of public comment was "regrettable," but that it did not "lessen the danger to democracy of this glorification of mob violence and this distortion of history."[61] In a press release issued several days after White's letter to Milliken, the NAACP indicated "Hays made no comment" on the matter.[62] On the other hand, in a letter to R. B. Eleazer, secretary of the Commission on Interracial Cooperation, another representative from the Hays office, F. S. Harmon, wrote:

> On March 29, 1937, in a letter to R. H. King, then Chairman of the Executive Committee of the Commission on Interracial Cooperation, it was stated that 'it is significant of the improvement in standards and increased sense of responsibility on the part of the motion picture industry that this picture would have to be materially changed before it could receive certificate of approval.' This continued to be our position here.[63]

In addition, the NAACP later reported it received word from the MPPDA "that the 'Birth of a Nation' in its original form could not be passed by the Hays office."[64] However, the controversy was moot because Epoch did not remake the film. Thus, in three instances individuals protesting The Birth petitioned self-regulatory agencies within the motion picture industry to no avail.

Film As An Extra-Legal Tactic

At least two films were presented as positive alternatives to the negative black stereotypes shown in The Birth of a Nation. One was a short epilogue added to The Birth supposedly to silence black protests because it depicted black progress since Reconstruction. The other film was a positive statement concerning blacks to counteract the negative statement of The Birth.

Epilogue

Little is known of the epilogue "showing the progress of the colored people in this country since the Civil War" added to The Birth on April 16, 1915.[65] The epilogue apparently has not survived. Nevertheless, this interesting sequence is important in the history of censorship of The Birth for several reasons. First, the film apparently was added to The Birth at least in part because of black protests against the film. The Christian Science Monitor reported Griffith was convinced by friends to add the footage because "while the story of the carpetbaggers and the Negro excesses during Reconstruction were historically correct, in all fairness the advancement of the race since that time should be shown."[66] Second, the addition of the epilogue was one reason Monroe Trotter and a number of blacks were at the Tremont Theatre to see the film April 17, 1915. (See Chapter IV.) Trotter and other blacks were arrested that evening and of the arrests several front-page headlines reported in an alarming fashion that a "near-riot" had taken place.[67] Third, the epilogue was mentioned in affidavits attesting to the positive educational value of the film. The affidavits were supportive evidence in at least one censorship controversy. Finally, the sequence itself was controversial and censored at least once.

Sources consulted paint a conflicting picture of the origin and nature of the epilogue. For example, the Boston Morning Journal announced Griffith produced the segment stressing accomplishments of individual blacks like Frederick Douglas and Booker T. Washington.[68]

Griffith also was credited for producing the epilogue in the Christian Science Monitor.[69] Film scholar Fred Silva concluded from a comment in the New York Mail that the sequence was shot at the Hampton Institute, probably by Griffith.[70] Historian Thomas Cripps confirms the footage was shot at Hampton, but does not directly attribute the film to Griffith.[71] At least one source indicated the footage was shot at the Tuskegee Institute, but did not attribute the footage to Griffith.[72]

Primary sources indicate the footage was indeed shot at Hampton, not Tuskegee. Although Tuskegee head Booker T. Washington apparently was approached by Philip Allston, National Business League representative, about the possibility of adding Tuskegee footage to The Birth, Washington refused to allow Tuskegee to be tied to the film. In his communication to Washington, Allston said he spoke with Griffith in the Tremont Theatre lobby and Griffith said: "Mr. Allston, what do you think of my reproducing in pictures Tuskegee?"[73] Allston also indicated that Griffith was "considering the matter very seriously."[74] Washington answered Allston:

> From all that I hear of 'The Birth of a Nation' it is a hurtful, vicious play and I do not think Tuskegee would be helped by having any connection with it, in fact, I think that any connection that we might have with the play would be interpreted in the direction of an endorsement of the play. Certainly, the play is resulting in stirring up a lot of useless race prejudice wherever it has gone and I very much wish that the play might be stopped.[75]

Washington reaffirmed his position on the film in a letter to Florence Swell Bond. Washington told Bond he refused to have Tuskegee in any way connected with the film because ". . .such an exhibit would be an indirect endorsement of 'The Birth of a Nation.'"[76]

In spite of Washington's opposition to The Birth and the NAACP campaign against the film which was in full swing, representatives from the Hampton Institute apparently agreed to allow films of their institution to be added to The Birth. Mary Childs Nerney, who called the Hampton footage "adding insult to injury,"[77] indicated the footage was "added to the play at the suggestion of Mr. Schieffelin who is one of the trustees of Hampton."[78] Charles (?)llason said he spoke with Hampton representative Sidney Frissell who "felt exceedingly sorry" and believed that adding the footage was "a great mistake."[79] (?)llason said "Hampton went into it in good faith and the time for decision was short so they relied upon the advice of their New York friends.[80] The New York Age editorially commented that from its point of view the epilogue could "only injure Hampton and not improve the picture."[81] Nerney later reported that "although a certain member of the Board of Trustees of Hampton was in favor of this reel being shown many of the Board seriously objected, so much so that their Secretary was sent up to New York some months ago to see what could be done to get the pictures withdrawn."[82]

However, sources indicate Hampton was not successful in eliminating the footage from The Birth. Although one source said that "the film people do not regularly show the Hampton picture, but only show them when the spirit moves them," the footage apparently was shown with selected prints of The Birth outside of Boston until at least 1923.[83] For example, among the affidavits filed with the Ohio Supreme Court in 1925 supporting The Birth are at least four which mention the epilogue.[84] In his affidavit Norfolk, Virginia, Mayor Wyndham R. Mayo, indicated the epilogue was with *The Birth* when it was presented in his city during the week beginning September 27, 1915.[85] Of the epilogue specifically, Mayo said:

> Your deponent further avers that the concluding pictures show the present day Afro-American training in the different professions at Hampton Institute together with statistics showing the remarkable strides the race has made within the last fifty years, which is a tribute that has never been so forcibly presented to the American people.[86]

R. T. Thorp, Norfolk resident, also filed an affidavit mentioning the epilogue. In part Thorp said:

> Your deponent believes that the picture brings one to a better understanding of conditions in the South, and this is borne out by the concluding pictures showing the present day Afro-American training in the different professions in Hampton Institute. It also protrays (sic) the remarkable strides in the African race as made in the last fifty years, and in a way that, in your deponent's opinion, has never been so forcibly presented on the American stage.[87]

The epilogue was also with the version of *The Birth* shown in Allentown, Pennsylvania, in November, 1915. Of this segment of the film, C. J. Smith, representative of the *Allentown Morning Call*, said "the final scenes emphasize most clearly the evolution of the Afro-American since the days of the Civil War along educational lines and call to mind the fact that the Negro is rapidly taking his place in the national frame work of the nation."[88]

Likewise, the epilogue was shown with *The Birth* during a week's run at Jersey City's Majestic Theatre, beginning January 10, 1916. Speaking for the film the *Jersey City Journal*'s business manager, Walter InDear said:

In the final scenes due emphasis is given to the evolution of the Afro-American and it is clearly shown that the Negro has become a powerful factor in the national framework of this country and by education and training, is eminently able to combat unscrupulous methods of the cheap politician.[89]

A letter to the editor of the Philadelphia Tribune indicated the epilogue was with the film in Atlantic City, New Jersey, during the film's initial run there at the New Nixon Theatre. The author of the letter said: "While the last five or six minutes of Hampton School scenes and statements of the colored man's progress is inspiring this to my mind cannot heal the terrible indignities heaped upon us for the two hours preceding."[90]

Francis Grimke in his pamphlet The Birth of a Nation confirms the epilogue was with the film in Atlantic City. Of the footage Grimke said:

> The last part of the photo-play, as it is now presented, which is an afterthought,--the showing of the buildings of Hampton Institute and some of the students at work in the classrooms and the various industries,--doesn't help matters. This was no part of the original play, but was added afterwards, after the protests began to be heard, simply as a blind, to disguise the utterly unworthy purpose of it so far as it pertains to the Negro. I confess I was greatly surprised to find that Dr. Frissell and the authorities at Hampton were willing to lend the weight of their influence in giving countenance to a play that is so manifestly hostile to the Negro. That it is only a disguise, admitted simply for the purpose of getting the endorsement of an institution like Hampton, is evident from the length of time the statement 'THESE PICTURES ARE PRESENTED BY PERMISSION OF DR. FRISSELL,' is kept upon the canvas, and the rapidity with which the pictures themselves are crowded on and off.[91]

An article in the Kansas City Call indicated the epilogue was with the film in December 1923 in that state. The article said Kansas Governor Jonathan Davis saw no harm in The Birth and indicated there were "many good things in the picture toward the end that show the progress of the race . . ."[92]

The epilogue itself apparently was censored at least once. The Cleveland Gazette in June 1915 reported the epilogue (under the title The New Era) was banned from Cleveland "even though separated from the rest" of The Birth.[93] J. J. McCarthy, manager of the theatre scheduled to show The New Era, called it:

> . . .a vivid impression of the progress of the race . . . it shows that in the last 50 years since the passing of the carpetbaggers and his trail of evil influences over the colored people their wealth has increased from $17,000,000 to $300,000,000. It shows how the Hampton Institute is making valuable citizens. It shows the agricultural advance of the race. It exhibits progressive types of colored men and women. In fact, it is a tribute to the qualities of the race and their capabilities for INDUSTRIAL and SOCIAL progress.[94]

In spite of McCarthy's praise the footage was apparently not shown in Cleveland.

Counter Film

The film made at least in part to counteract The Birth of a Nation was The Birth of a Race. Of the latter, film historian Thomas Cripps wrote:

> To deal with the racist social propaganda of Birth of a Nation blacks needed to choose a tactic that allowed maximum control of rhetoric theme, imagery, much as Griffith and Thomas Dixon had controlled their movie--outside the conventional studios in New York and California.[95]

Although black leaders like Booker T. Washington and Mary White Ovington expressed interest in the production of a black answer to The Birth, it proved impossible to raise enough money from black backers to finance the project.[96] Individuals interested in the film eventually turned to money from white business people to salvage the project.[97] The white investors who backed the film took over control of is production and content.[98] Final sequences of the film were shot in Tampa, Florida, in 1918.[99] In December 1918, the film opened in Chicago.[100] It was received unfavorably by the critics and apparently quickly disappeared from view.[101]

Thus, in two instances films were generated as alternative communications to The Birth of a Nation. However, neither film resolved the controversy over The Birth.

Sermons

Sermons were another form of communication involved in The Birth of a Nation censorship controversies. Although it would probably be impossible to determine precisely how many sermons for or against The Birth were delivered, it is apparent from the sources consulted that such sermons were preached, particularly during the initial round of censorship controversies in 1915.

For example, the Boston press reported during the censorship controversy there in April 1915 that at least one minister preached favoring The Birth and a variety spoke against the film. A supporter was the Rev. Chauncey J. Hawkins. In one sermon Hawkins ". . . praised 'Birth of a Nation'and said there was nothing in it to suggest immorality to a normal mind."[102] Hawkins also called the movie a "masterful picturing of the nation's most momentous problems."[103]

However, press reports indicated more Boston clergy condemned the film than praised it. For example, one newspaper reported that "practically all of the white and colored ministers of this vicinity voiced protests against the film including Harvard president Dr. Charles W. Eliot.[104] Although it did not mention specific ministers, another Boston paper said "denunciation of the photoplay Birth of a Nation and severe criticism of Mayor Curley for failing to stop its production in Boston were expressed at several meetings Sunday. In only one instance reported did a minister who considered the topic defend the play."[105]

At least one member of the New York clergy preached against The Birth in March 1915. The New York clergyman, Dr. Stephen Wise, Free Synagogue, said the film "stirred hatred between the Negro and the White man."[106] Wise said the film should be suppressed because it was a "deliberate attempt to deepen and justify within the hearts of men the . . . prejudices which it is the business of an enlightened democracy . . . to challenge and convert."[107]

The press of St. Paul, Minnesota, reported local clergy opinions about The Birth during the October 1915 censorship controversy in that city. For example, Rev. Charles N. Pace, First Methodist Church, returned to the theatre complimentary tickets with a note indicating the film contained "elements which excite prejudices that are Unamerican."[108] In a sermon delivered at the First Methodist Church, Pace said the film appealed to the "partisan spirit" and was "hostile to the peace and prosperity of the nation."[109] On the other hand, St. Paul ministers Dr. S. T. Willis, First Christian Church, and the Rev. W. J. Robb, Atlantic Congregational Church, both preached supportive of The Birth. Robb called the film the greatest production ever staged in the moving picture world" and said:

> Because of class hatred and prejudice and politics, there is an attempt being made to prohibit it from being shown. The people have a right to see it and judge for themselves. I have seen the picture. Instead of stirring up class hatred, it will save the people from making mistakes which our fathers made and help us to live as the children of God.[110]

Willis called The Birth "wonderful," and said the "play is correct as a portrayal of history, at least its main features are correct."[111] Willis also praised the film for its "moral value:"

> . . . From the viewpoint of the artist and the mechanism of this panorama, the presentations of the scenes are well nigh perfect. It is simply marvelous. Everything is presented with such spectacular vividness that one senses of the beautiful experiences the deepest satisfaction. Much of it is beyond the power of words to tell. The scenes of intrigue and warfare move on with such terrific cumulative force that I found myself recoiling from it. It is too intense and it produces a feeling of awful intensity in one's soul as the play moves on and on sweeping thousands of men in untimely graves . . . The chief moral value of the play is in its vivid presentation, in the most spectacular and effective forms possible, the unspeakable horrors of war.[112]

The Chicago Defender reported at least one minister took a public stand from his pulpit against The Birth during the October 1915 controversy in that city. The Defender said Preston Bradley, Wilson Avenue People's Church, denounced The Birth as a "menace to higher nationalism and true patriotism."[113] Bradley also said the film should be stopped and that "education will untimately solve every problem including the race question."[114]

Thus, it can be seen that the pulpit was also a forum from which the acceptability of The Birth of a Nation was debated. Ministers publicly supported or attacked the film for a variety of reasons.

Pamphlets

Although both sides engaged in pamphleteering concerning The Birth's right to the screen, the tactic was used more frequently by those opposed. During the early years of controversy, at least six pamphlets against The Birth were published. Only one major document in favor of the film was found published as a pamphlet.

Support

The major document written in support of The Birth was authored by D. W. Griffith. In addition to quotations from individuals favoring The Birth, Griffith expressed in The Rise and Fall of Free Speech in America his belief that movies should have the same constitutional freedom as the printed press.[115] Griffith argued:

> The moving picture is simply the pictorial press. The pictorial press claims the same constitutional freedom as the printed press. Freedom of speech and publication is guaranteed in the Constitution of the United States, and in the constitutions of practically all the states. Unjustifiable speech or publication may be punished, but cannot be forbidden in advance.
>
> Today the censorship of moving pictures, throughout the entire country is seriously hampering the growth of the art. Had intelligent opposition to censorship been employed when it first made itself manifest it could easily have been overcome. But the pigmy child of that day has grown to be, not merely a man, but a giant, and I tell you who read this, whether you will or no, he is a giant whose forces of evil are so strong that he threatens that priceless heritage of our nation--freedom of expression.[116]

Griffith contended that film censorship was the first serious attack on freedom of expression in the United States since colonial times. The Birth's maker said individuals who would allow film to be suppressed would "unquestionably" allow all other forms of legitimate expression to be suppressed.[117] According to Griffith, the First Amendment meant that every American citizen had a constitutional right to publish in any form anything she/he pleased and be subject to liability only after publication for such things as obscenity and libel. Griffith said the distinction between this theory of the First Amendment and the reality of film's lack of First Amendment protection meant that all films could be censored before publication. In Griffith's opinion, that "directly controverts the most valuable of all our liberties under the Constitution."[118] Griffith concluded:

> It is said the motion picture tells its story more vividly than any other art. In other words, we are to be blamed for efficiency, for completeness. Is this justice? Is this common sense? We do not think so.
>
> We have no wish to offend with indecencies or obscenities, but we do demand, as a right, the liberty to show the dark side of wrong that we may illuminate the bright side of virtue--the same liberty that is conceded to art of the written word--that art to which we owe the _Bible_ and the works of Shakespeare.[119]

Thus, Griffith argued _The Birth_'s right to the screen specifically on First Amendment grounds. However, his interpretation of the First Amendment as it should apply to filmic expression has not yet been accepted by the U. S. Supreme Court (See Chapter II.), the pre-exhibition censorship status of the medium remains basically the same as when Griffith first published _The Rise and Fall of Free Speech in America_.

Opposition

Unlike Griffith's argument which addressed the constitutionality of film censorship specifically, pamphlets published against

The Birth attacked directly the film itself. One of the first major documents against The Birth was published in 1915 by the NAACP's Boston Branch after the film was approved by Boston's censorship board.

The Boston NAACP pamphlet, Fighting a Vicious Film: Protest Against The Birth of a Nation, is basically a compilation of essays by many individuals concerning the film and what the NAACP saw as related issues. In the introductory section of the publication, the Branch expressed its "grievous disappointment" that the agitation in Boston against The Birth failed to stop the film.[120] However, because the agitation resulted in securing a new censorship law for Boston and because "a series of public meetings, remarkable for the spirit of unity and brotherhood and a very pronounced desire to save every group of our varied citizenship from insult and indignity," had been generated by the protest, the struggle could not be considered a total defeat.[121] Within this frame, the group offered Fighting a Vicious Film "with a view to giving some idea of the scope of the agitation and the spirit in which it was conducted a few of the many letters, resolutions, and speeches produced by the opposition to the play in April are put in permanent form with the further purpose of aiding other communities in opposing this and all such productions."[122] More than 25 documents about the controversy were reproduced in the 47-page pamphlet. Thus, the NAACP's Boston Branch compiled and published a pamphlet to be used as a primer by other individuals interested in opposing The Birth. The document itself contained a number of statements by individuals who expressed a variety of arguments against the film and did not address the theoretical question of film censorship.

In addition, Frances Grimke published a short pamphlet against the film in October 1915. Grimke recorded his "impressions" of the film after viewing it in Atlantic City, New Jersey, in August 1915.[123] Grimke indicated the film was unacceptable. Grimke said his pamphlet was to "set forth clearly the spirit of the play, and the purpose of it."[124] Specifically, Grimke said the purposes of the film were to:

> I. . . . . revive the spirit of rebellion and to set it forth in such a light as to take the stigma from it which it rightly deserves. It aims to make the impression, that, after all the spirit that took the South out of the Union was a noble spirit, a spirit not to be condemned, but rather to be admired . . .
>
> II. . . . give respectability to a band of lawbreakers and murderers known as the Ku Klux Klan,--an organization that was inspired by hatred of the Negro, and that committed all kinds of outrages upon him. No blacker, fouler record was ever made than was made by this organization. And yet, according to the representations here, it represented the chivalry of the South! . . .
>
> III. . . . discredit the Negro, to present him in the most unfavorable light, with, as it seems to me, a fourfold object: 1) Of intensifying race prejudice, of making it all the harder for him to get along in his upward struggle in this country (2) Of showing that he is unworthy of citizenship, that it is not safe, not wise to entrust him with political power (3) That he was much happier in slavery, much better off in every way than he is now (4) That freedom has had only the effect of spoiling him, of filling him with false notions of himself and of his rights, which never can be realized in this country; and that under freedom he had degenerated, has become a less desirable element of the population.[125]

Grimke also said the scenes of the Hampton Institute did not offset the negative spirit of the film as a whole. Grimke concluded by attacking supporters and praising the opposition. He expressed the hope that the "good people of this land" would make the production of such films impossible in the future.[126] Thus, in this pamphlet one individual argued the film should be stopped because it presented blacks unfairly and glorified the Klan.

A similar attack on the film was launched by Rev. W. Bishop Johnson, Pastor of Washington, D. C. Second Baptist Church, in a speech at his church to a joint meeting of the Second Baptist Lyceum and Citizens Association on March 26, 1916.[127] Afterwards, Johnson published the speech as a pamphlet. In his eight-page document, Johnson developed the thesis that The Birth was a "monumental slander of American History; the Negro and the Civil War."[128] Johnson summarized the perceived historical inaccuracies in the film and called the film's mission "one of hatred, prejudice and oppression."[129] Johnson then analysed how Thomas Dixon expressed this mission in The Birth. According to Johnson, Dixon slandered the black race through racial stereotyping. Specifically, three types of black characters are given "undue prominence and made to represent vile and disgusting conditions."[130] These three unfavorable characterizations are represented by Lydia Brown, Salis (sic) Lynch, and Gus. To accomplish his purposes Dixon also "makes an effort to dignify that relic of barbarism--the Ku-Klux."[131] Johnson said Dixon gave the South "the maximum of the glory" in all battle scenes.[132] Johnson interpreted this emphasis as an attempt to "stir sectional strife by reviving the spirit of the rebellion and emphasizing the awful sacrifice that Southern family life made without the least suggestion that all parties suffered."[133] Johnson concluded, outlining the advances of the black race since reconstruction and asserting that in spite of his tremendous effort, Thomas Dixon would not be able to drive blacks "out of this country that has been enriched by our blood and toil."[134] Griffith is not mentioned; Dixon bears the brunt of the attack. The film is discussed only as a graphic example of Dixon's racist philosophy. In this instance, the author spoke against the film because of its alleged historical inaccuracy and its racial stereotyping.

An empassioned plea for racial equality was made by Isaac L. Thomas' pamphlet <u>The Birth of a Nation a Hyperbole Versus A Negro's Plea for Fair Play</u>.[135] Although Thomas attacked <u>The Birth</u> in the pamphlet, he utilized the 64-page document to summarize racial discrimination and ask for its erradication. In this context, <u>The Birth</u> is unacceptable because it was a vehicle to continue racial prejudice. Thomas indicated because America was founded on the principles of equality and because blacks were given equality under the law through the Fourteenth Amendment, <u>The Birth</u> violated the spirit of America by teaching "to hate without a cause."[136] Indeed, Thomas argued the film was treasonous because it "has for its motive the destruction of the government by the weakening of one of its factors."[137] Thomas contended the film "materially" damaged the United States because it humiliated and injured ten percent of the country's population.[138] Thomas said:

The various scenes representing the Negro in the play would not be put upon canvas by men who had the welfare of the people of the United States at heart, even if they were true. And when they are creations of the imagination and shown to the American people as if they really took place they reveal the fact what men will do for the almighty dollar, and are willing to see even the nation go down and help to send it for a piece of silver. They are not thinking of the peace of the nation but what they can get out of it for themselves.[139]

Next, Thomas called <u>The Birth</u> "a mere creation intended to intensify race feeling and incite white men, North and South, to dislike the Negro with a hatred that upon the slightest misrepresentation they will feel justified in shooting the Negro down like a mad dog."[140]

Next Thomas argued that <u>The Birth of a Nation</u> violated the constitutional rights of blacks guaranteed by the Fourteenth Amendment:

> . . . It is a sad situation when a nation allows race prejudice to make it ignore its constitution. The Fourteenth Amendment to the Constitution . . . provides that by no qualification or discrimination on account of race or color or previous condition of servitude and for no other reasons than by due process of law or according to the law of the land which shall be applicable alike to every part of the sixty millions of citizens and to the most favored by reason of any common law, custom or said enactment against the citizens of the United States of African descent by constitutional deprivation of the full and unqualified enjoyment of all such immunities and privileges; that the citizens of African descent by virtue of being citizens of the United States are clothed with immunity from, and protection against, all discrimination on account of race, color, or previous condition and as a citizen of the United States he is entitled to all the privileges and immunities which are accorded to every one of their most favored citizens as fundamental rights of citizenship.
>
> . . . A continued disregard of many of the constitutional rights of the Negro as an American citizen as such fire brands as 'The Birth of a Nation' can have but one

end--race strife and race feeling, when there should be
a mutual co-operation and goodwill of white and colored
Americans.[141]

Thomas also argued the final scenes of The Birth which show Christ blessing "all races of mankind" were sacrilegious because "Christ has no connection with anything that is a wicked device."[142] In other lengthy sections not directly mentioning The Birth, Thomas discussed the place of blacks in American society at the time, indicated positive contributions of blacks to American society, and asked that blacks be treated equally with whites.

As a document in the history of controversy surrounding The Birth, this pamphlet is unique. First, it primarily discussed the film as a vehicle for carrying its larger message. Second, it is the only document found which argued in great detail that the film violated the constitutional rights of blacks. Third, the document reflected the Supreme Court opinion in the Mutual case that film was a business.

At least two other short pamphlets against The Birth were published and used as a resource document during censorship battles. For example, as part of its protest the NAACP's Providence, Rhode Island, Branch published A Statement of Facts Regarding the Photo-Play The Birth of a Nation in 1915.[144] The one-page flyer summarized the branch's efforts against the film and suggested extending the protest. The folder also reproduced a letter from Samuel Gee, secretary of the Providence Board of Police Commissioners, assuring the branch the commission would not approve The Birth. In the flyer, the branch indicated it opposed the film because it was historically incorrect, reflected negatively upon black people, and was a "meance to peaceful race relations."[145] The flyer instructed individuals opposed to The Birth to:

> Continue to protest by letter, word, and act. Make our attitude clear by handing one of the circulars to an uninformed friend. Request your pastor to make some mention of this important matter every Sunday. Let our protest be dignified, uncompromising, and unyielding.
>
> At the hours of two and eight, whether at home or work, lift your hearts in prayer to the Father of us all that He will interpose that Justice may be accorded a people who from the real birth of the Nation to the present day have been loyal and law-abiding citizens. PASS IT ON.[146]

Although the Police Commission did ban the film (See Chapters II and V), the controversy was resolved when Griffith secured an injunction, enjoining the commission from interfering with the film.

The other circular against The Birth was published by the NAACP in 1921. Stop the KKK Propaganda in New York specifically attacked the film as Klan propaganda. The one-sheet flyer summarized the revival of the Klan in four southern states and denounced Klan activities,[147] It indicated The Birth's 1921 revival would aid the Klan in its concurrent revival. The flyer asked: "Are you going to allow Ku Klux Klan propaganda to be displayed in the movies in New York?"[148] The flyer was distributed by individuals picketing the Capitol Theater during The Birth's 1921 New York revival. The picketers (See Chapter IV) were arrested and charged with distributing materials in violation of a New York law which forbade the distribution of commercial or business advertising material in public places.[149] Although the individuals were convicted originally, the convictions were reversed on appeal. In this decision Judge Alfred Tally, New York County General Sessions Court, said the individuals were within their rights in making public their protest against the film through the distribution of the leaflets.[150]

Thus, two NAACP affiliates suggested tactics for stopping the film, because it engendered racial prejudice and was historically inaccurate. Although the other document did not actually suggest action against the film, individuals were arrested for distributing it. The authors opposed the film because it glorified the Ku Klux Klan.

Demonstrations

Demonstrations primarily in the forms of picketing and parading were tactics included in several censorship controversies. Because the forms of demonstration differ, each will be discussed individually.

Parades

During the time period studied, at least three protest parades were planned. However, at least one was cancelled because of lack of a parade permit. This aborted effort was planned by the NAACP as part of its original New York protest against The Birth in March 1915. Although NAACP representative Paul Kennaday apparently co-ordinated the parade plans, Mary Childs Nerney helped. Specifically, the parade was scheduled as part of the organization's protest to New York Mayor John Mitchell. The NAACP arranged for a hearing with

Mitchell on the film and wished to preface the hearing with a parade from Union Square down Broadway to City Hall Park and from there to Mitchell's office.[151] Several groups were asked to participate. For example, Nerney wrote Major R. C. Wendall:

> I am wondering if the Boy Scouts would not like to take part in the parade, and if you would not interest as many of our friends as possible. There will be no women in the parade. It is our object to have a very dignified procession of representative people. We feel that it is quality rather than quantity that matters.[152]

Nerney also wrote that the association secured "the proper permits from the bureau of Licenses, the Police Department, and the Park Commissioner" and had been "assured by them of protection."[153] Nerney's letter to Wendall is dated March 26, 1915. On the same day Kennaday wrote New York Park Commissioner, Cabot Ward, and requested "a permit to enter City Hall from Broadway on Tuesday March 30 between 11 and 12."[154] Kennaday also wrote he had already "applied to the Police Department" for a parade permit.[155] Thus, it appears that Nerney was working with insufficient or incorrect data when she wrote Wendall. In any event, the Police Department notified the NAACP that it would not issue the permit "for the reason that the streets can only be used for processions on holidays and Saturdays."[156] Nerney immediately announced the parade was cancelled.[157]

One source indicated a protest parade was planned for Philadelphia in September 1915. In this instance the Chicago Defender reported the "men" of Philadelphia had been granted a permit to have a "big demonstration and protest parade against 'The Birth of a Nation' on Wednesday evening September 15th."[158] There is no confirmation that the parade took place.[159]

Harry Smith reported in the Cleveland Gazette that a protest "parade demonstration" against The Birth took place in Cleveland some time in 1917.[160] However, Smith did not record details.

Picketing

Sources indicated that during the time period studied at least three theatres were picketed for showing The Birth. The first recorded incident of organized picketing occurred in New York in 1921. Several picketers were arrested (See Chapter IV). The NAACP enlisted "several ex-service men and women" to picket.[161] Several carried signs reading "We represented America in France, why should The Birth of a Nation misrepresent us here."[162] Others distributed the circular, Stop the KKK Propaganda in New York.[163] As discussed, the five picketers were arrested for distributing the leaflets, but the charges were eventually dismissed.[164]

The NAACP also picketed the Beverly Theatre in New York when The Birth was revived there in 1950.[165] In spite of the pickets, manager Henry Raymond reported there were "no disturbances and . . . business was good."[166]

More than 40 NAACP organized pickets demonstrated in front of the Lansdowne Theatre in Philadelphia during a 1965 revival of The Birth.[167] Variety reported the picketing was "orderly and the participants carried signs with slogans as "We Shall Overcome 'The Birth of a Nation" and "Is This Pennsylvania or Alabama?"[167] Lansdowne Theatre manager Don Scott commented:

> I can't object to the demonstrators any more than they should have objected to this film. Movies in general are an art form and as such should be entitled to a certain amount of freedom of expression. Where's all this freedom everyone is yelling about? This year makes Nation's 50 anniversary and it is being shown to old film fans and curious new ones all over the country.[169]

Scott also said "racist" parts had been eliminated from the film.[140]

Mass meetings

During the time period studied, there were several other mass meetings concerning the film. One of the largest occurred in Boston in April 1915 when more than a thousand people gathered at the Massachusetts State House and protested the film's Boston production to Massachusetts Governor David Walsh.[171] Walsh met with representatives from the delegation and expressed sympathy.[172] (See Chapter V.)

A more violent demonstration against The Birth apparently took place in front of Philadelphia's Forrest Theatre in September 1915.[173] The protesters were apparently called to the theatre that evening by an announcement circulating in predominantly black sections of Philadelphia which said in part a "dignified protest" against the film would begin at the theatre at 8 p.m.[174] About five hundred individuals were involved in the demonstration which erupted into violence when someone threw a brick through a theatre window.[175] At least four individuals were arrested, but all charges were dismissed (See Chapter IV).[176]

At least four other mass meetings were held in Boston during 1915 to protest The Birth. At one held by the Maverick Church Men's Club of East Boston, Dr. Charles Fleischer and Peter Fagan, newspaperman, debated the film's merits.[177] At another meeting, Harvard President Charles Eliot opposed the film at the First Parish Church, Cambridge, Massachusetts.[178] Two peaceful mass demonstrations against The Birth took place in Boston, May 2, 1915. That evening 2,500 people met at the Tremont Temple to protest the film's production.[179] The same evening, a mass meeting was held on the Boston Common.[180] Although one newspaper account indicated that "indirect threats of violence" were made by the speakers, the demonstrations were peaceful.[181]

Resolution

Rather than physically demonstrate against the film, several groups expressed displeasure by passing formal resolutions against the film. Representative ones will be cited. Several resolutions were passed by differing organizations during the April 1915, Boston censorship controversy. The directors of the Federation of Churches and Religious Organizations of Greater Boston unanimously expressed "in the strongest terms their disapproval of the photoplay 'The Birth of a Nation.'"[182] The group said The Birth was "contrary to good public policy and . . . injurious to public morality."[183] The group also articulated the "trust that some way will be found to prevent its further production."[184] The group also asked the state legislature to pass a new film censorship ordinance for Boston.[185] The Zion Methodist Church also held a mass meeting about the film and the arrests at the Tremont:

> Whereas, to act as ticket sellers or ticket takers for a
> theatre is not the proper function of a policeman whose
> salaries are paid by public taxation and whereas, for a
> policeman to stop a citizen in the entrance lobby of a
> theatre is illegal and for a policeman to demand to see
> and scrutinize the theatre ticket to check a citizen at
> the door is a violation of personal liberty, resolved
> that we protest such action by the Boston police at the
> Tremont Theatre during the run of 'Birth of a Nation' and
> that we demand a cessation of such invasion of the public
> rights that any play which is deemed to make such police
> action necessary be stopped at once.[186]

After The Birth was approved by the Boston censors, the executive committee of the city's NAACP Branch expressed its "profound regret" that the film had been approved.[187] The NAACP resolution said in part:

> We deplore this decision as a rejection of the just claims
> of our colored fellow citizens to be protected against a
> malicious misrepresentation of their race in a play involving
> a perversion of our national history and a glorification of
> lynching.
>
> We deplore the insidious influence of this play in the manner
> of its presentation--before audiences whose judgment is misled
> and whose passions are inflamed by a most clever combination
> of spectacular and musical art with the inevitable result of
> increased racial and sectional antagonism . . .
>
> We deplore the sinister circumstances connected with the contro-
> versy over this play in Boston--the enormous capital invested
> in its preparation; the lavish use of advertising space in
> newspapers whose editoral (sic) columns with very few excep-
> tions have been silent; the extraordinary police protection
> employed to prevent anticipated outbreaks at the performances;
> all these things revealing the formidable commercial interests
> involved--while the opposition to the play, with no unworthy
> motive has sought only to further justice, truth, and peace.[188]

On the positive side, the association said: "we congratulate ourselves on the great increase of interest in the cause of human rights . . . which has been aroused by the recent discussions" and urged "fair-minded" individuals in other parts of the country to work for the "legal suppression" of The Birth.[189]

The St. Louis, Missouri, Federation of Colored Women's Clubs and Mothers Congress resolved against The Birth in September 1915. In their protest, the clubs called the film "detrimental to peace and harmony between the white and Negro races."[190] The clubs also opposed the film because it "deals with times and scenes that belong to the happily forgotten past" and said the film should be suppressed.[191]

The Grand Army of the Republic Post also requested suppression of The Birth. The resolutions adopted by the Post in December 1915 were made public through George H. Thomas Post No. 2, Department of California and Nevada.[192] The resolutions charged The Birth "slanderously misrepresents the federal soldier engaged in suppressing the rebellion."[193] The Post also objected to the film because it glorified the Klan and had as its tendency engendering hatred against the Negro race and "against the colored troops who fought gallantly for their own freedom."[194]

Likewise, the George H. Thomas Grand Post No. 5 Department of Illinois, appointed a committee to investigate The Birth. The committee recommended a resolution against the film. It was unanimously adopted. The resolution said The Birth was a "remarkable work of art" but because its chief purposes were to intensify race hatred and glorify the Klan, it should not be exhibited.[195]

At least two New York City groups passed resolutions against the film during the initial censorship controversy there in 1915.

For example, the Committee on Education and Publicity of the New York Progressive Club passed resolutions critical of The Birth in March 1915. The resolutions attacked the film for presenting blacks unfairly and for exciting racial prejudice.[196] A set of resolutions condemning The Birth were passed at a joint meeting of the Salem Civic Committee, the Civic League, and the Equal Rights League in March 1915. The joint meeting took place in New York's Salem Methodist Church.[197]

The Colored Baptist Churches of Ohio also passed a resolution supporting censorship of The Birth in 1915. The resolution was passed at the churches regular convention and condemned " . . . all such film productions as tending only to stir up ill feeling between the races and thus hindering both religious and moral progress in this state."[198]

Editorials and Letters to the Editor

Newspapers not only reported The Birth of a Nation censorship controversies, but entered into the fray through the use of editorial columns and letters to the editor. Using the press as a vehicle to win support for its drive to suppress The Birth waa advocated by the NAACP. Early in its compaign against the film, the NAACP urged its membership "to bring the sinister nature of this play to the attention of the public through the press."[199] The association also urged individuals to make their objections public through a letter to the editor. For example, Mary Childs Nerney suggested in a letter to Mrs. A. J. Erdman that Erdman "send your protest against 'The Birth of a Nation' to the 'N. Y. Evening Mail' or the 'New York Globe.'"[200]

Nerney also thanked the Bishop Alexander Walters for "writing to the 'Herald' as we requested."[201]

Apparently, both sides were prolific in writing letters about The Birth because at least two newspapers decided they had published enough letters about the issue and would print no more. For example, the St. Paul Pioneer Press said:

> The Pioneer Press is in receipt of a bushel basket of letters to the mailbag dealing with the question of the fitness and unfitness of The Birth of a Nation and discussing both sides of the proposition to prohibit the production. Much space has been devoted lately both in the Pioneer Press and Dispatch to this issue and the argument is exhausted. The council has decided to permit the exhibition with the elimination of most of the scenes to which objection has been registered and the incident may be considered closed. Further discussion in the mailbag at this time would accomplish no purpose, and it may as well end with the closing of the incident.[202]

The New York Evening Post also ended discussion of the topic in its letters to the editor column with a note ". . . discussion of this subject must be brought to a close."[203]

In spite of reasonable discussion in the letters to the editor columns, the NAACP was dissatisfied with press coverage of the controversy surrounding the film. Mary Childs Nerney noted the New York press other than the Call and the Evening Post were "closed" to the NAACP.[204] The association was particularly irritated with the press for not commenting upon an interview with Jane Addams sent to them for that purpose.[205] Nerney indicated her disgust with the situation in a letter to Rev. William P. Hayes. In part Nerney said: "The press, except the Evening Post . . . are all carrying advertisements and apparently nothing else from their silence on the enclosed inter-

view with Miss Addams . . ."[206] The association was also less than
enthusiastic about press coverage given the issue during the 1915
Boston controversy. The organization's Boston Branch observed:

> The 'Traveller' is fine, true from the beginning. 'Post'
> fair. The others all bought over by the huge advertise-
> ments . . . The papers have misrepresented as much as
> they dare.[207]

Because letters to the editor and editorials differ in the
voice represented, each is discussed separately. Editorial campaigns opposing The Birth are considered first. Next, editorial campaigns favoring the film are reviewed. Letters to the editor follow.
Although all issues of all newspapers read for the study were also
searched for editorials about The Birth, those editorials discussed
here cannot be considered all that were no doubt published during the
years of this study. Rather, the editorials and letters to the editor
analysed here present a range of published opinion about the film's
right to the screen and indicate the variety of approaches taken to
the subject.

Editorials Against The Birth

Editorials against The Birth were published in a variety of
newspapers. Those discussed here either originated or were reprinted
by one of a number of newspapers.

One of the first editorials against The Birth of a Nation
appeared in the Western Outlook immediately after the film opend at
the Los Angeles Auditorium. This editorial summarized the Los Angeles battle fought by blacks against The Birth and reprinted the ad-

vice given to the film's opponents by the judge who issued the restraining order which forbade interference with the film's production in Los Angeles.[208] The judge told the film's opponents they should "wholly disregard" the matter because "constant agitation" would only bring attention to the film (See Chapter III).[209] The editorial echoed the judge's advice and said the appropriate tactic against the film was to "totally ignore it."[210] In this was "box office receipts will not fatten . . . and in the end we shall reap greater satisfaction."[211]

A different tactic was evident in the manner the N. Y. Age editorially commented on The Birth. Because the paper generated its own editorials opposing the film, ran editorial columns critical of the film, and reprinted editorials against the film from other papers, it is evident the editors of the N. Y. Age did not agree with the policy of silence championed by the Western Outlook.

In its first major editorial, the Age said a partial victory had been won locally because "two of the obnoxious scenes" had been cut from The Birth.[212] The Age also offered the following advice to those mayors who wished to censor the film, but could find no precedent:

> To Mayor Mitchell and other mayors who seem to be up a tree as to what vests them with the power to forbid the exhibition of this and other vicious pictures we suggest that they apply the same laws which gave them power in New York City and in other cities to put a ban on all fight pictures in which Jack Johnson came out victorious in the fight with his white opponents. Then the mayors issued orders that the Johnson pictures should be suppressed as they would create racial antagonism. We are asking that The Birth of a Nation be stopped for the same reason.[213]

In its next comment about The Birth, the Age in an editorial paragraph said "the attempt to break up The Birth of a Nation at the Liberty Theatre did not succeed very well."[214] However, the Age noted a similar attempt at Boston's Tremont Theatre had "succeeded somewhat better" because "more people went to jail."[215]

The last major Age editorial concerning directly The Birth during the 1915 controversy was published May 27. In this statement, the newspaper said the summons against the producers of the film had been dismissed by the court, ending local efforts to restrain the film legally. On the negative side, the Age noted " . . . notwithstanding all efforts very little" had been accomplished.[216] Also, the Age said:

> . . . the front put up will have some effect. Sentiments have been sown that will somewhere . . . and at some time bear fruit. Words have been spoken by such powerful papers as the 'World,' the 'Evening Post,' the N. Y. 'Globe' and others that have gone straight to some hearts and they will at some time produce results. A complete victory has not been won, but the effort put forth by the NAACP, the 'Crisis,' the 'Age' and the other Negro publications, together with a body of representative citizens was not one to be ashamed of.[217]

The Age concluded, expressing the hope that others would have "complete success" against the film.[218]

Later, the Age editorially used The Birth as partial justification for its support of a controversial New York state censorship law.[219] The Age said in a "civilized community there should not be any necessity for such extra regulation," but the film industry had "grown too powerful" and therefore such legislation was justified.[220]

The Age also published at least seven editorial columns against The Birth during 1915. Four of these columns were written by James W. Johnson and three, Lester A. Walton. Because the approaches of each man differ, each will be discussed separately.

In his role as contributing editorial writer James Johnson stressed the negative aspects of the film and analyzed press coverage of the controversy. For example, in his first column about The Birth, Johnson assaulted The Clansman in all forms: book, stage play, and film.[221] Johnson called the film a "serious attempt to hold the American Negro up before the whole country as a degraded brute" and called for all "law abiding citizens" to protest the film's production to legal authorities.[222]

In his next column on The Birth, Johnson reproduced a N. Y. World editorial critical of The Birth and considered generally the nature of press coverage given the issues by the New York press.[223] Johnson praised the World for breaking "the silence" of the "great New York dailies" concerning the production "of this famous picture."[224] Johnson noted that except for the Evening Post not even letters to the editor against the film had been given editorial space in the local press. He called for the New York press to editorialize on the issue and said:

> The combined influence of the great newspapers of this city could do what the mayor, the police and the courts say they are powerless to do; that is, stop the presentation of a picture which defames an entire race, which is incendiary and obscene, which breeds hatred in one class of American citizens against another, which makes its strongest appeal to the lowest and most dangerous of human passions, a picture that will fan the very fires of hell wherever it is shown.[225]

Johnson consluded by calling the World editorial "more than mere news-writing" because it "touches the same emotions . . . stirred by Lincoln's Gettysburg speech."[226]

The following week Johnson praised the N. Y. Globe for publishing three editorials during one week in opposition to The Birth.[227] Johnson quoted freely from the editorials and indicated the Globe also printed letters to the editor supporting the film. Johnson called The Birth "morally wrong" because it engendered racial hatred and reissued his call for "the press of the city" to "put the production in bad repute."[228]

Press coverage of The Birth was also the subject of Johnson's remaining 1915 column on the film. However, Johnson's approach to his subject matter this time was different because he criticized a newspaper which editorially commended the film. Johnson quoted from a Press editorial in which the editorial writer said she/he was at a loss "to understand the persistent attacks" upon The Birth.[229] Johnson called this "utter stupidity" and said he did not believe "any man could rise to an editorial writer on the Press and be so dull of understanding as not to be able to see the cause of the attacks upon Dixon's photoplay."[230] Johnson concluded emphasizing the historical inaccuracy of The Birth.

In his three editorial columns about The Birth, Lester Walton expressed a rather different approach to the subject matter. For example, in his initial editorial column about The Birth, Walton condemned New York blacks almost as severely as he condemned the film. Of blacks, Walton said: "sooner or later members of the race . . .

will learn that the Negro and not the white man is our worst enemy and that until we possess race consciousness and race respect . . . we must expect to be ridiculed and humiliated.[231] Walton continued, "the colored man in New York is long on talk, but short on the ammunition necessary to bring a fight to a successful issue."[232] Walton concluded that New York blacks were too "self-centered" and that until blacks overcame "our weakness" The Birth could not be defeated.[233]

In his next commentary about The Birth, Walton continued the theme that the blacks had to counter The Birth through action, but presented the message in a different context. Specifically, Walton advised black musicians touring England "to be on . . . good behavior" because "agencies" from America were at work in Europe to discredit the black just as The Birth was "seeking to create a false impression" of blacks in America.[234]

In his final column on the film, Walton blasted a Chicago Tribune editorial which praised the production. After reproducing the Tribune editorial virtually intact, Walton said the piece filled him "with utter amazement and deep chagrin."[235] Walton concluded his analysis of the film and the editorial by saying the "sin" of the film "is its viciousness, its distortion of history, and its uncalled assault on a race that was loyal when such men as Thomas Dixon opposed the North."[236]

The remaining editorial comment in the Age about The Birth during the 1915 controversy was contained in an editorial reprinted from the World praising Charles W. Anderson, retiring New York 2nd District Collector of Internal Revenue. In the editorial the World said: ". . .In. . .'The Birth of a Nation'. . .a race is libelled. In the office of the Collector of Internal Revenue. . . that race may be judged by its fruits."[237]

As indicated in the Age's editorial columns, at least two other New York newspapers, the World and the Globe, editorially attacked The Birth during its premiere run in that city. In its editorial the World developed the theme that The Birth was "an outrage on a race."[238] However, the editorial did not specifically request censorship of the film. A similar approach was used in a Globe editorial. In part the Globe said:

> White men in this country have never been just to black men. We tore them from Africa and brought them over as s ves . . .The nation finally freed them, but has but slightly protected them in the enjoyment of the legitimate fruits of their freedom. We nominally gave them the vote, but looked on inactive when the right was invaded. We do not, in any state of the union, grant to the Negro economic and political economy . . .Then to the injury is added slander. To make a few dirty dollars men are willing to pander to depraved tastes and to foment a race antipathy that is the most sinister and dangerous of American life.[239]

However, like the World, the Globe did not explicitly call for censorship of the film.

The New York Age continued its early editorial efforts against The Birth until at least early 1916. In March of that year, the Age reprinted an editorial from the Lexington, Kentucky, Herald against The Birth. The Age praised the editorial and said "It is good to see this rot exposed by a leading southern newspaper."[240]

Like the N.Y. Age, the Chicago Defender used a combination of editorial formats against The Birth. In its editorial effort during 1915 the Defender included its own editorials, editorial cartoons, and reprints of editorials from other newspapers.

The Defender published an editorial against the film in May 1915: "whenever it becomes necessary to appeal to the baser instincts of men in order to extract from their purse a pitance, it is high time the law steps in and says so far shall you go and no further."[241] The Defender called The Birth "objectionable and detrimental to the whole race" and indicated it would not be good "public policy" to allow The Birth to be shown in Chicago.[242] In a tone of militancy, the writer said those who took "the law in their own hands. . . may be pardoned for their fight was not a selfish one."[243] The writer added "the motto of the race in Chicago is 'I will strike a telling blow whenever and wherever necessary at the demon prejudice.'"[244] In its next comment, the Defender saluted W. Monroe Trotter for his role in the Boston fight against The Birth.[245] Next, the newspaper celebrated a premature victory over The Birth. In an editorial published May 22, 1915, the paper said the film would not be allowed in Chicago because the Mayor forbade it. The Defender praised Mayor Thompson as "a friend who will guard our interest."[246] However, as discussed, Thompson was enjoined from interfering with the film's production. Indicating its disappointment, in a short editorial the Defender said the film should have been called "the dirt of a nation."[247]

A rather militant protest editorial against The Birth was run by the Defender in June 1915. In this statement, the paper said that "We, the American Negroes, prefer death rather than submit" to the "new slavery" represented by The Birth.[248] The paper called The Birth an attempt to "enslave the Negroes" by "America's moneyed interests."[249] With its own comments the paper ran a "supposedly sarcastic" editorial from "the world's greatest newspaper" which discussed the role of Chicago's mayor in the controversy.[250] The Defender urged blacks to continue the fight "against violation of our natural rights and despoilation of the privileges of our citizenship."[251] The paper also condemned the film as purely a money-making enterprise.

In September 1915, the Defender regenerated its editorial battle against The Birth. In a piece headlined "Keep Up The Fight," the paper encouraged people everywhere to continue the protest.[252] The editorial also encouraged Chicagoans to "show their displeasure . . .at some future election" with the judge who issued the injunction allowing The Birth.[253]

The following month the paper commented on the Philadelphia disturbance. The Defender said "It is unbelievable that in Philadelphia. . .400 policemen should be necessary to keep the peace before a theatre where 'The Birth of a Nation' was being presented."[254] The editorial concluded "may the hateful plant be uprooted and burned in the fire of justice and right."[255]

Shortly thereafter the Defender changed tactics concerning The Birth. In an editorial "Unwarranted Advertising," the newspaper said it did not intend to comment about the film further because "comment good or bad is advertising."[256] The paper said:

> A press agent is a valuable adjunct to any kind of a theatrical enterprise and the libe scribe likes nothing better than to get up a heated argument--provided it appears in print about the enterprise he represents. . .'The Birth of a Nation' has had thousands of dollars worth of free advertising and we have innocently added our might whether we have accomplished anything or not is a much mooted question. Chicago people have however come to their senses and are letting the subject severely alone. Our white friends are still on the firing line and after all it is more the Union soldiers and Northerners battle than it is ours.
>
> The best way to kill objectionable people is by ignoring them. The same with a production. . .Let us advertise our friends not our enemies. . .Discussion of this subject must be brought to a close.[257]

Thus, after battling the film through its pages for a year the Defender reached the same conclusion expressed by the Western Outlook in February 1915.[258]

Prior to its decision not to run any more editorial statements about The Birth, the Defender ran two editorial cartoons against the film. The first ran in July 1915 and was titled "The Melting Pot."[259] The cartoon featured a devilish looking figure with a stick marked "Birth of a Nation" stirring a kettle marked "Chicago."[260] The "brew" in the kettle is marked "race prejudice." The caption under the cartoon said "The Hon. (?) Thomas Dixon in proper costume. The South not satisfied with its persecution of the race below the Mason Dixon line sends its pimps broadcast through the land."[261]

The other anti-The Birth cartoon was titled "The Last Cat."[262] In this cartoon, a street scene with men leaning out of windows and yelling is presented. Five black men are shown throwing objects at four cats. Three cats, labeled Blease, Vardaman, and Tillman have been knocked over.[263] The fourth cat is labeled "Birth of a Nation" and has its back up screaming. One of the black men has a megaphone labeled public sentiment.

Also, during 1915 the Defender reprinted at least three editorials from other newspapers critical of The Birth. One of these editorials was from the Elizabeth City, North Carolina, Independent.[264] The Independent reasoned that just as a film presenting Jews in a negative light would be repugnant to its readers so should The Birth of a Nation because of its presentation of blacks. However, the editorial advised the film's opponents to ignore it rather than "advertise" the film through their opposition. The editorial also suggested that blacks devote their talents to producing messages which stressed black accomplishments.

In the same issue, the Defender reprinted an editorial from the Kansas City Times against the film. The Times condemned Dixon in particular for succeeding "in picturing the Negro as wholly degraded and bestial with unlimited possibilities of evil."[265] The editorial also said the tendency of The Birth was to arouse racial hatred and expressed the hope that the film "could be still further censored."[266]

In early November 1915, the _Defender_ reprinted an anti-_Birth_ editorial from "the Duluth, Minnesota Daily Sunday paper."[267] This editorial called _The Birth_'s title a misnomer. The editorial said the film would "never be permitted in Duluth" and the film's authorship was enough to condemn it.[268] The paper concluded that arousing racial prejudice was the purpose of the film and therefore it should not be allowed.

The _Defender_ also attacked _The Birth_ in a larger context. In front-page commentary, the paper tied _The Birth_ to the lynchings of four Texas men. The _Defender_ noted the lynchings of a father and his three sons had never been reported or criticized publicly before, but a postcard picturing the four hanged men was sent to the newspaper.[269] The _Defender_ said:

> This is the lesson that is being taught by 'The Birth of a Nation.' This is the thing the daily papers of America is (sic) upholding. Remember that any paper that carries the ad of that photoplay you should not buy. Any moving picture house that uses any of Griffith's plays should be boycotted. And, any woman of the race who is now living at the south like they had to do in slavery time should run out of your neighborhood or do as the race men have done in Savannah, Ga., call the white fiends to the door and shoot them.[270]

Unlike the _Defender_ and the N.Y. _Age_ editorial campaigns against _The Birth_ which included a combination of editorial formats, the St. Louis _Argus_ concentrated its efforts against the film entirely in its own editorials. From the time of _The Birth_'s release until the end of 1915 the _Argus_ published 10 such editorials. The ten editorials present a variety of arguments against the film.

In its initial efforts against the film, the Argus informed its readers of The Birth's existence and warned them to watch for the film locally. The Argus identified The Birth as based on one of Thomas Dixon's "vile books."[271] The paper said the film was not only "an insult to the whole Negro race with a tendency to foster . . .lawlessness and race retaliation," but also was "a menace to the morals of any community because of certain scenes that are criminally immoral."[272] The Argus told its readers to meet the film with "a unified determined protest," and to demand the film stopped.[273]

In late May 1915, the Argus ran the front-page banner headline "Protest Against 'The Birth of a Nation.'"[274] However, this head referred to an editorial on page four, rather than to a front-page story. The editorial was built around a protest against the film lodged with the St. Louis Board of Police Commissioners by Charlotte Rumbold, St. Louis Park Division Recreation head. In her argument, Rumbold asserted The Birth should not be shown in St. Louis because the community had been narrowly drawn between the north and the south during the Civil War. The Argus concurred and told its readers "every true citizen should protest to the Police Board. . .Do it today. Protest now!"[275]

One editorial attack was aimed directly at Thomas Dixon. The Argus said that Dixon presented his hateful message in book, play, and sermon form prior to The Birth and failed. The paper called the film the "arch triumph of fiendishness" and said that America was not "ready or willing to be converted to the Gospel according to Dixon."[276]

The focus of the Argus editorial campaign shifted during August 1915 because The Birth finally arrived in the city and the paper began fighting reality rather than possibility. The paper lamented it had "sounded the warning alarm" but "as usual our warning fell upon stony ground."[277] The Argus conceded it would now be difficult to stop the film, but advised its readers "in the name of justice, in the name of rights, in the name of religion, in the name of peace" to protest immediately to the mayor and chief of police.[278]

Next, the Argus praised St. Louis Mayor Kiel for attempting to stop the film.[279] The Argus said its protest to Kiel had been "justified and dignified" and the paper could only await the decision of the court hearing the case concerning the film's right to the screen locally.[280] The Argus concluded this editorial with another appeal to continue the protest. The Argus explained:

> Should the court decide against us and the injunction be made permanent then what we have done would be considered only the beginning. Our protests should be continuous, firm and dignified. Our aim must be to create a sentiment so strong that the white people can see the justice of our position. . .should our protests and our agitation end in no immediate result and no apparent good, we must be broad enough and farsighted enough to work for the uplift and advancement of the entire race and not only for this day and generation, but for our posterity. So, the protest and agitation which we have begun, we must continue.[281]

In its September 17, 1915, issue, the Argus ran two editorials on The Birth. One editorial criticized the local Negro Business League for failing to publicly condemn the film.[282] The other editorial attached a pamphlet "called the Home Defender. . .which is being distributed to the hundreds of spectators at every performance."[283] The Argus did not detail the content of this pamphlet, but did indicate the publication was "adding fuel to the flames" set by The Birth.[284] Specifically, the Argus labeled the pamphlet "another of the satanic moves of that diabolical collection of race-killers and city breakers known as the Welfare League."[285] The Argus advised its readers to learn to "fight fire with fire" and "be everlastingly on the watch."[286]

In its next film editorial, the Argus attacked Judge Hennings' decision to allow the film.[287] While vigorously stating opposition to the judge's decision, the Argus said he settled the question of the film's presentation locally.

Nevertheless, the Argus editorially commented at least twice more concerning The Birth during 1915. The next statement, a week after the Henning editorial, was about the "riot" in Philadelphia in connection with the film.[288] Somewhat militantly, the paper asked why a riot had occurred in Philadelphia, not St. Louis. Answering itself, the editorial said:

> It would have if the St. Louis Negro were not so afraid to resent an insult. Too long have we accepted the time-worn saying that we must wait and hope and trust in the law to get our rights. We do not advocate a riot, but we do feel that we should let the world know that we cannot be insulted. Of two evils, court and jail is less than insult and humiliation. Sometimes, a riot is a good thing and necessary.[289]

The final 1915 Argus editorial comment on The Birth criticized the film because it glorified the Ku Klux Klan.[290]

As mentioned in other chapters, Harry Smith, editor of the Cleveland, Ohio, Gazette, took an active role in The Birth 1915 censorship controversy in his state. In addition to writing letters and asking local officials to suppress the film, Smith also used his newspaper as an editorial voice against the film. Smith's editorial approach to the issue differed from that taken by the editors of the Argus, Defender, and Age. Rather than generate long editorials about the film, Smith published a number of brief editorial paragraphs. In addition, he tended to run the same editorial a number of times. Smith's approach also differed from his colleagues' in that he frequently criticized other newspaper editors for not being thorough enough in their efforts against The Birth.

Smith began his editorial campaign against The Birth by mentioning that blacks in Chicago and New York were vocally opposing the film and praising Ohio Governor Frank Willis for "thus far" keeping such "vicious" films out of the state.[291] Several days later with a report of the disturbance at Boston's Tremont Theatre, the Gazette commented:

> The South will NOT permit its moving picture theaters to exhibit such miserable photo-plays as 'The Birth of a Nation,' Thomas Dixon's infamous play. . .Gov. Willis has barred out of Ohio. Why do some of the Northern states tolerate them?[292]

The Gazette criticized Boston for allowing The Birth and continued its praise of Willis in an editorial paragraph on May 22.[293] In the July 3, 1915, Gazette, Smith warned his readers to "be on the lookout!" for The Birth. Smith said that although the film had been banned by the Ohio State Board of Censors, some theatres might try to show the film. If anyone found this, Smith advised to notify the governor or the state censors immediately.[294]

In its next brief editorial comment, the Gazette applauded those individuals continuing the fight against the film elsewhere and asked why the efforts had not continued in New York and Chicago.[295] Smith also criticized the Columbus, Ohio, correspondent for the N.Y. Age and Chicago Defender, and said that much the correspondent had written about the resolution of the Ohio controversy was "not true."[296]

In October 1915, the Gazette departed from its format of short editorial paragraphs concerning The Birth and ran a longer editorial, praising the victory over the film when it was officially rejected by the Ohio censors. In the editorial, Smith indicated he had not doubted Willis' assurances that the film would not be allowed in Ohio, but the actual victory was sweet. The Gazette credited the NAACP, Willis, the censors, the Lord, and itself with the victory. Of its own role in the controversy the Gazette said it was "always on the firing line when the race's rights, privileges, and interests are being assailed or are in danger and which accomplished results with the help of the loyal and active of the race."[297] The Gazette reprinted this editorial in six subsequent issues.[298]

After that, the Gazette returned to its shorter editorial paragraph format and once again asked why the race in New York, Chicago, and Boston had abandoned the fight against The Birth. Smith indicated he did not understand why efforts had not been made to have the injunctions dissolved in each city.[299]

Editorially, the Gazette mentioned The Birth in at least two other commentaries about film censorship in Ohio. First such mention came in an editorial paragraph against petitions apparently circulating in Ohio to eliminate state censorship of film.[300] The other editorial praised Willis for going on public record before a Knights of Pythias meeting in Columbus against any film which reflected negatively on any group of citizens.[301]

During 1915 the Gazette also reprinted at least two editorials from other newspapers opposing The Birth. One editorial praising Willis and criticizing the defeats in Massachusetts and New York was from the Springfield, Illinois, Forum.[302] Although the Gazette was concerned because The Birth presented a negative stereotype of blacks, it reprinted an editorial from the St. Paul Appeal which stereotyped a group of people. In this editorial paragraph, the paper commented: "The fact that three Jews have bought the rights for the film and that Jewish capitalists are exploiting the photoplay all over the country would cause our people to see that many of their most bitter enemies are Jews."[303]

Like the editorial campaigns of the Age and the Defender, the Philadelphia Tribune combined in-house generated editorials, editorial columns, and editorial reprints from other newspapers in its editorial campaign against The Birth. In its initial comment, the Tribune said The Birth was having "a rocky road to the cash receipts."[304] The paper criticized Thomas Dixon severely and said he was a man who "revels in strife and in creating strife as maggots revel in dead carcasses."[305] In a longer editorial in the same issue, the paper stated New Yorkers should be successful in their current battle against The Birth.[306] The editorial said that over $500,000 had been invested in the film, but its backers should be prepared to lose money because they invested in a "dirty proposition."[307] The editorial then criticized Dixon severely and concluded by saying "the death damp is already on his brow."[308]

In September 1915, the *Tribune* entered an editorial protest against the planned local opening of the film. The newspaper criticized local authorities who approved the film and commented that the ". . .power of God is against those who wrong the weak, who abuse them in their spirit and deed."[309] The *Tribune* also indicated those individuals who supported *The Birth* went against God in an editorial printed October 23, 1915.[310]

In an editorial column in the *Tribune*, L. T. Parker called the film a "nefarious production."[311] Parker condemned the film as "not in keeping with the spirit of the good thinking people" because it would incite race hatred and violence.[312]

The *Tribune* reprinted two editorials from other newspapers about *The Birth* on September 25, 1915. One was from the Philadelphia *Ledger* and concerned the disturbance outside the Forrest Theatre. This editorial attacked state censorship in Pennsylvania and said: "The rioting incidental to the presentation of a photoplay. . .emphasizes the intolerable position in which this city is placed by the state censorship."[313] The editorial asked that the state board be abolished and replaced by municipal boards which could better "conserve public morality."[314] The *Tribune* also reprinted an editorial from the Norfolk *Journal and Guide*. The *Journal and Guide* editorial said *The Birth* should be suppressed because it was a menace to society. The editorial also called *The Birth* a "perversion of history."[315] The Tribune added its own comments to the Journal and Guide editorial. Specifically, the Tribune criticized judges who did not consider the film illegal.

The Baltimore Ledger apparently did not give as much editorial space to The Birth during 1915 as the papers previously discussed. The Ledger published two editorials of its own about The Birth and published two editorial paragraphs discussing The Birth in other contexts. In addition, the Ledger reprinted a short editorial about the film from another newspaper.

The first editorial written by the Ledger specifically about The Birth was published in March 1915.[316] The newspaper criticized the film as existing "for no other purpose than to excite the prejudices of the northern people against the Negro and to bolster up the Southern idea of the proper way in which to treat a Negro."[317] The paper also called attention to an Atlanta, Georgia, ban on the play Uncle Tom's Cabin. In that instance the "daughters of the Confederacy" protested the exhibition of that play because it could only have "the effect of stirring up unpleasant memories and race prejudices which should be buried and forgotten."[318] Consequently, certain scenes were cut from the play. The Ledger reasoned it was inconsistent to allow The Birth to show uncut if Uncle Tom's Cabin had been censored for similar reasons. The newspaper also said the "black man in the south today is little less than a slave who has every privilege curtailed--even frequently the right to breathe through lynching mobs."[319]

The other major editorial run in the Ledger concerning The Birth summarized the national fight against the film and said it was "encouraging" that the film aroused opposition wherever it went.[320] The Ledger restated its belief that the film existed only to increase racial hatred and was critical of Thomas Dixon.

In its September 4, 1915, issue the Ledger said:

> 'The Birth of a Nation' writes Thomas Dixon. 'The Birth of a (dam)nation' suggests the St. Louis Fraternal Clarion. Which is just as appropriate as placing the damn before !'Birth.'[321]

The Ledger negatively mentioned The Birth within editorials about two other subjects. One such editorial indicated the books of Thomas Dixon were not on the shelves of the Enoch Pratt Public Library locally.[322] The Ledger asked the librarian about the omission and was told the library judged Dixon's works were "unworthy of a place in the collection."[323] The Ledger also used its editorial column to praise the efforts of Cleveland Gazette editor Harry C. Smith for his "persistent and effective war" against The Birth.[324]

Efforts by the Twin City Star and the St. Paul Appeal against the film were concentrated during October and November 1915. This time period coincided with censorship controversies in Minneapolis and St. Paul concerning the film. Each of these two newspapers used a variety of editorial formats against the film.

The Star generated at least three editorials against The Birth during October/November 1915. In one of its initial efforts against the film, the Star called upon Minneapolis Mayor Nye to hold "to his campaign pledges" and prevent the film locally.[325] The editorial was reprinted a month later with the phrase "and it came to pass" written below it.[326] Also, in October 1915 the Star editorialized, urging city blacks to be peaceful in protests against The Birth.[327] The newspaper stressed that even if the film were shown, militancy was wrong. The Star said the blacks in Boston, Chicago, and Philadelphia were different from the blacks in Minneapolis because:

> We are a small minority here and have no organization. Threats amount to nothing. We cannot demand anything because we represent so little. The good conduct of the Negroes will reflect great credit on the race everywhere. We have no record anywhere that the play of itself has done such a great harm to Negroes. It has been accepted by the public as a sensation which is the damnable fabrication of mercenary white promoters based on the 'Clansman' a novel written by Thos. Dixon, a white man, recognized as the modern type of American savagery. Agitation without organization is futile. Mob violence among any people must be discouraged. The exclusion of 'The Birth of a Nation' and other plays from Ohio was done legally and orderly. . .the editor of the Star hopes that the pictures will not be shown, but it they show, let us as Negroes, make the best of it. 'Suffer it to be so now' because of our unpreparedness.[328]

After Minneapolis Mayor Nye refused to censor The Birth, the Star criticized the mayor. The paper charged that Nye had "used his Negro FRIENDS and 'The Birth of a Nation' as a means to an end by securing a legal decision as to his power to revoke licenses. . ."[329] This action the paper termed "political suicide" and said it would have been better for Nye to allow the film originally without stirring up the controversy and giving the film so much free "advertising."[330] The Star concluded its commentary with a plea that "God direct Mayor Nye so that in the future he will use his discretionary power to differentiate so that we shall have a cleaner city government and a better citizenship."[331] On the same day the Star also reprinted an editorial from the St. Paul Pioneer Press which praised the efforts of Minneapolis attorney B. S. Smith against The Birth.[332]

During the same time period, the St. Paul Appeal generated two editorials against The Birth. One was written by a paper representative who witnessed a local screening of the film. The writer said the film "with ghoulish glee" delved "into the charnel houses of the buried past and brings to view the grinning skeletons that would much better be left to mold and decay."[333] The writer said the film could not help but "lower" individual estimates of black people and therefore should not be permitted.[334] In its other editorial on The Birth, the Appeal said "they had an awful hard fight and only secured partial success owing to the technicalities of the law which worked to the benefit of the producers."[335] However, the licenses in both cities had been revoked and the film would have to close. The paper praised John Steele, Henry McColl, and the St. Paul city council for helping resolve the controversy.[336] The Appeal also republished the St. Paul Pioneer Press editorial praising Brown S. Smith.[337]

Although the efforts of the Appeal were concentrated during the local controversy, the newspaper did run at least two other editorials concerning The Birth. In each case the editorials were printed in more than one edition of the paper. In June 1915, the Appeal pointed to what it considered an inconsistency in tactics used against the film in Chicago. The newspaper commented that while some of the "prejudice fighters" in Chicago were battling The Birth "some of the prominent colored people were giving a minstrel performance."[338] Of this behavior the Appeal said if "the colored people of Chicago wish to make an effective protest against prejudice breeding programs. . .they must stop burlesquing themselves and come clean."[339] This editorial was reprinted at least three times.[340] The Appeal also reprinted a letter written to the Chicago Tribune in opposition to The Birth written by a Major John R. Lynch.[341] This letter ran originally on June 12, 1915, and was reprinted at least five times.[342]

Although there was not apparently a controversy concerning The Birth's right to the screen in Indianapolis, Indiana, during 1915, that city's black newspapers ran several editorials against the film and also reported heavily the involvement of one of its reporters in a New York demonstration against the film. For example, April 17, 1915, the Freeman ran three editorials about The Birth. In the shortest of these, the newspaper alleged the film "was built on race prejudice and seemingly meant to inflame racial passion."[343] In a longer editorial, the Freeman condemned the play upon which The Birth was based and criticized Thomas Dixon for being willing "to plunge the nation in woe to line his pockets with silver or to perpetuate his name."[344] The editorial also discussed the cost of admission to the film and concluded that a $2.00 admission might mean a "war on the race begun in high places. . ."[345] The editorial also criticized the National Board of Censorship for approving the film. In the same issue the Freeman also reprinted a large portion of an editorial denouncing The Birth from the N.Y. Globe.[346]

In its next edition, the Freeman outlined the egg-throwing incident in the Liberty Theatre and said the eggs hitting the screen "may be like those of Fort Sumter that were heard around the world."[347] The Freeman also ran a commentary from one of its reporters in the theatre the night of the egg throwing. In his column about the incident, Cleveland Allan said The Birth had "aroused the ire of every decent and respectable man and woman of both races."[348] Allan said he created a disturbance in the theatre prior to the egg throwing, and he actually missed the incident because he was "making a speech in the theatre in which he bitterly scorned the management of the theatre for permitting such a play. . ."[349] Because of his speech, Allan said he was hurried into the street by police and "narrowly escaped arrest."[350] Of Allan's participation, the paper said "the Freeman representative was the only Negro to make the protest and the significance of the event has made him the hero of the hour."[351]

The Freeman's next comment about The Birth dealt with the demonstration at Boston's Tremont Theatre. The editorial traced events in Boston prior to the disturbance and called the movement in favor of The Birth "a propaganda of hate, a moving exposition conceived for the purpose of inflaming race prejudice."[352] The Freeman said it feared a "deep laid plan" existed to incite racial prejudice and that it could "only result in some dreadful outbreak if. . .not checked."[353] Because the film surely would lead to violence, the Freeman said the play should be prevented. The paper advised:

> It is up to the authorities to prohibit the things that are meant to breed such ills. It may be doing violence to business freedom in the meanwhile, but when it is known that men are commercializing, selling the peace of the nation, somehow they should be stopped. . .[354]

Several other newspapers editorialized against The Birth during 1915. The New York Outlook said the "evil" in the film lay in that "the play is both a denial of the power of development within the Negro and an exaltation of race war."[355] The Kansas City, Missouri, Times called the film a "scenic marvel" but questioned the advisability of presenting such a spectacle "founded on race hatred" in which the Negro was presented as "wholly degraded and bestial with unlimited possibilities of evil."[356] The Duluth, Minnesota, Daily, said the ridicule of blacks in The Birth was not analogous to the ridicule of other minorities such as "jews, farmers and what not" because such groups were "used to" it.[357] Also, such groups always were "friends of the audience."[358] Rather than fulfill this purely comic purpose the "whole aim" of The Birth was "not to caricature the black race, but to depict it as debased and brutal."[359]

Variety reported in December 1923 that the Kansas press had been giving "much space" to editorials condemning the Kansas censors and Kansas officials for allowing The Birth to be shown in that state for the first time.[360] The Kansas City Call was one of the papers which editorially spoke against the film. The Call advised its readers to protest the film's production to the Governor in December 1915.[361] The Call also said that the film's screening would probably lead to an increase in the number of lynchings.[362] The Kansas City Star said The Birth should be "discarded" and that all objections which had been raised against it were "entirely valid and should be respected by the state authorities."[363] The Topeka Daily Capital said the film was "an encourager of race hatred" and should therefore not be allowed.[364] The Wichita Protest supported the city ordinance passed specifically to keep the film from that city.[365]

Thus, it can be seen that during the years studied a variety of newspapers editorialized against The Birth. Most of the campaigns included the use of a variety of editorial formats. More editorials against The Birth were found during 1915 than any other year.

Editorials Neutral About Film

The St. Paul Pioneer Press ran two editorials specifically about The Birth censorship controversies in that city in 1915 without taking a stand on the film. One of these editorials praised the efforts of black attorney Brown S. Smith who argued the case of those wishing the film suppressed before the St. Paul city council. The editorial writer said s/he listened to Brown with an "impartial" ear and found:

> . . .aside from the merits of either side of the argument in which this man participated, his part in the real-life drama was an unanswerable argument in refutation of the theory, which even now finds exponents that education and enlightenment are bad for his race.[366]

The Pioneer Press also editorialized that the city council would "be damned either way" it decided on The Birth. The editorial said that if the council should decide to reject the film it would be criticized because it granted the license originally. If the film were permitted, the council would be criticized for levying a special tax on the production not required of other exhibitions at the same facility. The newspaper offered no solution, but said that "the councilman's life is not a happy one."[367]

Editorials Supportive of The Birth

Unlike the editorials in opposition to The Birth which usually attacked either the film itself or the individuals responsible for the film's production, editorials on the other side of the issue tended to speak more to the point of film censorship in general. Also, editorials of this nature were found more spread across the years of the study and not as concentrated in 1915 as those editorials opposed to the film. Also, more editorials against the film were found than editorials supportive of the film.

The Houston, Texas, Chronicle talked about film censorship in general. The Chronicle said that when the local board of censors:

> . . .assumes to deal with any picture such as 'The Birth of a Nation' which is free from immoral, lascivious, or prurient suggestiveness and which only portrays the truth of history and deals with questions of social and historical importance, then it passes beyond any legal line and entrenches upon the right of free born citizens who are capable of judging for themselves what they should see or should not see.[368]

The Chronicle advised "every man, woman, and child over ten years of age, black or white," to see the film. The Chronicle predicted The Birth would prove beneficial to blacks rather than harmful and concluded that "no Negro can seriously object to it."[369]

Other newspapers editorialized that black opposition to the film was unwarranted. For example, the Charlotte, North Carolina, Observer said it could see no reason "for the objections which the Negroes" are making about The Birth.[370] Likewise, the Bridgeport, Connecticut, Herald commented that most of the complaints lodged by blacks against the film were "unjust."[371] The Herald reasoned that just as there were no protests against films which depicted the early colonists of New England as superstitious witch-burners, there should be no complaints against The Birth.[372] Although the Hartford, Connecticut, Post did not speak specifically of The Birth, it said it was glad "to see the Pennsylvania censors taken down a peg" by a court decision which ruled in favor of a film after the censors ruled against the film.[373] The Fremont, Ohio, Messenger charged that motion picture censorship had been made a political football by Ohio Governor Frank Willis because Willis had ordered The Birth and similar films recalled after they had been passed by the state censors.[374] The Messenger said the only reason for banning The Birth was because "it was objectionable to certain manipulators of the colored vote."[375]

Several newspapers mentioned The Birth editorially when they discussed pending local or state censorship legislation. For example, the St. Paul Pioneer Press said to omit The Birth when considering the advisability of a new censorship ordinance under consideration. The Press said it would not be sound policy to pass the ordinance which gave the absolute power of censorship to the police commissioner.[376] In a second editorial the Press reaffirmed its belief that censorship by police censors was not appropriate.[377]

A variety of editorials against censorship and in favor of The Birth were published in the Massachusetts press during the 1915 Boston censorship controversy. For example, the Boston Evening Transcript called censorship "the curse of a nation."[378] The paper editorially attacked directly the Sullivan Bill introduced into the Massachusetts legislature to allow censorship of films like The Birth.[379] The editorial called this "offensive" and projected the Sullivan Bill would be "rejected by a decisive vote."[380] Of the bill, the Transcript said:

> Such petition would deliver a blow at religious freedom, the rights of the individual, and the liberty of the press. Were such a statute in operation. . .Jewish citizens could prohibit 'Merchant of Venice,' mill owners could drive off stage any play or from the screen any film portraying the horrors of child labor, our saloon keepers could force the Prohibitionists to give up the use of film in their crusade, Protestant citizens could end the exhibition of any film portraying the awful persecution of priests and nuns in Mexico. In short, the usefulness of the theatre as a place of amusement or education would be reduced to a ridiculous minimum. . .
>
> Any sort of censorship is irritating to the spirit of our people and only that regulation which is in the essential interest of public decency and public morals should ever be tolerated.[381]

The Boston Herald called the Sullivan Bill "hysterical legislation" which would ". . .do far more to limit the freedom of the individual, of the theatre, and of the church and the press than any citizen devoted to the best interests of the whole people could possibly desire."[382] The Springfield, Massachusetts, Republican ran a similar editorial under the head "the Menace of Censorship," reprinted in the Transcript.[383] The Transcript also ran an ad on its amusements page, "Kill the Sullivan Bill," with reprints of editorial comments opposing censorship from the aforementioned Massachusetts papers.[384]

When the Joint Judiciary Committee of the Massachusetts legislature offered its compromise censorship bill, the Transcript called the measure a "sensible solution" because the bill did not specifically define immorality and allowed "a representative board" to decide by "common sense" what violated "the canons of public decency."[385] The *Transcript* said the controversy over *The Birth* was useful because:

> Boston has suffered too long from a stupid, silly, and un-American censorship of its stage. It is high time in these . . .days that some of our excited citizens were reminded that they are living neither in Germany nor Russia but in the U.S. in that state of all others where the liberty of the individual, the freedom of the press and a decent regard for the rights and opinions of other men have ever been cherished as among the most precious of the rights safeguarded by the fathers in the framing of our Constitution. . .Any limitation upon freedom of the stage which would not be imposed on any similar agency of publicity is in effect a blow at freedom of the press.[386]

In one of the few editorials noted specifically in praise of *The Birth*, the *Boston Morning Journal* called the film "one of the most remarkable achievements that the people of Boston have ever seen."[387] The *Journal* also said the film was "exceptionally inspiring from the standpoint of broad and true Americanism."[388] The *Journal* said black-led opposition to the film was "a serious diversion" which "obscured temporarily" the "strength, beauty, and inspiration of the whole."[389]

Although it did not specifically support *The Birth*, the *Washington Bee* commented in May 1915 that "the colored Americans in this city are civilized and those who manage the different movies to portray the colored people in an uncomplimentary manner are only demonstrating their own folly and ignorance."[390] The *Bee* concluded *The Birth* would disturb neither blacks nor whites in Washington.

In connection with The Birth of a Nation censorship controversies, the Chicago Tribune editorialized against motion picture censorship in both 1915 and 1924. During the 1915 controversy, the Tribune said The Birth was the greatest piece of work done for the films by American Producers."[391] The Tribune asserted the film was neither "immoral nor coarse" nor offensive for "any of the reasons which usually cause the prohibition of picture plays. . ."[392] The Tribune said it opposed "interference with freedom of expression" and the only "sin" of the film was its effectiveness.[393] The Tribune concluded:

> All censorship is an infringement of that perfect freedom of thought and expression which is dear to the liberal as an ideal if not always acceptable as a fact. . .Censorship of information and of debate is allowed only in extreme cases as under martial law. Censorship of literary expression also is permitted only within relatively narrow limits. . .Censorship often accomplishes concrete benefits and may be conceded to be necessary, but we ought never to lose sight of the fact that if necessary it is a necessary evil which we are right in regarding jealously. . .[394]

In 1924, the Tribune criticized the Jackson law passed specifically to allow censorship of The Birth (See Chapter VI) and praised the film itself.[395] Of the Jackson law, the Tribune said:

> The law passed to bear it (The Birth) out of the state has a specific intent but a general effect. It might be used under a stupid or prejudiced construction to prevent the playing of 'The Merchant of Venice' or even 'Othello.' Such a law could interfere with the artistic and intellectual freedom of people. It might permit prejudices to be converted into dictates. In this present case we are well aware of the dangers of provocation. No intelligent person likes to see the principles of free speech within the bounds of public decency restricted for adults and if we were all sensible adults it would not need be. Sensible adults do not need censors. They exercise censorship without statues. They withhold their patronage from what offends them.

We know that it is next to impossible in this country to take an uncompromising stand for unrestricted liberty of utterance. You may defend the principle and be disturbed by a fact which will not be reconciled to the theory you defend. We are opposed in principle to the stopping of 'The Birth of a Nation.' If the purpose of showing were to arouse race prejudice and bring about trouble, we're opposed to the showing. Circumstances which are far from ideal force compromises. As a police expedient this interference with liberty must be justified every time it is used. . .[396]

In a 1965 editorial, the New York Times stated specifically The Birth was entitled to First Amendment protection. The Times also urged the NAACP to abandon attempts to censor the film.[397] The Times editorial came after the NAACP began fighting for a ban on the film in New York that year. The Times noted the NAACP had been promoting censorship of The Birth for 50 years. The Times said:

Negroes are not unique in trying to use police powers of the state to protect their own interests and sensibilities. But, films, like other forms of artistic expression are entitled to the free speech guarantees of the 1st Amendment. This is true even though they may mix bad history and brilliant artistry as does 'The Birth of a Nation.'[398]

The Times advised the NAACP to stop its censorship campaign and concluded: "In a country made up of so many diverse creeds and peoples such attempts to censor films, plays or books because they are obnoxious to one group or another could only deform art."[399]

Letters to the Editor

During the time period studied, letters to the editor were also found to be an extra-legal tactic in The Birth of a Nation censorship controversies. As noted, the tactic was so heavily engaged in by individuals, that in at least three instances newspaper editors ran statements closing the letters-to-the-editor column to the subject.[400]

During the 1915 censorship controversy in St. Paul, the Pioneer Press closed its letters to the editor column to the subject in the midst of a glut of mail. Before ending the discussion, the Pioneer Press printed a number of letters which either condemned or praised The Birth.

For example, a letter "from a southern subscriber" called Thomas Dixon a "traitor" and said the film should be banned to "uphold the dignity of" America's black citizens.[401] Another subscriber who identified herself as a "southern woman" said Dixon should be "tarred and feathered" for producing a work that incited to violence and gave the incorrect impression that the south hated blacks.[402] Clarence M. Tibbs wrote The Birth should be banned because blacks objected to it and that in such cases "the golden rule" should apply.[403] A.J. Broddy said The Birth should not be allowed at the Auditorium because it was a public building supported by tax money in part paid by blacks who would thus be forced to subsidize something which offends them.[404] Broddy also said the film would incite racial hatred.[405] Charles E. Mackean also opposed The Birth's Auditorium showing because "nothing should be allowed in a public building which insults or affronts any race or nationality."[406] The auditorium as the place for The Birth's screening also came under fire from an individual who signed a letter "Citizen."[407] An individual who signed a letter "B" objected to The Birth because the film would only "beget prejudice in the white man and humiliation in the Negro. . ."[408] "S.V.W." attacked the historical inaccuracy of the film and said its main purpose was to glorify the Klan.[409]

On the other side, "A White Woman" wrote she couldn't understand how a "fair-minded person" could become prejudiced against blacks by seeing The Birth.[410] An individual who signed her letter "Naomi" said she did not understand how "fair-minded" people could possibly object to The Birth because she had seen the film twice and found it to be "wonderful."[411] "Naomi" suggested the "narrow-minded slow people" who objected to the film should stay home and let the "broad-minded" have the "privilege and pleasure of seeing it."[412] D. T. Stetson said the film would teach children more history in one viewing then "they can get out of books in the next five years."[413] Stetson also asserted those who favored censorship of The Birth would support the removal of history textbooks from school rooms.[414] C. Calsin wrote he opposed censorship of The Birth as a matter of principle. In part, Calsin said "The idea of someone else judging what play or photoplay I shall or shall not see is not one that appeals to me. . ."[415] Willis Drummond wrote he had "no objection" to the film and could not understand the "narrow-mindedness" of those who did oppose the film. Drummond said although the film contained several scenes "repulsive to my black abolitionist heart" he was "not thin-skinned or bigoted enough to want to deprive my fellow men of the opportunity to witness with their own eyes this most wonderful and beautiful product of the camera."[416] "Dingbat" attacked specifically St. Paul Commissioner of Public Safety Henry McColl and said The

Birth was one of the "greatest and costliest" films ever produced.[417] "Y.R.U." called the film a "masterpiece" and said the purpose of the film was an "anti-war lesson" which overshadowed "any harm that may come. . .from showing the film."[418] "One Who Has Seen" also praised The Birth as the "greatest argument in favor of world peace" because it so graphically presented the horrors of war.[419]

The New York Age ran three letters to the editor critical of Thomas Dixon. One writer said he knew Dixon personally and that for over a decade Dixon "made it his wicked business to capitalize the savage instincts in the white man of this country by appealing to this race prejudice."[420] The writer called The Birth "absolutely false" and said it was an "outrageous slander of an innocent, helpless struggling race."[421] Another writer said Dixon "sought to undo all that the Civil War had accomplished" and was willing to coin race prejudice into money.[422] Rosalie M. Jonas wrote her hatred "for that dangerous hypocrite" Thomas Dixon was intensified a "thousand fold" by seeing The Birth.[424] Jonas concluded Dixon would eventually meet with "universal contempt" because he sought to degrade Lincoln and also engaged in sacrilege.[425]

In October 1915, the Age ran an exchange of comments between Rev. Christian Reisner and Rev. Wm. H. Brooks. Brooks began the correspondence by criticizing Reisner for showing The Birth at a church efficiency gathering at Reisner's Church. Brooks called the film "a travesty on history" and dubbed the church screening an "unholy marriage."[426] Reisner replied that he did not believe the production of the film could injure the black race. Reisner explained a committee had arranged to show the film "wholly with the purpose of showing what marvelous productions are now possible through motion pictures."[427]

In a letter to the Philadelphia Public Ledger, Rev. Carl E. Grammer said he had never seen "a great theme" handled "more crudely and cruelly" than in The Birth.[428] Grammer said the film presented an unfriendly portrait of blacks and should not be allowed. Grammer's letter was reprinted in the Baltimore Ledger and the Philadelphia Tribune.[429]

D. R. Wallace asked Oakland, California, citizens not to use violence against The Birth in a letter to the editor of the Western Outlook. Wallace advised those who opposed the film to "stay away" from the film because it would hurt their feelings and said restraint must be exercised because any actions would reflect upon the "entire race in this community."[430]

Beulah Kennard "earnestly" protested the film's production to the editor of the New York Sun.[431] J. C. Jenkins told the editor of the Evening Post that The Birth was a "pernicious and insidious attack" upon both blacks and whites.[432] Mary Jane Revier "emphatically protested" the production of The Birth because it degraded blacks and tended to excite racial prejudice in a letter to the editor of the New York Tribune.[433]

In addition to varied statements for and against The Birth, major letters in defense of the film were written by Thomas Dixon and D. W. Griffith and one major letter in protest was written by Booker T. Washington. Dixon and Griffith each wrote a letter in reply to the N.Y. Globe editorials which attacked The Birth. In his letter to the Globe, Dixon said he took "full moral responsibility" for the purpose and effects of the film.[434] Dixon said the film had been submitted to a jury of three representative New York clergy who agreed the film did the following six things:

1) Reunited all sections of the country
2) Taught the priceless inheritance of the sacrifices made during the Civil War and Reconstruction
3) Tended to prevent the lowering of the standard of our citizenship by its mixture with Negro blood
4) Showed the horror and futility of war
5) Reaffirmed Lincoln's solution of the Negro problem
6) Gave Daniel Webster his true place in American history as the inspiring creator of the modern nation.[435]

In his letter, Dixon also attacked Thaddeus Stevens because of Stevens' alleged relationship with a quardoon mistress.[436] Dixon concluded by saying he was not "attacking the Negro of today" but rather "recording faithfully the history of fifty years ago."[437] In his reply to the Globe, Griffith attacked the newspaper for saying The Birth had been exhibited for purely sordid reasons.[438] Griffith said the film had been brought forth to "reveal the beautiful possibilities of the art of motion pictures and to tell a story which is based upon truth in every vital detail."[439] Griffith called the Globe editorial an insult to the "intelligence and the human kindness of nearly 100,000 of the best people in New York City who have seen the play."[440] Griffith asserted the NAACP objected to The Birth primarily because it believed the film would lead to anti-intermarriage legislation.[441]

Dixon also wrote the editor of the Boston Journal and requested "fair play for The Birth. . ."[442] In a rather long letter,

430

Dixon defended The Birth and criticized the censorship bills introduced into the Massachusetts legislature. Dixon called the censorship legislation a "violation of every principle of freedom and democracy" for which the country "has stood for 200 years."[443] Dixon said he could not believe the Massachusetts lawmakers would "deliberately deny to a Southern white man freedom of speech on the Boston Common merely because a few Negro agitators differ from his historical conclusions."[444] Dixon said the law would lead to the suppression of more than just The Birth. Dixon defended at length the historical accuracy of The Birth and said the film "was not written to stir race hatred."[445] He concluded that the censorship bill would be "an incredible insult to the 25,000,000 of Southern white people whom I represent."[446]

In a letter to the editor of the Chicago Defender, Booker T. Washington urged "our people everywhere to take time by the forelook and adopt in advance such measures" as would prevent the production of The Birth.[447] Washington said to wait until the play was already presented was a "serious and grave mistake" because it gave the film undue advertising.[448] Washington suggested "each town where there is a possibility the" film would be shown should have a committee of citizens "representing the churches, schools, businesses" lodge a complaint with the appropriate local authorities.[449] Washington called The Birth "fundamentally wrong" and said no matter what the film's artistic merits the ultimate result of it would be "to intensify race prejudice and thereby do great and lasting harm to both races."[450]

Petitions to Exhibitors

During the time period studied, the film's opponents went directly to those individuals exhibiting The Birth and asked them to voluntarily censor the film. Commercial theatre managers, organizers of non-commercial showings, and individuals interested in showing the film on television all received such censorship petitions.

On at least six occasions the NAACP petitioned commercial theatre managers directly with requests that they voluntarily not show the film. In two cases theatre managers agreed not to show the film; in two instances theatre managers rejected the NAACP's request; and, in two cases the reactions of the theatre managers to the petitions are unclear.

The two decisions to voluntarily not show the film were made by theatre managers in New York and San Antonio, Texas. The first theatre manager to agree not to show The Birth was the organizer of a 1941 Bundles for Britain benefit in New York.[451] The benefit screening was cancelled "to avoid possible embarrassment" after the NAACP protested the presentation.[452] Similarly, a 1965 revival of The Birth planned for San Antonio, Texas, was cancelled after that city's NAACP branch requested and received promises that the film would not show in their theatres from the managers of two theatre chains.[453]

The two decisions to show the film in spite of protests were made by theatre managers in New York and Philadelphia. In 1950, the NAACP requested that Harry Raymond, manager of the Beverly Theatre, in New York, not show the film.[454] Raymond refused and the NAACP picketed the theatre during the film's run.[455] The NAACP also picketed the Lansdowne Theatre in a Philadelphia, Pennsylvania, suburb after theatre manager Don Scott refused to remove the film from the screen in 1965.[456]

The responses of two other theatre managers asked to voluntarily censor the film are unclear. For example, the NAACP Ithaca, New York, Branch wrote to the manager of the Willard Straight Theatre asking him not to show The Birth as an endeavor to better racial understanding.[457] However, the manager's response is unclear.[458] The Des Moines, Iowa, NAACP regional office asked a local theatre owner not to show The Birth in 1970 because the NAACP contended the film's presentation could only intensify already deteriorating race relationships in our communities."[459] Again, the response of the theatre manager is unclear.[460]

Non-commercial showings of The Birth have also been protested. For example, in 1960 the film was withdrawn from a program sponsored by the Newark State Teachers College Fine Arts Club after a group of students protested the screening.[461] In 1966, the film was shown on the University of Massachusetts campus despite the protests of the Springfield, Massachusetts, NAACP Branch and the local organization of the Congress of Racial Equality.[462]

The NAACP also opposed the showing of the film on television. The organization asked Sterling Television not to show the film on television after Sterling purchased the broadcast rights in 1959. In a letter to Sterling, NAACP representative Roy Wilkins said that

if the film were shown on television "it will plant hatred and lies
in" individuals who "know nothing of the truth or falsity of the
historical period it claims to depict."[463] Wilkins also asserted
the film would "encourage violence because the film advocates and
glorifies violence (of the KKK) as a means of controlling Negro
citizens."[464] Sterling advised Wilkins that it had "never had any
intention of releasing 'The Birth of a Nation' in its original
version."[465] In a letter to Wilkins, Sterling president, Saul J.
Turell, said the company intended to use "certain excerpts" from the
film in a planned series on motion picture history.[466] In particular,
Turell indicated the "truly great battle sequences and the theme concerning the assassination of Lincoln" were being considered for the
series.[467] Turell also said that Sterling would invite the NAACP to
view the program before it was aired. Turell assured the NAACP that
his company would do nothing which in "any way" might "obstruct the
fight to establish complete and equal rights for the Negro in the
U.S."[468] Two years later Sterling announced The Birth was "too
dangerous a picture" for television and abandoned plans to show the
film in any form.[469]

Other

The film was withdrawn at least once by a theatre manager not
specifically petitioned to censor the film. However, in this instance
an individual shot at the screen during a showing of the film. After
an unidentified individual "fired several shots at the silver sheet
during the showing of D. W. Griffith's 'The Birth of a Nation,'"

Variety reported that the manager of the Senate Theatre withdrew the film in 1924.[470] Variety noted that the cancellation came at an "apropos moment" because "business was poor anyway; the theatre was guarded by cops; children are forbidden."[471]

Spinoff Efforts

There were at least two spinoff efforts which attempted to capitalize on the film in 1915. For example, the Boston Morning Journal serialized the film and ran it in story form beginning May 3, 1915.[472] In an ad promoting the series, the Journal called the film "the sensation of the hour in Boston" and noted that Gertrude Stevenson had followed the "structural narrative of the film" in her newspaper adaptation.[473]

A St. Louis land developer also used The Birth for his own commercial purposes in autumn 1915. The developer ran ads for a development called East Kinloch which began "The Birth of a Nation' is a great picture depicting a past history. . .The Birth of East Kinloch is the picture of a future history to be written by a Negro historian."[474] The ad concluded: "Come out and see the Birth of East Kinloch and forget all about 'The Birth of a Nation.'"[475] The ad was run at least ten times in the St. Louis Argus.[476] It is interesting to note that the Argus ran this ad at the same time it was conducting an editorial campaign urging people to keep up the protest against The Birth.[477]

Summary

During the time period 1915-1973, a variety of extra-legal tactics were used in The Birth of a Nation censorship controversies by individuals who supported or opposed the film. Extra-legal tactics included such things as appeals to motion picture self-regulatory agencies, asking motion picture exhibitors to voluntarily not show the film, production of films to counter The Birth, and various forms of communication like sermons, pamphlets, demonstrations, editorial campaigns, and letters to the editor. Extra-legal tactics were used for two purposes: to accomplish controversy resolution and to influence public opinion about the film's acceptability. However, the majority of extra-legal actions were designed to mobilize public opinion for one side or the other, rather than to accomplish controversy resolution. Specifically, only 17 of the 181 extra-legal actions discussed in this chapter were aimed directly toward controversy resolution.[478]

Regardless of focus, extra-legal tactics existed as part of specific censorship controversies at all levels and also existed independently of individual censorship controversies. In five controversies, censorship of the film at the national level was specifically at issue. In two controversies state censorship of the film was debated. In 25 controversies, local censorship of The Birth was discussed. In the remaining instances, 23 extra-legal tactics were directed toward the film's right in general to the screen and were not tied to specific censorship controversies in a given locale.

Extra-Legal Tactics Designed to Resolve Controversies

Extra-legal tactics aimed toward controversy resolution included: asking motion picture industry self-regulatory bodies not to approve the film; asking the individuals responsible for a specific screening not to show the film; exerting editorial pressure against censorship; and picketing theatres in which the film was being screened. Specifically, four censorship petitions were sent to motion picture self-regulatory bodies; 10 requests for censorship were directed to individuals responsible for the film's screening; two theatres were picketed,; and one newspaper editorialized against censorship. These 17 actions were taken during 15 controversies. In each case extra-legal tactics were the only tactics employed to accomplish controversy resolution. Nine of the controversies were resolved by the extra-legal tactics and six were not. These figures are not significant ($x^2 = .6$, $>.02$). Therefore, extra-legal tactics did not accomplish controversy resolution with a frequency differing from chance. One of the controversies was resolved by the action of a motion picture industry self-regulatory body and the remaining eight were resolved by actions taken by individuals responsible for the film's screening. Two controversies resolved through extra-legal means concerned screenings at the national level. The remaining seven controversies resolved through extra-legal means were at the local level. Controversies in which censorship of The Birth was sought by extra-legal means by year and resolution are presented in table 18.

TABLE 18

CONTROVERSIES IN WHICH CENSORSHIP SOUGHT THROUGH
EXTRA-LEGAL MEANS BY YEAR AND RESOLUTION

Year	Censorship	No Censorship	Unclear	Total
1915	1	0	0	1
1924	1	0	0	1
1930	0	0	1	1
1937	0	0	1	1
1939	0	0	1	1
1940	0	0	1	1
1941	1	0	1	1
1950	0	1	0	1
1959	1	0	0	1
1960	1	0	0	1
1965	1	1	1	3
1966	0	1	0	1
1970	0	0	1	1

As evident in table 18, although extra-legal actions were taken with the purpose of accomplishing controversy resolution across almost all the years studied, the tactic was somewhat more effective in accomplishing controversy resolution after the 1952 Supreme Court ruling in the Burstyn[279] case than it was before 1952. Specifically, prior to 1952, the tactic was used nine times and accomplished controversy resolution in four instances. After 1952, the tactic was implemented seven times and was successful in accomplishing controversy resolution in five cases. However, these numbers were judged too small to determine reliable statistical significance.

Also as presented in table 18, six controversies were resolved with some form of censorship. Specifically, prior restraint was exercised against the film three times; subsequent restraint twice; and subsequent restraint partial once. The film was not censored in three controversies resolved through extra-legal means. The resolution of the remaining six controversies in which extra-legal tactics were employed for the purpose of controversy resolution are unclear.

In 14 controversies, extra-legal resolution was sought by the film's opponents and in one controversy resolution was sought by the film's supporters through an extra-legal tactic. Whenever extra-legal tactics were used to accomplish controversy resolution by the film's opponents, the tactics were based on the rationale that the film would engender racial prejudice. However, in no instance did the individuals ordering censorship state they were doing so because they agreed with that rationale. For example, one group responded it would not show the film to avoid "embarrassment" although the actual nature of the potential embarrassment is unclear. One group said it considered the film "too dangerous" for national television showing. However, specifically what this danger was is unclear. One group indicated racial prejudice was not an appropriate censorship rationale but ordered subsequent restraint partial based on the rationale that certain scenes were immoral. One individual specifically rejected the rationale that the film would engender racial prejudice and screened the film in total. The rationales for action or inaction of the remaining agents asked to censor the film are unclear. The extra-legal argument in favor of the film was based on the rationale that the film was entitled to free speech protection. However, the resolution of this controversy is unclear.

Extra-Legal Tactics Used To Influence Public Opinion

The remaining extra-legal actions studied were used either as support tactics in individual censorship controversies or existed independently of any controversy to influence general public opinion concerning the film. Specifically, 17 controversies included 141 extra-legal actions used as support tactics and 23 extra-legal actions existed independently of individual screening debates.

Individuals opposing The Birth used extra-legal tactics more frequently to influence opinion than did individuals supporting the film. Specifically, 128 extra-legal efforts against the film were made; the tactic was used in support of the film 32 times; and in four cases extra-legal tactics were related to censorship controversies but did not take a position pro or con concerning censorship. Of the actions against the film, 111 were controversy specific and 18 were controversy independent. Of the actions supporting the film, 26 were controversy specific and five were controversy independent. All extra-legal actions judged neutral were controversy specific. Not only did individuals opposed to The Birth use extra-legal tactics more frequently to influence opinion, they also used a wider range of tactics than did individuals supporting the film. The number of extra-legal actions by category of extra-legal tactic and the position taken concerning the film by the action are shown in table 19.

TABLE 19

RANGE OF EXTRA-LEGAL TACTICS AND POSITION CONCERNING FILM

Tactic	Support Film	Oppose Film	Neutral on Censorship	Total
Editorials	15	82	2	99
Letters to Editor	12	18	0	30
Resolutions	0	9	0	9
Demonstrations	0	8	0	8
Pamphlets	1	6	0	7
Sermons	3	4	0	7
Miscellaneous	0	0	2	2
Film	0	2	0	2
Total	31	129	4	164

As is evident in table 19, extra-legal tactics were used with varying frequency. Editorials and letters to the editor were used more frequently than all other forms of extra-legal actions combined. Specifically, over 60 percent of extra-legal actions taken to influence opinion were editorials, and slightly over 18 percent were letters to the editor. However, over five times as many editorials opposed the film as supported it and this was not the case for letters to the editor. Letters to the editor were reasonably equally split between those which opposed censorship of the film and those which supported censorship.

Extra-legal actions to influence opinion rather than specifically to resolve controversies were taken only during the time period

1915-1924.

TABLE 20

EXTRA-LEGAL TACTICS BY YEAR

Tactic and position on film	1915	1916	1917	1918	1921	1923	1924
Editorials							
Against	77	1	0	0	0	4	0
Favor	13	1	0	0	0	0	1
Neutral	2	0	0	0	0	0	0
Letters to the Editor							
Against	18	0	0	0	0	0	0
Favor	12	0	0	0	0	0	0
Resolutions							
Against	8	1	0	0	0	0	0
Demonstrations							
Against	6	0	1	0	1	0	0
Pamphlets							
Against	3	2	0	0	1	0	0
Favor	0	1	0	0	0	0	0
Sermons							
Against	4	0	0	0	0	0	0
Favor	3	0	0	0	0	0	0
Film							
Against	1	0	0	1	0	0	0
Other							
Neutral	2	0	0	0	0	0	0

As evident from table 20, different types of extra-legal tactics were employed to influence opinion with unequal frequency across the years studied. The range of extra-legal tactics was greatest and most concentrated during 1915. Specifically, 149 of the 164 actions taken to influence opinion occurred during 1915. No extra-legal tactics were found to be used to influence opinion after 1924.

A variety of arguments for and against the film were presented through extra-legal tactics. The argument most frequently presented in extra-legal form against the film was that it would engender racial prejudice. Rationales underlying extra-legal actions to influence opinion against the film are presented by year in table 21. Rationales underlying extra-legal actions to influence opinion in favor of the film by year are presented in table 22. As evident in table 21, a wide range of arguments was used against the film. However, the argument most frequently presented was that the film would engender racial prejudice. Although the rationale was most frequently expressed during 1915, it was used to influence opinion against the film across the years in which extra-legal tactics were found to be used for this purpose. Second in terms of number of times used to sway opinion against the film were extra-legal communications critical of Thomas Dixon. As evident in table 22, the argument used most frequently to support the film was that it should be entitled to the free speech protections guaranteed by the Constitution. Second in terms of number of times used to influence opinion in favor of the film was that black opposition to the film was unwarranted.

TABLE 21

RATIONALES UNDERLYING EXTRA-LEGAL ACTIONS DESIGNED
TO SWAY PUBLIC OPINION AGAINST THE FILM BY YEAR

Rationale	1915	1916	1917	1918	1921	1923
Engender racial prejudice	54	2	0	1	0	2
Critical of Tom Dixon	11	1	0	0	0	0
Praise censor efforts	9	0	0	0	0	1
Discuss protest incidents	9	0	0	0	0	0
Criticize protest efforts	8	0	0	0	0	0
Glorifies Klan	3	1	0	0	1	0
Stop free advertising for film	4	0	0	0	0	0
Hostile to peace	2	0	0	0	0	1
Press coverage inadequate	3	0	0	0	0	0
Historically inaccurate	2	0	0	0	0	0
Justification for censor legislation	2	0	0	0	0	0
Unpatriotic	1	0	0	0	0	0
Advocate peaceful protest	1	0	0	0	0	0
Unfit for public building	1	0	0	0	0	0
Attacking pamphlet	1	0	0	0	0	0
Immoral	1	0	0	0	0	0
Unclear	5	0	1	0	1	0

TABLE 22

RATIONALES UNDERLYING EXTRA-LEGAL TACTICS DESIGNED
TO SWAY OPINION IN FAVOR OF THE FILM BY YEAR

Rationale	1915	Year 1916	1924
Film should be protected speech	12	2	1
Black opposition unwarranted	7	0	0
Anti-War Statement	3	0	0
Praise Film	5	0	0
Historically accurate	2	0	0
Not immoral	1	0	0

Extra-Legal Tactics To Influence
Opinion: Controversy Specific

As mentioned previously a majority of the extra-legal actions taken to influence opinion were tied to specific censorship controversies. Specifically, 133 extra-legal actions taken to influence opinion were controversy specific. The actions were tied to 17 controversies occurring between 1915 and 1924. As evident in table 23, the actual degree of extra-legal involvement varied from controversy to controversy. The controversy found to have the most extra-legal tactics tied to it was the 1915 New York controversy. This controversy which was actually resolved by the city's mayor who exercised subsequent partial restraint against the film included at least 29 extra-legal actions in the forms of editorials, letters to the editor, demonstrations, sermons, and resolutions. Although the 1915 Boston controversy involved fewer extra-legal tactics, the range of tactics utilized was found to be the greatest of any controversy. In this instance the 16 extra-legal actions were divided among editorials, letters to the editor, demonstrations, sermons, pamphlets, resolutions, and miscellaneous.[479] The number of extra-legal actions in each controversy and the censor/no censor decision resolving the controversy are presented in table 23.

TABLE 23

EXTRA-LEGAL TACTICS TO INFLUENCE OPINION BY YEAR, CONTROVERSY, AND CENSOR OR NO CENSOR RESOLUTION

	1915 Baltimore	Boston	Chicago	Los Angeles	Minneapolis	New York	Oakland	Ohio	Philadelphia	Providence	St. Louis	St. Paul	Washington, D.C.	1917 Cleveland	1921 New York	1923 Kansas	1924 Chicago
Editorials																	
For film	0	5	1	0	0	0	0	1	0	0	0	2	1	0	0	0	1
Against	5	0	10	1	3	15	0	10	7	0	10	5	1	0	0	4	0
Neutral	0	0	0	0	0	0	0	0	0	0	0	2	0	0	0	0	0
Letters to the Editor																	
For film	0	1	0	0	0	3	0	0	0	0	0	8	0	0	0	0	0
Against	0	0	1	0	0	7	1	0	1	0	0	8	0	0	0	0	0
Demonstrations																	
Against	0	3	0	0	0	1	0	0	2	0	0	0	0	1	1	0	0
Resolutions																	
Against	0	3	1	0	0	2	0	1	0	0	1	0	0	0	0	0	0
Sermons																	
For film	0	1	0	0	0	0	0	0	0	0	0	2	0	0	0	0	0
Against	0	1	1	0	0	1	0	0	0	0	0	1	0	0	0	0	0
Pamphlet																	
Against	0	1	0	0	0	0	0	0	0	1	0	0	0	0	1	1	0
Miscellaneous																	
Neutral	0	1	0	0	0	0	0	0	0	0	1	0	0	0	0	0	0
Resolution	NC	C	C	NC	NC	C	NC	C	NC	NC	NC	C	NC	NC	NC	NC	NC

446

As evident in table 23, 12 controversies which included extra-legal tactics were resolved with decisions supporting no censorship and five were resolved with decisions supporting censorship. These figures are not significant (x^2 = 2.88, .02). Therefore, the censorship/no censorship resolutions could have occurred by chance. Thus, there appears to be no consistent dependency between extra-legal tactics and censorship/no censorship decisions resolving controversies.

Extra-Legal Tactics To Influence Opinion: Controversy Independent

Extra-legal tactics designed to influence opinion, but not tied to specific censorship controversy took one of four major forms: editorial; pamphlet; resolution; film. Eighteen of these actions supported censorship of the film and five supported the film. Controversy independent extra-legal actions are presented in table 24.

TABLE 24

CONTROVERSY INDEPENDENT EXTRA-LEGAL ACTIONS BY POSITION REGARDING FILM

Tactic	Against Film	Support Film	Total
Editorial	12	4	16
Pamphlet	3	1	4
Resolution	1	0	1
Film	2	0	2

These extra-legal tactics were employed during the time period 1915-1918. The majority of the actions took place during 1915. Specifically, 14 extra-legal efforts against the film and three in support of the film were taken during 1915. Three extra-legal actions were taken against the film in 1916 and that year two were presented in defense of the film. The remaining controversy independent action was taken against the film in 1918. Because these tactics existed to influence opinion concerning the film's right to the screen. the actual effectiveness of the tactics could not be evaluated.

Conclusions

During the time period 1915-1973, extra-legal tactics were used by both those individuals who wished The Birth suppressed and those who championed the film's right to the screen. However, because the majority of extra-legal tactics were designed to influence public opinion concerning the film rather than to resolve the censorship controversy, it is not possible to measure the effectiveness of most of the extra-legal tactics. Also, the extra-legal actions cited are not an exhaustive list. Efforts have been made to include as wide a range of tactics as possible from the sources available to complete the portrait of efforts to suppress this controversial and important film. However, certain records important to this aspect of the study have been lost. For example, it is highly unlikely that Monroe Trotter was editorially silent concerning The Birth in the Boston Guardian during 1915. But, because the Guardian (with the exception of a few scattered clippings) is not extant for that time period, it is impossible to analyze what might have been an important extra-legal editorial campaign against the film. Therefore, reconstruction of the **extra-legal tactics used in Boston contains a facsimile of what occurred** because it reflects the range and tone of tactics used, but is probably incomplete because it contains only editorials published in the Boston majority press which supported the film specifically or opposed censorship generally. Nevertheless, this range of tactics is important in censorship history of The Birth because of the number and variety of action taken throughout the history of the film and therefore warrants discussion.

In the few instances when controversy resolution was attempted entirely through extra-legal means, the tactic was, with one exception, employed by those individuals who opposed the film. Individuals who wished to stop the film through extra-legal means utilized two primary techniques: petitioning a motion picture self-regulation agency to stop the film nationally, and asking individuals in charge of the film's screening not to show it. The former variety of extra-legal action was not particularly successful from the standpoint of those who utilized it. In only one instance of four did the agency petitioned respond by ordering partial suppression of the film and that agency used a different standard for censorship than the standard argued by those requesting censorship. This ruling is interesting because it was made in 1915 just after the U. S. Supreme Court's Mutual v. Ohio[480] decision by one of the first motion picture industry self-regulatory bodies which specifically rejected as an acceptable standard for censorship the argument that films might be stopped because of the racial images presented in them. Thus, even after the Supreme Court ruled that film was not protected by the First Amendment in any way, the film industry's self-policing agency was willing only to accept immorality as a reasonable standard for censorship.

When an extra-legal tactic took the form of petitioning individuals responsible for the film's screening, it was somewhat more successful from the film's opponents' point of view. Specifically, five of the 10 times this tactic resulted in total suppression of the film. In three cases the individuals petitioned refused to stop the film. However, the success or failure of the tactic in the remaining two instances is unclear. In each case the request was the only tactic used against the film. This approach to censorship of The Birth was used most frequently after 1952.

Therefore, it can be concluded that when extra-legal tactics were used in attempts to resolve The Birth censorship controversies, the tactics were used alone and were only somewhat successful in achieving censorship in highly specialized circumstances. Specifically, these circumstances were when individuals were asked not to show the film on a screening-by-screening basis.

The majority of extra-legal actions against The Birth occurred in the year of the film's release, 1915. Individual censorship controversies after 1915 were not found to have as many extra-legal tactics tied to them as the individual controversies in 1915. This may have been due in part to the acceptance of the assertion that any protest was free advertising for the film and therefore counterproductive. This decline in the use of extra-legal tactics may also have been due to a tactical shift of the major opposition to the film, the NAACP. As noted in Chapter V, the NAACP became discouraged after early concentrated efforts failed to stop The Birth and after 1915 directed the bulk of its energies elsewhere. Although the NAACP never gave up battling the film, its efforts after 1915 were less frequent.

After the Burstyn v. Wilson[481] decision in 1952, the year in which the most extra-legal actions (three) concerning The Birth were taken was 1965. In that year, two actions against the film and one in support of its right to the screen were taken. At least one of these actions in opposition to the film was taken concurrently with civil rights demonstrations in Alabama. Although the theatre showing the film was in Philadelphia, it was picketed by NAACP-organized demonstrators carrying signs indicating it was inappropriate to show the film because of discrimination against blacks in Alabama. In spite of the protest, the film was not withdrawn from the Philadelphia theatre.

When those individuals who supported the film asserted its right to the screen, the argument was usually based on First Amendment grounds regardless of the year in which the statement was made. For example, D. W. Griffith called film equivalent to print media in 1915 and asserted The Birth's right to First Amendment protection after the U. S. Supreme Court's Mutual ruling. In fact, only one statement concerning The Birth's right to First Amendment protection was made after the Burstyn ruling. This seems to indicate either a reluctance on the part of these individuals to accept the Supreme Court's ruling or perhaps a hope to influence future interpretations of the medium's First Amendment status. In the majority of cases, the argument that the film was entitled to First Amendment protection was made by newspaper editorial writers who interpreted the right to censor the film as a step toward the right to censor newspapers.

On the other hand, only once during the entire time period was an argument found in opposition to The Birth which reflected the Supreme Court's Mutual ruling. Why the film's opponents did not more frequently use the reasoning of the court in their arguments against the film is difficult to ascertain. Perhaps the opponents were unaware of the Court's ruling (which seems highly unlikely in the case of the NAACP). Perhaps the opponents did not think the decision gave them adequate ammunition against the film or perhaps they did not see any connection between the ruling and censorship of The Birth. Rather, the arguments against the film reflect the assumption that the film could be censored only if potential censors accepted as valid certain kinds of criteria. The rationale expressed most frequently by those individuals utilizing extra-legal tactics against the film was that the film would engender racial prejudice.

In the censorship controversies which included the use of extra-legal tactics to influence public opinion, there seems to be little connection between the number or type of extra-legal actions taken and the outcome of the censorship controversy. For example, in the controversy which had the most individual extra-legal actions against the film and also had few extra-legal actions in support of the film, subsequent partial restraint was exercised against the film. In another controversy which involved only slightly fewer efforts for the film than against, the outcome was the same, subsequent partial restraint. In one controversy in which the efforts against the film outnumbered the efforts for the film 16 to 1, the controversy was resolved by a court which ruled no one under 18 could view the film, but did not otherwise censor the film. Also, effectiveness of the technique did not change over time. Therefore, it can be concluded that there is no certain way to tie number or type of extra-legal actions to ultimate censorship controversy resolution in terms of censorship or no censorship of the film.

Notes to Chapter VII

¹Roger Baldwin to Walter White, 25 April 1939, ACLU Archives, Vol. 2157.

²Ibid.

³Walter White to Roger Baldwin, 1 May 1939, ACLU Archives, Vol. 2157.

⁴Resolution to ACLU, Minutes of the NAACP Board of Directors, 8 May 1939, NAACP Archives, File C300. See also, Walter White to Roger Baldwin, 17 June 1939, ACLU Archives, Vol. 2157, and Walter White to Roger Baldwin, 17 June 1939, NAACP Archives, File C302.

⁵Roger Baldwin to Walter White, 14 June 1939, ACLU Archives, Vol. 2157.

⁶Walter White to Roger Baldwin, 17 June 1939, ACLU Archives, Vol. 2157.

⁷Thurgood Marshall, Memorandum to Committee on Administration, 4 March 1940, NAACP Archives, File C302.

⁸Ibid.

⁹Ibid.

¹⁰Roger Bladwin to Roy Wilkins, 17 April 1940, ACLU Archives, Vol. 2157.

¹¹Roger Baldwin to Editor of the Crisis, 17 April 1940, ACLU Archives, Vol. 2157. See also, Roger Baldwin to Editor of the Crisis, 17 April 1940, NAACP Archives, File C302.

¹²Ibid.

¹³New Release, n.t., n.d., n.p., clipping in ACLU Archives, Vol. 2157.

¹⁴Mr. Pickens, Memorandum to Mr. White, undated, NAACP Archives, File C302.

¹⁵Ibid.

¹⁶As discussed Chapter II, the National Board of Censorship was formed in 1909 by a citizen's group interested in alternatives to formalized legal censorship. (See National Board of Censorship of Motion Pictures, The Question of Motion Picture Censorship (New York: National Board of Censorship, 1914), p. 4.) The board officially

stood "in favor of voluntary, non-official co-operative censorship in contrast to legal official pre-publicity by authorities, Federal, State, and local." (See Ruth Inglis, Freedom of the Movies (Chicago: University of Chicago Press, 1947), p. 76). Although the board lacked legal authority, its voluntary agreements with theatre owners at the time of The Birth's release assured that approximately 80 percent of the nation's theatres would not show a film rejected by the board (See John Collier, "Censorship in Action," Survey, 34, (7 August 1915): 23). Writer Paul Gallico who served on the board in its early years described it as follows: "That was a volunteer organization. At that time there was only state censorship, so the picture producers, to protect themselves and get a decent censorship on their pictures, paid this national board. It was sort of a charity organization. They paid them six dollars a reel to review pictures. We had about two hundred people and we would screen pictures all morning, all afternoon. I worked as review secretary with these committees. The idea was for the review secretary to control the meeting and see that nothing really smutty got by, but at the same time to keep the do-gooders and wowsers from taking out pieces of the picture which would gut it." See Jerome Holtzman, Ed., No Cheering in the Press Box (New York: Holt, Rinehart and Winston, 1973), p. 65. See also, "Censors Ban 'Birth of Nation," Western Outlook, 20 March 1915, p. 2.

[17] W. D. McGuire, "Correspondence," The New Republic, 10 April 1915, p. 262.

[18] Ibid.

[19] Ibid.

[20] E. Burton Ceruti to Mary Childs Nerney, 3 February 1915, NAACP Archives, File C299.

[21] NAACP Los Angeles Branch to The Honorable The City Council of the City of Los Angeles, State of California, 2 February 1915, NAACP Archives, File C299.

[22] E. Burton Ceruti to Mary Childs Nerney, 3 February 1915, NAACP Archives, File C299.

[23] NAACP National to Rev. Charles Macfarland, 26 March 1915 NAACP Archives, File C299.

[24] Ibid.

[25] McGuire, p. 262. See also, W. D. McGuire to Mary Childs Nerney, 15 March 1915, NAACP Archives, File C299.

[26] Lester F. Scott to Dr. J. E. Springarn, 12 April 1915, NAACP Archives, File C299. It is interesting to note that the NAACP anticipated it would object to the film if "as reported, it depicts the attack of a colored man on a white girl and his murder afterwards by the Klu (sic) Klux Klan, we cannot be too strong in our condemnation of the apparent attempt to relate this abhorrent crime to the colored race or the subtle justification of lynching such a picture would suggest to the average unthinking person. Statistics prove that less than ten percent of the lynchings in this country can be shown to have as their alleged cause an attack upon white women. These lynchings have so increased within the last few years that in Georgia and Louisiana the State authorities are now making investigations. Lynchings now include among their victims women and children and in one instance recently a whole family was wiped out." See Mary Childs Nérney, Memorandum, 27 February 1915, NAACP Archives, File C299.

[27] The board promised the twelve tickets before it had arranged for a special showing of the film. (See Nerney, Memorandum, 27 February 1915). Apparently, logistical problems developed as the screening was arranged. Later the board reported that although promised the review, it could not arrange for an independent screening. The board said it had trouble gaining access to a theatre in which to show the film and also had trouble acquiring a print for review as "one film was lost in the snows of the Rockies and the other was being worked on in New York." (See NAACP To Rev. Charles MacFarland, 26 March 1915). However, Aitken and Griffith had arranged for an advance matinee performance of the film "for the press, their friends, and other producers." (See Lester Scott to Dr. J. E. Spingarn). When Griffith and Aitken learned of the protest, they agreed to allow members of the board to attend the performance. The board later told the NAACP that the screening was "no way a performance under the control or at the request of any individual of the National Board." (See Lester Scott to Dr. J. E. Spingarn). The board said it was later notified by the producers that only two tickets beyond the number needed by the General Committee would be issued. These were the two tickets sent to the NAACP. However, three NAACP representatives actually got tickets. This occurred because W. D. McGuire learned that one member of the General Committee would be out of the city at the time of the screening. McGuire sent this individual's ticket to John Haynes Holmes, NAACP National Vice-President, who had previously been invited to meetings of the board. (See McGuire to Nerney, 27 February 1915). Nerney reported that W. A. Barrett, Board Assistant Secretary, came to her office and told her no blacks would be admitted (See NAACP to Rev. Charles MacFarland).

[28] McGuire to Nerney.

[29] Ibid.

[30] Lester Scott to Dr. J. E. Spingarn.

[31] W. D. McGuire, "Correspondence," p. 262.

[32] Ibid.

[33] Ibid., p. 263.

[34] The association reported Dr. Howe gave the unofficial notification and that although it immediately requested an official statement from the board it did not receive the written notice until 15 March 1915. See NAACP to Rev. Charles MacFarland.

[35] Mary Childs Nerney to Dr. Jacques Loeb, 3 March 1915, NAACP Archives, File C299.

[36] Mary Childs Nerney, telgram to E. Burton Ceruti, 2 March 1915, NAACP Archives, File C299.

[37] See "Censors Ban 'Birth of Nation," Western Outlook; "This is Material Success," Cleveland Gazette, 6 March 1915, p. 2; "Clansman Back in Moving Pictures," Defender, 13 March 1915, p. 4; "Censors Bar 'The Birth of a Nation," Baltimore Afro-American, 6 March 1915, p. 1.

[38] Ibid.

[39] W. D. McGuire to Mary Childs Nerney, 15 March 1915, NAACP Archives, File C299.

[40] Ibid.

[41] Mary Childs Nerney to Jane Addams, 13 March 1915, NAACP Archives, File C299.

[42] Lester Scott to Dr. J. E. Spingarn.

[43] See "Another Fight Over Photo-Play," Cleveland Gazette, 10 April 1915, p. 2; "Clansman Is Kicked Out of New York," Chicago Defender, 27 March 1915, p. 1; "Censorship Board Splits on Dixon's Clansman Film," N. Y. World, 24 March 1915, n.p., clipping in Griffith's The Birth of a Nation scrapbook, MOMA Archives. Nerney later reported the New York press ignored the controversy until it published the story of the split. See "Fighting Race Calumny," in Fred Silva, ed. Focus on The Birth of a Nation (Englewood, N. J.: Prentice-Hall, 1971), p. 69.

[44] "Censor Board Splits on Dixon's Film," N. Y. World; "Clansman is Kicked Out of New York," Defender.

[45] Ibid.

[46] NAACP to Rev. Charles MacFarland.

[47] Lester Scott to Dr. J. E. Spingarn.

[48] Ibid.

[49] Ibid.

[50] Ibid.

[51] Formed in the early 1920's to regulate the film industry, the MPPDA chose Will Hays, then Postmaster-General in Harding's cabinet, as its first head. Hays was given "absolute authority to police the morals of the industry and to reform or rather establish its public relations." However, the "absolute authority" vested in Hays was totally extra-legal. See Richard Griffith and Arthur Mayer, The Movies, Revised Edition (New York: Siman & Schuster, 1970), p. 182.

[52] "Movies Turn Deaf Ear to Colored Plea," Christian Century, 24 September 1930, p. 38.

[53] Ibid.

[54] Ibid.

[55] "Resolution," Minutes of the Meeting of the NAACP Board of Directors, 8 May 1939, p. 6, NAACP Archives. See also Walter White to Roger Baldwin, 17 June 1939. See also "Birth of a Nation' Fight to be continued," Press Release, 12 May 1939, NAACP Archives, File C302.

[56] Walter White to Will Hays, 21 March 1940, NAACP Archives, File C302. A copy of the letter is in ACLU Archives, Vol. 2157.

[57] Ibid.

[58] Walter White to "Organizations," 22 March 1940, NAACP Archives, File C302. See also Walter White to Roger Baldwin, 22 March 1940, ACLU Archives, Vol. 2157.

[59] "Nationwide Protests on 'Birth of a Nation' Is Sent To Hays Office," Press release, 29 March 1940, NAACP Archives, File C302.

[60] Carl E. Milliken to Walter White, 25 March 1940, ACLU Archives, Vol. 2157.

[61] Walter White to Carl E. Milliken, 27 March 1940, ACLU Archives, Vol. 2157.

[62]"Nationwide Protests on 'Birth of a Nation' Is Sent To Hays Office."

[63]F. S. Harmon to R. B. Eleazer, 29 March 1940, NAACP Archives, File C302.

[64]"Letters from Readers," n.t., August 1940, clipping in ACLU Archives, Vol. 2157.

[65]"Theatre Notes," Christian Science Monitor, 17 April 1915, p. 19.

[66]Ibid.

[67]"Birth of Nation' Causes Near-Riot . . . Alleged Plot to Destroy Film Results in Wild Scenes and 11 Arrests," Boston Sunday Globe, 18 April 1915, p. 1.

[68]"New Film Shows Negroes Progress," Boston Morning Journal, 17 April 1915, p. 6.

[69]"Theatre Notes," Christian Science Monitor, 17 April 1915, p. 4.

[70]Fred Silva, Ed., Focus on The Birth of a Nation, p. 4.

[71]Thomas R. Cripps, "The Reaction of the Negro to the Motion Picture 'Birth of a Nation," The Historian 26 (1963); 357. It is interesting to note that even though the newspapers generally attributed the production of this epilogue to Griffith, no mention of it is made in the standard sources listing Griffith's words such as Iris Barry's D. W. Griffith: American Film Master (New York: Museum of Modern Art, 1965) which includes an annotated list of Griffith films compiled by Eileen Bowser and Robert M. Henderson, D. W. Griffith: The Years at Biograph (New York: Farrar, Straus, & Girous, 1970). Henderson also does not mention this sequence in his biography of Griffith, D. W. Griffith: His Life and Work (New York: Oxford University Press, 1972).

[72]"Gov. Davis Sees No Harm in Klan Film," Kansas City Call, 14 December 1923, p. 1.

[73]Philip Allston to Booker T. Washington, 12 April 1915, Booker T. Washington Papers, Box 75, Library of Congress Manuscript Collection, Washington, D. C. (Hereafter referred to as Booker T. Washington Papers).

[74]Ibid.

[75] Booker T. Washington to Philip Allston, 25 April 1915, Booker T. Washington Papers, Box 75.

[76] Booker T. Washington to Florence Swell Bond, 30 June 1915, Booker T. Washington Papers, Box 75. Thomas Cripps indicates in his article "The Reaction of the Negro to the Motion Picture, 'Birth of a Nation,'" the Negro Business League in which Washington and Allston were both involved had a "factional fight over endorsing the Griffith movie." The controversy developed when Samuel E. Courtney reported to Washington that Allston and another member of the Business League, Dr. Alexander Cox, "voluntarily" endorsed The Birth and gave the film representatives the impression that they spoke for Washington (See S. E. Courtney to Booker T. Washington, 19 April 1915, Booker T. Washington Papers, Box 75). Cripps indicated a resolution to endorse the film was "blocked in a meeting of the executive council, but even so he (Washington) had to manipulate the rebel group into remaining in the organization so as to continue the public impression of Negro unity." See Thomas Cripps, "The Reaction of the Negro to the Motion Picture, 'Birth of a Nation,'" p. 357. See also, "No Thanks for Mayor Curley," Baltimore Ledger, 28 August 1915, p. 1.

[77] Mary Childs Nerney to R. Granville Curry, 21 September 1915, NAACP Archives, File C300.

[78] Mary Childs Nerney to Desha Breckinridge, 20 September 1915, NAACP Archives, File C300.

[79] Charles E. (?)llason to Booker T. Washington, 1 June 1915, Booker T. Washington Papers, Box 75.

[80] Ibid. From these comments and the fact that nowhere does Griffith take credit for the footage, it is possible to speculate that either Hampton shot the sequence or the footage was already in existence.

[81] "'Birth of Nation' Case Dismissed," New York Age, 27 May 1915, p. 4.

[82] Mary Childs Nerney to Desha Breckinridge.

[83] Charles E. (?)llason to Booker T. Washington.

[84] With Epoch's application in behalf of The Birth filed in the Supreme Court of Ohio in 1925 were approximately ninety affidavits in favor of the film. See Epoch Production Corp. v. Vernon M. Riegel, No. 19030, Answer & Certified Transcript of Record Filed 19 March 1925 by Seba Miller, Clerk of the Supreme Court of Ohio, "Exhibit C," in Ohio State Historical Society Archives, Columbus, Ohio (Hereafter referred to as Ohio State Historical Society Archives).

[85] Wyndham R. Mayo, Affidavit in Support of The Birth of a Nation, filed 6 April 1916, in "Exhibit C" Epoch Production Corp. v. Riegel.

[86] Ibid.

[87] R. T. Thorp, Affidavit in support of The Birth of a Nation, Filed 6 April 1916, in "Exhibit C," Epoch Production Corp. v. Riegel.

[88] C. J. Smith, Affidavit in support of The Birth of a Nation, Filed 20 January 1916, in "Exhibit C," Epoch Production Corp. v. Riegel.

[89] Walter InDear, Affidavit in support of The Birth of a Nation, Filed 15 January 1916, in "Exhibit C," Epoch Production Corp. v. Riegel.

[90] John P. Turner to Editor, Philadelphia Tribune, 31 July 1915, p. 4.

[91] Francis J. Grimke, The Birth of a Nation (Washington, D. C.: Francis Grimke, 1915), p. 2.

[92] "Governor Davis Sees No Harm in Klan Film."

[93] "Still Fighting . . . For the Production of the Infamous Photo-Play, 'The Birth of a Nation," Cleveland Gazette, 12 June 1915, p. 3.

[94] Ibid.

[95] Thomas R. Cripps, "The Birth of a Race' Company: An Early Stride Toward a Black Cinema," The Journal of Negro History 59 (January 1974), 29.

[96] Ibid., pp. 33-35.

[97] Carroll Carroll, "White Investors Wrecked Blacks Answer to 'Birth of a Nation," Variety, 8 May 1974, p. 71.

[98] Thomas Cripps, "The Birth of a Race' Company," p. 35-36.

[99] Sharon Cohen, "When the Hillsborough River Became the Nile," Florida Accent, 8 December 1974, pp. 10-11.

[100] Ibid.

[101] Thomas Cripps, "The Birth of a Race' Company," p. 36.

[102] "Pathetic Appeal in Photo-play," *Boston Morning Journal*, 26 April 1915, p. 4. See also "Says Negro Is Not a Ward of the Country," *Boston Morning Journal*, 3 May 1915, p. 6.

[103] Ibid.

[104] "Still Fighting Obnoxious Movies," *Baltimore Ledger*, 1 May 1915, p. 1.

[105] "Photoplay Much Condemned," *Boston Evening Transcript*, 26 April 1915, p. 2.

[106] "Dr. Wise Sees Evil in Film," *New York Sun*, 15 March 1915, n.p., clipping in Griffith's *The Birth of a Nation* scrapbook, MOMA Archives.

[107] "Film Play a Crime Against Two Races," *New York Evening Post*, 15 March 1915, n.p., clipping in Griffith's *The Birth of a Nation* scrapbook, MOMA Archives.

[108] "Opinions Vary on 'Birth of Nation,'" *St. Paul Pioneer Press*, 18 October 1915, p. 5.

[109] "Minister Says Film Shows Partisan Aim," *St. Paul Pioneer Press*, 25 October 1915, p. 7.

[110] "Birth of Nation' Defended by Robb," *St. Paul Pioneer Press*, 18 October 1915, p. 5.

[111] "Divine Sees Good in Discussed Film," *St. Paul Pioneer Press*, 25 October 1915, p. 5.

[112] Ibid.

[113] "Birth of Nation' Assailed by Leading White Pastor," *Chicago Defender*, 9 October 1915, p. 1.

[114] Ibid.

[115] D. W. Griffith, *The Rise and Fall of Free Speech in America* (n.p.: D. W. Griffith, 1916). It is interesting to note Griffith did not copyright the work and in a prefatory note said "The press is invited to freely use its contents."

[116] D. W. Griffith, "The Rise and Fall of Free Speech in America," excerpted in Harry Geduld, *Focus on D. W. Griffith* (Englewood Cliffs, N. J.: Prentice Hall, 1971), pp. 43-44.

[117] Ibid., p. 44.

[118] Ibid., p. 45.

[119] Ibid.

[120] Boston Branch of the NAACP, *Fighting a Vicious Film: Protest Against The Birth of a Nation* (Boston: Boston Branch of the NAACP, 1915), p. 8.

[121] Ibid., p. 6.

[122] Ibid., p. 8.

[123] Francis Grimke, *The Birth of a Nation*.

[124] Ibid., p. 3.

[125] Ibid., pp. 1-2.

[126] Ibid., p. 4.

[127] W. Bishop Johnson, *The Birth of a Nation: A Monumental Slander of American History; The Negro and The Civil War By Thomas Dixon Analytically and Critically Considered* (n.p.: n.p., 1916).

[128] Ibid.

[129] Ibid., p. 2.

[130] Ibid., p. 3.

[131] Ibid., p. 5.

[132] Ibid., p. 6.

[133] Ibid.

[134] Ibid., p. 8.

[135] Isaac L. Thomas, *The Birth of a Nation: A Hyperbole Versus a Negro's Plea for Fair Play* (Philadelphia: William Watson, 1916).

[136] Ibid., p. 6.

[137] Ibid., p. 6.

[138] Ibid.

[139] Ibid., p. 13.

[140] Ibid., p. 20.

[141] Ibid., pp. 22-24.

[142] Ibid., p. 49.

[143] *Mutual Film Corporation v. Ohio*, 236 U. S. 230.

[144] Providence Branch of the NAACP, *A Statement of Facts Regarding The Photo-Play 'The Birth of a Nation' By The Providence Branch of the NAACP To The Providence Board of Police Commissioners*, n.d., NAACP Archives, File C302.

[145] Ibid.

[146] Ibid.

[147] *Stop The KKK Propaganda in New York*, n.d., NAACP Archives, File C301.

[148] Ibid.

[149] *People of the State of New York v. Kathryn Johnson, Helen Curtis, Laura Rollock, Edward Frasier and Llewelyn Rollock*, Court of General Sessions of the Peace In and For the County of New York. Copy of the opinion rendered by Judge Alfred Tally, 31 November 1921, p. 2, NAACP Archives, File C301.

[150] Ibid.

[151] Mary Childs Nerney to Major R. C. Wendall, 26 March 1915, NAACP Archives, File C302.

[152] Ibid.

[153] Ibid.

[154] Paul Kennaday to Hon. Cabot Ward, 26 March 1915, NAACP Archives, File C299.

[155] Ibid.

[156] Mary Childs Nerney to Rev. W. H. Brooks, 27 March 1915, NAACP Archives, File C299.

[157] Ibid.

[158] "Protest Parade Against 'Birth of Nation," *Chicago Defender*, 18 September 1915, p. 4.

[159] Most notably the Philadelphia North American which covered the Philadelphia controversy extensively did not mention a parade. See issues of the Philadelphia American, September 1-30, 1915.

[160] "The Birth of a Nation," Cleveland Gazette, 12 October 1918, n.p., clipping in NAACP Archives, File C301.

[161] James W. Johnson to Lester A. Walton, 20 May 1921, NAACP Archives, File C301.

[162] "Negroes Oppose Film," New York Times, 7 May 1921, p. 8.

[163] Ibid.

[164] "Birth of Nation' Pickets Freed By Higher Court," New York Call, 5 November 1921, n.p., clipping in NAACP Archives, File C301.

[165] No Head, The Daily Compass, 17 May 1950, p. 5, clipping in Lincoln Center Archives, Birth of a Nation File.

[166] No Head, New York Times, 19 May 1950, n.p., clipping in Lincoln Center Archives, Birth of a Nation File.

[167] "Coincident with Alabama Ruckus 'Birth of Nation' Opens in Philly," Variety, 24 March 1965, p. 2.

[168] Ibid.

[169] Ibid., pp. 2 & 82.

[170] Ibid., p. 2.

[171] "Big Negro Mass Meeting Denounces Photo-Play," Boston Morning Journal, 19 April 1915, p. 1.

[172] Ibid.

[173] "100 Cops Fight Negro Mobs in Broad Street Riot," Philadelphia North American, 21 September 1915, p. 1.

[174] Ibid. See also "Colored Women Run 'Birth of Nation' Out of Philadelphia," Chicago Defender, 25 September 1915, p. 1.

[175] Ibid.

[176] Ibid.

[177] "Negro Worse Used In North Than in South," Boston Morning Journal, 6 May 1915, p. 3.

[178] "Eliot Protests 'Birth of Nation," Boston Morning Journal, 26 April 1915, p. 4.

[179] "Fighting Race Calumny," The Crisis 10 (June 1915), p. 88.

[180] Ibid.

[181] "Negroes Flying Flag of Truce They Declare," Boston Morning Journal, 3 May 1915, p. 6.

[182] "Negroes Charge An Attempt to Bribe Salons," Boston Morning Journal, 30 April 1915, p. 4.

[183] Ibid.

[184] Ibid.

[185] Ibid.

[186] "Meeting Zion Methodist Church," Boston Morning Journal, 26 April 1915, p. 26.

[187] NAACP Boston Branch, "Resolutions of Executive Committee," 8 June 1915, NAACP Archives, File C300.

[188] Ibid.

[189] Ibid.

[190] "Public Protest Against 'The Birth of a Nation," St. Louis Argus, 3 September 1915, p. 1.

[191] Ibid.

[192] "The Grand Army Post Puts Ban on Clansman," New York Age, 2 December 1915, p. 1.

[193] Ibid.

[194] Ibid.

[195] "The Birth of a Nation' George H. Thomas Post Appropriately Denounces It," Cleveland Gazette, 11 September 1915, p. 2.

[196] "Promise to Tone Down," New York Age, 1 April 1915, p. 1.

[197] "News of Nations Metropolis," Indianapolis Freeman, 23 March 1915, p. 8.

[198] "The Resolutions," Cleveland Gazette, 23 October 1915, p. 3.

[199] Mary Childs Nerney to Hudson Quin, 15 September 1915, NAACP Archives, File C300.

[200] Mary Childs Nerney to Mrs. A. J. Erdman, n.d., NAACP Archives, File C299.

[201] Mary Childs Nerney to Bishop Alexander Walters, 20 March 1915, NAACP Archives, File C299.

[202] "Editorial Note," St. Paul Pioneer Press, 28 October 1915, p. 8.

[203] "Unwarranted Advertising," Chicago Defender, 13 November 1915, p. 8.

[204] Mary Childs Nerney to Verne E. Sheridan, 24 March 1915, NAACP Archives, File C299.

[205] Mary Childs Nerney to Rev. William P. Hayes, 17 March 1915, NAACP Archives, File C299. In the article sent a number of newspapers Jane Addams called The Birth a "pernicious caricature of the Negro race." She said the film was "unjust and untrue" and appealed to race prejudice. The article was published in the New York Evening Post and reprinted in the Chicago Defender. See "Birth of a Nation' Arouses Ire of Miss Jane Addams," Chicago Defender, 29 March 1915, p. 1.

[206] Mary Childs Nerney to Rev. William P. Hayes.

[207] Mrs. J. P. Lord to Mary Childs Nerney, 10 May 1915, NAACP Archives, File C300.

[208] "The Clansman," Western Outlook, 20 February 1915, p. 2.

[209] Ibid.

[210] Ibid.

[211] Ibid.

[212] "A Partial Victory," New York Age, 1 April 1915, p. 4.

[213] Ibid.

[214] "Editorial Paragraphs," New York Age, 22 April 1915, p. 4.

[215] Ibid.

[216] "Birth of Nation' Case Dismissed," New York Age, 27 May 1915, p. 4.

[217] Ibid.

[218] Ibid.

[219] "Movie Censorship," New York Age, 28 May 1915, p. 4.

[220] Ibid.

[221] James W. Johnson, "Uncle Tom's Cabin and The Clansman," New York Age, 4 March 1915, p. 4.

[222] Ibid.

[223] James W. Johnson, "Views and Reviews," New York Age, 1 April 1915, p. 4.

[224] Ibid.

[225] Ibid.

[226] Ibid.

[227] James W. Johnson, "Views and Reviews," New York Age, 15 April 1915, p. 4.

[228] Ibid.

[229] James W. Johnson, "Views and Reviews," New York Age, 22 April 1915, p. 4.

[230] Ibid.

[231] Lester Walton, "The Ulterior Motive," New York Age, 26 March 1915, p. 6.

[232] Ibid.

[233] Ibid.

[234] Lester A. Walton, "Bojangles Wins Harlem," New York Age, 6 May 1915, p. 6.

[235] Lester A. Walton, "A Patron of the Arts," New York Age, 3 June 1915, p. 6.

[236] Ibid.

[237] "A Splended Editorial Tribute," New York Age, 8 April 1915, p. 4.

[238] James W. Johnson, "Views and Reviews," New York Age, 1 April 1915, p. 4.

[239] "Capitalizing Race Hatred," New York Globe, 6 April 1915, Reprinted in Silva, Focus on Birth of a Nation, pp. 73-75.

[240] "False History," New York Age, 16 March 1916, p. 4.

[241] "The Death of a Movie," Chicago Defender, 1 May 1915, p. 8.

[242] Ibid.

[243] Ibid.

[244] Ibid.

[245] "Editorial Paragraph," Chicago Defender, 15 May 1915, p. 8.

[246] "Killing a Film" Chicago Defender, 22 May 1915, p. 2.

[247] "A Misnomer That's All," Chicago Defender, 29 May 1915, p. 8.

[248] "The Dirt of a Nation," Chicago Defender, 5 June 1915, p. 3.

[249] Ibid.

[250] Ibid.

[251] Ibid.

[252] "Keep Up The Fight," Chicago Defender, 11 September 1915, p. 8.

[253] Ibid.

[254] "Editorial Paragraph," Chicago Defender, 30 October 1915, p. 8.

[255] Ibid.

[256] "Unwarranted Advertising," Chicago Defender, 13 November 1915, p. 8.

[257] Ibid.

[258] "The Clansman," Western Outlook, 20 February 1915, p. 2.

[259] "The Melting Pot," Chicago Defender, 24 July 1915, p. 8.

[260] Ibid.

[261] Ibid.

[262] "The Last Cat," Chicago Defender, 23 October 1915, p. 9.

[263] Ibid. The individuals probably represented are W. K. Vardaman, Ben Tillman, and Cole L. Blease. Vardaman was a Mississippi politician who in one speech said "The way to control the nigger is to whip him when he does not obey without it and another is never to pay him more wages than is actually necessary to buy food and clothing." (See W. J. Cash, The Mind of the South (New York: Vintage Books, 1969), p. 253. Historian W. J Cash identified South Carolinan Tillman as the archtypical southern demagogue who "brought his nigger-baiting down to the levels of the more brutal sort." (See Cash, p. 253). South Carolinan Blease defended lynching and in one speech said "Whenever the Constitution comes between me and the virtue of the white women of the South, I say to hell with the Constitution." (See Cash, p. 253). Cash said the Negrophobia of these three Southern politicians represented the "most brutal viewpoint in Dixie." (See Cash, p. 254).

[264] "Editorial on 'Birth of a Nation' Reprinted from 'The Independent," Chicago Defender, 30 October 1915, p. 8.

[265] "Birth of Nation' Denounced Vitriolic Editorial From Kansas City, Mo. Leading Daily," Chicago Defender, 30 October 1915, p. 1.

[266] Ibid.

[267] "Duluth Editor Shows Broad Mind," Chicago Defender, 6 November 1915, p. 1.

[268] Ibid.

[269] "Father and Three Sons Assassinated For Raising The First Cotton," Chicago Defender, 30 October 1915, p. 1.

[270] Ibid. The photo of the dead men suspended from a tree is reproduced with the commentary.

[271] "The Birth of a Nation," St. Louis Argus, 16 April 1915, p. 2.

[272] Ibid.

[273] Ibid.

[274] "Protest Against 'The Birth of a Nation," St. Louis Argus, 28 May 1915, p. 1.

[275] "Protest Now," St. Louis Argus, 28 May 1915, p. 4.

[276] "Can The Leopard Change His Spots?", St. Louis Argus, 11 June 1915, p. 4.

[277] "The Birth of a Nation," St. Louis Argus, 27 August 1915, p. 4.

[278] Ibid.

[279] "Keep Up The Protest," St. Louis Argus, 3 September 1915, p. 4.

[280] Ibid.

[281] Ibid.

[282] "Why Not Protest?", St. Louis Argus, 17 September 1915, p. 4.

[283] "A Contributory Evil," St. Louis Argus, 17 September 1915, p. 4.

[284] Ibid.

[285] Ibid.

[286] Ibid.

[287] "Judge Hennings Decision," St. Louis Argus, 24 September 1915, p. 4.

[288] "The Fallacy Proven," St. Louis Argus, 1 October 1915, p. 4.

[289] Ibid.

[290] "The KKK and 'Birth of a Nation," St. Louis Argus, 19 November 1915, p. 4.

[291] "Editorial Graph," Cleveland Gazette, 17 April 1915, p. 2.

[292] "Editorial Graph," Cleveland Gazette, 24 April 1915, p. 2.

[293] "Editorial Graph," Cleveland Gazette, 22 May 1915, p. 2.

[294] "Be on the Lookout!", Cleveland Gazette, 3 July 1915, p. 2.

[295] "The Birth (Dirt) of a Nation," Cleveland Gazette, 18 September 1915, p. 2. Smith specifically charged the black newspapers in Chicago and New York with lying.

296Ibid. Smith was extremely critical of the N. Y. Age and the Chicago Defender and said "When will the editors of those newspapers tumble." Smith was specifically referring to columns by Ralph W. Tyler published in the Defender and the Age and the Pittsburgh Courier. Smith was critical of Tyler because Tyler credited "a white man Daniel J. Ryan" for leading the battle against The Birth in Cleveland because Tyler attacked Ohio Governor Frank Willis (See Ralph Tyler, "Why 'Birth of Nation' Should Not Be Allowed to Play," Chicago Defender, 9 October 1915, p. 3). In one editorial statement attacking Tyler directly Smith called him "a versatile curse." (See "These dispose of Tyler's 'Stories," Cleveland Gazette, 9 October 1915, p. 2, reprinted under same head Cleveland Gazette, 16 October 1915, p. 1). In another editorial comment Smith called Tyler's writing "rot" and said it was obvious several black papers had not "yet realized the mean, low, and contemptable advantage" Tyler was taking of them. Smith also called Tyler a "chronic grouch and marplot." (See "Special to the New York Age," Cleveland Gazette, 20 November 1915, p. 2. Reprinted under same head, 27 November 1915, p. 2).

297"Another Great Victory," Cleveland Gazette, 2 October 1915, p. 2.

298See "Another Great Victory," Cleveland Gazette on following dates and pages: 9 October 1915, p. 3; 16 October 1915, p. 1; 23 October 1915, p. 1; 6 November 1915, p. 2; 20 November 1915, p. 2; and, 27 November 1915, p. 2.

299"Editorial Graph," Cleveland Gazette, 23 October 1915, p. 2. Smith again asked the newspaper editors in those cities to answer his question.

300"Editorial Graph," Cleveland Gazette, 7 August 1915, p. 2.

301"Birth of a Nation," Cleveland Gazette, 28 August 1915, p. 2.

302"Governor Willis of Ohio," Cleveland Gazette, 22 May 1915, p. 1. Although not really editorials nor letters to the editor, the Gazette also ran a number of letters Smith wrote to various people in opposition to the film. For example, Smith wrote letters to Willis and to Wallace D. Yaple in opposition to The Birth and reproduced those protest letters in the Gazette. (See Harry Smith to Frank Willis, Cleveland Gazette, 10 April 1915, p. 2, and Harry Smith to Wallace Yaple, 10 April 1915, p. 2). Smith also reproduced a letter he had written to the editor of the Cleveland Plain Dealer. In this letter Smith commented on the nature of protests concerning The Birth in other cities and said Monroe Trotter did not "stir up" the Boston disturbance and that "politics had absolutely nothing to do with the Philadelphia demonstration."

(See Harry Smith to Editor Plain Dealer, <u>Cleveland Gazette</u>, 12 February 1916, p. 2). Perhaps of most interest within the context of this research was a letter written by Smith to Julian Solomon. In this letter Smith said that "freedom of speech an American institution sounds nice but there is certain kind of speech freedom the American government and none other tolerate and that is the sort of rot some photoplays contain that make censorship absolutely necessary." Thus, Smith specifically stated <u>The Birth</u> was not entitled to free speech protection. (See Harry Smith to Julian Solomon, <u>Cleveland Gazette</u>, 16 October 1915, p. 2).

[303] "Reprinted From St. Paul Appeal," <u>Cleveland Gazette</u>, 18 September 1915, p. 2.

[304] "Editorial Graph," <u>Philadelphia Tribune</u>, 10 April 1915, p. 4.

[305] Ibid.

[306] "The Birth of a Nation," <u>Philadelphia Tribune</u>, 10 April 1915, p. 4.

[307] Ibid.

[308] Ibid.

[309] "The Birth of a Nation in Philadelphia Now," <u>Philadelphia Tribune</u>, 11 September 1915, p. 4.

[310] "The Birth of a Nation Still in the Making," <u>Philadelphia Tribune</u>, 23 October 1915, p. 4.

[311] L. T. Parker, "Let All Cry--Away With 'The Birth of a Nation," <u>Philadelphia Tribune</u>, 27 March 1915, p. 1.

[312] Ibid.

[313] "No Censorship," <u>Philadelphia Tribune</u>, 25 September 1915, p. 4.

[314] "The Bad Blood That Makes for Race Strife," <u>Philadelphia Tribune</u>, 25 September 1915, p. 4.

[315] Ibid.

[316] "Consistency," <u>Baltimore Ledger</u>, 20 March 1915, p. 4.

[317] Ibid.

[318] Ibid.

[319] Ibid.

[320] "The Birth of a Nation," Baltimore Ledger, 5 June 1915, p. 4.

[321] "Editorial Graph," Baltimore Ledger, 4 September 1915, p. 4.

[322] "Editorial Graph," Baltimore Ledger, 18 September 1915, p. 4.

[323] Ibid.

[324] "Editorial Graph," Baltimore Ledger, 23 October 1915, p. 4.

[325] "A Damnable Photoplay," Twin City Star, 16 October 1915, p. 4.

[326] "A Damnable Photoplay," Twin City Star, 27 November 1915, p. 2.

[327] "A Peaceful Protest," Twin City Star, 16 October 1915, p. 4.

[328] Ibid.

[329] "A Means To An End," Twin City Star, 27 November 1915, p. 4.

[330] Ibid.

[331] Ibid.

[332] "Attorney B. S. Smith of Minneapolis Makes An Eloquent Address Against Exhibition of 'The Birth of a Nation," Twin City Star, 27 November 1915, p. 1.

[333] "The Birth of a Nation," St. Paul Appeal, 23 October 1915, p. 2.

[334] Ibid.

[335] "It Pays to Agitate," St. Paul Appeal, 20 November 1915, p. 2.

[336] Ibid.

[337] "Lament 'The Birth of a Nation," St. Paul Appeal, 30 October 1915, p. 2.

338"Must Come Clean," St. Paul Appeal, 12 June 1915, p. 2.

339Ibid.

340See "Must Come Clean," St. Paul Appeal, on the following dates and pages, 19 June 1915, p. 2; 26 June 1915, p. 2; 3 July 1915, p. 2.

341"The Birth of a Nation," St. Paul Appeal, 12 June 1915, p. 2.

342See "The Birth of a Nation," St. Paul Appeal on the following dates and pages, 19 June 1915, p. 2; 26 June 1915, p. 2; 3 July 1915, p. 2; 25 September 1915, p. 2; 2 October 1915, p. 1.

343"Editorial Paragraph," Indianapolis Freeman, 17 April 1915, p. 4.

344"The Birth of a Nation," Indianapolis Freeman, 17 April 1915, p. 4.

345Ibid.

346"Tom Dixon Tries to Defend the Clansman," Indianapolis Freeman, 17 April 1915, p. 1.

347"Editorial Graph," Indianapolis Freeman, 24 April 1915, p. 4.

348"News of the Nations Metropolis," Indianapolis Freeman, 24 April 1915, p. 1.

349Ibid.

350Ibid.

351Ibid.

352"The Birth of a Nation," Indianapolis Freeman, 1 May 1915, p. 4.

353Ibid.

354Ibid.

355Monroe Work, Negro Yearbook 1914-1916 (n.p.: Negro Yearbook, 1916), p. 48.

356Ibid.

[357] Ibid.

[358] Ibid.

[359] Ibid.

[360] "Still Protesting 'Birth," *Variety*, 20 December 1923, p. 20.

[361] "Protest Film," *Kansas City Call*, 7 December 1923, p. 1.

[362] "A New Era of Good Will and Racial Co-Operation," *Kansas City Call*, 8 February 1924, p. 4.

[363] Ibid.

[364] "An Encourager of Race Hatred," *Topeka Daily Capital*, 19 June 1923, n.p., reproduced in Press Release, 29 June 1923, NAACP Archives, File C302.

[365] "Wichita, Kansas Bars 'Birth of Nation' After *Protest* and N.A.A.C.P. Take Action," 8 June 1923, Press Release in NAACP Archives, File C302.

[366] "A Champion Worth While," *St. Paul Pioneer Press*, 28 October 1915, p. 8.

[367] "Will Be Damned Either Way," *St. Paul Pioneer Press*, 27 October 1915, p. 8.

[368] Federal Motion Picture Commission Hearings on H. R. 456, p. 226.

[369] Work, *Negro Yearbook*, p. 47.

[370] Ibid.

[371] Ibid.

[372] Federal Motion Picture Commission Hearings, p. 223.

[373] Ibid., p. 224

[374] Ibid.

[375] Ibid.

[376] "Better Think That Over," *St. Paul Pioneer Press*, 16 October 1915, p. 6.

[377] "The Police As Censors," St. Paul Pioneer Press, 19 October 1915, p. 8.

[378] "The Curse of a Nation," Boston Evening Transcript, 23 April 1915, p. 12.

[379] Ibid.

[380] Ibid.

[381] Ibid.

[382] "Kill The Sullivan Bill," Boston Evening Transcript, 26 April 1915, p. 17.

[383] "Menace of Censorship," Springfield Republican, reprinted in Boston Evening Transcript, 26 April 1915, p. 12.

[384] "Kill The Sullivan Bill."

[385] "A Sensible Solution," Boston Evening Transcript, 30 April 1915, p. 10.

[386] Ibid.

[387] "The Birth of a Nation," Boston Morning Journal, 23 April 1915, p. 8.

[388] Ibid.

[389] Ibid.

[390] "The Nigger," Washington Bee, 1 May 1915, p. 4.

[391] Lester A. Walton, "A Patron of the Arts."

[392] Ibid.

[393] Ibid.

[394] Ibid.

[395] "The Birth of a Nation," Chicago Tribune, 6 February 1924, p. 8.

[396] Ibid.

[397] "Birth of a Nation," New York Times, 17 February 1915, p. 42.

[398] Ibid.

[399] Ibid.

[400] "Editorial Note," St. Paul Pioneer Press, 28 October 1915, p. 8.

[401] A Southern Subscriber to The Editor, St. Paul Pioneer Press, 27 October 1915, p. 8.

[402] A Subscriber to The Editor, St. Paul Pioneer Press, 25 October 1915, p. 6.

[403] Clarence M. Tibbs to The Editor, St. Paul Pioneer Press, 26 October 1915, p. 6.

[404] J. Broddy to The Editor, St. Paul Pioneer Press, 11 October 1915, p. 6.

[405] Ibid.

[406] Charles E. Mackean to The Editor, St. Paul Pioneer Press, 22 October 1915, p. 12.

[407] Citizen to The Editor, St. Paul Pioneer Press, 22 October 1915, p. 12.

[408] B. to The Editor, St. Paul Pioneer Press, 22 October 1915, p. 12.

[409] S. V. W. to The Editor, St. Paul Pioneer Press, 21 October 1915, p. 8.

[410] A White Woman to The Editor, St. Paul Pioneer Press, 23 October 1915, p. 8.

[411] Naomi to The Editor, St. Paul Pioneer Press, 20 October 1915, p. 10

[412] Ibid.

[413] D. T. Stetson to The Editor, St. Paul Pioneer Press, 19 October 1915, p. 8.

[414] Ibid.

[415] C. Calsin to The Editor, St. Paul Pioneer Press, 19 October 1915, p. 8.

[416] Willis Drummond to The Editor, St. Paul Pioneer Press, 18 October 1915, p. 4.

[417] Dingbat to The Editor, St. Paul Pioneer Press, 18 October 1915, p. 4.

[418] Y. R. U. to The Editor, St. Paul Pioneer Press, 27 October 1915, p. 8.

[419] One Who Has Seen to The Editor, St. Paul Pioneer Press, 26 October 1915, p. 6.

[420] Some Personal Notes to The Editor, New York Age, 20 May 1915, p. 1.

[421] Ibid.

[422] William H. Keller to The Editor, New York Age, 14 October 1915, p. 4.

[423] Ibid.

[424] Rosalie M. Jonas to The Editor, New York Age, 25 March 1915, p. 4.

[425] Ibid.

[426] "The Dixon Play at Dr. Reisners Church," New York Age, 21 October 1915, p. 1.

[427] Ibid.

[428] Rev. Grammer to The Editor, Baltimore Ledger, 9 October 1915, p. 7.

[429] Ibid.

[430] D. R. Wallace to The Editor, Western Outlook, 15 May 1915, p. 2.

[431] Beulah Kennard to The Editor, New York Sun, 13 March 1915, n.p., clipping in D. W. Griffith's personal scrapbook, MOMA Archives.

[432] J. C. Jenkins to The Editor, Evening Post, 14 March 1915, n.p., clipping in MOMA Archives, D. W. Griffith's Personal Birth of a Nation scrapbook.

[433] Mary Jane Review to The Editor, New York Tribune, 15 March 1915, n.p., clipping in MOMA Archives, D. W. Griffith Personal Birth of a Nation scrapbook.

[434]Thomas Dixon to The Editor, New York Globe, 10 April 1915, Reprinted in Silva, pp. 75-77.

[435]Ibid.

[436]Ibid.

[437]Ibid.

[438]D. W. Griffith to The Editor, New York Globe, 10 April 1915, reprinted in Silva, pp. 77-79.

[439]Ibid.

[440]Ibid.

[441]Ibid.

[442]Thomas Dixon to The Editor, Boston Morning Journal, 26 April 1915, p. 4.

[443]Ibid.

[444]Ibid.

[445]Ibid.

[446]Ibid.

[447]Booker T. Washington to The Editor, Chicago Defender, 22 May 1915, p. 1.

[448]Ibid.

[449]Ibid.

[450]Ibid.

[451]"Griffith Film Protested," New York Times, 4 February 1941, n.p., clipping in Lincoln Center Archives, Birth of a Nation folder.

[452]Ibid.

[453]"Not Showing in San Antonio," Variety, 24 March 1965, p. 82.

[454]No Head, The Daily Compass, 17 May 1950.

[455]No Head, New York Times, 19 May 1950.

[456] "Birth of Nation' Opens in Philly; 40 Pickets Against 150 Patrons," *Variety*, 24 March 1965, pp. 2 & 82.

[457] M. M. Payne to Manager Willard Straight Theatre, 23 November 1937, copy of letter in MOMA Archives, D. W. Griffith Personal Papers.

[458] The information was not included in the sources consulted for this research listed in the bibliography.

[459] "Des Moines Showman Books 'Birth of Nation' Disclaims Race Bias," *Variety*, 16 December 1970, n.p., clipping in Lincoln Center Archives, *Birth of a Nation* folder.

[460] The information was not included in the sources consulted for this research listed in the bibliography.

[461] "Film Withdrawn," *Newark Evening News*, 15 November 1960, n.p., clipping in Lincoln Center Archives, *Birth of a Nation* Folder. See also, "1914 Film Stirs Student Protest At College in N. J.," *New York Herald Tribune*, 13 November 1960, n.p., clipping Lincoln Center Archives, *Birth of a Nation* Folder.

[462] "Protest Showing of 1915 Film," *New York World Journal Tribune*, 28 September 1966, n.p., clipping in Lincoln Center Archives, *Birth of a Nation* Folder.

[463] "NAACP Implores Sterling Lay Off 'Birth of Nation," *Variety*, 13 May 1959, n.p., clipping in Lincoln Center Archives, *Birth of a Nation* Folder.

[464] Ibid.

[465] Paul Killiam, "Sterling Sets NAACP's Mind At Rest On Use of 'Birth of Nation," *Variety*, 3 June 1959, n.p., clipping in Lincoln Center Archives, *Birth of a Nation* Folder.

[466] Ibid.

[467] Ibid.

[468] Ibid.

[469] "Birth' Too Deadly for TV," *Variety*, 7 June 1961, n.p., clipping in Lincoln Center Archives, *Birth of a Nation* Folder.

[470] "Shoot At Screen: 'Birth of Nation' in Irish-Jewish Neighborhood Causes Rumpus," *Variety*, 4 June 1924, p. 3.

[471] Ibid.

[472]"The Birth of Nation' In Story Form By Gertrude Stevenson," *Boston Morning Journal*, 3 May 1915, p. 1.

[473]"Beginning in Monday's Journal 'The Birth of Nation' In Story Form Written by Gertrude Stevenson," *Boston Morning Journal*, 30 April 1915, p. 7.

[474]Advertisement for East Kinloch, *St. Louis Argus*, 10 September 1915, p. 2.

[475]Ibid.

[476]The advertisement was repeated in the *Argus* on the following dates and pages: 17 September 1915, p. 2; 24 September 1915, p. 2; 1 October 1915, p. 2; 8 October 1915, p. 2; 15 October 1915, p. 2; 22 October 1915, p. 2; 29 October 1915, p. 2; 5 November 1915, p. 2; 12 November 1915, p. 2.

[477]For example, see "Protest Against 'The Birth of a Nation," *St. Louis Argus* and "Protest Now," *St. Louis Argus*.

[478]In this chapter, each individual extra-legal action was counted only once. Thus, even if an editorial was run more than one time or was reprinted in another newspaper, it was only counted as one extra-legal action.

[479]As discussed in the Conclusions section of this chapter, this figure is probably misleading because the *Boston Guardian* is not extant for this time period. It is highly probable that the *Guardian* editorialized against the film.

[480]236 U.S. 230

[481]*Joseph Burstyn, Inc. v. Wilson*, 343 U.S. 495, 96 L. Ed. 1098, 72 S. Ct. 777 (1952).

CHAPTER VIII

ANALYSIS AND CONCLUSIONS

During the time period 1915-1973, _The Birth of a Nation_'s right to the screen was challenged at least 120 times. Five major tactics were implemented within the resulting censorship controversies fought at the local, state and national levels. Tactics employed to accomplish controversy resolution were: initiating court action or criminal proceedings; petitioning officials to use administrative power; seeking censorship legislation; and, utilizing extra-legal means. These five tactics were operationalized through individual actions. Specifically, the number of actions taken regarding the film in the 120 controversies studied is 356. In a majority of the controversies (111) censorship of the film was debated directly. In the remaining nine instances the controversy manifested itself as a drive for legislation which could later be used against the film. In addition, 20 extra-legal actions existed independently of the 120 controversies. Thus, rather than being tied to a specific screening, 20 actions were designed to mobilize public opinion either for or against the film's right to the screen in general.

In order to answer the questions posed by this research, it is necessary to perform several levels of analysis on the data. First, controversies in which censorship was debated directly will be analyzed in terms of ultimate resolution. Next, tactics will be analyzed to determine overall effectiveness in relation to controversy resolution. Finally, actions which did not resolve controversies will be discussed.

Resolution of Controversies in Which Censorship Debated Directly

As indicated previously, 111 controversies concerning directly the film's right to the screen in a given community are discussed in this study. The ultimate resolution in terms of the film's right to the screen was recorded in the sources consulted for 94 of the 111 controversies. The remainder of this section of the analysis refers only to the 94 controversies with documented resolutions. Seventy-five controversies with known resolutions concerned censorship at the local level, 17 controversies involved censorship at the state level, and two controversies of known resolution dealt with censorship at the national level. Total or partial censorship of The Birth resolved 59 controversies. In the remaining 35 controversies the film was not censored. These figures are significant (x^2 = 6.13, $<.02$). From this it can be concluded that the film was censored with a frequency that differs from random. Specific types of actions resolving controversies are presented in table 25.

TABLE 25

TYPES OF SPECIFIC ACTIONS RESOLVING CONTROVERSIES

Prior Restraint	Prior Restraint Partial	Subsequent Restraint	Subsequent Restraint Partial	No Censorship
35	4	15	5	35

The figures presented in table 25 are highly significant ($x^2 = 50.4$, $< .001$). In addition to supporting the generalization that controversies were more likely than not to be resolved with some form of censorship, these figures indicate that controversies tended to be resolved by actions regarding the film as a whole. Also, if the categories prior restraint partial, subsequent restraint, subsequent restraint partial, and no censorship are combined the resulting total indicates that the film in some form or for some time was screened in 59 of the 94 controversies. When the number of times the film was screened is compared with the number of times the film was not screened for any time or in any form, the resulting differences are significant ($x^2 = 6.127$, $< .02$). Therefore, throughout the years of this study in terms of individual censorship controversies, the film was screened either in its entirety, with modifications, or for some time with a frequency that differs from random. Thus, even though the film was censored with a frequency that differed from random, the film was more likely than not to be screened in some form or for some time during each controversy. Therefore, prior restraint _per se_ cannot be considered a highly effective weapon against the film during the years studied. To determine whether the above generalizations hold for all controversies regardless of tactic employed, controversy level, or year of resolution, it is necessary to extend the data analysis.

As discussed previously, the number of The Birth censorship controversies for which resolution could be documented was 94. In 88 instances controversy resolutions were accomplished through the direct implementation of one of four major tactics. Specifically, as indicated in table 26, 56 controversies were resolved by administrative intervention, 22 controversies were resolved by court decisions, nine controversies were resolved through extra-legal means, and three were resolved by criminal proceedings. Two controversies were not specifically resolved by the implementation of any tactic. Rather, in these two cases the controversies ended when the film's opponents after trying various approaches acquiesced to the film's supporters. The ultimate status of the film's right to the screen in the remaining two cases is documented, but the manner in which these decisions were made is unclear in the sources consulted.[1] Because legislative action was not directed toward individual controversy resolution, that tactic is not considered in this section of the analysis. Censorship/no censorship decisions resolving controversies by tactic are presented in table 26.

TABLE 26

CONTROVERSY RESOLUTION BY TACTIC

Tactic Resolving Controversy	Censorship	No Censorship	Total
Official	43	13	56
Court	6	16	22
Extra-legal	6	3	9
Acquiesce	0	2	2
Criminal proceeding	2	1	3
Unclear manner of resolution	2	0	2

The figures shown in table 26 regarding the number of controversies resolved by officials in favor of censorship and the number resolved in favor of the film are significant ($x^2 = 16.06$, $< .02$). Therefore, it can be seen that officials resolved controversies in favor of censorship with a frequency that differs from chance. On the other hand, the figures indicating the censorship/no censorship decisions rendered by court action are not significant ($x^2 = 4.54$, $> .02$). Thus, courts resolved controversies in favor of censorship/no censorship with a frequency that did not differ from chance. The number of controversies resolved by each of the other major tactics, criminal proceedings and extra-legal means, was too small for independent statistical analysis. However, if the two categories are combined, the resulting figures are not significant ($x^2 = 1.33$, $> .02$). The number of controversies resolved through acquiescence and for which the tactic resolving the controversy is unknown were judged too small for independent analysis even when combined. However, two-thirds of these decisions supported the film and one-third supported censorship. Therefore, the overall study finding (that in resolved controversies, the film was censored with a frequency that differs from chance) applies independently only to the tactic of administrative intervention. It appears that if a controversy was resolved by any means other than administrative intervention, the resulting decision would support the film or censorship with a frequency that does not differ from chance. Thus, in general tactics other than administrative intervention were not successful in reliably accomplishing the goals of either the film's supporters or opponents.

It is possible to magnify this finding by analyzing specific types of actions taken. Specific actions resolving controversies by tactic are shown in table 27. When considered individually, differences among the specific types of decisions made by courts and by officials are significant (for officials, $x^2 = 30.9$, $< .001$; for courts, $x^2 = 33.92$, $< .001$). Because the number of controversies resolved by criminal proceedings and by extra-legal means was judged too small for independent analysis, the categories were combined. The resulting figures are not significant ($x^2 = 2.6$, $> .02$). The number of controversies resolved through acquiescence and through unclear means was judged too small for independent analysis even when combined. However, all controversies resolved through acquiescence ended with no censorship. In one case resolved through unclear means, prior restraint was exercised against the film and in the remaining case subsequent restraint was exercised. Thus, the individual types of decisions rendered by officials and by courts supported the overall study finding that controversies were more likely than not to be resolved by some form of censorship and that the controversies tended to be resolved by actions regarding the film as a whole. Also, the controversies resolved through acquiescence and for which the manner of resolution is unclear seem to support the findings.

To determine whether the finding indicating that the film was more likely than not to be screened during each controversy held regardless of the manner in which the controversy was resolved, the categories prior restraint partial, subsequent restraint, subsequent restraint partial, and no censorship were combined and compared to the category of prior restraint for each agency resolving controversies. The resulting figures are significant for controversies resolved by courts ($x^2 = 8.9$, $< .001$) but not for controversies resolved by officials ($x^2 = .071$, $> .02$). Controversies resolved through extra-legal means and through criminal proceedings were considered together and the resulting figures were not significant ($x^2 = .4$, $> .02$). Again, the number of controversies resolved through acquiescence and through uncertain means was judged too small to determine independent statistical significance. However, because the film was screened in five controversies and not screened in only one, these two categories seem to support the overall finding.

TABLE 27

ACTIONS RESOLVING CONTROVERSIES BY TACTIC

Controversy Resolved By	Prior Restraint	Prior Restraint Partial	Subsequent Restraint	Subsequent Restraint Partial	No Censorship
Official	27	3	10	3	13
Court	3	1	1	1	16
Extra-Legal	4	0	1	1	3
Criminal proceedings	0	0	2	0	1
Acquiescence	0	0	0	0	2
Unclear	1	0	0	0	0

Thus, the film was more likely than not to be screened during any controversy resolved by a court decision. However, the film was screened or not screened in some form or for some time during controversies resolved by officials, extra-legal means, or criminal proceedings with a frequency that does not differ from random.

In summary, the overall findings of the study concerning censorship actions resolving controversies were found to be true regarding certain tactics resolving controversies but not for others. The finding that the film was censored with a frequency differing from random was true independently only for those controversies resolved by administrative intervention. Controversies resolved through all other means ended in censorship/no censorship decisions with frequencies not differing from random. The finding concerning the likelihood that the film would be screened during any controversy with a frequency differing from chance applied independently only to those controversies resolved by court action. When considered together, controversy resolutions reached through acquiescence and through unclear means also appear to support this finding. However, during controversies resolved by officials, by criminal proceedings, or by extra-legal means, the film was screened/not screened with a frequency not differing from random.

Resolved controversies included debates over screenings at the local, state, and national levels. Resolved controversies at the local level outnumbered resolved controversies at the state level by more than four to one. Only two controversies were resolved at the national level. One national controversy concerned a proposed television showing of the film and one national controversy was resolved through the actions of a motion picture industry self-regulatory body. Because the number of controversies at the national level was so small, these figures were not tested for independent statistical significance. The number of controversies by level and resolution are presented in table 28.

When the overall frequencies of controversies resolved at the state and local levels are tested for independence, the resulting figure is not significant ($x^2 = .716, > .02$). Therefore, it can be concluded that in general controversy resolution functioned independently of controversy level. However, when considered individually, censorship decisions rendered at the local level differ from chance ($x^2 = 5.88, < .02$); but decisions at the state level do not differ from chance ($x^2 = .058, > .02$). Thus, controversies at the local level were more likely to be resolved by some form of censorship action than they were to be resolved by an action supporting the film. This finding is consistent with that found for controversy resolution regardless of level. However, state controversies were not resolved in favor of censorship or in favor of the film with a frequency that differs from random. Thus, the resolution of controversies at the state level does not support the overall study finding concerning controversy resolution.

TABLE 28

CONTROVERSY RESOLUTION BY LEVEL

Level	Censorship	No Censorship	Total
Local	48	27	75
State	9	8	17
National	2	0	2
Total	59	35	94

To further dissect this finding it is possible to analyze controversy resolutions by level and specific action taken. Specific actions taken regarding the film by level are shown in table 29. Again, when controversy level and specific actions are analyzed for independence, the resulting figure is not significant ($x^2 = 9.88$, $> .02$). Therefore, it can be concluded that specific actions taken were independent of controversy level. However, once again differences among the frequencies of actions at the local level are significant ($x^2 = 36.9$, $< .001$), but differences among actions taken at the state level are not significant ($x^2 = 9.88$, $> .02$). From this it can be concluded that the manner in which controversies were resolved at the state level did not differ from chance. However, the manner in which controversies were resolved at the local level did. These finding reinforce the conclusion that at the local level controversies were more likely than not to be resolved by some form of censorship action. However, at the state level censorship/no censorship decisions were made with a frequency that does not differ from random. Regardless of level, controversies tended to be resolved by actions dealing with the film as a whole. The number of controversies resolved at the national level was judged too small for independent statistical analysis. However, both decisions supported some form of censorship.

TABLE 29

SPECIFIC ACTIONS RESOLVING CONTROVERSIES BY LEVEL

Level	Prior Restraint	Prior Restraint Partial	Subsequent Restraint	Subsequent Restraint Partial	No Censorship
Local	27	3	14	4	27
State	7	1	0	0	8
National	1	0	0	1	0

To determine whether the film was screened or not screened during controversies with a frequency that differed by level, the categories prior restraint partial, subsequent restraint, subsequent restraint partial, and no censorship were combined for each level. The resulting figures indicate that at the local level the film was screened in some form or for some time in 48 controversies and not screened in 27. These figures are significant (x^2 = 5.88, $<.02$). Therefore, although local controversies were resolved with some form of censorship with a frequency that differs from random, the film was also likely to be screened during each controversy for some time or in some form with a frequency that differs from chance. However, at the state level, the film was screened in 10 controversies and not screened in 7. These figures are not significant (x^2 = .2647, $>.02$). Therefore, the film was as likely as not to be screened during each state controversy. Again, independent statistical analysis was not performed on national controversies because the number of such resolved controversies was too small.

Overall, controversy resolution was found to be independent of controversy level. However, when levels were considered individually, the overall findings of the study concerning censorship actions were found to apply to controversies resolved at the local level but not to controversies resolved at the state level. Local controversies were found to be resolved by actions supportive of censorship with a frequency differing from random. State controversies were not. Also, the finding concerning the likelihood that the film would be screened during any controversy with a frequency differing from chance was true for local controversies but not for state. Regardless of level, controversies tended to be resolved by actions considering the film as a whole.

Resolved controversies were also analyzed according to year of resolution. Controversies were found to be resolved from 1915-1966. Censorship/no censorship decisions by year are presented in table 30. From table 30 it can be seen that more censorship controversies were resolved during 1915 than any other year studied. During 1915, The Birth's right to the screen was debated at least 31 times. Fourteen controversies were resolved with some form of censorship and 17 were resolved with no censorship. These differences are not significant ($x^2 = .29$, $> .02$). Therefore, during 1915, controversies were resolved with censorship or no censorship with a frequency that does not differ from chance. The number of controversies

TABLE 30

CONTROVERSY RESOLUTION BY YEAR

Year	Censorship	No Censorship	Total
1915	14	17	31
1916	1	1	2
1917	0	2	2
1918	8	2	10
1920	1	0	1
1921	3	2	5
1922	2	0	2
1923	0	1	1
1924	4	4	8
1925	4	1	5
1930	1	0	1
1931	9	1	10
1938	2	0	2
1939	2	0	2
1940	1	0	1
1941	1	0	1
1950	0	1	1
1952	1	0	1
1958	0	1	1
1959	2	0	2
1960	1	0	1
1961	1	0	1
1965	1	1	2
1966	0	1	1

resolved in only two other years, 1918 and 1931, was judged large enough for independent statistical analysis. In 1918, eight controversies were resolved with some form of censorship and two were resolved with a decision in favor of the film. These figures are not significant ($x^2 = 2.25$, $> .02$). However, in 1931, nine controversies were resolved with some form of censorship and one was resolved with a ruling in favor of the film. These figures are significant ($x^2 = 6.4$, $< .02$). Thus, controversies were resolved during 1931 in a pattern consistent with the overall study finding that controversies were resolved with censorship with a frequency differing from random. However, if a controversy was resolved during either 1915 or 1918, the decision would support censorship with a frequency that does not differ from chance. The number of controversies resolved during each of the remaining years studied was not large enough for independent analysis. However, if the categories are collapsed the resulting figures are not significant ($x^2 = 2.59$, $> .02$). It is interesting to split the time analysis into two segments, pre-Burstyn 1915-1951, and post-Burstyn 1952-1973. During the pre-Burstyn period 53 controversies were resolved with censorship and 32 were resolved by no censorship. These figures are not significant ($x^2 = 5.188$, $> .02$). During the post-Burstyn period, 1952-1973, six controversies were resolved with censorship and three were resolved with no censorship. These figures are also not significant ($x^2 = .44$, $> .02$). Therefore, during both the pre- and post-Burstyn time periods, controversies were resolved in favor of censorship or in favor of the film with a frequency not differing from random. Thus, it appears that overall controversy resolution was independent of controversy year.

To determine whether tactics accomplishing controversy resolution were concentrated in any given time period, the two factors were compared. The resulting figures are presented in table 31. From table 31, it appears that most tactics accomplishing resolution did not concentrate in certain time periods. Rather, tactics successful in controversy resolution tended to span the years of the study. For example, administrative intervention resolved controversies from 1915-1961. Court decisions resolved controversies from 1915-1952. The success of extra-legal tactics spanned the years in which resolved controversies were identified, 1915-1966.

Decisions to censor or not to censor the film were justified with a variety of rationales. Specifically, at least nine rationales justifying censorship were found to be expressed in 35 of the controversies resolved. In the remaining eight controversies resolved with censorship, the rationales for censorship are unclear. On the other hand, the rationales underlying 15 decisions not to censor the film are unclear. The remaining 16 decisions not to censor were explained by one of five rationales. Because rationales justifying censorship and justifying no censorship differed, the two types of actions are split for this analysis.

During the time period studied, the rationale expressed most frequently by those ordering censorship in resolved controversies

TABLE 31

TACTICS RESOLVING CONTROVERSIES BY YEAR

Year	Official	Court	Extra-Legal	Acquiescence	Criminal Proceedings	Unclear
1915	20	10	1	0	0	0
1916	0	1	0	0	1	0
1917	1	1	0	0	0	0
1918	7	3	0	0	0	0
1920	0	0	0	0	0	1
1921	2	1	0	1	0	1
1922	2	0	0	0	0	0
1923	1	0	0	0	0	0
1924	4	2	1	1	0	0
1925	3	2	0	0	0	0
1930	1	0	0	0	0	0
1931	9	1	0	0	0	0
1938	1	0	0	0	1	0
1939	2	0	0	0	0	0
1940	0	0	0	0	1	0
1941	0	0	1	0	0	0
1950	0	0	1	0	0	0
1952	0	1	0	0	0	0
1958	1	0	0	0	0	0
1959	1	0	1	0	0	0
1960	0	0	1	0	0	0
1961	1	0	0	0	0	0
1965	0	0	2	0	0	0
1966	0	0	1	0	0	0

was that the film would engender racial prejudice. Specifically, 17 controversies were resolved by individuals expressing this rationale. An additional 14 controversies were resolved with censorship orders which came directly after black protests. Other rationales justifying censorship were: the film was immoral or obscene; the film was unpatriotic; the film was detrimental to public peace; the film was not harmless; the film violated blacks' moral rights; the film was unfit for decent people; and, the film's screeners violated some procedural element. In order to determine whether certain types of rationales were used more frequently to justify certain types of actions, resolved controversies were analyzed by rationales and censorship action. The resulting figures are presented in table 32.

TABLE 32

RATIONALES JUSTIFYING CENSORSHIP BY SPECIFIC ACTION

Rationale	Prior Restraint	Prior Restraint Partial	Subsequent Restraint	Subsequent Restraint Partial	No Censorship
Racial prejudice	9	1	6	1	17
After black protest	12	0	2	0	14
Immoral/ obscene	1	1	0	2	4
Patriotism	2	0	0	0	2
Detrimental public peace	1	0	0	0	1
Procedural	2	1	2	1	6

Unfit decent people	1	0	0	0	1
Violates blacks' moral rights	0	0	0	0	1
Not harmless	1	0	0	0	1
Other	1	0	1	0	2
Unclear	5	1	4	0	10

Although it is evident from table 32 that six rationales were used exclusively to justify censorship of the film as a whole, the number of times all but one of the rationales were used was judged too small to determine individual statistical significance. The one rationale category containing enough controversies for analysis (after black protest) indicated that the finding was significant ($x^2 = 23.7$, $< .001$). Thus, if censorship of the film was justified by this rationale action was taken against the film as a whole with a frequency differing from random. Also, the action taken against the film would more likely than not be prior restraint. Although the number of controversies resolved by each of the following rationales was too small to determine reliable statistical significance, the frequencies with which the film was considered as a whole would appear to support this finding: patriotism, detrimental to public peace, other, unfit for decent people, and not harmless. One rationale, violates black moral rights, was used only to justify partial suppression of the film. However, because only one controversy was resolved by each rationale, statistical significance was not computed for these figures. Only three rationales were used to justify both total and partial suppression of the film. These

rationales were: engender racial prejudice, procedural, and immoral/
obscene. Although the differences among the actions taken against
the film justified by the rationale that the film would engender
racial prejudice do not differ from chance ($x^2 = 8.53$, $> .02$),
actions taken concerning the film as a whole based on this rationale
outnumbered partial censorship actions 15 to 2. Also, it appears
that if this rationale was used equally to justify prior restraint
and subsequent restraint. On the other hand, the rationale immoral/
obscene was used to justify partial censorship, three times and
total suppression once. Procedural decisions concerning the film
as a whole outnumbered procedural decisions ordering partial censorship 5 to 1. Also, a majority of the censorship actions for which
the rationale was unclear were taken against the film as a whole
and these actions were equally split between prior restraint and
subsequent restraint. Thus, the overall finding that actions tended
to be taken against the film as a whole is reinforced. Also, types
of actions taken appear to be related in some degree to rationales
used to justify the action.

It is also possible to analyze rationales by tactic. The
number of times each rationale was used by each tactic to resolve
a controversy is presented in table 33. From table 33, it can be
seen that the distribution of rationales used across tactics resolving controversies was not even. For example, no rationale
was used by all tactics. The highest number of tactics justifying
censorship with the same rationale was two. Two tactics used each

of the following rationales: racial prejudice; after black protest; immoral/obscene; and, procedural. However, in only two instances were the number of controversies resolved by different rationales large enough to test for independent statistical analysis: racial prejudice and after black protest. In both cases, the figures are significant (for racial prejudice, $x^2 = 32.04$, $<.001$; for after black protest, $x^2 = 19.14$, $<.001$). Thus, in these two cases the frequencies with which the rationales were used/not used by tactic differed from chance. Although the number of times each rationale was used by tactic in the remaining instances were not large enough for individual analysis, the frequencies tend to support this finding. Therefore, it appears that rationales were to some degree tactic dependent.

TABLE 33

RATIONALES FOR CENSORSHIP BY TACTIC

Rationale	Official	Court	Extra-Legal	Criminal Proceeding	Other
Racial prejudice	15	0	0	2	0
After black protest	11	0	4	0	0
Immoral/obscene	3	0	1	0	0
Patriotism	2	0	0	0	0
Detrimental to public peace	1	0	0	0	0
Not harmless	1	0	0	0	0
Procedural	1	5	0	0	0

Unfit for decent folk	1	0	0	0	0
Violates black moral rights	1	0	0	0	0
Other	0	0	1	0	0
Unclear	7	1	0	0	2

It is also possible to determine whether rationales justifying censorship varied by year of controversy resolution. These figures are presented in table 34.

TABLE 34

RATIONALES JUSTIFYING CENSORSHIP BY YEAR

Year	Racial Prejudice	After Black Protest	Immoral/ Obscene	Patriotism	Procedural	Other	Unclear
1915	4	0	2	0	2	3	3
1916	0	0	0	0	0	0	1
1917	1	2	0	2	2	0	1
1920	0	0	0	0	0	0	1
1921	1	0	0	0	0	0	2
1922	0	1	1	0	0	0	0
1924	1	1	0	0	0	0	0
1925	0	3	0	0	1	0	0
1930	1	0	0	0	0	0	0
1931	3	4	0	0	0	0	2
1938	2	0	0	0	0	0	0
1939	1	0	1	0	0	0	0
1940	1	0	0	0	0	0	0
1941	0	1	0	0	0	0	0
1952	0	0	0	0	1	0	0
1959	1	1	0	0	0	0	0
1960	0	1	0	0	0	0	0
1961	1	0	0	0	0	0	0
1965	0	1	0	0	0	0	0

From table 34 it can be seen that rationales used against the film did not concentrate in any time period. The two rationales used most frequently to justify censorship, engender racial prejudice and after black protest, were spread across the years of the study as were all other rationales used against the film.

In summary, it can be concluded that in selected instances type of censorship action and the rationale justifying that action did not function independently. For example, with certain rationales, the film as a whole was censored and with other rationales only partial restraint was exercised against the film. Only in a minority of cases were rationales used to justify both total and partial suppression. Also, there appeared to be some relationship between tactic and rationale expressed to justify censorship. On the other hand, rationale usage was not time dependent.

Rationales for actions supportive of the film were stated in only 17 of the 35 controversies decided in favor of the film. Nine no censorship decisions were based on specific rejections of arguments used against the film. Six no censorship decisions were made on procedural grounds and two no censorship resolutions were based on the rationale, no authority to act. Rationales used to justify no censorship by tactic are presented in table 35.

TABLE 35

RATIONALES JUSTIFYING NO CENSORSHIP BY TACTIC

Rationale	Official	Court	Extra-Legal	Criminal Proceeding	Acquiescence
No authority	2	0	0	0	0
Reject racial prejudice	1	4	1	1	0

Reject immoral	1	0	0	0	0
Procedural	0	6	0	0	0
Reject detrimental peace	0	1	0	0	0
Unclear/not given	9	5	2	0	2

Because the number of controversies with known rationales was smaller than the number with unknown rationales, statistical significance was not determined. However, it can be seen that in a majority of cases rationales for action regardless of tactic were either not given or were unclear from the sources consulted. This suggests that in many cases individuals resolving controversies in favor of the film were not compelled to publicly justify their actions. It appears that most court decisions rejecting censorship did so on procedural rather than content grounds. Rationales used to justify no censorship decisions by year are presented in table 36. From table 36, it can be seen that expressed rationales justifying censorship were most heavily concentrated during 1915. The only no censorship decisions which spanned the years of the study were those with rationales unclear or not given.

In summary, it is difficult to draw conclusions concerning rationales underlying no censorship decisions because in over half the cases, rationales were either not given or unclear. This was true regardless of tactic. Only nine no censorship decisions were based on rationales which specifically rejected arguments concerning the film's content. The remaining no censorship decisions with known rationales were made on procedural rather than content grounds. Expressed rationales were most heavily concentrated during 1915. Not given or unclear rationales spanned the years of the study. In no case was a no censorship decision based specifically on First Amendment grounds.

TABLE 36

RATIONALES JUSTIFYING NO CENSORSHIP BY YEAR

Year	No Authority	Not Immoral	Not Prejudice	Procedural	Not Detrimental	Unclear
1915	2	1	3	4	0	6
1916	0	0	1	0	0	0
1917	0	0	0	1	0	1
1918	0	0	0	1	0	1
1921	0	0	0	1	0	1
1923	0	0	0	0	1	1
1924	0	0	1	0	0	3
1925	0	0	0	0	0	1
1931	0	0	0	0	0	1
1950	0	0	0	0	0	1
1958	0	0	0	0	0	1
1965	0	0	1	0	0	0
1966	0	0	0	0	0	1

Actions Resolving and Not Resolving Controversies

To extend the data analysis, it is possible to compare the actions resolving controversies already discussed with actions taken but not resolving controversies. Within this context, it is necessary to first divide actions taken regarding the film into those designed to resolve a given controversy and those actions designed to accomplish some purpose other than controversy resolution. Then, the overall effectiveness of actions in terms of avowed purpose can be analyzed.

Of the 356 actions documented in this research, 174 were designed to directly resolve a specific censorship controversy. The remaining 182 actions were intended for purposes other than direct controversy resolution. The 174 actions intended to accomplish controversy resolution were taken in 111 specific controversies. The ultimate resolutions of 96 of the 111 controversies were recorded in the sources consulted. The majority of actions taken fell within the general tactic of petitioning officials to use administrative power to resolve a controversy. Specifically, 113 officials were asked to resolve 91 controversies. Second in terms of number of times implemented was the tactic court action. Specifically, 39 courts were asked to resolve 28 controversies. Seventeen extra-legal actions were designed to resolve 15 controversies. Five criminal proceedings were initiated to resolve five controversies. From these figures and the controversy resolution statistics discussed previously, it is possible to determine the effectiveness of both general tactics and specific actions in terms of controversy resolution.

First, to determine the overall effectiveness of each general tactic in terms of controversy resolution, the number of controversies in which a given tactic was employed was compared with the number of controversies resolved and not resolved by that tactic. The resulting figures are presented in table 37. Since tactic effectiveness is the factor under consideration, the two controversies with the manner of resolution unclear are not included in this section of the analysis.

TABLE 37

SUCCESS OF TACTICS IN ACHIEVING CONTROVERSY RESOLUTION

Tactic	Controversies Resolved by Tactic	Controversies Not Resolved But Tactic Used	Total Number of Controversies in which Tactic Used
Official	56	35	91
Court	22	6	28
Criminal Proceeding	3	2	5
Extra-Legal	9	6	15

From table 37 it can be seen that officials resolved 56 controversies in which they were involved, but did not resolve 35. These figures are not significant ($x^2 = 4.88$, $>.02$). Thus, officials did not resolve controversies with a frequency differing from chance. However, courts resolved 22 of the 28 controversies in which they were involved. These figures are significant ($x^2 = 9.14$, $<.01$). Therefore, courts resolved controversies with a frequency differing from chance. Extra-legal tactics resolved nine controversies and did not resolve six. These figures are not significant ($x^2 = .6$, $>.02$). Thus, extra-legal means did not resolve controversies with a frequency greater than chance. Although there were insufficient numbers in the category criminal proceedings to determine statistical significance, the figures do not appear to differ from a chance distribution. Therefore in terms of accomplishing controversy resolution, the tactic of court action was the only one which resolved controversies with a frequency differing from chance. All other tactics were found to be successful in terms of accomplishing controversy resolution with a frequency not differing from random

From the data it is also possible to determine how frequently one tactic accomplished controversy resolution in a specific instance when another tactic or tactics could not. For example, of the controversies in which officials were involved but did not resolve, 19 were resolved by court action, two were resolved through acquiescence, one was resolved by a criminal proceeding, one was resolved through extra-legal means and the resolutions of the remaining 12 are unknown. If the findings of unknown resolutions are dropped, the resulting figures are significant (x^2 = 19.66, <.001). Thus, it appears that if an official did not resolve a controversy, that controversy would be resolved by a court with a frequency differing from chance. Conversely, of the six instances in which courts did not resolve the controversies in which they were involved, five were resolved by officials and one was resolved through acquiescence. These figures are not significant (x^2 = 1.5, >.02). Of the controversies involving criminal proceedings but not resolved by them, one was resolved through acquiescence and one was resolved by a court action. These numbers were too small to determine reliable statistical significance. Therefore, it appears that only one tactic consistently overruled another.

It is also interesting to compare the actual number of actions taken within each tactic with the number of controversies resolved by that tactic. For example, the 28 controversies including the tactic of court action actually included 39 different petitions to court officials. Of these 39 petitions, 22 were successful in accomplishing controversy resolution. These figures are not significant ($x^2 = .641, > .02$). Thus, in terms of individual petitions for resolution, court actions did not resolve controversies with a frequency differing from chance. Likewise, in terms of petitioned officials, 113 were asked to resolve 91 controversies. Only 55 such petitions proved successful in achieving controversy resolution. These figures are also not significant ($x^2 = .14, > .02$). Thus, in terms of individual petitions for resolution, an official was as likely as not to resolve a controversy. Of the 17 extra-legal action intended to accomplish the resolution of 15 controversies, nine did so and six did not. These figures are not significant ($x^2 = .05, > .02$). Five attempts were made to resolve five controversies through criminal proceedings. Three controversies were resolved by criminal proceedings and two were not. These numbers were judged too small to test for statistical significance, but the resolution/no resolution differences do not appear to differ from chance. Thus, in terms of individual actions taken, no tactic resolved controversies with a frequency differing from chance.

In summary, the only general tactic which resolved controversies with a frequency differing from random was court action. However, as noted previously, courts resolved controversies in favor of censorship or in favor of the film with a frequency not differing from random. Thus, although this tactic was effective in terms of actual controversy resolution, it could not be reliably employed by either side. On the other hand, administrative intervention did not accomplish controversy resolution with a frequency differing from chance. However, if an official did resolve a controversy, the result was some form of censorship with a frequency differing from chance. Thus, if the film's opponents were willing to chance that an official would resolve a controversy, the tactic of administrative intervention could be considered somewhat successful in achieving that goal. All other tactics did not resolve controversies with a frequency differing from chance; and, if controversy resolution was accomplished by any other tactic, the decision would be in favor of the film or in favor of censorship with a frequency not differing from random. In terms of individual actions taken, no tactic resolved controversies with a frequency differing from random. Thus, it can be concluded that more often than not multiple actions were necessary to achieve controversy resolution. Therefore, no tactic when considered as individual actions could be reliably utilized by either side. To see if this pattern held regardless of the year of controversy resolution, the individual actions taken were analyzed by year. The resulting distribution of individual actions across time are presented in table 38.

As evident in table 38, the split by year between the number
of times each tactic was implemented and the number of times each
tactic was implemented but did not accomplish controversy resolution
is reasonably equal for all tactics. Thus, the success rate of any
tactic in terms of controversy resolution does not seem to be time
dependent. This supports the general finding that overall tactics
did not resolve controversies with a frequency differing from random.
However, it is interesting to note that after 1952, **extra-legal
action was the tactic** used most frequently.

TABLE 38

ACTIONS RESOLVING (R) AND NOT RESOLVING (NR) CONTROVERSIES
BY YEAR AND TACTIC

Year	Official R	Official NR	Court R	Court NR	Extra-Legal R	Extra-Legal NR	Criminal Proceedings R	Criminal Proceedings NR
1915	20	27	10	8	1	0	0	1
1916	0	3	1	1	0	0	1	0
1917	1	2	1	2	0	0	0	0
1918	7	5	3	0	0	0	0	0
1920	0	1	0	0	0	0	0	0
1921	2	5	1	0	0	0	0	0
1922	2	1	0	0	0	0	0	0
1923	1	3	0	0	0	0	0	0
1924	4	2	2	1	1	0	0	1
1925	3	2	2	2	0	0	0	0
1930	1	0	0	0	0	1	0	0
1931	8	4	1	3	0	0	0	0
1937	0	0	0	0	0	1	0	0

1938	1	1	0	0	0	0	1	0
1939	2	0	0	0	0	0	0	0
1940	0	0	0	0	0	1	1	0
1941	0	0	0	0	1	0	0	0
1950	0	1	0	0	1	1	0	0
1952	0	1	1	0	0	0	0	0
1958	1	0	0	0	0	0	0	0
1959	1	0	0	0	1	0	0	0
1960	0	0	0	0	1	0	0	0
1961	1	0	0	0	0	0	0	0
1965	0	0	0	0	2	2	0	0
1966	0	0	0	0	1	1	0	0
1970	0	0	0	0	0	1	0	0

Of the 84 actions not resolving a controversy, 31 made a specific censorship decision concerning the film. Specifically, 24 of the 31 actions supported total or partial suppression of the film. While not taking direct actions concerning the film, an additional 17 times petitioned individuals helped facilitate controversy resolution or indicated they were in sympathy with the film's opponents. In 11 cases, petitioned individuals indicated they were without authority to act concerning the film. Five court involvements did not resolve controversies because the cases were not adjudicated. Two criminal proceedings did not influence the status of the film. In the remaining 18 instances actions taken or not taken regarding the film are unclear. Actions not resolving controversies by tactic are presented in table 39.

TABLE 39

ACTIONS NOT RESOLVING CONTROVERSIES BY TACTIC

Tactic	Censor Total	Censor Partial	No Censor	No Authority	Facilitated	Not Adjudicated	No Influence	Unclear
Official	18	1	2	8	17	0	0	12
Court	4	1	4	3	0	5	0	0
Extra-Legal	0	0	0	0	0	0	0	6
Criminal Proceeding	0	0	0	0	0	0	2	0

A majority of the actions taken for the purpose of controversy resolution were initiated by the film's opponents. Specifically, 127 actions were initiated by the film's opponents and 27 were begun by the film's supporters. Also, the opposite sides of the issue did not use tactics equally. For example, when intended for controversy resolution, criminal proceedings, official intervention, and extra-legal means were used only by the film's opponents. Court action was used by both sides. However, the film's supporters utilized court action with greater frequency than did the film's opponents. Specifically, 27 court actions were initiated by the film's supporters as opposed to 10 court actions begun by the film's opponents. In terms of accomplishing controversy resolution as has already been discussed, criminal proceedings, official intervention, and extra-legal means did not resolve controversies with a frequency differing from chance. However, if an official did resolve a controversy, the decision would support censorship with a frequency differing from chance. Thus, within a rather limited frame, this one tactic was successful for the film's opponents. On the other hand, court action did resolve controversies with a frequency differing from chance. Of the 22 court actions resolving controversies, 20 were begun by the film's supporters and two were initiated by the film's opponents. Of the resulting court decisions, 16 supported no censorship and all of these cases were brought by the film's supporters. Six court decisions resolving controversies supported some form of censorship of the film. Four of these cases were brought by the film's supporters and two were begun by the film's opponents. Therefore, from the standpoint of the film's supporters initiating court action was a good tactic. Courts resolved controversies in their favor 16 times and against them only four. These differences are significant ($x^2 = 7.2$, $< .01$). The number of controversies resolved by court actions initiated by the film's opponents in favor of ecnsorship was judged too small to determine statistical significance. Also, in terms of accomplishing controversy resolution, initiating court action was a tactic used by the film's supporters with a frequency differing from chance. Specifically, the tactic was utilized by the film's supporters 27 times. Twenty of the resulting actions resolved controversies and seven did not. These figures are significant ($x^2 = 6.25$, $< .02$). However, the tactic was not successful in accomplishing controversy resolution for the film's opponents. Specifically, only two of 12 court actions brought by the film's opponents ended in controversy resolution. These figures are not significant ($x^2 = 5.33, > .02$). Therefore, initiating court actions was a good tactic for the film's supporters but not for the film's opponents.

In summary, the majority of actions taken during the course of The Birth of a Nation censorship controversies were initiated by the film's opponents. In terms of achieving controversy resolution, three tactics were used exclusively by the film's opponents and one tactic was used by both the film's supporters and opponents. The three tactics used solely by the film's opponents did not achieve controversy resolution with a frequency differing from chance. The tactic used by both the film's supporters and opponents did accomplish controversy resolution successfully from the standpoint of the film's supporters, but not from the standpoint of the film's opponents.

Actions Not Designed Specifically to Resolve Controversies

The 182 actions not intended to directly resolve censorship controversies were in the form of one of three tactics: legislative, extra-legal, and criminal proceedings. Actions not intended to resolve controversies took place at the local, state, and national levels. The purposes underlying the actions varied. For example, of the 14 legislative actions, 12 actions were designed to establish censorship standards which could later be used against the film; one action was designed as a renunciation of the film; and one action was intended to ban the film. The criminal proceedings not intended to accomplish controversy resolution appear to have been either attempts to discourage public protests against the film or to terminate allegedly illegal acts. In all four cases of this nature, the individuals arrested were engaging in some form of protest action during a raging censorship controversy. Extra-legal actions not designed to accomplish controversy resolution existed primarily to influence public opinion concerning the film. Of the 164 extra-legal actions within this category, 141 were tied to specific controversies and 23 were not controversy specific. To amplify the analysis of actions taken for purposes other than direct controversy resolution, the actions will be discussed by tactic.

Legislative Actions

During the time period studied, there were at least 14 attempts to pass legislation tied to The Birth. Five such actions occurred during the course of an ongoing censorship controversy and nine occurred independently of individual screening debates. All legislative actions were initiated by the film's opponents. Five attempts to pass legislation were at the local level; six such attempts were at the state level; and, three were at the national level. All five actions at the local level concerned the passage of ordinances which could be used against the film. All five actions resulted in the passage of the proposed ordinances. Four were passed during 1915 and one was passed in 1923. Five of the state actions concerned bills which were intended to establish state censorship statutes which could be used against the film. Two of these bills became law and three did not. The bills which became law were passed in 1917 and 1919. Two such bills failed during 1915 and one failed in 1916. One state legislative action dealt with the establishment of a new censorship agency for a city within that state. This action was successful in establishing a municipal censorship board in 1915 to consider The Birth and all other films. The three remaining legislative actions took place in the U. S. Congress. One action was in the form of a bill to establish a federal censorship standard which could be used against the film. One action was designed as a Congressional renunciation of the film. The remaining action was a resolution instructing the District of Columbia governing body to ban the film from the District. All three measures were introduced into Congress during 1916 and all three died in committee.

The eight laws passed to allow for censorship of The Birth were used inconsistently against the film. For example, in at least four instances the film was shown in spite of legislation passed specifically to censor it. In one of these cases, the ordinance involved was declared null and void by a court and the film shown. In another case, the censorship board established specifically to stop the film refused to do so. In one instance, the film was shown in spite of an ordinance designed to stop it. In another case, an attempt to apply the legislation indirectly to the film through criminal proceedings proved unsuccessful. Three of these cases occurred at the local level and one at the state level. Also,

TABLE 40

NATURE OF EXTRA-LEGAL ACTIONS TIED TO SPECIFIC CONTROVERSIES

Action	Support Censorship	Support Film	Neutral	Total
Editorial	70	11	2	83
Letters to Editor	18	12	0	30
Demonstration	8	0	0	8
Resolution	8	0	0	8
Pamphlet	3	0	0	3
Sermons	4	3	0	7
Other	0	0	2	2
Total	111	26	4	141

These extra-legal actions were not equally distributed among the 17 controversies in which they were employed nor were they equally distributed across the years of the study. The largest number of extra-legal actions tied to a specific controversy was 29 and the smallest was one. All extra-legal actions tied to controversies occurred during the time period 1915-1924. A majority of the actions were taken during 1915. Specifically, 133 actions were tied to censorship controversies which occurred during 1915. Although the majority of extra-legal actions taken supported censorship, of the 17 controversies which included extra-legal actions, 12 were resolved with decisions supporting the film's right to the screen. Only four controversies in which extra-legal actions were used as support tactics were resolved with some form of censorship. In one instance individuals interpreting censorship laws changed over time and one group of censors might approve the film while a second group functioning under the same legislation might reject it. This occurred at least once during the time period studied. On the other hand, at least one state law passed to stop the film did so effectively for several years. Thus, in general legislative action even as a secondary or indirect tactic in terms of controversy resolution was not a particularly effective tool from the standpoint of the film's opponents.

Extra-Legal Actions

Extra-legal actions were used as support tactics in individual censorship controversies or existed independently of any controversy to influence general public opinion concerning the film. Specifically, 17 controversies included 141 extra-legal actions as support tactics and 23 extra-legal actions existed independent of screening debates. Of the 141 extra-legal actions tied to censorship controversies, a majority were initiated by the film's opponents. Specifically, 111 were in opposition to the film and 26 were in support of the film. Four actions of this nature were neutral concerning the film's acceptability. Of the 23 extra-legal actions existing independently, 18 supported censorship and five supported the film.

Extra-legal actions tied to specific controversies took a variety of forms. Actions by form and number of times used for and against the film are presented in table 40.

including extra-legal tactics, the ultimate resolution of the controversy is unclear.

Extra-legal actions not tied to specific controversies were in one of four major forms. Such actions by form and position regarding the film are presented in table 41.

TABLE 41

EXTRA-LEGAL ACTIONS NOT CONTROVERSY SPECIFIC

Form	Support Censorship	Support Film	Total
Editorial	12	4	16
Pamphlet	3	1	4
Resolution	1	0	1
Film	2	0	2

These extra-legal efforts took place during the time period 1915-1918. Again, the majority of these actions took place during 1915. Specifically, 18 of the 23 extra-legal actions which were not controversy specific occurred during 1915. However, because these actions existed to influence public opinion concerning the film, the effectiveness of the tactics could not be accessed.

Criminal Proceedings

Four criminal proceedings existed independently of controversy resolution. All four took place during raging censorship controversies which were being fought directly through other means. In each case, individuals were arrested for participating in some form of demonstration against the film. Three of these cases took place in 1915 and one occurred in 1921. Of the four controversies in which criminal proceedings existed as a secondary tactic, one was resolved by a court, one was resolved by a municipal censorship board, one was resolved by a mayor, and one was resolved through acquiescence. Three of these decisions supported the film and one supported partial subsequent restraint.

First Amendment Arguments

Although this research documented 120 censorship controversies fought over The Birth of a Nation's right to the screen, only three controversies were defined in First Amendment terms and apparently none was specifically decided on these grounds. The First Amendment question was not directly asked in a specific controversy until 1939/40, when the ACLU contended that an ordinance prohibiting the presentation of films which might engender racial prejudice violated the free speech/press guarantees of the U. S. Constitution. At issue was the arrest of a theatre manager who allegedly violated the ordinance by showing The Birth. The ACLU entered the controversy as a friend of the court and argued that the motion picture medium had progressed considerably since the time of the Mutual decision in 1915. Because of this development, film should be entitled to First Amendment protection. The NAACP countered that communications like The Birth were not and should not be granted First Amendment protection. In spite of these arguments, the case was not decided on First Amendment grounds.

Rather, the case ended when the defendant agreed to plead guilty to a lesser charge and received a reduced fine. A First Amendment right to the screen was asserted for the film in a 1952 court resolved controversy. However, although the case was adjudicated after the Burstyn decision, it was apparently decided on procedural rather than free speech grounds. The other controversy defined by at least one party in First Amendment terms occurred in New York in 1965. In this instance, the New York Times editorially asserted that The Birth was protected by the First Amendment and advised those attempting to ban the film to direct their efforts elsewhere. The actual resolution of this controversy is unclear.

Although these were the only three controversies in which a First Amendment argument was made in an attempt to resolve the controversy, The Birth's right to free speech/press protection was mentioned at least 13 additional times. All were in the form of extra-legal tactics. In nine cases, the free speech/press argument was contained in newspaper editorials related to the film and published between 1915 and 1924. Three of these editorials denounced film censorship in rather general terms. Six specifically attacked all forms of censorship as infringements on freedom of speech and the press and indicated that the only acceptable reason for censorship was obscenity. Since The Birth was clearly not obscene, these editorials reasoned that any censorship of the film was a free speech violation. Thus, these editorials considered film as part of the press of the country--a status the Supreme Court had specifically rejected in the Mutual decision.

The argument that the film medium was equivalent to the country's press was made most strongly by D. W. Griffith. Griffith defended The Birth on First Amendment grounds in at least one pamphlet and one letter to the editor. In these communications, Griffith argued that the medium should be freed entirely of the burden of prior restraint. Thomas Dixon also argued that the film should be protected by the First Amendment in a letter to the editor.

The First Amendment right of the individual to see the film as opposed to the film's First Amendment right to the screen was central to at least two extra-legal actions regarding The Birth. In these two instances, one an editorial and one a letter to the editor, the authors stated that the individual should have the right to decide whether or not to see the film. One author said specifically that he did not approve of someone deciding what he could or could not see and indicated that this violated what he believed to be his Constitutional right to receive information.

At least one other incident in the history of The Birth of a Nation hinged on a First Amendment question. However, in this case the question concerned the right of the film's opponents to picket and distribute literature denouncing the film. In this instance individuals who had been arrested for picketing a theatre screening The Birth and distributing a pamphlet against the film contended that their arrests were invalid because their actions against the film were within the free speech guarantee of the Constitution. The trial court disagreed with the demonstrators, but an appeal court reversed. Thus, in at least one case rather than the film's right to the screen or an individual's right to see the film being questioned, the right to public protest was affirmed.

Conclusions

From the analysis, the research questions can be answered. Because the secondary questions guiding the research provided the data with which the primary question could be answered, the secondary questions will be considered first.

Secondary questions

1) Has there been a change in the U. S. Supreme Court's interpretation of the First Amendment as it applies to filmic expression, 1915 to 1973?

During the time period studied, there was one major change in the Supreme Court's interpretation of the First Amendment as it applies to the motion picture medium. In its first consideration of the question concerning the medium's right to First Amendment protection in its 1915 Mutual decision, the Court exempted the medium from free speech protection. In 1952, in the Burstyn ruling, the Court again considered the First Amendment status of the medium and extended limited free speech protection to film. Since 1952, the Court has continued to hold that as long as appropriate procedural guidelines are followed, prior restraint of the motion picture medium per se is not an unconstitutional abridgement of free speech.

that The Birth took on more of a symbolic meaning to the film's opponents and protests against the film took a form consistent with other civil rights tactics.

   8) Were tactics other than court action, administrative intervention, legislative action, and extra-legal means used for and against The Birth of a Nation during debates over the film's right to the screen, and if so, how did these tactics follow the direction of the U. S. Supreme Court in dealing with restraints against filmic expression?

In addition to court action, administrative intervention, legislative action, and extra-legal means, criminal proceedings were used as a tactic in the debates over The Birth of a Nation's right to the screen. Criminal proceedings were part of nine controversies. In five cases criminal proceedings were initiated to accomplish controversy resolution and in four instances criminal proceedings were not intended to accomplish controversy resolution. Only two of the criminal proceedings documented were argued specifically on First Amendment grounds. Both controversies occurred under the Supreme Court's Mutual decision and only one asserted a First Amendment right for the film, which was denied. The other controversy asserted a First Amendment right for protesters to publicly demonstrate against the film. This right was upheld by a court in a decision not dealing with film censorship. Thus, the criminal proceedings instigated to resolve controversies did not seem to be in conflict with the direction set by the Supreme Court in Mutual.

Primary Question

Did arguments for and against censorship of The Birth of a Nation change from 1915-1973 as the Supreme Court's inter-

2) What kind of restraint (prior restraint, subsequent restraint, prior restraint partial, subsequent restraint partial) have been used against The Birth of a Nation during the film's history, 1915 to 1973?

During the time period studied, censorship controversies were resolved with prior restraint, prior restraint partial, subsequent restraint, subsequent restraint partial, and no censorship decisions. These decisions were accomplished through the implementation of four major tactics: court action; criminal proceedings; administrative intervention; and, extra-legal means. In terms of individual actions taken, no tactic accomplished controversy resolution with a frequency differing from chance. However, in terms of controversies rather than individual actions, the tactic of court action resolved controversies with a frequency greater than chance. Regardless of tactic implemented, controversies were more likely than not to be resolved by decisions supportive of some form of censorship with a frequency greater than chance. This finding would tend to support the direction established by the Supreme Court in the Mutual decision, that because film was not protected by the First Amendment it was possible to censor films for a variety of reasons. Censorship controversies were fought at the local, state, and national levels. However, controversy resolution was found to be dependent neither on controversy year nor on controversy level. In terms of overall ability to achieve controversy resolution, the tactic of court action proved most effective during the time period studied. Court action was the only tactic studied which resolved the controversies in which it was employed with a frequency differing from chance.

3) What arguments have been presented in courts at all levels for and against censorship of The Birth of a Nation from 1915-1973, and how do these follow the direction of the U. S. Supreme Court in dealing with restraints against filmic expression?

Arguments used for and against censorship of The Birth in courts at all levels centered on content, procedural, or effects issues. The film's opponents tended to stress in their arguments against The Birth that the film's content was objectionable and that if shown the film would have a negative effect. The film's supporters tended to argue that censorship of the film violated established procedural guidelines concerning film censorship, that the film would have a positive or neutral effect, and that the film's content was not objectionable. In only one case was the film's First Amendment right asserted. All but one court decision concerning the film were made prior to the Supreme Court ruling in the Burstyn case. The decisions made under the Mutual guidelines basically were in harmony with the direction established by the Supreme Court. The Mutual decision did not deal with the content of any film and indicated that the censorship procedures used in the state of Ohio were reasonable because film was not guaranteed any free speech protections. In dicta, the decision also indicated that film was capable of producing a negative effect and could also be curbed for this reason. Also, the decision reasoned that the medium was a business rather than a legitimate organ of public opinion. Acting in the shadow of this directive the courts which considered The Birth's right to the screen based a majority of their decisions on procedural grounds. In only one instance was the Mutual decision directly mentioned in dicta accompanying a decision concerning The Birth. In this decision a judge mentioned that since the method of film censorship in that state had been upheld by the Supreme Court in the Mutual decision, a mayor acted inappropriately by banning the film after it had been approved by the state's censorship board. This decision was one of three which indicated that once a film had been ruled on at the state level, local authorities could not contradict that decision. These decisions were rendered before the Supreme Court dealt with the question of what it meant by a community in terms of community standards concerning obscenity. Thus, in these three cases judges in essence defined community as the state rather than as a city or as the nation. Therefore, if state censorship existed it was considered supreme and a film approved by a state board could not be stopped by a lesser authority. In a different decision concerning The Birth, a court indicated that it was appropriate to have one censorship standard for adults and another for juveniles. This preceded by 53 years the Supreme Court ruling that it was acceptable to have one standard for juveniles and another for adults at least in terms of obscenity in the Ginsberg case.

There were at least three court decisions concerning The Birth which may have differed somewhat from the direction established by the court in the Mutual decision. In these three cases judges specifically rejected the censorship standard of engendering racial prejudice. Thus, although the Mutual decision indicated that basically any censorship standards could be established to judge the medium by since it was not protected by the First Amendment, these judges said no, certain standards are not legitimate. In one of these cases a judge specifically declared a censorship ordinance null and void because it included this standard. In the remaining cases the ordinances were not erased, but the judges indicated that the criteria included in the ordinances was inappropriate. On the other hand, several other judges indicated in their decisions that censorship because a film might engender racial prejudice was appropriate. One judge specifically ruled that a statute including this standard was valid (However, the judge also ruled that The Birth did not violate that standard). Because no written opinion in the only controversy resolved by a court after the Burstyn decision was found, it is difficult to guage the impact of the Burstyn decision. However, the court ruling after Burstyn upheld the right of the state censorship board involved to censor the film. This decision was rendered only weeks after the Burstyn decision and whether or not the validity of the censorship standard used against the film was considered by the court is unclear. After the Burstyn decision the number of censorship controversies concerning The Birth was relatively small. It is possible that the decision and subsequent Supreme Court rulings concerning the film medium indicated to the film's opponents that they would have little chance against the film if censorship decisions were challenged in the courts. It is also possible that relatively few controversies occurred after Burstyn because the film was old and its commercial value diminished.

4) When administrative bodies acted in a quasi-judicial capacity concerning The Birth of a Nation, did they follow the direction of the U. S. Supreme Court in dealing with restraint of filmic expression?

Officials using the administrative power of office concerning the film seem to have followed the general direction of the Mutual decision but seem to have in several cases departed from the Burstyn guidelines. Prior to the Burstyn decision, officials who resolved controversies supported censorship of the film with a frequency differing from chance. However, in terms of individuals petitioned, officials did not resolve controversies with a frequency differing from chance. Officials tended to make censorship decisions concerning the film based on content or effect criteria. In fact, only one decision made by an official body regarding the film was made on procedural grounds. Officials used a wide range of arguments to justify actions against the film. Officials were more consistent than courts in accepting the standard of engendering racial prejudice as legitimate.

Petitioning authorities was the primary tactic used by the film's opponents. In terms of accomplishing the goal of censoring the film, the tactic could not be considered particularly successful. On the other hand, the tactic was also not consistent in achieving no censorship resolutions. However, in more controversies than not in which officials were involved, the film was screened in some form or for some time. Thus, in terms of accomplishing prior restraint, the tactic was not effective.

In two cases after the Burstyn decision, authorities ordered censorship of the film based on the grounds that the film would engender racial prejudice. Although the Supreme Court had never ruled specifically concerning the constitutionality of this censorship standard, it would appear on the basis of Burstyn and later decisions that the standard is overbroad. Thus, it appears that in these two cases officials ordering censorship of the film were in violation of the Burstyn doctrine. However, the decisions were not challenged in the courts.

5) Does the legislative history of specific censorship laws suggest that these laws were designed specifically to restrain The Birth of a Nation?

The legislative history of at least eight censorship laws suggests that these laws were designed specifically to restrain The Birth. However, the effectiveness of these laws in accomplishing that purpose was not great. In general, the statutes were not consistently interpreted regarding The Birth. One official interpreting the law might use it against the film, and another official interpreting the same law might decide that The Birth did not violate the statute. The constitutionality of such statutes was also interpreted inconsistently by the courts. As mentioned previously, one such statute was declared void by a court and another statute was upheld.

6) What interest groups advocated censorship of the film and what arguments did they offer to support restraint of the film, and what interest groups supported the film and what arguments did they offer in support of the film's right to the screen?

The primary interest group advocating censorship of The

public opinion concerning the film. Within this context the First Amendment status of the film medium was discussed several times. Specifically, when establishment newspapers editorially considered The Birth, they tended to do so within the context of a freedom of expression argument regardless of the year of the editorial. Thus, newspapers were arguing that film should have some free speech protection long before the Burstyn decision. On the other hand, black newspapers tended to editorially attack the film on content and effects grounds and did not consider the free speech issue. In the black press, the tendency was to indicate that in certain circumstances it was appropriate to curb freedom of expression and The Birth fit well within those circumstances. In one extra-legal effort against the film, the argument was made that the film itself violated the Fourteenth Amendment rights of blacks. Thus, although not considered consistently by either courts or officials, constitutional questions concerning the film were discussed in a minority of extra-legal actions.

Extra-legal actions were also taken with the purpose of controversy resolution. In this context, extra-legal actions were not particularly effective. However, it is interesting to note that the majority of actions were taken after the Burstyn decision were extra-legal in nature. Thus, it is possible that the film's opponents interpreted Burstyn to indicate that legal channels were closed to them and a redirection of effort needed. It is also possible that as civil rights activities increased during the 1960's in particular

Birth throughout the years studied was the National Association for the Advancement of Colored People (NAACP). The NAACP began its opposition to The Birth in 1915 and continued it through 1973. The NAACP consistently argued that the film should be restrained because of the negative images of blacks it presented. According to the NAACP, films like The Birth which engendered racial prejudice were not entitled to First Amendment protection. Although the organization's argument against the film did not change during the years studied, its tactics did somewhat. After the Burstyn decision, the NAACP used extra-legal tactics more than any other against the film.

The primary interest group advocating the film's right to the screen was the American Civil Liberties Union (ACLU). However, ACLU's support of The Birth was more concentrated during the time period studied than was the NAACP's opposition. ACLU support of The Birth occurred primarily during 1939-1940. The ACLU supported the film completely on First Amendment grounds. Although the ACLU said it did not approve of communications which engendered racial prejudice, prior restraint of film represented an unconstitutional abridgement of free speech. D. W. Griffith also argued that The Birth and all films should be absolutely protected by the First Amendment.

7) What kind of extra-legal actions have been taken for and against censorship of The Birth of a Nation and how do these follow the direction of the U. S. Supreme Court in dealing with restraints against filmic expression?

A variety of extra-legal actions were taken regarding The Birth. The majority of these actions were intended to influence pretation of the First Amendment applied to filmic expression changed?

From the data analyzed, it can be concluded that arguments for and against censorship of The Birth of a Nation basically did not change from 1915-1973 as the U. S. Supreme Court's interpretation of the First Amendment as it applies to filmic expression changed.

Although most censorship actions concerning The Birth took place before the Supreme Court extended First Amendment protection to the medium in 1952, those censorship decisions occurring both during the 1915-1951 period and the 1952-1973 period supported censorship or the film with a frequency not differing from random. It has been asserted by at least one researcher that at least two censorship orders issued against the film after the Burstyn ruling were in violation of that doctrine, but the rulings were not challenged. Also, tactics used in support of and against the film were reasonably evenly spread across the years of the study. However, a minor shift did seem to occur after the Burstyn decision. From 1952 on, the majority of actions taken concerning the film were within the tactic extra-legal means. Although the numbers are not large enough to determine statistical significance, this would indicate that perhaps at least a portion of the film's opponents interpreted the ruling to mean that extra-legal tactics would be most effective concerning the film given its First Amendment status.

In the Burstyn decision Justice Tom Clark concluded that accepting as valid a censorship standard as broad as sacrilegious would cast the censor "adrift upon a boundless sea amid a myriad of conflicting currents. . .with no charts but those provided by the most vocal and powerful orthodoxies."[2] It appears that this is precisely what has happened throughout the censorship history of The Birth. Censors have banned and not banned the film with frequencies not differing from random basically regardless of controversy level, tactic employed to accomplish controversy resolution, controversy year, or rationales justifying the actions. Thus, during the time period studied neither the film's opponents nor the film's supporters could enter into censorship debate with a hope of victory greater than chance.

Thus, although the study must accept the null hypothesis, its importance is not diminished. The research indicates that at least in terms of one of history's most important films, the Supreme Court has failed to provide adequate guideposts for film censorship, and, with the 1974 Billy Jenkins v. Georgia[3] decision the Court may have muddled the situation even further. At least during most of the battles over The Birth's right to the screen, courts defined community censorship standards as either state standards or national standards. However, the Jenkins decision indicated that community standards were not necessarily national, state, or local standards and that in each case the jury should be given an adequate definition of community during the trial.[4] Under Jenkins, it is possible that a film could be censored in one city and shown in another only miles away. This happened to The Birth and it is as absurd today as it was then.

The study also illustrates the confusion resulting from the Court's failure to face squarely the question of the constitutionality of censorship because of stereotypes presented. This question continues to be an issue. As recently as 1971, a resolution was introduced into the U. S. Congress which asked the film and broadcast industries to voluntarily remove negative stereotypes of ethnic, racial, and religious groups from all programs.[5] If the voluntary effort failed, the resolution contained a provision for federally enforced censorship.[6] Even more recently, the U. S. Civil Rights Commission asked the Federal Communications Commission to take regulatory action to halt stereotyping of minorities and women on television.[7] For the FCC, Richard Wiley responded that the commission could not deal with "such a complex and highly subjective concept as stereotyping without becoming deeply involved in the reviewing of program materials."[8] Wiley concluded that such a role for the FCC was contrary to the Communications Act of 1934 which established the commission, ". . .the Constitution, and the overall best interests of our free society."[9] Although Wiley is speaking more of the FCC's role than he is about the actual acceptability of stereotyping as a censorship standard, his remarks reflect a lesson apparent from the censorship history of The Birth. Censorship based on stereotypes cannot be fairly and consistently enforced, and, in the author's opinion, is a violation of the First Amendment and not in the best interests of a free society.

All censorship denies at least two free speech rights: the right to communicate information and the right to receive information. All censorship controversies concerning The Birth were waged over the first right. Perhaps the battleground which will resolve the issue in the future lies withing the second.

Suggestions for further research

As with most research inquiries, as many questions have been raised with this effort as have been answered. Several deal more generally with the First Amendment and several concern more specifically The Birth. In terms of the First Amendment generally, more investigation should be done in the area of censorship allowed or disallowed because of stereotypes presented. Do censorship decisions concerning stereotypes follow the inconsistent resolution pattern found for The Birth or are there consistencies to the decisions? What other films have been challenged because of stereotypes presented and how have these controversies been resolved? Has censorship been justified because of the presentation of positive rather than negative stereotypes? What rationales other than stereotyping and obscenity have been used by courts to justify film censorship and how do these decisions follow the direction established by the Supreme Court's interpretation of film's First Amendment status? The majority of decisions rendered by courts concerning The Birth were procedural rather than free speech or content decisions. Perhaps it would be beneficial to investigate whether this tendency for procedural rather than free speech or content decisions holds for other film censorship cases.

Specifically, relating to The Birth, it was noted several times during the research that newspaper accounts of events important in the history of the film varied. The greatest variance appeared to be between accounts in black newspapers and accounts in establishment newspapers. It would be interesting to compare press coverage of these important events with other records to determine whether the black press or the establishment press recorded events more accurately. Also, several white newspapers editorially supported The Birth on First Amendment grounds, no black newspaper was found to do so. Therefore, the black press stand on freedom of expression would be an interesting area to investigate. Did the black press generally support freedom of expression but justify prior restraint only to eliminate negative stereotypes? How did this compare with stands taken by the white press on similar issues? There were, no doubt, other controversies over The Birth's right to the screen. In might be beneficial to track these down and determine if the resolutions of these controversies are consistent with the findings of this study. Finally, it would be interesting to investigate further the Hampton epilogue to determine the origin of the footage, the fate of the footage and whether any censorship controversies other than the one documented by this research occurred.

[1] The information was not included in the books, newspapers, magazines and other sources consulted for this research and listed in the bibliography.

[2] *Joseph Burstyn, Inc. v. Wilson*, 343 U. S. 495, 504.

[3] *Billy Jenkins v. State of Georgia*, 418 U. S. 153, 94 S. Ct. 2750, 41 L. Ed. 2d 642.

[4] Ibid., at 154.

[5] *Hearings Before the Subcommittee on Communication and Power of the Committee on Interstate and Foreign Commerce House of Representatives, Ninety-Second Congress First Session on H. Con. Res. 9 and H. Con. Res. 182 Expressing the Sense of Congress Relating to Films and Broadcasts Which Defame, Stereotype, Ridicule, Demean or Degrade Ethnic, Racial, and Religious Groups, April 27 and 28, 1971* (Washington, D. C.: U. S. Government Printing Office, 1971), p. 3.

[6] Ibid., p. 4.

[7] "TV Censorship Threat Cited," *Tulsa Tribune*, 17 August 1977, Section C, p. 15.

[8] Ibid.

[9] Ibid.

BIBLIOGRAPHY

Primary Sources

Legal Citations

Alexander v. Virginia, 413 U.S. 836, 37 L.Ed.2d 993, 93 S.Ct. 2803 (1973).

Bainbridge v. Minneapolis, 131 Minn. 195, 154 N.W. 964 (1915).

Beauharnais v. Illinois, 343 U.S. 250, 72 S.Ct. 725, 96 L.Ed. 919 (1952).

Billy Jenkins v. Georgia, 418 U.S. 153, 94 S.Ct. 2750, 41 L.Ed. 2d 642 (1974).

Block v. Chicago, 239 Ill. 251, 87 N.E. 1011 (1909).

Bookcase, Inc. v. Broderick, 18 N.Y. 2d 71, 271 N.Y.S.2d 947, 218 N.E. 2d 668 (1965).

Commercial Pictures Corp. v. Regents of the University of the State of New York, 305 N.Y. 366, 113 N.E.2d 502 (1953).

Epoch Producing Corp. v. Harry L. Davis, Mayor of the City of Cleveland, et. al., 19 Ohio NISI Pruis Reports 465 (1917).

Epoch Producing Corp. v. Herman F. Schuettler, 280 Ill. 310, 117 N.E. 479 (1917).

Epoch Producing Corp. v. Herman F. Schuettler, 209 Ill.Sup. 596 (1918).

Epoch Producing Corp. v. The Industrial Commission of Ohio, et. al., 95 Ohio 400, 117 N.E. 10 (1916).

Frank Dyson v. Brent Stein, 401 U.S. 200, 91 S.Ct. 769, 27 L.Ed.2d 781 (1971).

Freedman v. Maryland, 380 U.S. 51, 13 L.Ed.2d 649, 85 S.Ct. 734 (1965).

Garret Byrne v. Serafim Karalex, 401 U.S. 216, 91 S.Ct. 777, 27 L.Ed. 2d 792 (1971).

Gelling v. Texas, 156 Tex.Crim. 516, 247 S.W.2d 95 (1952).

Gelling v. Texas, 343 U.S. 960, 72S.Ct. 1002, 96 L.Ed. 1359 (1952).

Ginsberg v. New York, 390 U.S. 629, 20 L.Ed.2d 195, 88 S.Ct. 1274 (1968).

Ginzburg v. U.S. 383 U.S. 463, 16 L.Ed.2d 31, 86 S.Ct. 942 (1966).

Heller v. New York, 413 U.S. 483, 37 L.Ed.2d 745, 93 S.Ct. 3689 (1973).

Higgins v. La Croix, 119 Minn. 145, 137 N.W. 417 (1912).

Interstate Circuit v. City of Dallas, 390 U.S. 676, 88 S.Ct. 1298 20 L.Ed.2d 225 (1968).

Jacobellis v. State of Ohio, 378 U.S. 184, 84 S.Ct. 1676, 12 L.Ed.2d 793 (1964).

Joseph Burstyn, Inc. v. Wilson, 303 N.Y. 242, 101 N.E.2d 665 (1951).

Joseph Burstyn, Inc. v. Wilson, 343 U.S. 495, 72 S.Ct. 777, 96 L.Ed. 1098 (1952).

Kaplan v. California, 413 U.S. 115, 93 S.Ct. 2680, 37 L.Ed.2d 492 (1973).

Kingsley International Pictures Corp. v. Regents, 4 N.Y.2d 349, 551 N.E. 2d 197 (1958).

Kingsley International Pictures Corp. v. Regents, 360 U.S. 684, 79 S.Ct. 1362, 3 L.Ed.2d 1512 (1959).

Leander H. Perez, Jr. v. August M. Ledesma, Jr., 401 U.S. 82, 91 S.Ct.

Manual Enterprises, Inc. v. Day, 370 U.S. 478, 82 S.Ct. 1432, 8 L.Ed. 2d 639 (1962).

Marvin Miller v. California, 413 U.S. 15, 93 S.Ct. 2607, 37 L.Ed.2d 419 (1973).

Memoirs of a Woman of Pleasure v. Massachusetts, 383 U.S. 413, 86 S.Ct. 975, 16 L.Ed.2d 1 (1966).

Mishkin v. New York, 383 U.S. 502, 86 S.Ct. 958, 16 L.Ed.2d 56 (1966).

Mutual Film Corp. v. Hodges, 236 U.S. 248 (1915).

Mutual Film Corp. v. Industrial Commission of Ohio, 205 Fed.Rep. 138 (1914).

Mutual Film Corp. v. Industrial Commission of Ohio, 236 U.S. 230,

35 S.Ct. 387, 59 L.Ed. 552 (1915).

Paris Adult Theatre I v. Slaton, 413 U.S. 39, 93 S.Ct. 2628, 37 L.Ed. 2d 446 (1973).

People v. Doris, 14 App.Div. 117, 43 N.Y. Supp. 571 (1st Dept., 1897).

People v. Gayner, 77 Misc. 576, 137 N.Y.Supp. 196 (Sup. Ct. N.Y. County, 1912).

People of California v. Alberts, 138 Cal.App.2d Supp. 999, 292 F.2d 90 (1956).

People of the State of Illinois, ex. rel. Walter Konzack v. Herman F. Schuettler, 209 Ill.App. 588 (1918).

RD-DR Corp. v. Smith, 183 F.2d 562, 89 Fed.Supp. 596 (1950).

RD-DR Corp. v. Smith, 340 U.S. 853, 71 S.Ct. 80, 95 L.Ed. 625 (1950).

Redrup v. New York, 386 U.S. 767, 87 S.Ct. 1414, 18 L.Ed.2d 515 (1967).

Roaden v. Kentucky, 413 U.S. 496, 93 S.Ct. 2796, 37 L.Ed.2d 757 (1973).

Roth v. U.S.; Alberts v. People of California, 354 U.S. 476, 77 S.Ct. 1304, 1 L.Ed.2d 1498 (1957).

Stanley v. Georgia, 394 U.S. 557, 89 S.Ct. 1243, 22 L.Ed.2d 542 (1969).

State of Kansas ex. rel. S.M. Brewster v. L.M. Crawford, 103 Kansas 76 (1918).

Superior Films v. Department of Ohio, 159 Ohio St. 315, 112 N.E.2d 311 (1953).

Superior Films v. Department of Education of Ohio, 346 U.S. 587 74 S.Ct. 286, 98 L.Ed. 329 (1954).

Times Film Corp. v. Chicago, 355 U.S. 35, 78 S.Ct. 115, 35 L.Ed.2d 403 (1961).

Theatre Company v. Weaver, 18 Penn.Dist.R. 794 (1911).

United Artists v. Board of Censors of City of Memphis, 225 S.W.2d 550 (1949).

United Artists Corp. v. Board of Censors of the City of Memphis, 339 U.S. 952, 70 S.Ct. 839, 94 L.ED. 1365 (1950).

U.S. v. One Book Called Ulysses, 72 F.2d 705 (2d Circ. 1934).

U.S. v. Orito, 413 U.S. 139, 93 S.Ct. 2674, 37 L.Ed.2d 513 (1973).

U.S. v. Paramount Pictures, 334 U.S. 131, 68 S.Ct. 915, 92 L.Ed. 1260 (1948).

U.S. v. Reidel, 402 U.S. 351, 91 S.Ct. 1410, 28 L.Ed.2d 813 (1971).

U.S. v. Roth, 237 F.2d 796 (2d Circ. 1956).

U.S. v. Thirty-Seven Photographs, 402 U.S. 363, 91 S.Ct. 769, 28 L.Ed. 2d 822 (1971).

U.S. v. 12 200 ft. Reels of Super 8mm Film, 413 U.S. 123, 93 S.Ct. 2665, 37 L.Ed.2d 500 (1973).

Valentine v. Chrestensen, 316 U.S. 52, 62 S.Ct. 920, 86 L.Ed. 1262 (1942).

Winters v. New York, 333 U.S. 507, 68 S.Ct. 665, 92 L.Ed. 840 (1948).

Published Primary Sources

British Film Institute. National Film Archive Catalogue Part III: Silent Fiction Films 1895-1930. London: British Film Institute, 1966.

Boston Branch of the National Association for the Advancement of Colored People. Fighting a Vicious Film: Protest Against The Birth of a Nation. Boston: Boston Branch of the NAACP, 1915.

Chicago Commission. The Negro in Chicago. Chicago: University of Chicago Press, 1922.

"The Great Films Society Presents The Birth of a Nation." Beverly Hills: Beverly Vista School, 1948.

Griffith, D.W. The Rise and Fall of Free Speech in America. Los Angeles: D.W. Griffith, 1916.

Johnson, W. Bishop. The Birth of a Nation: A Monumental Slander of American History; The Negro and the Civil War by Thomas Dixon Analytically and Critically Considered. Washington, D.C.: W. Bishop Johnson, 1916.

National Board of Censorship of Motion Pictures. *The Policy and Standards of the National Board of Censorship of Motion Pictures.* New York: National Board of Censorship, 1914.

_____. *The Question of Motion Picture Censorship.* New York: National Board of Censors, 1914.

New York Branch of the National Association for the Advancement of Colored People. *Stop the KKK Propaganda in New York.* New York: New York Branch of the NAACP, 1921.

Pennsylvania. State Board of Censors (of Motion Pictures). *Rules and Standards: Act Passed May 15, 1915, P.L. 534.* Harrisburg, Pa.: Wm. Stanley Ray, 1915.

Providence, Rhode Island, Branch of the National Association for the Advancement of Colored People. *Statement of Facts Regarding the Photo-Play 'The Birth of a Nation' by the Providence Branch of the NAACP to the Providence Board of Police Commissioners.* Providence, Rhode Island: Providence Branch of the NAACP, n.d.

Rosenberg, James N. *Censorship in the U.S.: An Address Before The Association of the Bar of the City of New York on March 15, 1928.* New York: The Court Press, n.d.

Thomas, Isaac L. *The Birth of a Nation: A Hyperbole Versus A Negro's Plea for Fair Play.* Philadelphia: William Watson, 1916.

U.S. Copyright Office. Library of Congress. *Catalog of Copyright Entries of Motion Pictures 1912-1939.* Washington, D.C.: GPO, 1951.

Statuory Materials

Atlanta, Georgia. *The Charter, Related Laws and Code of General Ordinances,* Chapter 56, Article IV (1953).

_____. *Ordinance Governing the Exhibition of Motion Pictures,* Sect. 1-12 (1944).

Charleston, West Virginia. *Code of Ordinances,* Sect. 596 (1924).

Chicago, Illinois. *City of Chicago Charter,* Art. 5, Cl. 45 (1907).

Chicago, Illinois. *Ordinances,* Sect. 1625 (1915).

Denver, Colorado. *Ordinances,* Chapter 48, Sect. 1282 (1915).

Illinois. *Revised Statutes*, Chapter 38, Paragraph 456 (1923).

Kansas. *General Statutes*, Chapter 294 (1913).

Massachusetts. *Laws and Resolves*, Chapter 494 (1914).

Massachusetts. House of Representatives. *Documents Printed by the Order of the House of Representatives of the Commonwealth of Massachusetts During the General Court of 1915*. Boston: Wright & Potter Printing Co., 1915.

Massachusetts. House of Representatives. *Journal of the House of Representatives of the Commonwealth of Massachusetts 1915*. Boston: Wright & Potter Printing Co., 1915.

Memphis, Tennessee. *Municipal Code*, Sect. 1131-1139 (1925).

Minneapolis, Minnesota. *City Charter*, Chapter 4, Subchapter 16 (1915).

_____. *Special Laws*, Chapter 76, Subchapter 4 (1915).

New York, New York. *Code of Ordinances*, Section 15, Article 2, Chapter 22 (1920).

New York. *Education Law* (McKinney's Con. Laws), Book 16, Sects. 122-9 (1954).

Ohio. *Code*, Sect. 154-47-154-471 (1943).

Ohio. *Constitution*. Article 1, Section 11.

Ohio. *Laws*, Chapter 103, Sect. 399 (1913).

Pennsylvania. *Act of May 15, 1915, P.L. 534 as amended by Act of May 8, 1929, P.L. 1655, 4 P.S. Sect. 41* (1929).

San Francisco. *Ordinances*, No. 761 New Series, as Amended by Ordi- No. 826, New Series (1909).

Tacoma, Washington. *City Ordinance No. 5864*, Sect. 1 (1914).

_____. *City Ordinance No. 6179*, Sect. 1 (1915).

U.S. Congress. House. *A Bill to Prohibit Exhibition or Use of Films or Pictorial Representation Calculated to Reflect on Any Race or Nationality*. H.R. 14668, 64th Cong., 1st Sess., 1916.

_____. House. Committee on Education. *Hearings Before The Committee on Education, House of Representatives, 64th Congress,

1st Session on H.R. 456, A Bill To Create a New Division of the Bureau of Education, To Be Known as the Federal Motion Picture Commission and Defining its Powers and Duties, Jan. 13, 14, 15, 17, 18, and 19, 1916, 64th Congress, 1st Session, 1916.

_____. House. Committee on Education. Report No. 697 To Accompany H.R. 15462, A Bill to Create a Federal Motion Picture Commission, 64th Congress, 1st Session, 1916.

_____. House. Committee on Interstate and Foreign Commerce. Hearings Before the Committee on Interstate and Foreign Commerce, House of Representatives, 73rd Congress, 2nd Session, on H.R. 6097 to Provide for Inspecting, Classifying, and Cataloging Motion Pictures, Both Silent and Talking, Before They Enter Interstate or Foreign Commerce To Create a Federal Motion Picture Commission To Define Its Powers and for Other Purposes, March 19, 1934, 73rd Congress, 2nd Session, 1934.

_____. House. Committee on Interstate and Foreign Commerce, Sub-Committee on Communications and Power. Hearings Before the Committee on Interstate and Foreign Commerce, Subcommittee on Communication and Power, 92nd Congress, 1st Session, on H. Con. Resolution 9 and H. Con. Resolution 182 Expressing the Sense of Congress Relating to Films and Broadcasts Which Defame, Stereotype, Ridicule, Demean, or Degrade Ethnic, Racial, and Religious Groups (and all identical resolutions) April 27 and 28, 1971, 92nd Congress, 1st Session, 1971.

_____. House. A Joint Resolution: The Birth of a Nation Picture. H.J.R. 222, 64th Congress, 1st Session, 1916.

_____. House. A Joint Resolution To Instruct the Commissioners of the District of Columbia to Forbid the Display of The Birth of a Nation in the District of Columbia. H.J.R. 221, 64th Congress, 1st Session, 1916.

U.S. Constitution. Amendment I.

U.S. Constitution. Amendment XIV.

West Virginia. Laws, Chapter 37 (1919).

West Virginia. Senate. A Bill Relating to Showing Or Exhibiting Any Picture or Theatrical Act in Any Theatre or Other Place of Public Amusement Tending to Arouse Feeling Between the Races. S.B. 176 (1919).

Wilmington, Delaware. An Ordinance to Prohibit the Exhibition of any

<u>Moving Picture Likely to Cause Ill-Feeling Between the White and Black Races</u> (1915).

Unpublished Materials

Columbus, Ohio. Ohio State Historical Society Archives. <u>Birth of a Nation</u> Papers.

Madison, Wisconsin. Wisconsin State Historical Society. Manuscript Collection. Aitken Papers.

Madison, Wisconsin. Wisconsin State Historical Society. Manuscript Collection. O'Brien Legal File.

Madison, Wisconsin. Wisconsin State Historical Society. Manuscript Collection. United Artists Papers.

Madison, Wisconsin. Wisconsin State Historical Society. Microform Collection. American Civil Liberties Union Papers.

New York, New York. New York City Archives. John P. Mitchell Mayoral Papers.

New York, New York. Lincoln Center Archives. <u>Birth of a Nation</u> Papers.

New York, New York. Museum of Modern Art Archives. <u>Birth of a Nation</u> Papers.

New York, New York. Museum of Modern Art Archives. D.W. Griffith Papers.

Washington, D.C. Library of Congress. Manuscript Collection. Booker T. Washington Papers.

Washington, D.C. Library of Congress. Manuscript Collection. Moorfield Storey Papers.

Washington, D.C. Library of Congress. Manuscript Collection. National Association for the Advancement of Colored People Papers.

Washington, D.C. Library of Congress. Manuscript Collection. William Allen White Papers.

Selected Secondary Sources

Articles in Periodicals

"Bigoted and Bettered Pictures." <u>Scribners Monthly</u>, September 1924, pp. 231-236.

"The Birth of a Nation." Confederate Veteran, May 1916, p. 237.

"Birth of a Nation." Outlook, 14 April 1915, p. 854.

"Birth of a Nation." Outlook, 7 January 1931, p. 32.

"Birth of a Nation Revived Draws Protest." Crisis, March 1938, p. 84.

"Boston and Movie Censorship." Survey, 17 April 1920, pp. 108-109.

Brown, James Mason. "Wishful Banning." Saturday Review, 12 March 1949, pp. 24-26.

Brown, Sterling A. "Negro Character As Seen By White Authors." Journal of Negro Education 2 (April 1933): 179-203.

Brychta, Ivan. "The Ohio Film Censorship Law." Ohio Law Journal 13 (Spring 1952): 350-411.

Calverton, V.F. "Cultural Barometer." Current History 49 (September 1938): 45-47.

Carter, Elmer Anderson. "Of Negro Motion Pictures." Close-Up, August 1929, pp. 118-122.

Carter, Everett. "Cultural History Written With Lightening: The Significance of 'The Birth of a Nation." American Quarterly 12 (1960): 347-357.

Casty, Alan. "The Films of D.W. Griffith: A Style for the Times." Journal of Popular Film 1 (Spring 1972): 67-79.

"Censorship and the National Board." Survey, 2 October 1915, pp. 9-14.

"Censorship of Motion Pictures." Yale Law Journal 49 (November 1939): 87-113.

"Censorship of the Movies." Forum, April 1923, pp. 4-14.

"The Civil War In Film." Literary Digest 50 (20 March 1915): 608-609.

"The Clansman: An Editorial." Crisis, May 1915, p. 33.

Collier, John. "Censorship in Action." Survey, 7 August 1915, pp. 23-25.

_____. "Learned Judges and the Films." Survey, 4 September 1915, pp. 513-516.

Cook, Raymond. "The Man Behind 'The Birth of a Nation." North Carolina Historical Review 29 (1962): 519-540.

Cranstone, E.L. "The Birth of a Nation' Controversy." Sight and Sound 16 (Autumn 1947): 119.

Cripps, Thomas. "The Birth of a Race' Company: An Early Stride Toward Black Cinema." Journal of Negro History 59 (January 1974): 28-37.

_____. "The Reaction of the Negro to the Motion Picture 'Birth of a Nation." The Historian 26 (1963): 244-262.

Crowther, Bosley. "The Birth of 'The Birth of a Nation." New York Times Magazine, 7 February 1965, sec. 6, p. 84.

_____. "The Strange Case of 'The Miracle." Atlantic, April 1951, p. 35.

"Editor Note." Sight and Sound 17 (Spring 1948): 50.

Emerson, A.J. "The Birth of a Nation." Confederate Veteran, March 1916, p. 141.

Everson, William K. "Griffith and Realism: Apropos 'The Birth of a Nation." Cinemages 5 (1955): 14-17.

"Fighting Race Calumny." Crisis, May 1915, pp. 40-41.

_____. Crisis, June 1915, pp. 87-88.

"Film Censors and Other Morons." Nation, 12 December 1923, p. 678.

"Films and Births and Censorship." Survey, 3 April 1915, pp. 4-5.

"Freedom of Speech and Assembly: The Problem of the Hostile Audience." Columbia Law Review 49 (December 1949): 118-1124.

Gordon, Henry Stephen. "The Story of David Wark Griffith." Photoplay, October 1916, pp. 90-94.

Grant Signey S. and Angoff, E.S. "Massachusetts and Censorship." Boston University Law Review 10 (January 1930): 36-60.

Griffith, David Wark. "Are Motion Pictures Destructive of Good Taste?" Arts and Decoration, September 1923, pp. 12-13.

Hackett, Francis. "Birth of a Nation." New Republic, 20 March 1915, pp. 185-186.

Hardwick, Leon. "Negro Stereotypes on the Screen." Hollywood Quarterly 1 (January 1946): 234-236.

Holmes, John Haynes. "Sensitivity as Censor." Saturday Review, 26 February 1949, pp. 9-10, 23.

Kupferman, Theodore and O'Brien, Philip. "Motion Picture Censorship and the Memphis Blues." Cornel Law Quarterly 36 (Winter 1951): pp. 275-287.

Lasker, Edward. "Censorship of Motion Pictures Pursuant to Recent Supreme Court Decisions." UCLA Law Review 1 (1954): 582-592.

McAnany, P.D. "Motion Picture Censorship and Constitutional Freedom." Kentucky Law Journal 50 (1962): 427-458.

McGuire, W.D. "Censoring Motion Pictures." The New Republic, 10 April 1915, pp. 262-263.

MacKaye, Milton. "The Birth of a Nation." Scribners Magazine, November 1937, pp. 40-46; 69.

Mcmanus, John T. and Kronenberger, Louis. "Motion Pictures, the Theatre, and Race Relations." Annals of the American Academy 244 (March 1946): 152-166.

Merritt, Russell L. "Dixon, Griffith and the Southern Legend." Cinema Journal 12 (Fall 1972): 26-45.

Metzger, Charles. "Pressure Groups and the Movie Picture Industry." Annals of the American Academy 254 (November 1947): 110-115.

Moore, John Hammond. "South Carolina's Reaction to the Photoplay, 'The Birth of a Nation." Proceedings of the South Carolina Historical Association 33 (1963): 30-40.

"More and Worse Censorship." Independent, 10 April 1926, p. 408.

"Motion Pictures and the First Amendment." Yale Law Journal 60 (1951): 696-719.

"Movies Turn Deaf Ear to Colored Plea." Christian Century, 24 September 1930, pp. 1140-1141.

Nelsen, Anne K. and Nelsen, Hart M. "The Prejudicial Film: Progress and Stalemate, 1915-1967." Phylon 31 (Summer 1970): 142-149.

"The Negro and the Movies." Negro Digest 2 (August 1940): 19-21.

Nimmer, Melville B. "The Constitutionality of Official Censorship of the Motion Picture." University of Chicago Law Review 25 (1958): 625-657.

Noble, Peter. "A Note on an Idol." Sight and Sound 15 (Autumn 1946): 81-82.

"Paris Suppresses An American Film." Literary Digest 78 (29 September 1923): 28-29.

Potamken, Harry A. "The Afroamerican Cinema." Close-Up, August 1929, pp. 107-117.

"Progressive Protest Against Anti-Negro Film." Survey, 5 June 1915, pp. 209-210.

"Protest." Time, 30 May 1938, p. 49.

Reddick, L.D. "Educational Programs for the Improvement of Race Relations: Motion Pictures, Radio, The Press, and Libraries." Journal of Negro Education 13 (Summer 1944): 367-389.

"Regulation of Films." The Nation, 6 May 1915, pp. 486-487.

Rumbold, Charlotte. "Against 'The Birth of a Nation." New Republic, 5 June 1915, p. 125.

Seldes, Gilbert. "Law, Pressure and Public Opinion." Hollywood Quarterly 1 (July 1946): 422-426.

Shary, Dore. "Censorship and Stereotypes." Saturday Review, 30 April 1949, pp. 9-10.

Sidney, P. Jay. "Anti-Negro Propaganda in Films." Film Comment 1 (Spring 1962): 22-23.

Simcovitch, Maxim. "The Impact of Griffith's 'The Birth of a Nation' on the Modern KKK." Journal of Popular Film. 1 (Winter 1972): 45-54.

Stern, Seymour. "The Birth of a Nation." Special Supplement to Sight and Sound. Index Series No. 4 (July 1945).

_____. "The Birth of a Nation' In Retrospect." The International Photographer, April 1935, pp. 4-5; 23-24.

_____. "Cinemages Special Issue No. 1: The Birth of a Nation." Cinemages. Special Issue No. 1 (April 1955).

_____. "The Cold War Against D.W. Griffith." Films In Review, February 1956, pp. 49-59.

_____. "Griffith: The Birth of a Nation Part 1." Film Culture 36 Special Griffith Issue (Spring-Summer 1965).

_____. "The Griffith Controversy." *Sight and Sound* 17 (Spring 1948): 49-50.

_____. "An Index to the Creative Work of David Wark Griffith: Part II: The Art Triumphant." *Special Supplement to Sight and Sound*. Index Series No. 7 (August 1946).

Stern, Seymour and Griffith, D.W. "A Reply to Peter Noble's Article in Autumn 'Sight and Sound." *Sight and Sound* 16 (Spring 1947): 32-35.

Rose, S.E.F. "The KKK and 'The Birth of a Nation." *Confederate Veteran*, April 1916, p. 157.

"Uncle Tom in Hollywood." *Crisis*, November 1934, p. 329.

Velie, Lester. "You Can't See That Movie: Censorship in Action." *Colliers*, 6 May 1950, p. 11.

Williams, Robert. "Stereotypes of Negroes in Film." *Film Comment* 1 (Summer 1962): 67-69.

"Without Comment." *Sight and Sound* 16 (Spring 1947): 35.

Bibliographies

Bukalski, Peter J., comp. *Film Research; a Critical Bibliography With Annotations and Essay*. Boston: G.K. Hall, 1972.

Christenson, Frances Mary. *A Guide to the Literature of the Motion Picture*. Los Angeles: University of Southern California Press, 1938.

Gerlach, John. *The Critical Index; a Bibliography of Articles on Film in English, 1946-1973*. New York: Teachers College Press, 1974.

Index to Periodical Articles by and about Negroes. Boston: G.K. Hall, 1950--.

Writers Program. *The Film Index, a Bibliography*. New York: H.W. Wilson and Museum of Modern Art Film Library, 1941.

Books

Aitken, Roy and Nelson, Al P. *The Birth of a Nation Story*. Middleburg, Va.: Denlinger Books, 1965.

Alexander, Charles. *The Ku Klux Klan in the Southwest*. Lexington: University of Kentucky Press, 1965.

Barry, Iris and Bowser, Eileen. *D.W. Griffith: American Film Master*. New York: Museum of Modern Art, 1940.

Berkhofer, Robert. *A Behavioral Approach to Historical Analysis*. New York: Macmillan, 1970.

Blumer, Herbert. *Movies and Conduct*. New York: Macmillan, 1933; reprint edition, New York: Arno Press and The New York Times, 1970.

Bogle, Donald. *Toms, Coons, Mulattoes, Mammies and Bucks*. New York: Bantam Books, 1973.

Brown, Karl. *Adventures With D.W. Griffith*. Edited by Kevin Brownlow. New York: Farrar, Straus & Giroux, 1973.

Bullock, Henry Allen. *A History of Negro Education in the South From 1619 to the Present*. Cambridge, Massachusetts: Harvard University Press, 1967.

Cannon, Lucuis H. *Motion Picture Laws, Ordinances and Regulations on Minors and Other Related Subjects*. St. Louis: St. Louis Public Library, 1920.

Carmen, Ira Harris. *Movies Censorship and the Law*. Ann Arbor: University of Michigan Press, 1966.

Cash, W.J. *The Mind of the South*. New York: Vintage Books, 1969.

Chafee, Zechariah. *Free Speech in the United States*. Cambridge, Massachusetts: Harvard University Press, 1941.

Chalmers, David. *Hooded Americanism: The First Century of the Ku Klux Klan, 1865-1965*. New York: Prentice-Hall, 1965.

Chase, Clinton I. *Elementary Statistical Procedures*. New York: McGraw-Hill, 1967.

Chesnutt, Helen M. *Charles Waddell Chesnutt*. Chapel Hill: University of North Carolina Press, 1952.

Clark, David and Blankenburg, William. *You and Media*. San Francisco: Canfield Press, 1973.

Cook, Raymond. *Fire From the Flint*. Winston Salem, North Carolina: John T. Blair, 1968.

_____. *Thomas Dixon*. New York: Twayne, 1974.

Cowie, Peter. *Seventy Years of Cinema*. New York: A.S. Barnes & Company, 1969.

Cripps, Thomas. "The Death of Rastus: Negroes in American Films Since 1945." In White Racism and Black Americans, pp. 605-616. Edited by David G. Gromley and Charles F. Longino, Jr. Cambridge, Massachusetts: Schenkmen Publishing Co., 1972.

_____. "The Myth of the Southern Box Office: A Factor in Racial Stereotyping in American Movies, 1920-1940." In The Black Experience In America, pp. 116-144. Edited by James Curtis and Lewis L. Gould. Austin: University of Texas Press, 1970.

Crowther, Bosley. Movies and Censorship, Pamphlet No. 332. New York: Public Affairs Committee, Inc., 1962.

Croy, Homer. Starmaker: The Story of D.W. Griffith. New York: Duell, Sloan and Pearce, 1959.

Dixon, Thomas. The Clansman. New York: Grosset & Dunlap, 1905.

_____. The Leopards Spots. New York: Doubleday, 1902.

Ellison, Ralph. Shadow and Act. New York: Random House, 1953.

Ernst, Morris. The First Freedom. New York: Macmillan, 1946.

Ernst, Morris and Lorentz, Pare. Censored: The Private Life of the Movies. New York: Jonathan Cape and Harrison Smith, 1930.

Fischer, David Hackett. Historians Fallacies. New York: Harper and Row, 1970.

Forman, Henry James. Our Movie Made Children. New York: Macmillan, 1935; reprint edition, New York: Arco Press, 1970.

Fox, Stephen R. The Guardian of Boston: William Monroe Trotter. New York: Atheneum, 1970.

Francois, William E. Mass Media Law and Regulation. Columbus, Ohio: GRID, 1975.

Franklin, John Hope. "The Two Worlds of Race: A Historical View." In The Negro American, pp. 47-68. Edited by Talcott Parsons and Kenneth B. Clark. Boston: Beacon Press, 1960.

Gallico, Paul. "Paul Gallico." In No Cheering in the Press Box, pp. 61-80. Edited by Jerome Holtzman. New York: Holt, Rinehart and Winston, 1973.

Geduld, Harry M., ed. Focus on D.W. Griffith. Englewood Cliffs, N.J.: Prentice-Hall, 1971.

Gessner, Robert. *The Moving Image: A Guide To Cinematic Literacy*. New York: E.P. Dutton & Co., 1968.

Gillmor, Donald and Barron, Jerome A. *Mass Communication Law: Cases and Comment*. St. Paul: West, 1969.

Gish, Lillian. *The Movies, Mr. Griffith, and Me*. With Ann Pinchot. Englewood Cliffs, N.J.: Prentice-Hall, 1969.

Goodman, Ezra. *The Firty-Year Decline and Fall of Hollywood*. New York: Simon and Schuster, 1961.

Gottschalk, Louis. *Understanding History: A Primer on Historical Method*. New York: Alfred A. Knopf, 1964.

Griffith, David Wark. *The Man Who Invented Hollywood: The Autobiography of D.W. Griffith*. Edited and Annotated by James Hart. Louisville, Kentucky: Touchstone Press, 1972.

Griffith, Linda Arvidson. *When the Movies Were Young*. New York: E.P. Dutton, 1925.

Griffith, Richard and Mayer, Arthur. *The Movies*, rev. ed. New York: Simon and Schuster, 1970.

Grimke, Francis J. *The Birth of a Nation*. Washington, D.C.: Francis Grimke, 1915.

Henderson, Robert M. *D.W. Griffith: His Life and Work*. New York: Oxford University Press, 1972.

_____. *D.W. Griffith: The Years at Biograph*. New York: Farrar, Straus, and Giroux, 1970.

Hofstadter, Richard, ed. *The Progressive Movement 1900-1915*. Englewood Cliffs, N.J.: Prentice-Hall, 1963.

Huff, Theodore. *A Shot Analysis of D.W. Griffith's The Birth of a Nation*. New York: The Museum of Modern Art, 1961.

Hughes, Langston. *Fight for Freedom: The Story of the NAACP*. New York: W.W. Norton and Co., 1962.

Hunnings, Neville March. *Film Censors and the Law*. London: George Allen & Unwin, Ltd., 1967.

Inglis, Ruth. *Freedom of the Movies*. Chicago: University of Chicago Press, 1947.

Jacobs, Lewis. *The Emergence of the Film Art*. New York: Hopkinson & Blake, Publishers, 1969.

Link, Arthur S. *Woodrow Wilson and The Progressive Era 1910-1917.* New York: Harper & Row, 1954; reprint edition, New York Harper & Row, 1963.

Jarvie, I.C. *Movies and Society.* New York: Basic Books, Inc., 1971.

Jerome, V.J. *The Negro in Hollywood Films.* New York: Masses and Mainstream, 1950.

Kellog, Charles Flint. *NAACP: A History of The National Association For The Advancement of Colored People Vol. I (1909-1920).* Baltimore: John Hopkins Press, 1967.

Knight, Arthur. *The Livliest Art.* New York: The New American Library, Inc., 1957.

Lawson, John Howard. *Film: The Creative Process*, 2nd ed. New York: Hill and Wang, 1967.

Lindsay, Vachel. *The Art of the Moving Picture.* New York: Macmillan, 1915.

MacDonald, Dwight. *On Movies.* Englewood Cliffs, N.J.: Prentice-Hall, 1967.

Mack, James R. *Censorship 1917.* Princeton, N.J.: Princeton University Press, 1941.

Mapp, Edward. *Blacks in American Films Today and Yesterday.* Metuchen, N.J.: Scarecrow Press, 1972.

Maynard, Richard A., ed. *The Black Man on Film: Racial Stereotyping.* Rochelle Park, N.J.: Hayden Book Co., 1974.

Meier, August. *Negro Thought in America, 1880-1915.* Ann Arbor: University of Michigan Press, 1970.

Miller, Seba H. *The Law and Practice in Error Proceedings and In Original Action In The Supreme Court of Ohio.* Cincinnati: W.H. Anderson, Co., 1924.

Murray, James. *To Find An Image.* Indianapolis: Bobbs Merrill, 1973.

Nelson, Harold L. and Tetter, Dwight L., Jr. *Law of Mass Communications: Freedom and Control of Print and Broadcast Media*, 2nd ed. Mineola, N.Y.: Foundation Press, 1973.

Newby, I.A. *Jim Crow's Defense: Anti-Negro Thought in America.* Baton Rouge, Louisiana: Louisiana State University Press, 1965.

New York Times Film Reviews: A One Volume Selection. New York: Quadrangle Books, 1971.

Noble, Peter. The Negro in Films. London: Skelton, Robinson, 1948.

O'Dell, Paul. Griffith and the Rise of Hollywood. New York: A.S. Barnes, 1970.

Ovington, Mary White. The Walls Came Tumbling Down. New York: Harcourt, Brace & Co., 1947.

Pember, Don. Mass Media in America. Chicago: Science Research Associates, 1974.

Petersen, Ruth C. and Thurston, L.L. Motion Pictures and the Social Attitudes of Children. New York: Macmillan, 1935.

Ramsaye, Terry. A Million and One Nights. Vol. II. New York: Simon and Schuster, 1926.

Randall, Richard S. Censorship of the Movies: The Social & Political Control of a Mass Medium. Madison: The University of Wisconsin Press, 1968.

Rhode, Eric. Tower of Babel, Speculation on the Cinema. New York: Chilton Books, 1967.

Rivers, William, Peterson, Theodore, and Jensen, Jay. The Mass Media and Modern Society, 2nd ed. San Francisco: Rinehart Press, 1971.

Ross, Joyce. J.E. Spingarn and the Rise of the NAACP, 1911-1939. New York: Atheneum, 1972.

Sandburg, Carl. The Chicago Race Riots. New York: Harcourt, Brace and Howe, 1919.

Sarris, Andrew. The Primal Screen. New York: Simon and Schuster, 1973.

Schumach, Murray. The Face on the Cutting Room Floor. New York: William Morrow & Co., 1964.

Silva, Fred, ed. Focus on The Birth of a Nation. Englewood Cliffs, N.J.: Prentice-Hall, 1971.

Tindall, George B. The Emergence of the New South, 1913-1945. Baton Rouge, Louisiana: Louisiana State University Press, 1967.

Tuttle, William M., Jr. Race Riot: Chicago in the Red Summer of 1919. New York: Atheneum, 1970.

Tyler, Parker. Sex Psyche Etcetera In The Film. New York: Horizon Press, 1969.

Vardac, Nicholas. State to Screen. Cambridge, Massachusetts: Harvard University Press, 1949.

Wagenknecht, Edward. Movies in the Age of Innocence. Norman: University of Oklahoma, 1962.

Wagenknecht, Edward and Slide, Anthony. The Films of D.W. Griffith. New York: Crown, 1975.

Waskow, Arthur I. From Race Riot to Sit-In. Garden City, New York: Doubleday & Co., 1966.

Webster's New Twentieth Century Dictionary of the English Language, Unabridged 2nd ed. Cleveland: World Publishing, 1973.

Work, Monroe N., ed. Negro Yearbook: An Annual Encyclopedia of the Negro, 1916-1917. Tuskegee Institute, Alabama: The Negro Yearbook Co., 1916.

_____. Negro Yearbook: An Annual Enclcyopedia of the Negro, 1918-1919. Tuskegee Institute, Alabama: The Negro Yearbook Publishing Co., 1919.

Young, Donald Ramsey. Motion Pictures: A Study in Social Legislation. Philadelphia: Westbrook Publishing, 1922.

Dissertations and Other

Bloom, S.W. "A Social Psychological Study of Motion Picture Audience Behaviour: A Case Study of the Negro Image in Mass Communication." Ph.D. dissertation, University of Wisconsin, 1956.

Carmen, Ira Harris. "State and Local Motion Picture Censorship and Constitutional Liberties With Special Emphasis on Communal Acceptance of Supreme Court Decision-Making." Ph.D. dissertation, University of Michigan, 1964.

Fleener-Marzec, Nickieann. "Censorship of 'The Birth of a Nation': The Revival Years." Seminar Paper, University of Wisconsin, 1974.

_____. "A Chapter in the History of 'The Birth of a Nation." Seminar Paper, Indiana University, 1972.

Giglio, Ernest David. "The Decade of 'The Miracle' 1952-1962; A Study in the Censorship of the American Motion Picture." D.S.S. dissertation, Syracuse University, 1964.

Gorenc, Robert Edward. "Public Law Aspects of Motion Picture Censorship, 1956." M.S. thesis, University of Wisconsin, 1956.

Jowett, Garth Samuel. "Media Power and Social Control: The Motion Picture in America, 1894-1936." Ph.D. dissertation, University of Pennsylvania, 1972.

Hutchins, Charles Larry. "A Critical Evaluation of the Controversies Engendered by D.W. Griffith's The Birth of a Nation." M.A. thesis, University of Iowa, 1961.

Merritt, Russell Lamont. "The Impact of D.W. Griffith's Motion Pictures from 1908-1914 On Contemporary American Culture." Ph.D. dissertation, Harvard University, 1970.

Randall, Richard. "Control of Motion Pictures In The United States." Ph.D. dissertation, University of Wisconsin, 1967.

Randall, Richard. "The Licensing of Motion Pictures." M.S. thesis, University of Wisconsin, 1962.

Reardon, Robert William. "Banned in Boston: A Study of Theatrical Censorship in Boston From 1630-1950." Ph.D. dissertation, Stanford University, 1952.

Short, Ralph. "A Social Study of the Motion Picture." M.A. thesis, Iowa State University, 1916.

White, Tom Murray. "The 'Birth of a Nation' An Analysis of Its Sources, Content And Assertations About Reconstruction." M.A. thesis, University of Chicago, 1952.

Yodelis, Mary Ann. "Boston's Second Major Paper War: Economics, Politica, and the Theory and Practice of Political Expression in the Press, 1763-1775." Ph.D. dissertation, University of Wisconsin, 1971.

Newspapers

Atlantic City Advocate. 10, 11 August 1915.

Baltimore Afro-American Ledger. 20 February-15 June, 1915; 1 August-31 December 1915.

Baltimore Morning Sun. 15 May-30 June, 1952; 15-30 October, 1958.

Boston American. 1-30 April 1915.

Boston Evening Transcript. 15 March-30 June 1915.

Boston Globe. 15 March -30 June 1915.

Boston Guardian. 24 April 1915; 22 February 1947.

Boston Herald. 1 April -30 May 1915.

Boston Morning Journal. 15 March -30 June 1915; 15-30 October 1915.

Chicago Defender. 15 March-30 November 1915; 1 February-31 March 1924.

Chicago Tribune. 1 February -15 March 1924; 12 December 1939.

Christian Science Monitor. 1-30 April 1915.

Cleveland Gazette. 1 April-31 December 1915; 15 January-15 February 1916; 15-31 October 1916.

Cleveland Press. 1 March-31 May 1915.

Daily Compass. 17 May 1950.

Florida Accent. 8 December 1974.

Indianapolis Freeman. 1 April-15 May 1915.

Kansas City Call. 1-31 December 1923; 1 January-15 February 1924.

Los Angeles Examiner. 15-31 May 1915.

Los Angeles Times. 1-28 February 1915.

Madison Badger Herald. 24-27 October 1974.

Minneapolis Tribune. 1 October-30 November 1915.

Newark Evening News. 15 November 1960.

New York Age. 10 February-31 December 1915; 16 March 1916.

New York Evening Post. 14-15 March 1915.

New York Herald. 12 March 1915.

New York Herald Tribune. 20 April 1939; 19 December 1949; 13 November 1960.

New York Mail. 13 March 1915.

New York News. 18 March 1915.

New York Sun. 12-15 March 1915.

New York Telegraph. 3 June 1915; 17 May 1950.

New York Times. 15 March-15 June 1915; 7 May 1921; 1-15 December 1922; 3 February 1924; 4 February 1941; 19 May 1950; 24 May 1952; 14 June 1952; 13 December 1954; 15 January-28 February 1965; 19 January 1975.

New York Tribune. 15 March 1915; 15 January 1916.

New York World. 24 March 1915.

New York World Journal Tribune. 28 September 1966.

New York World Telegram. 18 May 1939.

Oakland Sunshine. 25 September-31 October 1915.

Philadelphia Evening Telegram. 12 March 1915.

Philadelphia Inquirer. 1 September-1 October 1915.

Philadelphia North American. 1 September-1 October 1915.

Philadelphia Tribune. 1 March-31 May 1915; 15 July-30 November 1915.

Pittsburgh Dispatch. 31 August-3 September 1915.

Pittsburgh Gazette Times. 7 September 1915.

Pittsburgh Post. 31 August-5 September 1915.

St. Louis Argus. 1 April-31 December 1915.

St. Paul Appeal. 1-30 June 1915; 1 October-30 November 1915.

St. Paul Pioneer Press. 1-31 October 1915.

Sacramento Bee. 28 May 1915.

San Francisco Call. 6 September 1915.

Topeka Daily State Journal. 1-31 December 1923; 1-15 January 1924.

Twin City Star. 12 March 1915; 1 October-31 November 1915.

Variety. 1 March-31 December 1915; 1 May-31 December 1921; 1 March-31 December 1922; 1 January-31 December 1923; 1 January-31 December 1924; 1 June 1938; 15-30 April 1939; 1 March-30 April 1940; 16 July 1944; 5 November 1958; 1 May-15 June 1959; 1 April-30 June 1961; 15 March-15 April 1965; 15 April 1970; 16 December 1970; 8 May 1974.

Washington Bee. 1 May 1915.

Western Outlook. 15 February-30 May 1915; 1-31 October 1915.

DISSERTATIONS ON FILM 1980

An Arno Press Collection

Allen, Robert C. **Vaudeville and Film 1895-1915: A Study in Media Interaction** (Doctoral Dissertation, The University of Iowa, 1977). 1980

Bordwell, David. **French Impressionist Cinema: Film Culture, Film Theory, and Film Style** (Doctoral Dissertation, The University of Iowa, 1974). 1980

Brown, Kent R. **The Screenwriter as Collaborator: The Career of Stewart Stern** (Doctoral Dissertation, The University of Iowa, 1972). 1980

Cozyris, George Agis. **Christian Metz and the Reality of Film** (Doctoral Dissertation, The University of Southern California, 1979). 1980

Curran, Trisha. **A New Note on the Film: A Theory of Film Criticism Derived from Susanne K. Langer's Philosophy of Art** (Doctoral Dissertation, Ohio State University, 1978). 1980

Daly, David Anthony. **A Comparison of Exhibition and Distribution Patterns in Three Recent Feature Motion Pictures** (Doctoral Dissertation, Southern Illinois University, 1978). 1980

Diakité, Madubuko. **Film, Culture, and the Black Filmmaker: A Study of Functional Relationships and Parallel Developments** (Doctoral Dissertation, Stockholm University, 1978). 1980

Editors of *Look*. **Movie Lot to Beachhead: The Motion Picture Goes to War and Prepares for the Future**. 1945

Ellis, Reed. **A Journey Into Darkness: The Art of James Whale's Horror Films** (Doctoral Dissertation, The University of Florida, 1979). 1980

Fleener-Marzec, Nickieann. **D.W. Griffith's** *The Birth of a Nation*: **Controversy, Suppression, and the First Amendment as it Applies to Filmic Expression, 1915-1973** (Doctoral Dissertation, The University of Wisconsin, 1977). 1980

Garton, Joseph W. **The Film Acting of John Barrymore** (Doctoral Dissertation, New York University, 1977). 1980

Gehring, Wes D. **Leo McCarey and the Comic Anti-Hero in American Film** (Doctoral Dissertation, The University of Iowa, 1977). 1980

Kindem, Gorham Anders. **Toward a Semiotic Theory of Visual Communication in the Cinema: A Reappraisal of Semiotic Theories from a Cinematic Perspective and a Semiotic Analysis of Color Signs and Communication in the Color Films of Alfred Hitchcock** (Doctoral Dissertation, Northwestern University, 1977). 1980

Manvell, Roger. **Ingmar Bergman: An Appreciation.** 1980

Moore, Barry Walter. **Aesthetic Aspects of Recent Experimental Film** (Doctoral Dissertation, The University of Michigan, 1977). 1980

Nichols, William James. **Newsreel: Documentary Filmmaking on the American Left** (Doctoral Dissertation, The University of California, Los Angeles, 1975). 1980

Rose, Brian Geoffrey. **An Examination of Narrative Structure in Four Films of Frank Capra** (Doctoral Dissertation, The University of Wisconsin, 1976). 1980

Salvaggio, Jerry Lee. **A Theory of Film Language** (Doctoral Dissertation, The University of Michigan, 1978). 1980

Simonet, Thomas Solon. **Regression Analysis of Prior Experiences of Key Production Personnel as Predictors of Revenues from High-Grossing Motion Pictures in American Release** (Doctoral Dissertation, Temple University, 1977). 1980

Siska, William Charles. **Modernism in the Narrative Cinema: The Art Film as a Genre** (Doctoral Dissertation, Northwestern University, 1976). 1980

Stewart, Lucy Ann Liggett. **Ida Lupino as Film Director, 1949-1953: An Auteur Approach** (Doctoral Dissertation, The University of Michigan, 1979). 1980

Strebel, Elizabeth Grottle. **French Social Cinema of the Nineteen Thirties: A Cinematographic Expression of Popular Front Consciousness** (Doctoral Dissertation, Princeton University, 1973). 1980

Veeder, Gerry K. **The Influence of Subliminal Suggestion on the Response to Two Films** (Doctoral Dissertation, Wayne State University, 1975). 1980

Vincent, Richard C. **Financial Characteristics of Selected 'B' Film Productions of Albert J. Cohen, 1951-1957** (Masters Thesis, Temple University, 1977). 1980

Williams, Alan Larson. **Max Ophuls and the Cinema of Desire** (Doctoral Dissertation, The State University of New York, Buffalo, 1977). 1980

KF 4300.F54 1980

	DATE DUE	